THE DIARY OF
SAMUEL PEPYS

THE DIARY
OF
SAMUEL PEPYS

A new and complete
transcription edited by

ROBERT LATHAM
AND
WILLIAM MATTHEWS

CONTRIBUTING EDITORS
WILLIAM A. ARMSTRONG · MACDONALD EMSLIE
SIR OLIVER MILLAR · the late T. F. REDDAWAY

VOLUME VI · 1665

HarperCollins*Publishers*

Published in 1995 by
HarperCollins College Division
An imprint of HarperCollins*Publishers* Ltd, UK
77-85 Fulham Palace Road
Hammersmith
London W6 8JB

First published in 1971 by Bell & Hyman Limited

British Library Cataloguing in Publication Data
A catalogue record for this book is available from the British Library

ISBN 0 00 499026 9

Printed and bound by Scotprint Ltd, Musselburgh, Scotland

PRINCIPAL EDITORS

ROBERT LATHAM, C.B.E., M.A., F.B.A.
Fellow and Pepys Librarian, Magdalene College, Cambridge

WILLIAM MATTHEWS, M.A., Ph.D., D.Lett.
Late Professor of English, University of California, Los Angeles
Fellow of Birkbeck College, University of London

CONTRIBUTING EDITORS

(*Theatre*)

WILLIAM A. ARMSTRONG, M.A., Ph.D.
Professor of English Literature, Birkbeck College, University of London

(*Music*)

MACDONALD EMSLIE, M.A., Ph.D.
Reader in English Literature, University of Edinburgh

(*Pictures and Works of Art*)

SIR OLIVER MILLAR, K.C.V.O., F.B.A.
Surveyor of the Queen's Pictures

(*London Topography*)

the late T. F. REDDAWAY, M.A., F.S.A.
Late Professor of the History of London, University College,
University of London

* * *

(*Text assistant*)

LOIS MATTHEWS, B.A.

CONTENTS

LIST OF ILLUSTRATIONS

READER'S GUIDE

This section is meant for quick reference. More detailed information about the editorial methods used in this edition will be found in the Introduction and in the section 'Methods of the Commentary' in vol. I, and also in the statements preceding the Select Glossary at the end of each text volume and the Large Glossary in the *Companion*.

I. THE TEXT

The fact that the MS. is mostly in shorthand makes exact reproduction (e.g. of spelling, capitalisation and punctuation) impossible.

Spelling is in modern British style, except for those longhand words which Pepys spelt differently, and words for which the shorthand indicates a variant pronunciation which is also shown by Pepys's longhand elsewhere. These latter are given in spellings which reflect Pepys's pronunciations.

Pepys's capitalisation is indicated only in his longhand.

Punctuation is almost all editorial, except for certain full-stops, colons, dashes and parentheses. Punctuation is almost non-existent in the original since the marks could be confused with shorthand.

Italics are all editorial, but (in e.g. headings to entries) often follow indications given in the MS. (by e.g. the use of larger writing).

The **paragraphing** is that of the MS.

Abbreviations of surnames, titles, place names and ordinary words are expanded.

Single **hyphens** are editorial, and represent Pepys's habit of disjoining the elements of compound words (e.g. Wh. hall/White-hall). Double hyphens represent Pepys's hyphens.

Single **angle-brackets** mark additions made by Pepys in the body of the MS.; double angle-brackets those made in the margins.

Light **asterisks** are editorial (see below, Section II); heavy asterisks are Pepys's own.

Pepys's **alterations** are indicated by the word 'replacing' ('repl.') in the textual footnotes.

II. THE COMMENTARY

1. Footnotes deal mainly with events and transactions. They also identify MSS, books, plays, music and quotations, but give only occasional and minimal information about persons and places, words and phrases. The initials which follow certain notes indicate the work of the contributing editors. Light asterisks in the text direct the reader to the Select Glossary for the definition of words whose meanings have changed since the time of the diary.

2. The **Select List of Persons** is printed unchanged in each text volume. It covers the whole diary and identifies the principal persons, together with those who are described in the MS. by titles or in other ways that make for obscurity.

3. The **Select Glossary** is printed at the end of each text volume. It gives definitions of certain recurrent English words and phrases, and identifications of certain recurrent places.

4. The **Companion** (vol. X) is a collection of reference material. It contains maps, genealogical tables, and a Large Glossary, but consists mainly of articles, printed for ease of reference in a single alphabetical series. These give information about matters which are dealt with briefly or not at all in the footnotes and the Select Glossary: i.e. persons, places, words and phrases, food, drink, clothes etc. They also treat systematically the principal subjects with which the diary is concerned: Pepys's work, interests, health etc. References to the *Companion* are given only rarely in the footnotes.

III. DATES

In Pepys's time two reckonings of the calendar year were in use in Western Europe. Most countries had adopted the New Style – the revised calendar of Gregory XIII (1582); Britain until 1752 retained the Old Style – the ancient Roman, or Julian, calendar, which meant that its dates were ten days behind those of the rest of Western Europe in the seventeenth century. 1 January in England was therefore 11 January by the New Style abroad. On the single occasion during the period of the diary when Pepys was abroad (in Holland in May 1660) he continued to use the Old Style, thus avoiding a break in the run of his dates. In the editorial material of the present work dates relating to countries which had adopted the new reckoning are given in both styles (e.g. '1/11 January') in order to prevent confusion.

It will be noticed that the shortest and longest days of the year occur in the diary ten days earlier than in the modern calendar. So, too, does Lord Mayor's Day in London – on 29 October instead of 9 November.

For most legal purposes (from medieval times until 1752) the new year in England was held to begin on Lady Day, 25 March. But in accordance with the general custom, Pepys took it to begin on 1 January, as in the Julian calendar. He gives to all dates within the overlapping period between 1 January and 24 March a year-date which comprehends both styles – e.g. 'January 1 16$\frac{59}{60}$.' In the present commentary a single year-date, that of the New Style, has been used: e.g. '1 January 1660'.

THE DIARY
1665

JANUARY. 166$\frac{4}{5}$.

1. *Lords day.* Lay long in bed, having been busy late last night. Then up and to my office, where upon ordering my accounts and papers with respect to my understanding my last year's gains and expense, which I find very great, as I have already set down yesterday. Now this day, I am dividing my expense, to see what my clothes and every perticular hath stood me in; I mean, all the branches of my expense.

At noon, a good venison pasty and a turkey to ourselfs, without anybody so much as invited by us – a thing unusual for so small a family of my condition – but we did it and were very merry. After dinner to my office again, where very late alone upon my accounts, but have not brought them to order yet; and very intricate I find it, notwithstanding my care all the year to keep things in as good method as any man can do.

Past 11 a-clock, home to supper and to bed.

2. Up, and it being a most fine hard frost, I walked a good way toward White-hall; and then being overtaken with Sir W. Penn's coach, went into it, and with him thither and there did our usual business with the Duke. Thence, being forced to pay a great deal of money away in boxes[1] (that is, basons at White-hall), I to my barbers, Gervas's, and there had a little opportunity of speaking with my Jane alone, and did give her something; and of herself she did tell me a place where I might come to her on Sunday next, which I will not fail; but to see how modestly and harmlessly she brought it out was very pretty. Thence to the Swan, and there did sport a good while with Herbert's young kinswoman[2] without hurt though, they being abroad, the old people. Then to the hall, and there agreed with Mrs. Martin, and to her lodgings which she hath now taken to lie in, in*a* Bow streete – pitiful poor things, yet she thinks them pretty;

a MS. 'in in'

---

1. Christmas or New Year boxes (for tips).   2. Probably Sarah Udall: below, p. 65.

and so they are for her condition I believe, good enough.   Here
I did ce que je voudrais avec her most freely; and it having cost
me 2s in wine and cake upon her, I away, sick of her impudence –
and by coach to my Lord Brunkers by appointment, in the piazza
in Covent-Guarding – where I occasioned much mirth with a
ballet I brought with me, made from the seamen at sea to their
ladies in town[1] – saying Sir W. Penn, Sir G Ascue, and Sir J
Lawson made them.   Here a most noble French dinner and
banquet, the best I have seen these many a day, and good discourse.   Thence to my bookseller's and at his binders saw Hookes
book of the Microscope,[2] which is so pretty that I presently
bespoke it; and away home to the office, where we met to do
something; and then, though very late, by coach to Sir Ph. Warwickes; but having company with him, could not speak with him.
So back again home, where, thinking to be merry, was vexed with
my wife's having looked out a letter in Sir Ph. Sidny about
jealousy for me to read,[3] which she industriously and maliciously
caused me to do; and the truth is, my conscience told me it was
most proper for me, and therefore was touched at it; but took
no notice of it, but read it out most frankly.   But it stuck[a] in
my stomach; and moreover,[b] I was vexed to have a dog brought
to my house to lime our little bitch, which they make him do
in all their sights; which God forgive me, doth stir my Jealousy
again, though of itself the thing is a very immodest sight.
      However, to Cards with my wife a good while, and then to bed.

a   repl. symbol rendered illegible   *b*   repl. 'the'

---

1. The ballad 'To all you ladies
now at land', written (probably in
1664) by Lord Buckhurst, later Earl
of Dorset. A ballad-sheet, now untraced, was entered in the Stationers'
Register, 30 December 1664, entitled
'*The Noble seamans complaint to the
Ladies at London*, to the tune of
Shackerley Hay': *Trans. Stat. Reg.*,
ii. 351. There is no copy in the PL.
(E).
      2. Robert Hooke's *Micrographia*
(1665; PL 2116). For a note on its
binding, see H. M. Nixon in the

forthcoming catalogue of the PL.
Pepys later had it embellished with
an index and marginal notes in the
hand of an amanuensis. It is re-
printed (from the 1745 edition) in
Gunther, vol. xiii. The bookseller
was Joshua Kirton, of St Paul's
Churchyard.
      3. In the third Eclogue of the third
book of the *Arcadia* ('a Jealous husband made a Pander to his own wife').
Pepys retained the 1674 edition:
PL 2214.

3. Up, and by coach to Sir Ph. Warwickes, the street being full of footballs, it being a great frost.[1] And find*a* him and Mr. Coventry walking in St. James park. I did my errand to him about the felling of the King's timber in the forests, and then to my Lord of Oxford, Justice in Eyre, for his consent thereto, for want whereof my Lord Privy Seale stops the whole business.[2] I found him in his lodgings, in but an ordinary furnished house and room where he was, but I find him to be a man of good discreet replies.

Thence to the Coffee-house, where certain news that the Dutch have taken some of our Colliers to the north – some say four, some say seven.[3]

Thence to the Change a while, and so home to dinner and to the office, where we sat late, and then I to write my letters. Then to Sir W. Batten's, who is going out of town to Harwich tomorrow, to set up a Light-house there which he hath lately got a patent from the King to set up, that will turn much to his profit.[4] Here very merry, and so to my office again, where very late, and then home to supper and to bed – but sat up with my wife at cards till past 2 in the morning.

4. Lay long; then up and to my Lord of Oxford's, but his Lordshipp was in bed at past 10 a-clock: and Lord help us, so rude a dirty family I never saw in my life. He sent me out word

a repl. 'then'

---

1. Play would be possible since the streets would be empty of horse-traffic. Regulations against football in the streets were periodically issued (e.g. in January 1669: Mdx R.O., Sessions Bk 253, p. 22) but are said to have ceased at about this time: M. Marples, *Hist. Football*, ch. vii, esp. p. 83. Warwick lived in the Outer Spring Garden.

2. Oxford was Warden and Chief Justice in Eyre of the royal forests south of Trent; he lived in the Piazza, Covent Garden. Timber in royal forests was felled under the supervision of naval purveyors on the authority of the Treasurer authenticated by privy seal warrants: cf.

CSPD 1664–5, p. 129. By mid-February the work was under way: ib., p. 200; *Shorthand Letters*, pp. 25, 27.

3. Capt. Banckert had taken four, according to *The Newes*, 12 January, p. 31.

4. Cf. above, v. 314. The patent (24 December 1664) allowed him to erect two lighthouses, and secured the revenue to him and his assigns for 61 years. The tolls levied were to be ½d. per ton on English ships, and 1d. a ton on foreign. PRO, C 66/3062, pt 12, no. 5; summary in *CSPD 1664–5*, p. 129. His will (1665) shows these revenues as forming a large part of his assets.

my business was not done, but should [be] against the afternoon.

I thence to the Coffee-house there, but little company; and so home to the Change, where I hear of some more of our ships lost to the Northward.[1] So to Sir W. Batten, but he was set out before I got thither; I sat long, talking with my Lady, and then home to dinner. Then came Mr. Moore to see me, and he and I to my Lord of Oxford's; but not finding him within, Mr. Moore and I to *Love in a tubb*; which is very merry, but only so by gesture, not wit at all, which methinks is beneath that house.[2]

So walked home, it being a very hard frost, and I find myself, as heretofore in cold weather, to begin to burn within and pimple and prick all over my body, my pores with cold being shut up.

So home to supper and to cards and to bed.

5. Up, it being very cold and a great snow and frost tonight. To the office, and there all the morning. At noon dined at home, troubled at my wife's being simply* angry with Jane our cook-maid (a good servant, though perhaps hath faults and is cunning) and given her warning to be gone. So to the office again, where we sat late; and then I to my office and there very late doing business. Home to supper and to the office again; and then late home to bed.

6. Lay long in bed, but most of it angry and scolding with my wife about her warning Jane our cook-maid to be gone – and upon that, she desires to go abroad today to look a place. A very good maid she is and fully to my mind, being neat – only, they say a little apt to scold; but I hear her not.

To my office all the morning, busy. Dined at home. To my office again, being pretty well reconciled to my wife; which I did desire to be, because she had designed much mirth today to

1. Two ships were taken off Bridlington: *The Newes*, 5 January p. 16.
2. *The comical revenge, or Love in a tub*, a comedy by Sir George Etherege, first acted and published in 1664. Many critics rank it as the first Restoration comedy of manners, and, according to Downes (pp. 24-5), it was acted by the Duke of York's Company at the LIF and 'got the Company more Reputation and Profit than any preceding Comedy' – a very different verdict from Pepys's. The cast listed by Downes includes Betterton as Lord Beaufort, Smith as Col. Bruce, Harris as Sir Frederick Frolic, Mrs Betterton as Graciana, and Mrs Davies as Aurelia. (A).

end Christmas with among her servants. At night home, being Twelfenight, and there chose my piece of cake,[1] but went up to my vial and then to bed, leaving my wife and people up at their sports, which they continue till morning, not coming to bed at all.

7. Up, and to the office all the morning. At noon dined alone, my wife and family most of them a-bed. Then to see my Lady Batten and sit with her a while, Sir W. Batten being out of town; and then to my office, doing very much business very late; then home to supper and to bed.

8. *Lords day.* Up betimes; and it being a very fine frosty day, I and my boy walked to White-hall and there to the chapel – where one Dr. Beaumont[2] preached a good sermon, and afterward a*a* brave anthem upon the 150 Psalm; where upon the word "Trumpet"[3] very good musique was made.

So walked to my Lady's and there dined with her (my boy going home), where much pretty discourse; and after dinner walked to Westminster and there to the house where Jane Welch had appointed me; but it being sermon time, they would not let me in[4] and said nobody was there to speak with me. I spent the whole afternoon walking into the church and abbey and up and down, but could not find her; and so in the evening took a coach and home – and there sat discoursing with my wife; and by and by at supper, drinking some cold drink I think it was, I was forced to go make water and had very great pain after it; but was well by and by and continued so, it being only, I think, from the drink or from my straining hard at stool to do more then my body would. So after*b* prayers, to bed.

9. Up, and walked to White-hall, it being still a brave frost and I in perfect good health, blessed be God. In my way saw a

a MS. 'and'   *b* repl. 'in'

---

1. Cf. above, i. 10 & n. 3.
2. Joseph Beaumont, Chaplain to the King; Master of Peterhouse, Cambridge, and Canon of Ely; later (1674) Regius Professor of Divinity. He was also a poet.

3. 'Praise him with the sound of the trumpet' (v. 3).
4. Alehouses were forbidden by law to open during the hours of church service.

woman that broke her thigh, in her heels slipping up upon the frosty street. To the Duke, and there we did our usual work. Here I saw the Royall Society*a* bring their new book, wherein is nobly writ their Charter and laws, and comes to be signed by the Duke as a Fellow; and all the Fellows' hands are to be entered there and lie as a monument, and the King hath put his, with the word "Founder".[1]

Thence I to Westminster to my barber's and found occasion to see Jane, but in presence of her mistress, and so could not speak to her of her failing me yesterday. And then to the Swan to Herberts girl, and lost time a little with her. And so took coach, and to my Lord Crews and dined with him; who receives me with the greatest respect that could be – telling me that he doth much doubt of the*b* success of this war with Holland; we going about it, he doubts, by the instigation of persons that do not enough apprehend the consequences of the danger of it – and therein I do think with him.

Holmes was this day sent to the tower – but I perceive it is made matter of jest only. But if the Dutch should be our maisters, it may come to be of earnest to him, to be given over to them for a sacrifice, as Sir W. Rawly was.[2]

Thence to White-hall to a Tanger Comittee; where I was accosted and most highly complimented by my Lord Bellasses our new Governor, beyond my expectation or measure I could imagine*c* he would have given any man, as if I were the only person of business that he intended to rely on, and desires my

a l.h. repl. l.h. rendered illegible   *b* repl. 'his'   *c* repl. 'am'

1. On 5 October 1664 the Society had ordered the compilation 'of a book to be called the Charter book, wherein forthwith is to be fairly written a copy of the charter, the statutes, and the register of the fellows and benefactors of the Society'. It was produced at the meeting of 11 January 1665: Birch, i. 472; ii. 4. It contains copies of the second charter of 1663 (and also of the third charter of 1669); 76 pages of statutes; and signatures, the first of which, that of the King as founder, is dated this day. Description in Sir H. Lyons, *Roy. Soc.*, pp. 53–4. The volume is still extant. A copy of the third charter and of the statutes of the Society is in PL 2831.

2. Holmes was imprisoned, and later held in custody, for his attack on Dutch W. Africa: see above, v. 283 & n. 1. He was released and pardoned in March, after the Dutch declaration of war. Ralegh had been executed in 1618 after attacking Spanish territory in S. America.

correspondence with him. This I was not only surprized at, but am well pleased with and may make good use of it. Our patent is renewed, and he and my Lord Barkely and Sir Tho. Ingram put in as commissioners.[1] Here some business happened which may bring me some profit.

Thence took coach; and calling my wife at her tailor's (she being come this afternoon to bring her mother some apples, neats tongues and brain) I home, and there at my office late with Sir W Warren and had a great deal of good discourse and counsel from him – which I hope I shall take, being all for my good in my deportment in[a] my office, yet with all honesty.

He gone, I home to supper and to bed.

10. Lay long, it being still very cold, and then to the office, where till dinner, and then home; and by and by to the office, where we sat and were very late, and I writing letters till 12 at night; and then after supper, to bed.

11. Up, and very angry with my boy for lying long a-bed and forgetting his Lute. To my office all the morning. At noon to the Change, and so home to dinner. After dinner to Gresham College to my Lord Brunker and Comissioner Pett, taking Mr. Castle with me, there to discourse over his draught of a ship he is to build for us[2] – where I first find reason to apprehend Comissioner Pett to be a man of any ability extraordinary in anything, for I found he did turn and wind Castle like a chicken in his business, and that most pertinently and master-like.[3] And

a repl. 'and every'

---

1. Belasyse was appointed Governor on 4 January. The commissioners' patent of 1662 (q.v. above, iii. 238 & n. 3) was now redrafted but not sealed until the following summer: PRO, SP 44/22, p. 217 (original and enrolment not traced). Berkeley of Stratton, one of the Commissioners of the Ordnance and Steward of the Duke of York's Household, had until recently been a Navy Commissioner. Ingram was Chancellor of the Duchy of Lancaster. Both were Privy Councillors and members of the Council of Trade.

2. The *Defiance*, a 3rd-rate, completed in the spring of the next year. This ship, together with several others built at this time, was copied from French and Dutch models, and was designed to carry the guns on the lower tier higher above the water than was usual.

3. Pett later condemned the *Defiance* 'for Baddness of Timber, Baddness of Scantlings . . .': NWB, p. 107 (31 January 1667).

great pleasure it was to me to hear them discourse, I of late having studied something thereon, and my Lord Brunker is a very able person also himself in this sort of business, as owning himself to be a master in the business of all lines and Conicall Sections.[1]   Thence home, where very late at my office, doing business to my content; though [God] knows with what a do it was that when I was out I could get myself to come home to my business, or when I was there, though late, could stay there from going abroad again.   To supper and to bed.

This evening, by a letter from Plymouth,[2] I hear that two of our ships, the *Leopard*, and another in the Streights, are lost by running aground, and that three more had like to have been so, but got off; whereof Captain Allen one – and that a Duch fleet are gone thither; which if they should meet with our lame ships, God knows what would become of them.[3]   This I reckon most sad news; God make us sensible of it. ⟨This night when I came home, I was much troubled to hear my poor Canary-bird that I have kept these three or four years is dead.⟩[a]

12.   Up, and to White-hall about getting a privy-seal for felling of the King's timber for the Navy, and to the Lords' House to speak with my Lord Privy Seal about it; and so to the Change – where to my last night's ill newes, I met more.   Spoke with a Frenchman who was taken, but released, by a Duch man-of-war of 36 guns (with seven more of the like or greater ships) off of the North Foreland, by Margett[4] – which is a strange attempt, that they should come to[b] our teeths.   But the wind being

---

a addition crowded in between entries   *b* repl. 'on'

---

1. Brouncker (first President of the Royal Society) was a considerable mathematician.   Some of his papers on the problems here referred to are in *Philos. Trans.*, iii (for 1668), pp. 645+; viii (for 1673), p. 6149.

2. John Lanyon to Pepys, 8 January: NMM, LBK/8, p. 147 (copy in Hewer's hand; printed *Further Corr.*, pp. 34–5).

3. The ships sunk were in fact the *Phoenix* and *Nonsuch*: see below, p. 10 & n. 1.   Four ships in all were stranded near Gibraltar on the night of 1–2 December through an error in navigation.   They thought they were well over to the African coast.   See Allin, i. 184–5, 218–24.

4. Pepys wrote to Sandwich this day to warn him about these ships: *Further Corr.*, pp. 35–6.

Easterly,[1] the wind that should bring our force from Portsmouth will carry them away home. God preserve us against them, and pardon our making them in our discourse so contemptible an enemy. So home and to dinner, where Mr. Hollyard with us dined.

So to the office and there late, till 11 at night and more, and then home to supper and to bed.

13. Up betimes, and walked to my Lord Bellasses lodging in Lincolns Inn fields, and there he received and discoursed with me in the most respectful manner that could be – telling me what a character of my judgment and care and love to Tanger he had received of me, that he desired my advice and my constant correspondence, which he much valued, and in my Courtship – in which, though I understand his design very well, and that it is only a piece of Courtship, yet it is a comfort to me that I am become so considerable as to have him need to say that to me; which if I did not do something in the world, would never have been. Here well satisfied, I to Sir Ph. Warwicke and there did some business with him. Thence to Jervas's and there spent a little idle time with him, his wife, Jane, and a sweetheart of hers. So to the Hall awhile and thence to the Exchange, where yesterday's news confirmed, though in a little different manner. But a couple of ships in the Straights we have lost, and the Duch have been in Margaret road. Thence home to dinner, and so abroad and alone to the King's house to a play, *The Traytor*,[2] where unfortunately I met with Sir W. Penn, so that I must be forced to confess it to my wife, which troubles me. Thence walked home, being ill-satisfied with the present actings of that house, and prefer the other house[3] before this infinitely.

To my Lady Batten's, where I find Pegg Pen, the first time that ever I saw her to wear spots.[4] Here very merry, Sir W. Batten being looked for tonight, but is not come from Harwich. So home to supper and to bed.

1. *Recte*, westerly.

2. A tragedy by James Shirley: see above, i. 300 & n. 1. (A).

3. The LIF used by the Duke's company under Davenant's management. The better discipline of the

Duke's Company and Pepys's great admiration for its leading actor, Betterton, help to explain his preference for its acting. (A).

4. For patches, see above, i. 234 & n. 3. Peg Penn was now 13.

14. Up, and to White Hall, where long waited in the Dukes chamber for a committee intended for Tanger; but none met, and so I home and to the office, where we met a little; and then to the Change, where our late ill news confirmed, in loss of two ships in the Straights; but are now the *Phœnix* and *Nonsuch*.[a][1] Home to dinner, and thence with my wife to the King's house, there to see *Vulpone*,[2] a most excellent play – the best I think I ever saw, and well acted. So with Sir W. Penn home in his coach, and then to the office; so home [to] supper and bed – resolving, by the grace of God, from this day to fall hard to my business again, after some, a week or fortnight's, neglect.

15. *Lords day.* Up; and after a little at my office to prepare a fresh draft of my vows for the next year, I to church, where a most insipid young coxcomb preached. Then home to dinner; and after dinner to read in Rusworths *Collections* about the charge against the late Duke of Buckingham,[3] in order to the fitting me to speak and understand the discourse anon before the King, about the suffering the Turkey merchants to send out their fleet at this dangerous time, when we can neither spare them ships to go, nor men nor King's ships to convoy them.[4]

At 4 a-clock with Sir W. Penn in his coach to my Lord Chancellors, where by and by Mr. Coventry, Sir W. Penn, Sir J Lawson, Sir G Ascue, and myself were called in to the King,

a rest of entry crowded into bottom of page

---

1. Cf. Pepys to Sandwich, 14 January: 'I have this day seen a letter from a master of a vessel lately come to Plymouth from Malaga, who in his way stopped at Gibraltar, where he found Captain Allen and 2 ships more safely got off, but the *Phoenix* and *Nonsuch* lost, all striking upon the great rock (as the letter says) that stands as you go into Gibraltar' (*Further Corr.*, pp. 36–7). Cf. above, p. 8, n. 2.

2. *Volpone, or The Fox*, a comedy by Jonson, acted in 1606 and published in 1608. The cast listed by Downes (p. 4) includes Mohun as Volpone. (A).

3. The reference is probably to the charge made in the impeachment of the 1st Duke of Buckingham (May 1628) that he had neglected the guard of the seas: John Rushworth, *Hist. Collections* (1659–1701), i. 307+, esp. pp. 312 and 385.

4. The Levant Company's negotiations with the King for a convoy are summarised in HMC, *Finch*, p. 363. An escort of six ships was granted in early February.

there being several of the Privy Council, and my Lord Chancellor lying at length upon a couch (of the goute I suppose); and there Sir W. Penn begun, and he had prepared heads in a paper and spoke pretty well to purpose, but with so much leisure and gravity as was tiresome – besides, the things he said was but very poor to a man in his trade after a great consideration. But it was to purpose endeed, to dissuade the King from letting*a* these Turkey ships to go out – saying (in short), the King having resolved to have 130 ships out by the spring, he must have above 20 of them merchantmen – towards which, he in the whole river could find but 12 or 14; and of them, the five ships taken up by these merchants were a part, and so could not be spared. That we should need 30000 to man these 130 ships; and of them in service we have not above 16000, so we shall need 14000 more. That these ships will with their convoys carry above 2000 men, and those the best men that could be got, it being the men used to the southward that are the best men for war, though those bred in the north among the Colliers are good for labour. That*b* it will not be safe for the merchants, nor honourable for the King, to expose these rich ships with his convoy of six ships to go, it not being enough to secure them against the Dutch, who without doubt will have a great fleet in the Straights. This, Sir J Lawson enlarged upon. Sir G Ascu, he chiefly spoke that the warr and trade could not be supported together – and therefore, that trade must stand still to give way to that.

This Mr. Coventry seconded, and showed how the medium of the men the King hath, one year with another, imployed in his Navy since his coming, hath not been above 3000 men, or at most 4000 men; and now having occasion of 30000, the remaining 26000 must be found out of the trade of the nation.

He showed how the Cloaths sending by these merchants to Turkey are already bought and paid for to the workmen, and are as many as they would send these twelve months or more; so the poor do not suffer by their not going, but only the merchant, upon whose hands they lie dead – and so the inconvenience is the less. And yet for them he propounded: either the King should, if his Treasure would suffer it, buy them, and showed the loss would not be so great to him – or dispense with the act of

a repl. 'sending'   *b* MS. 'That that'

Navigacion, and let them be carried out by strangers;[1] and ending, that he doubted not but when the merchants saw there was no remedy, they would and could find ways of sending them abroad to their profit.

All ended with a conviction (unless future discourse with the merchants should alter it) that it was not fit for them to go out, though the ships be loaded.

The King in discourse did ask me two or three Questions about my news of Allen's loss in the Straights; but I said nothing as to the business, nor am not much sorry for it, unless the King had spoke to me as he did to them, and then I could have said something to the purpose I think. So we withdrew, and the merchants were called in.

Staying without, my Lord Fitzharding came thither and fell to discourse of Prince Rupert, and made nothing to say that his disease was the pox[2] and that he must be Fluxed, telling the horrible degree of the disease upon him, with its breaking out on his head. But above all, I observed how he observed from the Prince that Courage is not what men take it to be, a contempt of death; "For," says he, "how Chagrin the Prince was the other day when he thought he should die – having no more mind to it then another man; but," says he, "some men are more apt to think they shall escape then another man in fight, while another is doubtful he shall be hit. But when the first man is sure he shall die, as now the Prince is, he is as much troubled and apprehensive of it as any man else. For," says he, "sence we told him that we believe he would overcome his disease, he is as merry, and swears and laughs and curses and doth all the things of a [man] in health, as ever he did in his life" – which methought was a most extraordinary saying, before a great many persons

---

1. The Navigation Act of 1660 forbade the use of foreign ships in these circumstances, but could be evaded by the exercise of the royal prerogative of dispensation or suspension.

2. This was the diagnosis favoured by Rupert's enemies. Denham in his *Directions to a painter* (1667) wrote of it as caused by some 'treach'rous *Jael*'. But Rupert was suffering from an old war wound received in Flanders and recently aggravated by the fall of a block on board ship in November 1664, for which he underwent three operations in 1664–7: *CSPD 1664–5*, p. 56; *CSPVen. 1664–6*, p. 63, n.; E. Warburton, *Mem. Rupert* (1849), iii. 486–7. He now recovered in time to take part in the spring campaign.

there of quality. So by and by with Sir W. Penn home again; and after supper to the office to finish my vows, and so to bed.

16. Up, and with Sir W. Batten and Sir W. Penn to Whitehall, where we did our business with the Duke. Thence I to Westminster hall and walked up and down. Among others, Ned Pickering met me and tells me how active my Lord is at sea[1] – and that my Lord Hinchingbrooke is now at Rome,[2] and by all reports a very noble and hopeful gentleman.

Thence to Mr. Povy's and there met Creed and dined well, after his old*a* manner of plenty and curiosity. But I sat in pain, to think whether he would begin with me again after dinner with his enquiry after my bill;[3] but he did not, but fell into other discourse, at which I was glad. But was vexed this morning, meeting of Creed, at some bye-questions that he demanded of me about some such thing; which made me fear he meant that very matter – but I perceive he did not.

Thence to visit my Lady Sandwich; and so to a Tanger Comittee, where a great company of the new Comissioners, Lords, that in behalf of my Lord Bellasses are very loud and busy, and call for Povy's accounts; but it was a most sorrowful thing to see how he answered to Questions so little to the purpose, but*b* to his own wrong. All the while, I sensible how I am concerned in my bill of 100*l* and somewhat more; so great a trouble is fear, though in a case that at the worst will bear enquiry.*c*

My Lord Berkely were very violent against Povy. But my Lord Ashly, I observe, is a most clear man in matters of accounts, and most ingeniously did discourse and explain all matters. We broke up, leaving the thing to a committee, of which I am one. Povy, Creed, and I stayed discoursing, I much troubled in mind seemingly for that business; but indeed, only on my own behalf, though I have no great reason for it, but so painful a thing is fear.

So after considering how to order business, Povy and I walked together as far as the New Exchange, and so parted and I by coach home. To the office a while; then to supper and to bed. This afternoon Secretary Bennet read to the Duke of Yorke

a repl. 'own'   *b* repl. 'to'   *c* repl. 'some'

---

1. On winter guard in St Helens Road. Pickering had left him on the 3rd: Sandwich, p. 161.   2. See above, ii. 142, n. 3.   3. See above, v. 340 & n. 2.

his letters, which say that Allen hath met with the Duch Smyrna fleet at Cales, and sunk one and taken three.[1] How true, or what these ships are, time will show; but it is good news – and the news of our ships being lost is doubted at Cales and Malaga. God send it false.

17. Up, and walked to Mr. Povy's by appointment, where I found him and Creed busy about fitting things for the committee; and thence we to my Lord Ashly's, where, to see how simply, beyond all patience, Povey did again, by his many words and no understanding, confound himself and his business to his disgrace and rendering everybody doubtful of his being either a fool or a knave – is very wonderful. We broke up, all dissatisfied, and referred the business to a meeting of Mr. Sherwin and others to settle.   But here it was mighty strange methought, to find myself to sit here in committee with my hat on, while Mr. Sherwin stood bare as a clerk, with his hat off to his Lord Ashly and the rest.[2]   But I thank God, I think myself never a whit the better man for all that.

Thence with Creed to the Change and Coffee-house – and so home, where a brave dinner, by having a brace of pheasants, and very merry about Povy's folly.

So anon to the office, and there sitting very late; and then after a little time at Sir W. Batten's, where I am mighty great, and could, if I thought it fit, continue so, I to my office again and there very late; and so home to the sorting of some of my books, and so to bed – the weather becoming pretty warm, and I think and hope the frost will break.

18. Up, and by and by to my bookseller's and there did give thorough direction for the new binding of a great many of my old books, to make my whole study of the same binding, within

1. On 19 December Allin had made an unprovoked attack on the Dutch merchantmen off Cadiz ('Cales'), and had taken two and sunk two: Allin, i. 191–3; *CSPD 1664–5*, p. 122; below, p. 19 & n. 2. This was the immediate cause of the war which followed.

2. Richard Sherwin had been an M.P. and a senior official of the Exchequer when Pepys had been a young clerk there. He was now secretary to Ashley.

very few.[1]   Thence to my Lady Sandwiches, who sent for me this morning.   Dined with her – and it was to get a letter of hers conveyed by a safe hand to my Lord's own hand at Portsmouth; which I did undertake.   Here my Lady did begin to talk of what she hath heard concerning Creed; of his being suspected to be a fanatic[2] and a false fellow.   I told her I thought he was as shrewd and cunning a man as any in England, and one that I would fear first should outwit me in everything – to which she readily concurred. Thence to Mr. Povy's by agreement; and there, with Mr. Sherwin, Auditor Beale, and Creede and I, hard at it very late about Mr. Povys accounts;   but such accounts I never did see, or hope again to see in my days.   At night late, they gone, I did get him to put out of this account our sums that are *in posse* only yet – which he approved of when told, but would never have stayed it if I had been gone.   Thence at 9 at night home; and so to supper, vexed and head akeing, and to bed.

19.   Up, and it being yesterday and today a great thaw, it is not for a man to walk the streets, but took coach and to Mr. Povys; and there meeting, all of us, again agreed upon an answer to the Lords by and by;   and then we did come to Exeter-house, and there was a witness of most*ᵃ* [angry] language against Mr. Povy from my Lord Peterburgh, who is most furiously angry with him, because the other, as a fool, would needs say that that 26000*l* was my Lord Peterburgh's account and that he had nothing to do with it.[3]

The Lords did find fault also with*ᵇ* our answer, but I think verily my Lord Ashly would fain have the outside of an Ex-

a repl. 'a'–   *b* repl. 'without'

---

1. See H. M. Nixon's account of the binding in the forthcoming catalogue of the PL.   The books would now presumably be bound in what Pepys has previously called his 'common binding' (see above, iv. 255 & n. 2).   The bookseller was Joshua Kirton of St Paul's Churchyard.

2. Cf. above, v. 108 & n. 1.
3. For these accounts, see above, p. 13; also above, v. 48 & n. 1. The £26,000 was in dispute between Povey as Treasurer of Tangier and Peterborough as Governor (1661–2), and appears to have represented payments made for the garrison.   Routh, p. 365; PRO, E 351/357.

chequer – but when we comes better to be examined.[1] So home by coach with my Lord Barkeley, who by his discourse I find doth look upon Mr. Coventry as an enemy, but yet professes great justice and pains.

At home, after dinner to the office and there sat all the afternoon and evening; and then home to supper and to bed.

Memorandum. This day and yesterday, I think it is the change of the weather, I have a great deal*a* of pain, but nothing like what I use to have – I can hardly keep myself loose; but on the contrary, am*b* forced to drive away my pain. Here, I am so sleepy, I cannot hold open my eyes nor pen,*c* and therefore must be forced to break*d* off this day's passages more shortly then I would and should have done.*e*

This day was buried (but I could not be there) my cousin Percivall Angier.[2] And yesterday I received the news that Dr. Tom Pepys is dead at Impington – for which I am but little sorry; not only because he would have been troublesome to us,[3] but a shame to his family and profession, he was such a coxcomb.

20. Up and to Westminster, where having spoke with Sir Ph. Warwicke, I to Jervas's and there do find them all in a great disorder about Jane, her mistress telling me secretly that she was sworn not to reveal anything, but she was undone. At last, for all her oath, she told me that she had made herself sure to a fellow that comes to their house that can only fiddle for his living – and did keep him company and had plainly told her that she was sure to him, never to leave him for anybody else. Now they were this day contriving to get her presently* to marry one Hayes that was there, and I did seem to persuade her to it, and at last got them to suffer me to advise privately, and by that means had

a repl. 'month'   *b* repl. 'is'   *c* repl. 'pan'   *d* repl. 'rise'
e The numerous errors and corrections in this paragraph testify to Pepys's weariness.

---

1. Possibly 'an Exchequer' is a slip for 'the Exchequer'. Some obscurities still remain (cf. above, note *e*), but the meaning may be that Ashley (Chancellor of the Exchequer) would prefer to have nothing to do with the Exchequer if accounts were not better presented for examination. (I owe this suggestion to Dr H. G. Roseveare.)

2. Percival Angier of London; a merchant.

3. As a creditor of Pepys's brother Tom: above, v. 85 & n. 1.

her company and I think shall meet her next Sunday; but I do verily doubt she will be undone in*a* marrying this fellow. But I did give her my advice, and so let her do her pleasure, so I have now and then her company.

Thence to the Swan at noon, and there sent for a bit of meat and dined and had my baiser of the*b* fille of the house there – but nothing plus. So took coach and to my Lady Sandwiches; and so to my booksellers and there took home Hookes book of Microscopy,[1] a most excellent piece,*c* and of which I am very proud.

So home, and by and by again abroad with my wife about several businesses; and met at the New Exchange, and there to our trouble find our pretty Doll is gone away to live, they say with her father in the country – but I doubt something worse.

So homeward, in my way buying a hare and taking it home – which arose upon my discourse today with Mr. Batten in Westminster-hall – who showed me my mistake, that my hares-foot[2] hath not the joynt to it, and assures me he never had his cholique since*d* he carried it about him. And it is a strange thing how fancy works, for I no sooner almost handled his foot but my belly begin to be loose and to break wind; and whereas I was in some pain yesterday and t'other day, and in fear of more today, I became very well, and so continue.

At home to my office a while, and so to supper – read, and to cards and to bed.

21. At the office all the morning. Thence my Lord Brunker carried me as far as Mr. Povy's and there I light and dined, meeting Mr. Sherwin, Creed, &c. there upon his accounts. After dinner they parted, and Mr. Povy carried me to Somersett-house and there showed me the Queen-mother's chamber and closet, most beautiful places for furniture and pictures;[3] and so

a MS. 'his'   *b* repl. 'his'   *c* repl. 'pr'—   *d* repl. 'more'

1. See above, p. 2, n. 2.
2. See above, v. 359 & n. 1.
3. There is no evidence about the furnishings and pictures in Henrietta-Maria's new rooms at Somerset House. Possibly they included some of the pictures which had hung there in the time of Charles I and which

may have been recovered at the Restoration. Such pictures were certainly hanging at Colombes when the Queen Mother died there in 1669, and are specifically described as such in the inventory of her possessions taken there at that time: PRO, SP 78/128, ff. 209–25. (OM).

down the great stone stairs to the garden and tried the brave
Eccho upon the stairs – which continues a voice so long as the
singing three notes, concords, one after another, they all three shall
sound in consort together a good while most pleasantly.   Thence
to a Tanger Comittee at White-hall, where*a* I saw nothing
ordered by judgment, but great heat and passion and faction
now, in behalf of my Lord Bellasses and to the reproach of my
Lord Tiviott, and dislike as it were of former proceedings.

So away with Mr. Povey, he carrying me homeward to Mark-
lane in his coach.   A simple fellow I now find him, to his utter
shame, in his business of accounts, as none but a sorry fool would
have discovered himself – and yet in little light sorry things, very
cunning; yet in the principal, the most ignorant man I ever met
with in so great trust as he is.

To my office till past 12, and then home to supper and to bed –
being now mighty well; and truly, I cannot but impute it to my
fresh Hares=Foote.   ⟨Before I went to bed, I sat up till 2 a-clock
in my chamber, reading of Mr. Hookes Microscopicall Observa-
cions, the most ingenious book that ever I read in my life.⟩*b*

22. *Lords day.*   Up, leaving my wife in bed, being sick of her
months, and to church.   Thence home, and in my wife's chamber
dined very merry, discoursing among other things of a design I
have come in my head this morning at church, of making a match
between Mrs. Betty Pickering and Mr. Hill my friend, the
merchant that loves musique and comes to me a-Sundays, a most
ingenious and sweet-natured and highly accomplished person.
I know not how their fortunes may agree, but their disposition
and merits are much of a sort, and persons, though different, yet
equally I think acceptable.[1]

After dinner walked to Westminster; and after being at the
Abbey and heard a good Anthem well sung there, I, as I had
appointed, to the Trumpett, there expecting when Jane Welsh
should come; but anon comes a maid of the house to tell me that
her mistress and maister would not let her go forth, not knowing

a   preceding part of paragraph crowded into bottom of page
b   addition crowded in between entries

1. Betty Pickering, Sandwich's   people) John Creed: below, p. 88,
niece, eventually married (of all   n. 2.

of my being here but to keep her from her sweetheart. So being defeated, away by coach home, and there spent the evening prettily in discourse with my wife and Mercer, and so to supper, prayers, and to bed.

23. Up, and with Sir W. Batten and Sir W. Penn to Whitehall; but there finding the Duke gone to his lodgings at St. James's for altogether, his*a* Duchesse being ready to lie-in,[1] we to him and there did our usual business. And here I met the great news, confirmed by the Dukes own relation, by a letter from Captain Allen[2] – first, of our loss of two ships, the *Phœnix* and *Nonesuch*, in the Bay of Gibraltar – then, of his and his seven ships with him, in the Bay of Cales or thereabouts, fight with the 34 Duch Smirna fleet – sinking the *King Salamon*, a ship worth 150000*l* or more, some say 200000*l*, and another, and taking of three merchant-ships. Two of our ships were disabled, by the Duch unfortunately falling against their will against them; the *Advice*, Captain W. Poole, and *Anthelop*, Captain Clerke. The Dutch men-of-warr did little service. Captain Allen did receive many shots at distance before he would fire one gun; which he did not do till he came within pistol-shot of his enemy. The Spaniards on shore at Cales did stand laughing at the Duch, to see them run away and fly to the shore, 34 or thereabouts against 8 Englishmen at most.[3] I do purpose to get the whole relation, if I live, of Captain Allen himself. In our loss of the two ships in the Bay of Gibraltar, it is observable how the world doth comment upon the misfortune*b* of Captain Moone of the *Nonsuch*, who did lose in the same manner the *Satisfaction*,[4] as a person that hath ill-luck attending him, without considering that the whole fleet was ashore: Captain Allen led the way, and Captain Allen himself writes that all the maisters of the fleet, old and young, were mistaken and did carry their ships

a repl. 'her'   *b* repl. 'mis' —

---

1. The Duke usually went there only for the summer.

2. Allin to Coventry, Cadiz Bay, 23 December: copy in Tanner 294, ff. 16*v*–17*v*.

3. Allin had eight men of war;

the Dutch 30 merchantmen and three warships. This was the action of 19 December: for other accounts, see above, p. 14 & n. 1; *The Intelligencer*, 23 January, p. 52.

4. See above, iii. 213 & n. 1.

aground.[1] But I think I heard the Duke say that Moone, being put into the *Oxford*, had in this conflict regained his credit, by sinking one and taking another. Captain Seale of the *Milford* hath done his part very well, in boarding the *King Salamon* – which held out half an hour after she was boarded – and his men kept her an hour after they did maister her; and then she sunk and drowned about 17 of her men.

Thence to Jervas's, my mind, God forgive me, running too much after sa fille, but elle not being within, I away by coach to the Change – and thence home to dinner; and finding Mrs. Bag-well waiting at the office after dinner,[a] away elle and I to a cabaret where elle and I have été before; and there I had her company toute l'après-dîner and had mon plein plaisir of elle – but strange, to see how a woman, notwithstanding her greatest pretences of love à son mari and religion, may be vaincue. Thence to the Court of the Turky Company at Sir Andr. Rickard's, to treat about carrying some men of ours to Tanger, and had there a very civil reception, though a denial of the thing, as not prac-ticable with them, and I think so too. So to my office a little; but being minded to make an end of my pleasure today, that I might fallow my business, I did take coach and to Jervas's again, thinking to avoir rencontré Jane; mais elle n'était pas dedans. So I back again and to my office, where I did with great content faire a vow to mind my business and laisser aller les femmes for a month;[2] and am with all my heart glad to find[b] myself able to come to so good a resolution, that thereby I may fallow my business, which, and my honour thereby, lies a-bleeding. So home to supper and to bed.

24. Up, and by coach to Westminster-hall and the Parliament-house, and there spoke with Mr. Coventry and others about business; and so back to the Change, where no news more then that the Dutch have, by consent of all the Provinces, voted no trade to be suffered for 18 months, but that they apply themselfs

a repl. 'day'   *b* repl. 'bring'

---

1. Allin wrote: 'Of so many ancient masters and officers never was such an oversight committed' (Allin, i. 185).

2. The oath seems to have been renewed on 23 February (his birth-day) and may be the oath which expired on 15 May.

wholly to the war.[1]   And they say it is very true but very strange, for we use to believe they cannot support themselfs without trade.

Thence home to dinner and then to the office, where all the afternoon and at night till very late; and then home to supper and bed, having a great cold, got on Sunday last by sitting too long with my head bare for Mercer to comb me and wash my eares.

25.   Up, and busy all the morning.   Dined at home upon a Hare=py, very good meat; and so to my office again, and in the afternoon by coach to attend the Council at White-hall, but come too late; so back with Mr. Gifford, a merchant, and he and I to the Coffee-house, where I met Mr. Hill and there he tells me that he is to bee Assistant to the Secretary of the Prize-office (Sir Ellis Layton),[2] which is to be held at Sir Rd. Fords – which methinks is but something low, but perhaps may bring him something considerable.   But it makes me alter my opinion of his being so rich as to make a fortune for Mrs. Pickering.

Thence home and visited Sir J. Mennes, who continues ill but is something better.   There he told me what a mad freaking fellow Sir Ellis Layton hath been and is – and once at Antwerp, was really mad.[3]

Thence to my office late, my cold troubling me and having, by squeezing myself in a coach, hurt my testicles; but I hope I will cease its pain without swelling.   So home, out of order, to supper and to bed.

26.   Lay, being in some pain, but not much, with my last night's bruise; but up and to my office, where busy all the morning; the like after dinner till very late; then home to supper and to bed.

1. An exaggeration. On 16/26 January two decrees had been issued: one prohibiting all imports from England, and the other stopping the Greenland trade.   At about the same time letters of marque were issued. All these measures were in retaliation against Allin's attack on the Dutch Smyrna fleet.   Colenbrander, i. 157; *The Newes*, 2 February, p. 78.

2. The Prize Office had been set up on 20-1 January: *CSPD 1664-5*, p. 175. For Leighton, see above, v. 300, n. 5.

3. This was in 1652, when he had gone first mad and then Papist: *CSPClar.*, ii. 162; *Nicholas Papers* (ed. G. F. Warner), i. 321.

My wife mightily troubled with the tooth-ake and my cold
not being gone yet; but my bruise yesterday goes away again,
and it chiefly occasioned, I think now, from the sudden change
of the weather from a frost to a great rayne on a sudden.

27. Called up by Mr. Creed to discourse about some Tanger
business. And he gone, I made me ready and find Jane Welsh,
Mr. Jervas his maid, come to tell me that she was gone from her
master and is resolved to stick to this sweetheart of hers, one
Harbing (a very sorry little fellow, and poor); which I did in a
word or two endeavour to dissuade her from. But being unwilling to keep her long at my house, I sent her away and by
and by fallowed her to the Exchange, and thence led her about
down to the Three Cranes, and there took boat for the Falcon
and at a house going into the fields there, took up and sat an
hour or two talking and discoursing and faisant ce que je voudrais
quant à la toucher; but she would not laisser me faire l'autre
thing, though I did what I pouvais to have got her à me*a* le laisser.
But I did enough to faire grand plaisir à moy-même. Thence,
having endeavoured to make her think of making herself happy
by staying out her time with her master, and other counsels;
but she told me she could not do it, for it was her fortune to
have this man, though she did believe it would be to her ruine –
which is a strange, stupid thing, to a fellow of no kind of worth
in the world and a beggar to boot.

Thence away to boat again, and landed her at the Three Cranes
again and I to the Bridge and so home; and after shifting myself,
being dirty, I to the Change and thence to Mr. Povys and there
dined; and thence with him and Creed to my Lord Bellassis
and there debated a great while how to put things in order against
his going;[1] and so with my Lord in his coach to White-hall, and
with him to my Lord Duke of Albemarle, finding him at cards.
After a few dull words or two, I away to White-hall again and
there delivered a letter to the Duke of Yorke about our Navy
business;[2] and thence walked up and down in the gallery, talking
with Mr. Slingsby, who is a very ingenious person, about the

a MS. 'me me'

1. To Tangier, as Governor.
2. Untraced: possibly Navy Board
to Duke of York (?1665), about, *inter*

alia, the growing debt of the navy
(*CSPClar.*, v. 523-4).

Mint and coynage of money.[1] Among other things, he argues that there being 700000*l* coined in the Rump time,[2] and, by all the Treasurers of that time, it being their opinion that the Rump money was in all payments, one with another, about a tenth part of all their money – "then," says he (to my question), "the nearest guess we can make is that the money passing up and down in business is 7000000*l*."[a]

To another question of mine, he made me fully understand that the old law of prohibiting[b] bullion to be exported is, and ever was, a folly and an injury, rather then good.[3] Arguing thus – that if the exportations[c] exceed importations, then the balance must be brought home in money; which, when our merchants know cannot be carried out again, they will forbear to bring home in money, but let it lie abroad for trade or keep in foreign banks. Or if our importations exceed our exportations, then to keep credit, the merchants will and must find ways of carrying out money by stealth, which is a most easy thing to do and is everywhere done, and therefore the law against it signifies[d] nothing in the world – besides, that it is seen that where money is free, there is great plenty; where it is restrained, as here, there is great[e] want, as in Spain.

These and many other fine discourses I had from him.

Thence by coach home (to see Sir J. Mennes first), who is still sick, and I doubt worse then he seems to be. Mrs. Turner here took me into her closet, and there did give me a glass of most pure water and showed me her Rocke,[f4] which endeed is a very noble thing, but a very bawble.

So away to my office, where late busy; and then home to supper and to bed.

a repl. figure rendered illegible   *b* repl. 'S'-   *c* repl. 'expr.'
d repl. 'signif'-   *e* repl. 'every'-   *f* l.h. superimposed on s.h. 'rock'

1. Henry Slingsby was Master of the Mint.

2. This figure was known because the Commonwealth money had been called in to the Mint by proclamation in 1661: cf. above, iv. 148; below, p. 326.

3. Pepys had been puzzled by a similar argument on a previous occasion: above, v. 70. Partial freedom of export had been allowed by an act of 1663, and the movement for a free market in bullion was now gaining strength. See Sir A. E. Feavearyear, *Pound Sterling*, p. 87. Thomas Mun's book advocating this policy (*England's treasure by foreign trade*), written under Charles I, was published in 1664.

4. Probably a distaff; or possibly rock-work made of shells: cf. above, i. 148 & n. 2.

28*a*.   Up, and to my office, where all the morning – and then home to dinner, and after dinner, abroad; walked to Pauls churchyard, but my books not bound, which vexed me;[1] so home to my office again, where very late about business; and so home to supper and to bed – my cold continuing in a great degree upon me still.

This day I receive a good sum of money, due to me upon one score or another from Sir G. Carteret, among others, to clear all my matters about colours, wherein a month or two since I was so embarrassed; and I thank God,*b* I find myself to have got clear, by that commodity, 50*l* and something more – and earned it with dear pains and care, and issuing of my own money, and saved the King near 100*l* in it.[2]

29.   *Lords day.*   Up, and to my office, where all the morning putting papers to rights, which now grow upon my hand.   At noon dined at home.   All the afternoon at my business again. In the evening comes Mr. Andrews and Hill, and we up to my chamber and there good Musique, though my great cold made it the less pleasing to me.   Then Mr. Hill (the other going away) and I to supper alone, my wife not appearing – our discourse upon the perticular vain humours of Mr. Povy, which are very extraordinary endeed.

After supper I to Sir W. Batten's, where I found him, Sir W. Batten, Sir J Robinson, Sir R. Ford and Captain Cocke and Mr. Fen Junior.   Here a great deal of sorry disordered talk about the Trinity-house men their being exempted from land service.[3]

a repl. '27'   *b* MS. 'Got'

1. The order had been given on the 18th and was completed on 10 February.

2. This was the matter of the calico flags which Pepys himself had arranged to supply: see above, v. 292, 295 & nn.   His claim to have saved money for the King ignores the fact that calico was inferior to bewpers: see B. Pool, *Navy Board contracts, 1660–1832*, p. 39.

3. In November 1664 Trinity House had protested to Sir John Robinson on behalf of one of the brethren of the corporation summoned to serve in the militia.   In March they petitioned the King and the Duke of York, and on 31 March the Privy Council ordered that members of the corporation were to enjoy their ancient exemption from service, except in cases when it might be commanded by council warrant: HMC, *Rep.*, 8/1/1/252*b*.   But in August 1667 similar complaints were made: ib., p. 253*b*.

But Lord, to see how void of method and sense their discourse was, and in what heat; insomuch as Sir Rd. Ford (who we judged, some of us, to be a little foxed) fell into very high terms with Sir W. Batten and then with Captain Cocke – so that I see that no man is wise at all times.

Thence home to prayers and to bed.

30. This is solemnly kept as a Fast[1] all over the City; but I kept my house, putting my closett to rights again, having lately put it out of order in removing my books and things in order to being made clean. At this all day, and at night to my office, there to do some business. And being late at it, comes Mercer to me to tell me that my wife was in bed and desired me to come home, for they hear, and have night after night lately heard, noises over their head upon the leads. Now, it is strange to think how, knowing that I have a great sum of money in my house,[2] this puts me into a most mighty affright, that for more then two hours I could not almost tell what to do or say, but feared this and that – and remembered that this evening I saw a woman and two men stand suspiciously in the Entry in the dark; I calling to them, they made me only this answer: the woman said that the men came to see her. But who she was I could not tell. The truth is, my house is mighty dangerous, having so many ways to be come to, and at my windows over the stairs, to see who goes up and down – but if I escape tonight, I will remedy it. God preserve us this night safe. So at almost 2 a-clock, I home to my house and in great fear to bed, thinking every running of a mouse really a thief – and so to sleep, very brokenly all night long – and found all safe in the morning.

31. Up, and with Sir W. Batten to Westminster, where to speak at the House with my Lord Bellasses, and am cruelly vexed to see myself put upon businesses so uncertainly, about getting ships for Tanger being ordered, a servile thing, almost every day.

So to the Change, back by coach with Sir W. Batten, and thence to the Crowne, a tavern hard by, with Sir W Rider and Cutler; where we alone, a very good dinner. Thence home to the office and there all the afternoon late. The office being up,

1. In commemoration of the execution of Charles I.   2. Over £1200: below, p. 26.

my wife sent for me; and what was it but to tell me how Jane carries herself and I must put her away presently. But I did hear both sides, and find my wife much in fault; and the grounds of all the difference is my wife's fondness of Tom, to the being displeased with all the house beside to defend the boy; which vexes me, but I will cure it. Many high words between my wife and I, but the wench shall go; but I will take a course with the boy, for I fear I have spoiled him already.

Thence to the office, to my accounts; and there, at once to ease my mind, I have made myself debtor to Mr. Povy for the 117*l*. 5*s*. got with so much joy the last month;[1] but seeing that it is not like to be kept without some trouble and Question, I do even discharge my mind of it; and so if I come now to refund it, as I fear I shall, I shall now be ne'er a whit the poorer for it – though yet it is some trouble to me to be poorer by such a sum then I thought myself a month since. But however, a quiet mind and to be sure of my owne is worth all. The Lord be praised for what I have, which is this month come down to 1257*l*. I stayed up about my accounts till almost 2 in the morning.

1. See above, v. 340 & n. 2.

FEBRUARY.

1. Lay long in bed; which made me, going by coach to St. James by appointment to have attended the Duke of Yorke and my Lord Bellasses, lose the hopes of my getting something by the hire of a ship to carry men to Tanger. But however, according to the order of the Duke this morning, I did go to the Change and there, after great pains, did light of a business with Mr. Gifford and Hubland[1] may bring me as much as I hoped for – which I have at large expressed in my stating the case of the *King's Fisher*, which is the ship that I have hired,[2] and got the Duke of Yorkes agreement this afternoon, after much pains and not eating a bit of bread till about 4 a-clock: going home, I put in to an ordinary by Temple barr, and there with my boy Tom eat a pullet; and thence home to the office, being still angry with my wife for yesterday's foolery. After a good while at the office, I with the boy to the Sun behind the Exchange, by agreement with Mr. Young the flag-maker, and there was met by Mr. Hill, Andrews, and Mr. Hubland, a pretty serious man. Here, two very pretty savoury dishes and good discourse. After supper, a song, or three or four (I having to that purpose carried Lawes's book);[3] and staying here till 12 a-clock, got the wach to light me home – and, in a continued discontent, to bed. After being in bed, my people came and say there is a great stink of Burning, but no smoake. We called up Sir J. Mennes's and Sir W. Batten's people, and Griffin and the people at the Mad=house,[4] but nothing could be found to give occasion to it; at this trouble we were till past 3 a-clock, and then the stink ceasing, I to sleep and my people to bed, and lay very long in the morning.

1. Probably James Houblon, jun., who became one of Pepys's closest friends in the period after the diary ends.
2. From Sir W. Warren: *CSPD 1664-5*, p. 51.
3. Pepys possessed Henry Lawes's three books of *Ayres and dialogues* (1653, 1655 and 1658): see above, iii. 27, n. 4; i. 76, n. 2; 164, n. 2. They were possibly bound up as a single volume. (E).
4. Possibly Penn's house (cf. Pepys's reference to Penn's 'simple talk', below, vii. 90). But if so, this is the only occasion on which Pepys gives it this nickname. There was no real madhouse close by.

2.[a] Then up and to my office, where till noon, and then to the Change; and at the Coffee-house alone Gifford, Hubland, the maister of the ship, and I read over and approved a Charter party for carrying goods for Tanger, wherein I hope to get some[b] money. Thence home, my head akeing for want of rest and too much business. So to the office. At night comes Povy, and he and I to Mrs. Blands to discourse about my serving her, to help her to a good passage for Tanger.[1] Here I heard her Kinswoman sing three or four very fine songs, and in good manner. And then home and to supper. My cook-mayd Jane and her mistress parted, and she went away this day. I vexed to myself – but was resolved to have no more trouble. And so after supper to my office and then to bed.

3.   Up, and walked with my boy (whom, because of my wife's making of him idle, I dare not leave at home); walked first to Salsbury court, there to excuse my not being at home at dinner to Mrs. Turner; who I perceive is vexed because I do not serve her in[c] something against the great feasting for her husband's reading in helping her to some good pennorths, but I care not.[2] She was dressing herself by the fire in her chamber, and there took occasion to show me her leg, which endeed is the finest I ever saw, and she not a little proud of it.

Thence to my Lord Bellases. Thence to Mr. Povys, and so up and down at that end of the town about several businesses, it being a brave frosty day and good walking; so back again on foot to the Change, in my way[d] taking my books from binding from my bookseller's: my bill for the rebinding of some old books, to make them suit with my study, cost me (besides other new books in the same bill) 3*l*[3] – but it will be very handsome.

---

a   entry crowded into bottom of page   b   repl. 'in'
c   repl. 'with'   d   MS. 'wife'

---

1. Her husband John, a merchant, became the first mayor of Tangier in 1668.

2. John Turner was Lenten Reader at the Middle Temple, and as such it was his duty to read lectures on a given theme (usually a statute), and also to provide feasts at great ex-pense, and for days on end. (Cf. below, p. 49 & n. 2.) His wife, a relative of Pepys, had hoped to get navy victuals cheaply through the Navy Office.

3. For bookbinding costs, see *A general note of the price of binding . . . August 2d 1669* (ed. W. A. Jackson).

At the Change did several businesses; and here I hear that news is come from Deale, that the same day my Lord Sandwich sailed thence with the fleet – that evening some Dutch men-of-war were seen on the back-side of the Goodwin, and by all conjecture, must be seen by my Lord's fleet – which if so, they must engage.[1]

Thence, being invited, to my uncle Wights, where the Wights all dined; and among the others, pretty Mrs. Margaret,[2] who indeed is a very pretty lady, and though by my vow[3] it cost me 12*d* a kiss after the first, yet I did adventure upon a couple.

So home; and among other letters, find one from Jane that is newly gone, telling me how her mistress won't pay her her Quarter's wages – and withal tells me how her mistress will have the boy sit three or four hours together in the dark, telling of stories – but speaks of nothing but only her indiscretion in undervaluing herself to do it. But I will remedy that – but am vexed she should get somebody to write so much, because of making it public. Then took coach and to visit my Lady Sandwich; where she discoursed largely to me her[a] opinion of a match, if it could be thought fit by my Lord, for my Lady Jemimah with Sir G Carteret's eldest son. But I doubt he hath yet no settled estate in land – but I will inform myself, and give her my opinion. Then Mrs. Pickering (after private discourse ended, we going into the other room) did at my Lady's command tell me the manner of a Masquerade before the King and Court the other day – where six women (my Lady Castlemayne and Duchesse of Monmouth being two of them) and six men (the Duke of Monmouth and Lord Aron[4] and Monsieur Blanfort[5] being three of them) in vizards, but most rich and antique dresses, did dance admirably and most gloriously.[6] God give us cause to continue that mirth.

So home; and after a while at my office, to supper and to bed.

a MS. 'how'

---

1. Sandwich searched for but could not find this fleet: Sandwich, pp. 165–6.

2. Their daughter, now aged about 19. She married John Perrier in 1668.

3. See above, p. 20 & n. 2.

4. The 1st Earl of Arran, son of the Duke of Ormond.

5. Marquis de Blanquefort, later (1676) 2nd Earl of Feversham.

6. Evelyn saw the masque on 2 February (Candlemas) when it was performed by '6 Gent: & 6 Ladys Surprizing his Majestie'. Gramont (pp. 119+) says that it had been arranged by the Queen, and that the dancers represented different nations.

4. Lay long in bed, discoursing with my wife about her maids, which, by Janes going away in discontent and against my opinion, doth make some trouble between my*a* wife and me. But those are but foolish troubles, and so not to be set to heart; yet it doth disturb me mightily, those things.

To my office, and there all the morning. At noon, being invited, I to the Sun behind the Change to dinner to my Lord Bellasses – where a great deal of discourse with him – and some good. Among other at table, he told us a very handsome passage of the King's sending him his message about holding out the town of Newarke, of which he was then governor for the King. This message he sent in a Slugg=bullet, being writ in Cypher and wrapped up in lead and swallowed. So the messenger came to my Lord and told him he had a message from the King, but it was yet in his belly; so they did give him some physic, and out it came. This was a month before the King's flying to the Scotts; and therein he told him that at such a day, being the 3 or 6 of May, he should hear of his being come to the Scotts, being assured by the King of France that in coming to them, he should be used with all the Liberty, Honour and safety that could be desired. And at the just day he did come to the Scotts.[1]

He told us another odd passage: how the King, having newly put out Prince Rupert of his Generallshipp upon some miscarriage at Bristoll, and Sir Rd. Willis of his governorshipp of Newarke at the entreaty of the gentry of the County, and put in my Lord Bellasses – the great officers of the King's Army mutinyed, and

a repl. 'us'

---

[1]. The letter (from Oxford; undated, early April 1646) is printed in HMC, *Ormonde*, n.s., ii. 392–3; and A. C. Wood, *Nottinghamshire in Civil War*, p. 115. It begins: 'If you discover the Secret I now import to you by this Extraordinary way of Conveyance. . . '. The King informed Belasyse that he would join the Scots besieging Newark on 4 or 5 May, 'till which time I conjure you to keep the place and hold out'. Montreuil, the French agent who had mediated in the negotiations, had been waiting since 5 April in the Scots' camp at Southwell. Belasyse, when examined by parliamentary forces in June 1646, gave an account of the letter and mode of its delivery, some time between 8 and 10 April. The messenger 'swallowed it in a billet and voided it twice': HMC, *Portland*, i. 377–8. The King arrived at Southwell on 5 May.

came in that manner, with swords drawn, into the market-place of the town where the King was[1] – which the King hearing, says, "I must to horse." And there himself personally, when everybody expected they would have been opposed, the King came and cried to the head of the Mutineers, which was Prince Rupert, "Nephew, I command you to be gone!" So the Prince, in all his fury and discontent, withdrew, and his company scattered – which they say was the greatest piece of mutiny in the world.[2]

Thence, after dinner, home to my office, and in the evening was sent to by Jane that I would give her her wages. So I sent for my wife to my office, and told her that rather then be talked on, I[a] would give her all her wages for this Quarter coming on, though two months is behind – which vexed my wife, and we begun to be angry; but I took myself up and sent her away. But was cruelly vexed in my mind, that all my trouble in this world almost should arise from my disorders in my family and the indiscretion of a wife that brings me nothing almost (besides a comely person) but only trouble and discontent.[b]

She gone, I late at my business; and then home to supper and to bed.

5. *Lords day.* Lay in bed most of the morning. Then up, and down to my chamber among my new books, which is now

a repl. 'we' *b* repl. 'shame'

1. Newark, Notts.
2. This incident belongs to October 1645; and Pepys's report differs in certain details from the contemporary or near-contemporary accounts summarised in S. R. Gardiner, *Hist. Great Civil War*, ii. 373+. Rupert had been out of favour since his surrender of Bristol in the previous month. Although relieved of his command and ordered abroad, he had come with a band of followers to Belvoir, and, again contrary to the King's express command, had joined Charles at Newark. There on 21 October he had been absolved by a Council of War. Willys was on 20 October transferred to another post, largely because of his inability to get on with the county commissioners. According to Gardiner's authorities, the 'mutiny' took place not in the market square, but in the room where the King was having dinner on 26 October. Rupert, Maurice, Willys and other officers insisted on seeing the King, and demanded that a council of war be held to hear the charges against Willys, who, in their allegation, was being dismissed only because he was a friend of Rupert. Charles refused, and next day they were all – to the number of about 200 – given passes to go abroad, and rode away to Belvoir. Cf. Clarendon, *Hist.*, iv. 122–6; A. C. Wood, op. cit., pp. 99+.

a pleasant sight to me, to see my whole study almost of one binding.*[a1] So to dinner, and all the afternoon with W. Hewer at my office, endorsing of papers there, my business having got before me much of late. In the evening comes to see me Mr. Sheply, lately come out of the country, who goes away again tomorrow – a good and a very kind man to me. There came also Mr. Andrews and Hill, and we sang very pleasantly; and so they being gone, I and my wife to supper, and to prayers and bed.

6. Up, and with Sir J. Mennes and Sir W. Penn to St. James, but the Duke is gone abroad. So to White-hall to him, and there I spoke with him. And so to Westminster, did a little business, and then home to the Change, where also I did some business; and went off and ended my contract with the *King-fisher*, hired for Tanger, and I hope to get something by it.

Thence home to dinner and visited Sir W. Batten, who is sick again, worse then he was, and I am apt to think is very ill.

So to my office; and among other things, with Sir W Warren four hours or more, till very late, talking of one thing or another, and have concluded a firm league with him in all just ways to serve him and myself all I can; and I think he will be a most useful and thankful man to me.[2] So home to supper and to bed.

This being one of the coldest days, all say, they ever felt in England;[3] and I this day under great apprehensions of getting an ague from my putting a suit on that hath lain by without ayring a great while, and I pray God it do not do me hurt.

7. Up, and to my office, where busy all the morning. And at home, at dinner, it being Shrove Tuseday, had some very good fritters. All the afternoon and evening at the office. And at night home to supper and to bed.

This day Sir W. Batten, who hath been sick four or five days, is now very bad, so as that people begin *b* to fear his death – and I at a loss whether it will be better for me to have him die, because he is a bad man, or live, for fear a worse should come.

a repl. same symbol blotted   *b* MS. 'being'

---

1. See above, p. 15, n. 1.
2. Warren was the most consider-able timber merchant in England. Pepys's league with him led to much

criticism both by his colleagues and in parliament: see e.g. above, v. 215–16 & n.

3. Cf. below, pp. 66–7 & n.

8. Up, and by coach to my Lord Peterburghs, where anon my Lord Ashly and Sir Tho Ingram met, and Povy, about his accounts; who is one of the most unhappy accountants that ever I knew in all my life, and one that if I were clear in reference to my bill of 117*l*.[1] he should be hanged before I would ever have to do with him. And as he understands nothing of his business himself, so he hath not one about him that doth.

Here late, till I was weary, having business elsewhere. And thence home by coach, and after dinner did several businesses and very late at my office; and so home to supper and to bed.

9. Up, and to my office, where all the morning very busy. At noon home to dinner, and then to my office again – where Sir Wm. Petty came, among other things, to tell me that Mr. Barlow is dead; for which, God knows my heart, I could be as sorry as is possible for one to be for a stranger by whose death he gets 100*l* per annum – he being a very*a* honest man.[2] But after having considered that when I come to consider the providence of God, by this means unexpectedly to give me 100*l* a year more in my estate, I have cause to bless God, and do it from the bottom of my heart. So home late at night, after 12 a-clock, and so to bed.

10. Up, and abroad to Paul's churchyard, there to see the last of my books new-bound – among others, my *Court of King James* and *The Rise and Fall of the Family of the Stewarts*;[3] and much pleased I am now with my study, it being methinks a beautiful sight.

Thence (in Mr. Greys Coach, who took me up) to Westminster, where I heard that yesterday the King met the Houses to pass the great bill for the 2500000*l*.[4] After doing a little business, I home, where Mr. Moore dined with me and evened our reckonings on my Lord Sandwiches bond to me for principal and interest.

a ? 'worthy'

---

1. See above, v. 340 & n. 2.
2. Thomas Barlow was Pepys's predecessor as Clerk of the Acts, whose claims on the office Pepys had bought out by an annuity of £100: above, i. 202 & n. 1.
3. Sir Anthony Weldon, *The court and character of King James . . .* (1650), and Sir Edward Peyton, *The divine catastrophe of the kingly family of* . . . *the Stuarts* (1652); bound up together: PL 62.
4. *LJ*, xi. 654. This was the 'Royal Aid' (16–17 Car. II c. 1) granted for the approaching war against the Dutch. Cf. above, v. 331 & n. 1. Mr. Grey was probably Thomas Grey, an M.P. and a member (with Pepys) of the Fishery Committee.

So that now, on both, there is remaining due to me 257*l*. 07*s*. 00*d*., and I bless God that it is no more.[1]

So all the afternoon at my office, and late home to supper – prayers, and to bed.

11. Up, and to my office, where all the morning. At noon to the Change by coach with my Lord Brunkerd; and thence, after doing much business, home to dinner; and so to my office all the afternoon, till past 12 at night, very busy. So home to bed.

12. *Lords day*. Up, and to church to St. Lawrence to hear Dr. Wilkins the great scholar, for curiosity, I having never heard him.[2] But was not satisfied with him at all. Only, a gentleman sat in the pew I by chance sat in, that sang most excellently, and afterward I found by his face that he hath been a paul's scholler, but know not his name – and I was also well pleased with the church, it being a very fine church. So home to dinner, and then to my office all the afternoon, doing of business; and in the evening comes Mr. Hill (but no Andrews) and we spent the evening very finely, singing, supping, and discoursing. Then to prayers and to bed.

13. Up, and to St. James's; did our usual business before the Duke. Thence I to Westminster and by water (taking Mr.*ᵃ* Stapely the rope-maker by the way) to his rope-ground and to Lime-house, there to see the manner of Stoves, and did excellently inform myself therein.[3] And coming home, did go on board

a repl. bracket

---

1. See above, ii. 61 & n. 5.

2. Dr John Wilkins (the mathematician; one of the founders of the Royal Society; Bishop of Chester, 1668–72) was Vicar of St Lawrence Jewry, 1662–8. Pepys in fact appears to have heard part of one of his sermons on 25 November 1660.

3. Cables and cordage generally were made from hemp which was spun into yarn, laid in tar and then twisted into rope. Long ropeyards were required for the last process. See J. Hollond, *Discourses* (ed. Tanner), ch. iv; *Elements . . . of rigging*

(for D. Steele, 1794), i. 55+; *Mar. Mirr.*, 43/170. The yarn was made pliable by exposure for about two days to slow heat over a charcoal fire in a stove-house. The Navy Board (distrustful of ready-made rope and greatly plagued during the previous winter by shortages) was planning new stovehouses for the King's yards, and Pepys now collected information from various sources about the several techniques: see e.g. NMM, LBK/8, pp. 152–4, 168–70. Cf. also his notes of Stapeley's information (30 December 1663) in NWB, p. 33.

Sir W Petty's *experiment*[1] – which is a brave roomy vessel – and I hope may do well. So went on shore to a Dutch [house] to drink some Mum, and there light upon some Dutchmen, with whom we had good discourse touching Stoveing and making of cables.[2] But to see how despicably they speak of us for our using so many hands more to do anything then they do, they closing a cable with 20 that we use 60 men upon.[3]

Thence home and eat something; and then to[a] my office, where very late; and then to supper and to bed. Captain Stokes, it seems, is at last dead at Portsmouth.[4]

14. *St. Valentine.* This morning comes betimes Dicke Pen[5] to be my wife's valentine, and came to our bedside. By the same token, I had him brought to my side, thinking to have made him kiss me; but he perceived me, and would not. So went to his Valentine – a notable, stout, witty boy. I up, about business; and opening the doore, there was Bagwell's wife, with whom I talked afterwards and she had the confidence to say she came with a hope to be time enough to be my Valentine, and so endeed she did – but my oath[6] preserved me from losing any time with her. And so I and my boy abroad by coach to Westminster, where did two or three businesses; and then home to the Change, and did much business there. My Lord Sandwich is, it seems, with his fleet at Alborough bay.[7] So home to dinner, and then to the office, where till 12 almost at night, and then home to supper and to bed.

15. Up, and to my office, where busy all the morning. At noon with Creed to dinner to Trinity-house to dinner, where

a repl. 'home'

1. See above, v. 353, n. 3.

2. Pepys refers to this talk in his letter to Coventry, 13 February: NMM, LBK/8, pp. 156–7; printed *Further Corr.*, pp. 37–8. Cf. Coventry to Pepys, 10 February: Rawl. A 174, ff. 466–7; and ib., ff. 489–90.

3. Hollond (op. cit., p. 196) had argued that only a large number of workmen could give strength to the cable.

4. On the 11th: *CSPD 1664–5*, p. 201.

5. Second son of Sir William; he died in 1673.

6. Pepys had sworn on 23 January 'laisser aller les femmes' for a month.

7. Aldeburgh Bay, Suff.

a very good dinner among the old Sokers – where an extraordinary discourse of the manner of the loss of the *Royall Oake*,
coming home from Bantam, upon the rocks of Scilly; many
passages therein being very extraordinary – and if I can, I will get
it in writing.[1]

Thence with Creed to Gresham College – where I had been
by Mr. Povy the last week proposed to be admitted a member;
and was this day admitted, by signing a book and being taken
by the hand by the Præsident, my Lord Brunkard, and some
words of admittance said to me.[2] But it is a most acceptable
thing to hear their discourses and see their experiments; which
was this day upon the nature of fire, and how it goes out in a
place where the ayre is not free, and sooner out where the ayre
is exhausted; which they showed by an engine on purpose.[3]
After this being done, they to the Crowne tavern behind the
Change, and there my Lord and most of the company to a club
supper – Sir P. Neale, Sir R. Murrey, Dr. Clerke, Dr. Whistler,
Dr. Goddard, and others of most eminent worth.[4] Above all,
Mr. Boyle[5] today was at the meeting, and above him Mr.
Hooke, who is the most, and promises the least, of any man in

1. The ship (an E. Indiaman; not
the royal ship of the same name) had
been wrecked on the Bishop and
Clerks' Rocks in a storm during the
night of 17–18 January, the survivors
taking refuge on the tallest of the
rocks. Fragments of their cargo –
boxes of pepper – were washed up
eventually on St Mary's, and two
days later boats were sent to their
rescue. Pepys kept among his
papers 'Mr. Daniel's report of the
losse of The Royall Oake . . .':
Rawl. A 195a, f. 180r–v.

2. Nominated on 8 February,
Pepys was now elected unanimous-
ly: Birch, ii. 13. The declaration
signed by fellows is in Sir H.
Lyons, *Roy. Soc.*, p. 38. Pepys later
served on the council of the
society and twice (1684–6) as its
President.

3. The official minute runs: 'Mr.
Hooke made an experiment with
charcoal inclosed in a glass, to which
nitre being put, and the hole suddenly
stopt again, the fire revived, though
no fresh air could get in' (Birch, ii.
15). The air-pump was usually called
a 'pneumatic engine'.

4. Fellows of the Royal Society
formed dining-clubs at an early date:
for evidence of one in 1676, see R.
Hooke, *Diary* (ed. Robinson and
Adams), pp. 260–1. A more formal
club, whose records begin in 1743, still
survives: Sir Archibald Geikie, *An-
nals of Roy. Soc. Club.*

5. Robert Boyle, a founder of
the Royal Society and one of the
most distinguished scientists of the
time.

the world that ever I saw.[1] Here,*a* excellent discourses till 10 at night, and then home – and to Sir W. Batten, where I hear that Sir Tho Harvy entends to put Mr. Turner out of his house and come in himself, which will be very hard to them.[2] And though I love him not, yet for his family's sake I pity him. So home and to bed.

16. Up, and with Mr. Andrews to White-hall, where a Comittee for Tanger; and there I did our vituallers' business for some more money, out of which I hope to get a little – of which I was glad.[3] But Lord, to see to what a degree of contempt, nay, scorn, Mr. Povy, through his prodigious folly, hath brought himself in his accounts, that if he be not a man of a great interest, he will be kicked out of his imployment for a fool – is very strange; and that most deservedly that ever man was. For never any man that understands accounts so little, ever went through so much; and yet goes through it with the greatest shame, and yet with confidence, that ever I saw man in my life. God deliver me, in my own business of my bill, out of his hands; and if ever I foul my fingers with him again, let me*b* suffer for it.

Back to the Change; and thence home to dinner, where Mrs. Hunt dined with me, and poor Mrs. Batters, who brought her little daughter with her, and a letter from her husband,[4] wherein, as a*c* token, the fool presents me very seriously with his daughter, for me to take the charge of bringing up for him and to make my owne. But I took no notice to her at all of the substance of the

a or 'Hear' *b* MS. 'be' *c* MS. 'he'

---

1. Robert Hooke was curator of experiments to the society: a melancholy, deformed, even sordid person, but a gifted experimentalist, and one of the most versatile and original virtuosi of his day.

2. Hervey had been appointed extra Commissioner of the Navy (*vice* Berkeley of Stratton) on 30 January. Thomas Turner, Clerk-General to the office, occupied a house next to Pepys's. Pepys obtained an allowance for him when he was turned out: below, viii. 63 & n. 1

3. Cf. Pepys to Lanyon, 16 February; copy (in Pepys's hand), Rawl. A 193, f. 207*v*.

4. Christopher Batters, gunner; later commander of a fireship.

letter, but fell to discourse and so went away – to the office, where all the afternoon till almost one in the morning; and then home to bed.

17. Up; and it being bitter cold and frost and Snow (which I had thought had quite left us), I by coach to Povy's; where he told me (as I knew already) how he is handled the other day, and is still, by my Lord Berkely. And among other things, tells me what I did not know, that my Lord will say openly that he hath fought more set fields then any man in England hath done.[1] I did my business with him, which was to get a little sum of money paid, and so home with Mr. Andrews, who met me there – and there to the office. At noon home, and there found Lewellin, which vexed me, out of my old jealous humour. So to my office, where till 12 at night, being only a little while at noon at Sir W. Batten's to see him, and had some high words with Sir J. Mennes about Sir W Warren, he calling him cheating knave; but I cooled him. And at night at Sir W Pen's, he being to go to Chatham tomorrow. So home to supper and to bed.

18. Up, and to the office, where sat all the morning. At noon to the Change, and thence to the Royall Oake taverne in Lumbard-Streete, where Sir Wm. Petty and the owners of the Doublebottomed boat (the *Experiment*) did entertain my Lord Brunkard,[a] Sir R. Murry, myself and others with marrow-bones and a chine of beefe of the victuals they have made for this ship – and excellent company and good discourse; but above all, I do value Sir Wm. Petty.

Thence home, and took my Lord Sandwiches Draught of the Harbour of Portsmouth[2] down to Ratcliffe to one Burston,[3] to make a plat for the King and another for the Duke and another for himself – which will be very neat.

a repl. 'Bellas'-

1. 'Set fields' could mean either duels or pitched battles: here duels seems more likely from Pepys's use of 'openly'. But Berkeley (of Stratton) had fought many battles – in the Scots War, the Civil War, and in the Low Countries. His vanity was notorious. Clarendon (*Hist.*, v. 229) remarks that 'by the custom of making frequent relations of his actions, [he] grew in very good earnest to think he had done many things which nobody else ever heard of.' Cf. also ib., iv. 266.

2. Untraced. Cf. Pepys to Sandwich, 18 February (*Shorthand Letters*, pp. 28–9); *Naval Minutes*, p. 39.

3. John Burston: 'the ablest man in *Towne*', according to Pepys (*Shorthand Letters*, p. 28).

So home, and till almost one a-clock in the morning at my office; and then home to supper and to bed.

My Lord Sandwich and his fleet of 25 ⟨ships⟩ in the Downes, returned from crucing; but could not meet with any Dutchmen.

19. Lay in bed, being Lords day, all the morning talking with my wife, sometimes pleased, sometimes displeased; and then up and to dinner. All the afternoon also at home and Sir W Batten's, and in the evening comes Mr. Andrews and we sung together; and then to supper (he not staying) and at supper, hearing by accident of my mayds their letting in a rogueing Scotch woman that haunts the office, to help them to wash and scour in our house, and that very lately, I fell mightily out, and made my wife, to the disturbance of the house and neighbours, to beat our little girle; and then we shut her down into the cellar and there she lay all night. So we to bed.

20. Up, and with Sir J. Mennes to attend the Duke; and then we back again and rode into the beginnings of my Lord Chancellors new house near St. James's, which common people have already called Dunkirke-house, from their opinion of his having*a* a good bribe for the selling of that town.[1] And very noble I believe it will be. Near that is my Lord Berkely beginning another on one side, and Sir J. Denham on the other.[2] Thence I to the House of Lords and spoke with my Lord Bellases; and so to the Change and there did business; and so to the Sun Taverne – having in the morning had some high words with Sir J Lawson about his sending of some bayled goods to Tanger; wherein the truth is, I did not favour him. But being conscious that some of my profit may come out, by some words that fell from him; and to be quiet, I have accommodated it. Here we dined, merry; but my club and the rest come to 7s. 6d, which was too much. Thence to the office and there found Bagwells wife, whom I directed to go home and I would do her business; which was to write a letter to my Lord Sandwich for her

a repl. 'taking'

---

1. This was Clarendon House in Piccadilly. The charge of bribery was baseless: cf. above, iv. 223 & n. 3. For prints of the house, see *Catalogue* of views of London collected by Frederick *Crace* (ed. J. G. Crace), p. 264.
2. Berkeley House and Burlington House respectively.

husband's advance into a better ship as there should be occasion – which I did; and by and by did go down by water to Deptford-yard, and then down further and so landed at the lower end of the town; and it being dark, did privately entrer en la maison de la femme de Bagwell,*ᵃ* and there I had sa compagnie, though with a great deal of difficulty; néanmoins, enfin je avais ma volonté d'elle. And being sated therewith, I walked home to Redriffe, it being now near 9 a-clock; and there I did drink some strong waters and eat some bread and cheese, and so home – where at my office, my wife comes and tells me that she hath hired a chamber-maid, one of the prettiest maids that ever she saw in her life, and that she is really jealous of me for her – but hath ventured to hire her from month to month. But I think she means merrily. So to supper and to bed.

21. Up, and to the office (having a mighty pain in my fore-finger of my left hand, from a strain that it received last night in struggling avec la *ᵇ* femme que je mentioned yesterday), where busy till noon; and then, my wife being busy in going with her woman to a hot-house¹ to bath herself, after her long being within doors in the dirt, so that she now pretends to a resolution of being hereafter very clean – how long it will hold, I can guess – I dined with Sir W. Batten and my Lady, they being nowadays very fond of me.

So to the Change, and off of the Change with Mr. Wayth to a cook's shop and there dined again, for discourse with him about Hamaccos² and the abuse now practised in tickets,³ and more like every day to be – also, of the great profit Mr. Fen⁴ makes of his place – he being (though he demands but ½ per cent of all he pays, and that is easily computed) but very little pleased with any man that gives him no more.

a s.h.   *b* repl. 'l'-

1. A public steam-bath establish-ment, used for hygienic and medicinal purposes, especially (perhaps exclus-ively) by women.
2. On 1 March Waith put in a tender for the supply of hammocks at 1s. 2d. to 2s. 4d. each: *CSPD 1665–6*, p. 130.
3. Cases of abuse of pay-tickets

('double-tickets', 'dead-pays', etc.) abound in the diary: e.g. above, iv. 152. Officers, seamen and clerks of the Ticket Office were all capable of malpractice.
4. John Fenn, Paymaster to the Navy Treasurer. For his profits, see below, p. 117, n. 1.

So to the office; and after office my Lord Brunkerd carried me to Lincoln's Inn fields, and there I with my Lady Sandwich (good lady), talking of innocent discourse of good housewifery and husbands for her daughters, and the luxury and looseness of the times and other such things, till past 10 a-clock at night; and so by coach home, where a little at my office, and so to supper and to bed.

My Lady tells me how my Lord Castlemayne is coming over from France, and is believed will be made*a* friends with his Lady again.

What mad freaks the mayds of Honour at Court have – that Mrs. Jennings, one of the Duchess's maids, the other day dressed herself like an orange-wench and went up and down and cried oranges – till falling down, or by such accident (though in the evening), her fine shoes were discerned and she put to a great deal of shame.[1]

That such as these tricks being ordinary and worse among them, and thereby few will venture upon them for wifes, my Lady Castlemayne will in merriment say that her daughter (not above a year old or two)[2] will be the first mayd in the Court that will be married.

This day my Lord Sandwich writ me word from the Downes that he is like to be in town this week.

22. Lay last night alone, my wife after her bathing lying alone in another bed – so cold all night. Up, and to the office, where busy all the morning. At noon at the Change, busy – where great talks of a Dutch ship, in the North, put on shore and taken by a troop of horse.[3] Home to dinner, and Creed with me. Thence to Gresham College,[4] where very noble discourse; and

a repl. 'mar'-

---

1. The incident appears to be referred to in Gramont, pp. 259+. Frances Jennings (elder sister of Sarah, later Duchess of Marlborough) married in this year George Hamilton, brother of Anthony Hamilton, author of the memoirs of Gramont.

2. Lady Charlotte Fitzroy, her daughter by Charles; born in September 1664.

3. Many canards of this sort began to gain currency at this time.

4. See the minute in Birch, ii. 16–18. The subjects discussed included weather-glasses, the late comet and the death of a dog whose spleen had been removed.

thence home, busy till past 12 at night, and then home to supper
and to bed.   Mrs. Bland came this night to take leave of me and
my wife, going to Tanger.

23.   This day, by the blessing of Almighty God, I have lived
32 years in the world – and am in the best degree of health at this
minute that I have been almost in[a] my life-time, and at this
time in the best condition of estate that ever I was in; the Lord
make me thankful.

Up, and to the office, where busy all the morning.   At noon to
the Change, where I hear the most horrid and astonishing news
that ever was yet told in[b] my memory – that De Ruiter, with his
fleet in guinny, hath proceeded to the taking of whatever we
have – forts, goods, ships, and men – and tied our men back to
back and thrown them all into the sea – even women and children
also.   This a Swede or Hamburger is come into the River and tells
that he saw the thing done.[1]   But Lord, to see the consternation
all our merchants are in is observable, and with what fury and
revenge they discourse of it – but I fear it will, like other things,
in a few days cool among us.   But that which I fear most is the
reason why he that was so kind to our men at first, should afterward, having let them go, be so cruel when he went further.
What I fear is that there he was informed (which he was not
before) of some of Holmes's dealings with his countrymen,[2] and
so was moved to this fury.   God grant[c] it be not so.

a MS. 'have'   b repl. 'almost'   c repl. 'willing'

---

1. The informant was a Dutch-
man named Petersen, posing as a
Swede, and he alleged that de Ruyter
disposed of 1500 in this way:
CSPVen. 1664–6, pp. 85 n., 90. His
tale – soon disproved (below, p. 43)
– caused such feeling that a guard had
to be put on the Dutch ambassador's
house: *The Intelligencer*, 27 February,
p. 136. In April the English envoy at The Hague reported stories
told there of the English in
W. Africa 'frying Dutch men by the
fire': qu. Lister, iii. 374.

2. For Robert Holmes's attack on
the Dutch in W. Africa, see above,
v. 160 & n. 4. He was held in
custody, in the Tower, and on
parole, between January and March
1665 while charges of exceeding his
instructions were investigated at the
instigation of the Royal African
Company. He had seized not only
forts but property, and had sent Dutch
traders packing back to Holland.
Cf. *CSPD 1664–5*, p. 170; R. Ollard,
Man of war, pp. 129–31.

But a more dishonourable thing was never suffered by Englishmen, nor a*ᵃ* more barbarous done by man, as this by them to us.

Home to dinner, and then to the office, where we sat all the afternoon; and then at night to take my finall leave of Mrs. Bland, who sets out tomorrow for Tanger. And then I back to my office till past 12, and so home to supper and to bed.

24. Up, and to my office, where all the morning – upon advising again with some Fishermen and the Waterbayliffe of the City, by Mr. Coventry's direction, touching the protections which are desired for the fishermen upon the River; and I am glad of the occasion to make me understand something of it.[1] At noon home to dinner, and all the afternoon, till 9 at night, in my chamber, and Mr. Hater with me (to prevent being disturbed at the office), to perfect my contract-book,[2] which for want*ᵇ* of time hath a long time lain without being entered in, as I used to do, from month to month.

Then to my office, where till almost 12, and so home to bed.

25. Up, and to the office, where all the morning. At noon to the Change; where just before I came, the Swede that had told the King and the Duke so boldly this great lie, of the Dutch flinging our men back to back into the sea at Guinny, so perticularly and readily and confidently, was whipped round the Change – he confessing it a lie, and that he did it in hopes to get something. It is said the judges, upon demand, did give it their opinion that the law would judge him to be whipped, to lose his eares, or to have his nose slit – but I do not hear that anything more is to be done to him.[3] They say he is delivered over to the Dutch Embassador to do what he please with him. But the

a repl. 'they' *b* repl. 'of'

1. The Board had consulted the city corporation to make sure that London's supplies of fish would not be dangerously reduced if some of the Barking and Greenwich fishermen were pressed into the navy. See below, p. 49 & n. 3. Coventry's letter to Pepys (16 February) is in Rawl. A 174, f. 464*r*. The water-bailiff was the official who executed the corporation's rights and duties in the river. Thomas Malyn now held the office: LRO, Rep. 70, f. 102*v*.

2. See above, iii. 65, n. 2.

3. Cf. above, p. 42 & n. 1. He lost his ears, according to a letter written this day by Sir T. Osborne: A. Browning, *Danby*, ii. 11.

world doth think that there is some design on one side or other, either of the Dutch or French – for it is not likely a fellow would invent such a lie to get money, whereas he might have hoped for a better reward by telling something in behalf of us to please us.

Thence to the Sun Taverne, and there dined with Sir W Warren and Mr. Gifford the merchant; and I hear how Nich. Colborne, that lately lived and got a great estate there, is gone to live like a prince in the country; and that this Wadlow, that did the like at the Devil by St. Dunstanes, did go into the country, and there spent almost all he had got, and hath now choused this Colborne out of his house, that he ⟨might⟩ come to his old trade again.[1]   But Lord, to see how full the house is, no room for any company almost to come into it.   Thence home to the office, where despatch much business; at night late home and to clean myself with warm water; my wife will have me, because she doth herself;[2] and so to bed.

26. *Sunday.* Up, and to church. And so home to dinner, and[a] after dinner to my office and there busy all the afternoon, till in the evening comes Mr. Andrews and Hill; and so home and to singing.   Hill stayed and supped with me; and very good discourse of Italy, where he was, which is alway to me very agreeable.   After supper, he gone, we to prayers and to bed.

27. Up, and to St. James's, where we attended the Duke as usual.   This morning I was much surprized and troubled with a letter from Mrs. Bland, that she is left behind; and much trouble it cost me this day to find out some way to carry her after the ships to Plymouth; but at last, I hope I have done it.[3]   At noon

a repl. 'al'-

1. Both were innkeepers and vintners. Nicholas Colborne had bought the manor of Esher for close on £10,000 in March 1663 and lived in style in the manor-house: O. Manning and W. Bray, *Hist. Surrey* (1804–14), ii. 747; J. Aubrey, *Nat. hist. and antiq. Surrey* (1719, 1718), iii. 104, 121. John Wadlow had an estate in Yorkshire: *CTB*, iii. 812.

2. One of the rare occasions on which Pepys records having washed.

3. She went by one of the ships of the Levant Company now bound for Smyrna – Capt. Hill's *Hannibal*: Pepys to Coventry, 2 March, *Shorthand Letters*, p. 31; *CSPD 1664–5*, p. 220. She gave Hill a piece of plate for his trouble and 40s. to distribute among his men. Her profuse and strangely spelt letters of thanks to Pepys (17, 21 March; from Yeabsley's house, Plymouth) are in Rawl. A 174, ff. 93r, 95r.

to the Change to enquire*ᵃ* what wages the Dutch give in their men-of-war at this day, and I hear for certain they give but twelve gilders at most, which is not full 24*s*, a thing I wonder at.[1]   At home to dinner; and then in Sir J. Mennes's coach, my wife and I with him, and also Mercer, abroad; he and I to White-hall, and he would have his coach to wait upon my wife on her visits – it being the first time my wife hath been out of doors (but the other day to bath her) several weeks.

We to a committee of the Council to discourse concerning pressing of men; but Lord, how they meet; never sit down – one comes, now another goes, then comes another – one complaining that nothing is done, another swearing that he hath been there these two hours and nobody came.   At last it came to this: my Lord Annesly, says he, "I think we must be forced to get the King to come to every committee, for I do not see that we do anything at any time but when he is here."   And I believe he said the truth.   And very constant*ᵇ* he is at the council table on council-days; which his predecessors, it seems, very rarely did.[2] But thus, I perceive, the greatest affair in the world at this day is likely to be managed by us.   But to hear how my Lord Berkely and others of them do cry up the discipline of the late times here, and in the former Dutch warr, is strange[3] – wishing with all their hearts that the business of religion were not*ᶜ* so severely carried on as to discourage the sober people to come among us, and wishing that the same law and severity were used against drunken-

a repl. 'list'   *b* repl. 'often'   *c* repl. 'so'

---

1. Cf. *CSPD 1664–5*, p. 249. This was the rate for ordinary seamen. In January it had been raised from 11 guilders: *The Newes*, 19 January, p. 54. In the English navy, the rates were 19*s*. a month for ordinary seamen, and 24*s*. for able seamen: *Cat.*, i. 140. But in April the Dutch again increased their rates: *CSPVen. 1664–6*, p. 112.

2. Unlike James I and Charles I, Charles II attended full council meetings (held in 1665 three times a week) with fair regularity.   The only committee he attended with equal fre-

quency was that for foreign affairs – ancestor of the modern cabinet. E. R. Turner, *Privy Council*, i. 101–3, 384; ii. 40–3, 207–8. In a letter of May 1682 to Hewer, Pepys contrasted the 'order, gravity and unanimity' of debate in the Scottish Privy Council (two meetings of which he had attended in Edinburgh) with the proceedings of its English counterpart: *Letters*, pp. 139–40.

3. Particularly since Berkeley had been in exile with the royalist court during the whole of that period.

ness as there was then – saying that our evil-living will call the hand of God upon us again. Thence to walk alone a good while in St. James park with Mr. Coventry, who I perceive is grown a little melancholy, and displeased to see things go as they do – so carelessly.

Thence I by coach to Ratcliffe high-way to the plat-maker's; and he hath begun my Lord Sandwiches plat very neatly.[1]   And so back again. Coming back, I met Collonell Atkins, who in other discourse did offer to give me a piece, to receive of me 20 when he proves the late news of the Dutch their drowning our men at Guiny. And the truth is, I find the generality of the world to fear that there is something of truth in it – and I do fear it too.

Thence back by coach to Sir Ph. Warwickes, and there he did contract with me a kind of friendship and freedom of communication, wherein he assures me, to make me understand the whole business of the Treasurers business of the Navy, that I shall know as well as Sir G Carteret what[a] money he hath; and will needs have me come to him sometimes, or he meet me, to discourse of things tending to the serving the King; and I am mighty proud and happy in becoming so known to such a man – and I hope shall pursue it.

Thence back home to the office, a little tired and out of order, and then to supper and to bed.

28. At the office all the morning. At noon dined at home. After dinner my wife and I to my Lady Batten's, it being the first time my wife hath been there, I think, these two years; but I have a mind in part to take away that strangeness, and so we did, and all very quiet and kind.

Came home; I to the taking my wife's kitchen account at the latter end of the month, and there find 7s wanting – which did occasion a very high falling out between us; I endeed too eagerly insisting upon so poor a thing, and did give her very provoking words, calling her "beggar" and reproaching her friends;* which she took very stomachfully, and reproached me justly with mine; and I confess, being myself, I cannot see what she could have done less. I find she is very cunning, and when

a   MS. 'what he'

---

1. See above, p. 38.

she least shows it, hath her wit at work; but it is an ill one, though I think not so bad but with good usage I might well bear with it; and the truth is, I do find that my being over-solicitous and jealous and froward, and ready to reproach her, doth make her worse. However, I find that now and then a little difference doth do no hurt – but too much of it will make her know her force too much. We parted, after many high words, very angry; and I to my office to my month's accounts, and find myself worth 1270*l* – for which the Lord God be praised.

So, at almost 2 a-clock in the morning, I home to supper and to bed.

And so ends this month, with great expectation of the Hollanders coming forth; who are, it seems, very high and rather more ready then we. God give a good issue to it.

MARCH.

1. Up – and this day being the day that, by a promise a great while ago made to my wife, I was to give her 20*l* to lay out in clothes against Easter, she did, notwithstanding[a] last night's falling-out, come to peace with me and I with her, but did boggle mightily at the parting with my money, but at last did give it her; and then she abroad to buy her things, and I to my office, where busy all the morning. At noon I to dinner at Trinity-house – and thence to Gresham College, where, first Mr. Hooke read a second very curious* Lecture about the late Comett, among other things, proving very probably that this is the very same Comett that appeared before in the year[b] 1618, and that in such a time probably it will appear again – which is a very new opinion – but all will be in print.[1]

Then to the meeting, where[c] Sir G Carterets two sons, his own and Sir N Slany,[2] were admitted of the Society. And this day I did pay my admission money – 40*s* – to the Society.

Here was very fine discourses – and experiments; but I do lack philosophy enough to understand them, and so cannot remember them. Among others, a very perticular account of the making of the several sorts of bread in France,[3] which is accounted the best place for bread in the world.

So home, where very busy getting an answer to some Questions of Sir Ph. Warwicke touching the expense of the navy; and that being done, I by coach at 8 at night by[d] coach with my wife and Mercer to Sir Ph. and discoursed with him[e] (leaving them in the

a repl. 'then'   b repl. same symbol badly formed   c repl. 'came'
         d repl. 'home'   e repl. 'them'

---

1. See Birch, ii. 19; the lecture was printed in *Philos. Trans.*, i (for 1665–6), pp. 3–4. His earlier lecture had been given in 1664; both were later printed, incompletely, in Hooke's *Lectures and collections* (1678), which also appeared as part of *Lectiones Cutlerianae* (1679). The latter is re-printed in Gunther, viii. 209+. For the comet, see above, v. 346 & n. 3.

2. I.e. Philip Carteret and Sir Nicholas Slaning, Sir George Carteret's son-in-law.

3. This was John Evelyn's paper on the subject ('Panificium, or the several manners of making bread in France, etc., where by general consent the best bread is eaten'), which was ordered to be entered in the Society's register: Birch, ii. 19.

coach); and then back with them home, and to supper and to bed.

2. Beginning this day to rise betimes, before 6 a-clock, and going down to call my people, find Besse and the girle with their clothes on, lying within their bedding upon the ground close by the fire-side – and a candle burning all night – pretending they would rise to scowre: this vexed me, but Besse is going and so she will not trouble me long. Up, and by water to Burston's about my Lord's Platt, and then home to the office. So there all the morning sitting. At noon dined with Sir W. Batten (my wife being gone again today to buy things, having bought nothing yesterday for lack of Mrs. Pierce's company) and thence to the office again, where very busy till 12 at night – and vexed at my wife's staying out so late, she not being at home at 9 a-clock. But at last she is come home, but the reason of her stay I know not yet. So shut up my books and home to supper and to bed.

3. Up, and abroad about several things; among others, to see Mr. Peter Honiwood, who was at my house the other day, and I find it was*a* for nothing but to pay me my Brother Johns Quarterage.[1] Thence to see Mrs. Turner, who takes it mighty ill I did not come to dine with the Reader, her husband; which she says was the greatest feast that ever was yet kept by a reader,[2] and I believe it was well – but I am glad I did not go, which confirms her in an opinion that I am grown proud.

Thence to the Change and to several places; and so home to dinner and to my office, where till 12 at night, writing over a discourse of mine to Mr. Coventry touching the Fishermen of the Thames, upon a reference of that business by him to me, concerning their being protected from presse.[3]

Then home to supper and to bed.

---

a repl. 'is'

1. See above, v. 142 & n. 3.
2. For readers' feasts at the Inns of Court, see above, p. 28, n. 2. They became extravagant in the 1660s and were shortly afterwards abandoned, along with the public readings themselves. Sir W. Dug-

dale, *Origines Juridiciales* (1666), p. 204; R. North, *Lives of Norths* (ed. Jessopp), i. 97–8; Sir W. Holdsworth, *Hist. Engl. law*, vi. 491–2.

3. Copy in NMM, LBK/8, pp. 161–5. Cf. above, p. 43 & n. 1.

4. Up very betimes; and walked, it being bitter cold, to Ratcliffe to the plat-maker's and back again. To the office, where we sat all the morning. I, with being empty and full of ayre and wind, had some pain today. Dined alone at home, my wife being gone abroad to buy some more things. All the afternoon at the office. Wm.*a* Howe came to see me, being come up with my Lord from Sea. He is grown a discreet but very conceited fellow. He tells me how little respectfully Sir W Pen did carry it to my Lord on board the Dukes ship at Sea – and that Captain Minnes, a favourite of Prince Ruperts,[1] doth show my Lord little respect – but that everybody else esteems my Lord as they ought. I am sorry for the folly of the latter, and vexed at the dissimulation of the former. At night home to supper and to bed. This day was proclaimed at the Change the war with Holland.[2]

5. *Lords day.* Up, and Mr. Burston bringing me by order my*b* Lord's plats,[3] which he hath been making this week, I did take coach, and to my Lord Sandwiches and dined with my Lord; it being the first time he hath dined at home since his coming from Sea. And a pretty odd demand it was of my Lord to my Lady before me: "How do you, sweetheart; how have you done all this week?" – himself taking notice of it to me, that he had hardly seen her the week before. At dinner he did use me with the greatest solemnity in the world, in carving for me and nobody else, and calling often to my Lady to cut for me, and all the respect possible.

After dinner looked over the plats; liked them mightily. And endeed, I think he is the most exact man in what he doth in the world of that kind.

So home again; and there, after a song or two in the evening with Mr. Hill, I to my office, and then home to supper and to bed.

---

a repl. 'Mr.'   *b* MS. 'the'

---

1. Myngs was critical of Sandwich over the prize goods affair, but was not a favourite of Rupert. 'Captain Holmes' is possibly meant here.
2. The declaration was dated 22 February: Steele, no. 3408; *CSPD*
1664-5, p. 214. Two heralds, with trumpeters, were to proclaim it at White-hall at 10 a.m. on 4 March, and afterwards at the accustomed places in the city: ib., p. 236.
3. See above, p. 38.

6. Up, and with Sir J. Mennes by coach (it being a most lamentable cold day as any this year) to St. James's, and there did our
business with the Duke. Great preparations for his speedy return
to sea. I saw him try on his buff coat and hat-piece[1] covered with
black velvet. It troubles me more to think of his venture then
of anything else in the whole warr. Thence home to dinner –
where I saw Besse go away – she having, of all wenches that
ever lived with us, received the greatest love and kindness and
good clothes, besides wages, and gone away with the greatest
ingratitude.[2] I then abroad to look after my Hamaccoes;[3] and so
home and there find our new chamber-maid, Mary, come; which
instead of handsome, as my wife spoke[4] and still seems to reckon,
is a very ordinary wench I think – and therein was mightily
disappointed.

To my office, where busy late; and then home to supper and
to bed – and was troubled all this night with a pain in my left
Testicle, that run up presently into my left Kidny and there kept
akeing all night – in great pain.

7. Up, and was pretty well; but going to the office, and I
think it was sitting with my back to the fire, it set me in a great
rage again, that I could not continue till past noon at the office,
but was forced to go home; nor could sit down to dine, but
betook myself to my bed; and being there a while, my pain begun
to abate and grow less and less. Anon I went to make water, not
dreaming of anything but my testicle, that by some accident I
might have bruised as I used to do – but in pissing, there came
from me two stones; I could feel them, and caused my water to
be looked into, but without any pain to me in going out – which
makes me think that it was not a fit of the stone at all; for my
pain was asswaged upon my lying down a great while before I
went to make water.[5] Anon I made water again very freely
and plentifully. I kept my bed in good ease all the evening;

1. Protective metal skull-cap.
2. She had served them since
September 1663.
3. See above, p. 40 & n. 2.
4. See above, p. 40.
5. Dr C. E. Newman writes:
'This was an attack of colic caused by
stones passing from the kidney into
the bladder (which would bring on
the pain which radiated from the back
into the testicle). Passage of the
stones through the urethra was sometimes painless.'

then rose and sat up an hour or two; and then to bed and lay till
《8.》 8 a-clock; and then, though a bitter cold day, yet I rose,
and though my pain and tenderness in my testicle remains a
little, yet I do verily think that my pain yesterday was nothing
else, and therefore I hope my disease of the stone may not return
to me, but void itself in pissing; which God grant – but I will
consult my physitian.

This morning is brought me to the office the sad[a] news of the
London, in which Sir J Lawsons men were all bringing her from
Chatham to the Hope, and thence he was to go to sea in her – but
a little a-this-side the buoy of the Nower, she suddenly blew up.
About 24 and a woman that were in the round-house and coach
saved; the rest, being above 300, drowned – the ship breaking all
in pieces – with 80 pieces of brass ordinance. She lies sunk, with
her round-house above water.[1] Sir J Lawson hath a great loss
in this, of so many good chosen men, and many relations among
them. I went to the Change, where the news taken very much
to heart. So home to dinner, and Mr. Moore with me; then
I to Gresham College and there saw several pretty experiments;[2]
and so home and to my office – and at night, about 11, home to
supper and to bed.

9. Up and to the office, where we sat all the morning.[b] At
noon to dinner at home and then abroad with my wife. Left
her at the New Exchange, and I to Westminster, where I hear
Mrs. Martin is brought to bed of a boy and christened Charles –
which I am very glad of, for I was fearful of being called to be a
godfather to it. But it seems it was to be done suddenly, and so

a MS. 'sad the'   b MS. 'afternoon'

---

1. The London was a 2nd-rate, one
of the largest ships in the navy, and
had until recently been Sandwich's
flagship. The accident happened on
the 7th. Cf. Pepys's note in NWB,
p. 86: 'It is true there is little room
left for enquiring, . . . but I do not
find that . . . any of us are concerned in the loss as if it were our
owne, but as soon as the tale was told
were as merry as ever.' Cf. other
accounts in BM, Stowe 744, f. 88r;
CSPD 1664–5, p. 249. Attempts

were made to salvage the entire
vessel, but only the guns were recovered. Shorthand Letters, p. 46;
CSPD 1665–6, p. 279.

2. E.g. a flaming spirit of wine
extinguished in the pneumatic engine, and tin filings cast over heated
nitre. At this meeting Pepys was
asked to enquire of Holmes about his
use of pendulum-watches for the de-
termination of longitude. Birch, ii.
21, 23; below, p. 57, n. 1.

I escaped. It is strange, to see how a liberty, and going abroad without purpose of doing anything, doth lead a man to what is bad; for I was just upon going to her, where I must of necessity have broken my oath[1] or made a forfeit. But I did not, company being (I heard by my porter) with her; and so I home again, taking up my wife, and was set down by her at Paules schoole, where I visited Mr. Crumlum[2] at his house. And Lord, to see how ridiculous a conceited pædagogue is, though a learned man – he is being so dogmaticall in all he doth and says. But among other discourse, we fall to the old discourse of Pauls Schoole; and he did, upon my declaring my value of it, give me one of Lillys grammer of a very old impression, as it was in the Catholique times; which I shall much set by.[3] And so after some small discourse, away and called upon my wife at a linen-draper's shop buying linen; and so home and to my office, where late, and home to supper and to bed. This night my wife had a new suit of Flowerd ash-Coloured silk, very noble.

10. Up, and to the office all the morning. At noon to the Change; where, very hot, people's proposal of the City giving the King another ship for the *London* that is lately blown up; which would be very handsome, and if well managed, might be done; but I fear, if it be put into ill hands or that the Courtiers do solicit it, it will never be done.[4] Home to dinner, and thence to the Committee of Tanger at White-hall, where my Lord Barkely and Craven and others; but Lord, to see how superficially things are done in that business of the Lottery;[5] which will be the disgrace of the Fishery, and without profit.

1. Made on 23 January for one month and presumably renewed.

2. Samuel Cromleholme, High Master of St Paul's School, 1657–72.

3. Cromleholme had one of the finest private libraries in London. The book was probably *Paules accidence. Iohannis Coleti . . . aeditio. Una cum quibusdam Guil. Lilii grammatices rudimentis*, n.d.; PL 424(5); largely in black-letter (the 'very old impression'), with an Ave Maria and a Paternoster, etc., printed at the beginning. Colet (d. 1519) had founded St Paul's School. The Latin

grammar compiled by the first High Master, William Lily (with help from Colet and Erasmus) long continued in use there and at other schools as the standard text-book. Altered only slightly, it was in use at Eton in the 1860s: M. L. Clarke, *Classical educ. in Brit. 1500–1900*, pp. 7, 51.

4. It was done; by voluntary subscription from the city. The *Loyal London* (another 2nd-rate) was completed in 1666. She was burnt by the Dutch at Chatham in June 1667.

5. See above, v. 323 & n. 2.

Home, vexed at my loss of time, and there to my office. Late at night comes the two Bellamys, formerly petty-warrant Victuallers of the Navy, to take my advice about a Navy debt of theirs, for the compassing of which they offer a great deal of money, and the thing most just.[1] Perhaps I may undertake it and get something by it, which will be a good jobb. So late home to bed.

11. Up, and to the office. At noon home to dinner, and to the office again, where very late; and then home to supper and to bed.

This day returned Sir W. Batten and Sir J. Mennes from Lee Roade, where they have been to see the Wrecke of the *London* – out of which, they say that guns may be got, but the Hull of her will be wholly lost, as not being capable of being weighed.[2]

12. *Lords day.* Up; and borrowing Sir J Minnes's coach, to my Lord Sandwiches, but he was gone abroad. I sent the coach back for my wife, my Lord a second time dining at home on purpose to meet me, he having not dined once at home but those times, since his coming from sea. I sat down and read over the Bishop of Chichesters sermon upon the anniversary of the King's death – much cried up, but methinks but a mean sermon.[3] By and by comes in my Lord, and he and I to talk of many things in the Navy, one from another. In general, to see how the greatest things are committed to very ordinary men, as to parts and experience, to do – among others, my Lord Berkely. We talked also of getting W. How to be put into the Muster-maistershipp in the room of Creed, if Creed will give way; but my Lord doth it without any great gusto, calling How a proud coxcomb

1. This was a debt dating back to 1658 (above, iv. 374, n. 2); no trace of its payment has been found. Petty-warrant victuals were bought independently of the navy victualler, on warrants from the clerks of the cheque. Thomas and Robert Bellamy were related to Pepys through the Trices.

2. For the method of weighing (raising) from the water, see above, i. 316, n. 1.

3. Dr Henry King had just published the sermon he had preached (on 2 Chron., xxxv. 24, 25) at Whitehall on the recent fast-day commemorating the execution of Charles I: *A sermon preached the 30th of January . . 1664* [1664/5]. He had published three similar sermons in the previous three years. Pepys did once enjoy hearing one of his sermons (above, iv. 69), but did not retain in the PL any of his sermons or poems.

in passion.[1]   Down to dinner, where my wife in her new Lace=
Whiske; which endeed is very noble and I much pleased with it,
and so my Lady also.   Here, very pleasant my Lord was at
dinner.   And after dinner did look over his plat, which Burston
hath brought him today, and is the last of the three that he will
have made.[2]   After satisfied with that – he abroad; and I, after
much discourse with my Lady about Sir G. Carteret's son, of
whom she hath some thoughts for a husband*a* for my Lady
Jem – we away home by coach again – and there sang a good
while very pleasantly with Mr. Andrews and Hill.   They gone,
we to supper, and betimes to bed.

13.   Up betimes, this being the first morning of my promise,
upon a forfeit, not to lie in bed a quarter of an hour after my first
waking.   Abroad to St. James's, and there much business – the
King also being with us a great while.   Thence to the Change;
and thence with Captain Taylor and Sir W. Warren dined at a
house hard by, for discourse sake; and so I home, and there
meeting a letter from Mrs. Martin desiring to speak with me, I
(though against my promise of visiting her) did go; and there
find her in her child-bed dress, desiring my favour to get her
husband a place.   I stayed not long; but taking Sir W Warren
up at White-hall, home;   and among other discourse, fell to a
business which he says shall, if accomplished, bring me 100*l*.[3]
He gone, I to supper and to bed.   ⟨This day my wife begun to
wear light-coloured locks, quite white almost;   which, though it
makes her look very pretty, yet not being natural, vexes
me, that I will not have her wear them.[4]   This day I saw my

a repl. 'son'

---

1. Howe was appointed: *CSPD*
1664-5, p. 443.   In the 1664 voyage
also he and Creed had contended for
the same place: above, v. 210 & n. 2.
2. See above, p. 38 & n. 2.
3. On the following day the Navy
Board, in consideration of the rise
in the costs of freight, authorised
Warren to hire ships, and promised

'to accept of the same upon his report
and reputacion': PRO, Adm. 106/
3520, f. 23r.   See also below, p. 70.
4. Cf. Pepys's views at 24 March
1662, where he finds the fashion
tolerable only because the additional
locks were made of his wife's own hair.

Lord Castlemayne at St. James, lately come from France.$\rangle^a$ 1

14. Up before 6. To the office, where busy all the morning. At noon dined with Sir W. Batten and Sir J. Mennes at the Tower with Sir J Robinson – at a farewell dinner which he gives Major Holmes at his going out of the Tower, where he hath for some time, since his coming from Guinny, been a prisoner[2] – and it seems had presented the Lieutenant with 50 pieces yesterday. Here a great deal of good victuals and company.

Thence home to my office, where very late; and home to supper and to bed, weary of business.

15. Up, and by coach with Sir W. Batten to^b St. James's; where among other things before the Duke, Captain Taylor was called in; and Sir J Robinson his accuser not appearing, was acquitted quite from his charge, and declared that he should go to Harwich; which I was very well pleased at.[3] Thence I to Mr^c Coventry's chamber, and there privately an hour with him in discourse of the office, and did deliver to him many notes[4] of things about which he is to get the Dukes command before he goes, for the putting of business among us in better order. He did largely own his dependence as to the office upon my care; and received very great expressions of love from him and so parted, with great satisfaction to myself. So home to the Change and thence home to dinner; where, my wife being gone down upon a sudden warning from my Lord Sandwiches daughters to the Hope with them to see the *Prince*,

a addition crowded in at bottom of page

b MS. 'by coach to'   c repl. 'the Change'

---

1. After quarrelling with his wife, the King's mistress, in 1662, he had gone abroad, travelling in France and Italy, and serving in 1664 in the Venetian fleet.

2. See above, v. 283 & n. 1. The warrant for his release was dated 6 March, his pardon 23

March: *CSPD 1664–5*, pp. 240, 268.

3. John Taylor, shipbuilder, the newly appointed Commissioner at Harwich, had been accused of being a fanatic: above, v. 326 & n. 1, 350.

4. Copy (in Hayter's hand) in NMM, LBK/8, pp. 171–2.

I dined alone. And after dinner to the office and anon to Gresham College; where among other good discourse, there was tried the great Poyson of Maccassa upon a Dogg, but it had no effect all the time we sat there.[1]

We anon broke up, and I home, where late at my office, my wife not coming home. I to bed, troubled, about 12 or past.[a]

16. Up, and to the office, where we sat all the morning – my wife coming home from the Water this morning – having lain with them on board the *Prince* all night. At noon home to dinner, where my wife told me the unpleasant Journy she had yesterday among the children – whose fear upon the water and folly made it very unpleasing to her. A good dinner, and then to the office again. This afternoon Mr. Harris the Sayle-maker sent me a noble present of two large silver Candlestickes and snuffers, and a Slice to keep them upon[b] – which endeed is very handsome.[2] At night came Mr. Andrews with 36*l* – the further fruits of my Tanger contract; and so to bed late, and weary with business but in good content of mind – blessing God for these his benefits.

17. Up, and to my office; and then with Sir W. Batten to St. James, where many came to take leave, as was expected, of the Duke; but he doth not go till Monday. This night my Lady Wood died of the small-pox, and is much lamented among the great persons for a good-natured woman and a good wife;

a followed by 'And then' struck through   *b* repl. 'in'

---

1. The powder was inserted on the point of a needle: see Birch, ii. 21, 23. A detailed account (by Samuel Butler) is in M. H. Nicolson, *Pepys' diary and the new science*, pp. 154–6. The poison (from the upas tree) was used in Malaya for making poisoned arrows. The only known antidote was human ordure taken internally: *Philos. Trans.*, ii (for 1667), p. 417. Cf. Birch, ii. 43–4, 318. At this same meeting Pepys reported that pendulum-watches (above, p. 52, n. 2) gave no better results, according to a ship's master, than 'vulgar reckoning'. He was also asked 'to bespeak a man, at Deptford, for diving'. Ib., p. 24.

2. On 28 March the Navy Board acknowledged receipt of 50 bolts of Holland duck at Deptford from John Harris, and on 4 May he tendered for the supply of 1500 hammocks: *CSPD 1664–5*, pp. 131, 132.

but for all that, it was ever believed she was as others are.[1]

The Duke did give us some commands, and so broke up, not taking leave of him. But the best piece of newes is that instead of a great many troublesome Lords, the whole business is to be left with the Duke of Albemarle, to act as Admirall in his stead; which is a thing that doth cheer my heart – for the other would have vexed us with attendance, and never done the business.[2]

Thence to the Committee of Tanger, where the Duke a little, and then left us and we stayed – a very great Committee – the Lords Albemarle, Sandwich, Barkely, Fitzharding, Peterborough, ⟨Ashley⟩, Sir Tho. Ingram, Sir G Carteret,[a] and others. The whole business was the stating of Povys accounts; of whom, to say no more, never could man say worse himself nor have worse said of him then was by that company to his face – I mean as to his folly, and very reflecting words to his honesty. Broke up without anything but trouble and shame – only, I got my businesses done, to the signing of two bills for the Contractors and Captain Taylor,[3] and so came away well pleased – and home, taking up my wife at the Change, to dinner. After dinner out again, bringing my wife to her father's again at Charing-cross. And I to the Comittee again, where a new meeting of trouble about Povy, who still makes his business worse and worse; and broke up with most open shame again to him – and high words to him of disgrace, that they would not trust him with any more money till he had given an account of this. So broke up.

Then he took occasion to desire me to step aside, and he and I by water to London together: in the way, of his own accord, proposed to me that he would surrender his place of Treasurer to me, to have half the profit. The thing is new to me; but the

a repl. 'A'-

---

1. Mary, second wife of Sir Henry Wood, Clerk of the Board of Green Cloth, had been a dresser to Queen Catherine. She died at the age of 38. Her reputation is glanced at in Marvell's reference to her husband as 'Knight of the Horn and Cane': *Last Instructions*, l. 162.

2. See Duke of York to Albemarle and to the Navy Board (both 22 March): Duke of York, *Mem. (naval)*, pp. 51+. The 'troublesome Lords' were the privy councillors who had acted in the Admiral's absence during the campaign of the previous year.

3. The victualling contractors (Lanyon and Yeabsley) and Capt. John Taylor, whose ships had been used.

more I think, the more I like it, and do put him upon getting it done by the Duke: whether it takes or no, I care not, but I think at present it may have some convenience in it.[1]

Home, and there find my wife come home, and gone to bed not well of a cold got yesterday by water. At the office Bellamy came to me again, and I am in hopes something may be got by his business.[2] So late home to supper *a* and bed.

18. Up, and to the office, where all the morning. At noon to the Change and took Mr. Hill along with me to Mr. Povy's, where we dined and showed him the house, to his good content – and I expect when we meet, we shall laugh at it. But I having business to stay, he went away, and Povy and Creed and I to do some business upon Povy's accounts, all the afternoon till late at night; where, God help him, never man was so confounded, and all his people about him in this world, as he and his are. After we had done something [to the] purpose – we broke up; and Povy acquainted me before Creed (having said something of it also this morning at our office to me) what he had done in speaking to the Duke and others about his making me Treasurer; and hath carried it a great way – so as I think it cannot well be set back. Creed I perceive envies me in it; but I think, as that will *b* do me no hurt, so, if it did, I am at a great loss to think whether *c* it were not best for me to let it wholly alone; for it will much disquiet me and my business of the Navy, which in this war will certainly be worth all my time to me. Home, continuing in this doubtful condition what to think of it; but God Almighty do his will in it for the best.

To my office, where late, and then home to supper and to bed.

19. *Lords day.* Mr. Povy sent his *d* coach for me betimes, and I to him and there to our great trouble do find that my Lord Fitzharding doth appear for Mr. Brunkard[3] to be pay-master

---

a repl. 'bed'   *b* repl. 'it'   *c* repl. 'where'   *d* repl. 'for'

---

1. Pepys's formal appointment followed in April. He remained Treasurer for Tangier until April 1680, when he was succeeded by Hewer. The profits which had now to be divided with Povey were from poundage – 1*d.* in each shilling and 2*d.* in each piece-of-eight of expenditure: NMM, AGC/XX/25.

2. See above, p. 54, n. 1.

3. Henry Brouncker, younger brother of Lord Brouncker, and Groom of the Bedchamber to the Duke of York.

upon Povy's going out – by a former promise of the Dukes, and offering to give as much as any for it.   This put us all into a great dump, and so we went to Creeds new lodging in the Mewes and there we found Creed with his parrot upon his shoulder, which struck Mr. Povy, coming by, just by the eye, very deep; which had it hit his eye, had put it out.   This a while troubled us; but not proving very bad – we to our business, consulting what to do.   At last, resolved; and I to Mr. Coventry and there had his most friendly and ingenuous advice – advising me not to decline the thing, it being that that will bring me to be known to great persons, while now I am buried among three or four of us, says he, in the Navy – "but do not make a declared opposition to my Lord Fitzharding".   Thence I to Creed, and walked talking in the park an hour with him, and then to my Lord Sandwiches to dinner.   And after dinner to Mr. Povy's – who hath been with*a* the Duke of Yorke, and by the mediation of Mr. Coventry the Duke told him that the business shall go on, and he will take off Brunkerd, and my Lord Fitzharding is quiet too.   But to see the mischief, I hear that Sir G Carteret did not seem pleased, but said nothing, when he heard me proposed to come in Povy's room; which may learn me to distinguish between the men that is a man's true and false friend.

Being very glad of this news, Mr. Povy and I in his coach to Hide parke, being the first day of the Tour[1] there – where many brave ladies.   Among others, Castlemayne lay impudently upon her back in her coach, asleep with her mouth open.   There was also my Lady Kerneeguy, once my Lady Anne Hambleton, that is said to have given the Duke a clap*b* upon his first coming over.[2] Here I saw Sir J Lawson's daughter and husband, a fine couple[3] – and also Mr. Southwell and his new lady, very pretty.[4]   Thence

a   repl. 'at'   b   repl. 'the'

1. The parade of coaches: see above, iv. 95 & n. 3.

2. Lady Anne Hamilton had married Lord Carnegie (cr. Earl of Southesk, 1669). Rumour had it that her husband arranged for her to give the Duke a clap: below, ix. 154–5 & n. Her affair with the Duke took place mostly in 1662: according to Gramont (p. 166) 'she had previously passed through the hands of several other gentlemen'.

3. Isabella and Daniel Norton of Southwick, Hants.

4. Robert Southwell, Privy Council clerk and clerk to the Prize Commissioners, had married (26 January 1665) Elizabeth, daughter of Sir Edward Dering of Surrenden, Kent.

back, putting in at Dr. Whore's, where I saw his lady, a very fine
woman.[1] So home, and thither by my desire comes by and by
Creed and lay with me, very merry – and full of discourse what
to do tomorrow, and the conveniences that will attend my having
of this place; and I do think they may be very great.

20.   Up, Creed and I, and had Mr. Povy's coach sent for us,
and we to his house – where we did some business, in order to the
work of this day.   Povy and I to my Lord Sandwich, who tells
me that the Duke is not only a friend to the business, but to me,
in terms of the greatest love and respect and value of me that can
be thought; which overjoys me.   Thence to St. James's, and
there was in great doubt of Brunkerd; but at last I hear that
Brunkerd desists, and the Duke did direct Secretary Bennet, who
was there, to declare his mind to the Committee that he approves
of me for Treasurer, and with a character of me to be a man
whose industry and discretion he would trust as soon as any man's
in England – and did the like to my Lord Sandwich.

So to White-hall to the Committee of Tanger – where there
was present: my Lord of Albemarle, my Lord Peterborough,
Sandwich, Barkely, Fitzharding, Secretary Bennet, Sir Tho.
Ingram, Sir John Lawson, Povy and I – where after other business,
Povy did declare his business very handsomely; that he was sorry
he had been so unhappy in his accounts as not to give their
Lordshipps the satisfaction he intended.   And that he was sure
his accounts were right, and continues to submit them to examination, and is ready to lay down in ready money the fault of his
account.[2]   And that for the future, that the work might be better
done and with more quiet to him, he desired, by approbation of
the Duke, he might resign his place to Mr. Pepys.   Whereupon,
Secretary Bennet did deliver the Dukes command; which was
received with great content and allowance beyond expectation –
the Secretary repeating also the Duke's character of me – and I
could discern my Lord Fitzharding was well pleased with me, and

---

1. William Hoare, F.R.S., a physician and amateur of music.
2. Povey's Tangier accounts were
at length declared in the Exchequer
on 9 December 1673, and cover 4
November 1662 to this day.   They
are in PRO, E 351/357 (summary in
Routh, p. 366), and are much less
detailed than those of Pepys, which
overlap and begin on 5 November
1664: PRO, ib. 358–60.

signified full satisfaction and whispered something seriously of me to the^a Secretary. And there I received their constitution under all their hands presently, so that I am already confirmed their Treasurer, and put into a condition of striking of Tallys.[1] And all without one harsh word or word of dislike; but quite the contrary – which is a good fortune beyond all imagination. Here we rose, and Povy and Creed and I, all full of joy, thence to dinner – they setting me down at Sir J Winter's by promise; and dined with him, and a worthy fine man he seems to be, and of good discourse. Our business was to discourse of supplying the King with Iron for Ancors, if it can be judged good enough. And a fine thing it is, to see myself come to the condition of being received by persons of this rank – he being, and having long been, Secretary to the Queene-mother.[2]

Thence to Povys, and there sat and considered of business a little; and then home, where late at it – W Howe being with me about his business of^b accounts for his money laid out in the fleet;[3] and he gone, I home to supper and to bed.

News is this day come of Captain Allen's being come home ⟨from the Straights⟩ as far as Portland, with 11 of the King's ships and about 22 of Merchant-men.[4]

21. Up; and my Taylor coming to me, did consult all my wardrobe, how to order my clothes against next summer. Then to the office, where busy all the morning. At noon to the Change and brought home Mr. Andrews; and there with Mr. Sheply dined, and very merry and a good dinner. Thence to

---

a repl. 'me'   *b* repl. 'and'

1. For tallies, see *Comp.*: 'Exchequer'. The power here referred to amounted to that of issuing promises to pay from public funds. Pepys's appointment was later confirmed by a privy seal of 20 April. For the conditions of his agreement with Povey, see below, p. 68, n. 2.

2. Sir John Winter had ironworks in and near Lydney, Glos., and was interested in technical improvements in manufacture. The Forest of Dean ironworks under his control had

supplied dockyards in the 1650s. He had been secretary to the Queen Mother since 1638.

3. Howe's bill of over £400 for expenses (as Deputy-Treasurer of Sandwich's fleet) was registered in the Navy treasury on 25 March: PRO, Adm. 20/6, p. 434.

4. Allin's convoy had made Portland Point by midday on 16 March, and he had thence sent letters to Coventry announcing his arrival: Allin, i. 215-16.

Mr. Povys to discourse about settling our business of Treasurer; and I think all things will go very fayre between us, and to my content. But the more I see, the more silly the man seems to me. Thence by coach to the Mewes, but Creed was not there. In our way the coach drove through a lane by Drury-lane, where abundance of loose women stood at the doors, which, God forgive me, did put evil thoughts in me but proceeded no further, blessed be God. So home and late at my office; then home, and there find a couple of state-cups, very large, coming*a* I suppose each to about 6*l* apiece – from Burrows the Slopseller.

22. Up, and to Mr. Povy's about our business, and thence I to see Sir Ph. Warwicke, but could not meet with him. So to Mr. Coventry, whose profession of love and esteem for me to myself was so large and free, that I never could expect or wish for more, nor could have it from any man in England that I should value it more. Thence to Mr. Povys, and with Creed to the Change and to my house; but it being washing-day, dined not at home, but took him (I being invited) to Mr. Hublands the merchant, where Sir W Petty and abundance of most ingenious men, owners and freighters of the *Experiment*, now going with her two bodies to sea.[1] Most excellent discourse. Among others, Sir Wm. Petty did tell me that in good earnest, he hath in his will left such parts of his estate to him that could invent such and such things – as among others, that could discover truly the way of milk coming into the breasts of a woman – and he that could invent proper Characters to express to another the mixture of relishes and tastes.[2] And says that to him that invents gold, he gives nothing for the Philosopher's stone; "for," says he, "they*b* that find out that will be able to pay themselfs – but," says he, "by this means it is better then to give to a lecture. For here my executors, that must part with this, will be sure to be well convinced of the invention before they do part with their money."

a repl. 'weighed'   *b* repl. 'if they'

---

1. For the ship, see above, v. 353 & n. 3. It was shortly afterwards wrecked in a storm, and Petty designed no more double-keeled ships for twenty years.

2. Petty's final will (2 May 1685, two years before his death) contains no such bequests: BM, Add. 15858, ff. 109–10.

After dinner Mr. Hill took me with Mrs. Hubland, who is a fine gentlewoman – into another room, and there made her sing; which she doth very well – to my great content.

Then to Gresham College and there did see a kitlin killed almost quite (but that we could not quite kill her) with sucking*a* away the Ayre out of a Receiver wherein she was put – and then the ayre being let in upon her, revives her immediately. Nay, and this ayre is to be made by putting together a Liquor and some body that firments – the steam of that doth do the work.[1]

Thence home, and thence to White-hall, where the House full of the Dukes going tomorrow; and thence to St. James, wherein these things fell out:

1 I saw the Duke. Kissed his hand. And had his most kind expressions of his value and opinion of me, which comforted me above*b* all things in the world.

2 The like from Mr. Coventry, most heartily and affectionately.

3 Saw, among other fine ladies, Mrs. Middleton, a very great beauty I never knew or heard of before;[2]

4 I saw Waller the Poet,[3] whom I never saw before.

So, very late, by coach home with W Pen, who was there.

To supper and to bed – with my heart at rest and my head very busy, thinking of my several matters now on foot – the new comfort of my old Navy business, and the new one of my imployment on Tanger.

23. Up, and to my Lord Sandwich, who fallows the Duke

a MS. 'such'-   *b* repl. 'about'

1. This was the second part of an experiment devised to find a way of breathing under water (In the first part a bird had been used. Pepys had perhaps arrived too late to see it.) The 'kitlin' (kitten) was put into a 'rarefying engine' from which the air was withdrawn. It appeared to expire but was revived by fumes of aquafortis (nitric acid) let into the chamber. Birch, ii. 25.

2. She was Jane, wife of Charles Myddelton of Ruabon, aged 20; later mistress of the Duke of York and of several others. 'Handsomely made, all white and golden' (Gramont, p. 109); 'the most beautiful woman in England' (French ambassador, 1676, qu. ib., loc. cit.); 'that famous & indeede incomparable beautifull Lady' (Evelyn, 24 August 1683). She was much painted by Lely: see, e.g., O. Millar, *Tudor, Stuart and early Georgian pictures in coll. H.M. Queen* (1963), no. 266, pl. 107.

3. Edmund Waller (d. 1687), M.P. for Hastings, Sussex.

this day by water down to the Hope, where the *Prince* lies. He received me, busy as he was, with mighty kindness and joy at my promotions, telling me most largely how the Duke hath expressed on all occasions his good opinion of my service and love for me. I paid my thanks and acknowledgment to him; and so back home, where at the office all the morning. At noon to the Change. Home, and Lewellin dined with me. I thence abroad; carried my wife to Westminster by coach. To the Swan, Herberts, and there had much of the good company of Sarah, and to my wish; and then to see Mrs. Martin, who was very kind. Three weeks of her month of lying-in is over.[1]

So took up my wife and home, and at my office a while and thence to supper and to bed.

Great*a* talks of noises of guns heard at Deale; but nothing perticularly, whether in earnest or not.

24. Up betimes, and by agreement to the globe taverne in Fleet-street to Mr. Clerke my sollicitor, about the business of my uncles accounts;[2] and we went with one Jefferys to one of the Barons (Spelman),[3] and there my accounts were declared and I sworn to the truth thereof to my knowledge – and so I shall, after a few formalities, be cleared of all.

Thence to Povy's and there delivered him his letters, of greatest import to him that is possible, yet dropped by young Bland (just come from Tanger) upon the road by Sittingburne; taken up and sent to Mr. Pett at Chatham. Thus, everything done by Povy is done with a fatal folly and neglect.

Then to our discourse with him, Creed, Mr. Viner, myself and Poyntz, about the business of the Workehouse at Clerkenwell; and after dinner went thither and saw all the works there. And did also consult the act concerning that business and other papers, in order to our coming in to undertake it with Povy,

a repl. 'Gat'

---

1. A month's lying-in was usual until the early 19th century or later, because of the risk of late sepsis. The churching of the mother then followed: cf. above, ii. 185.

2. Robert Pepys's accounts as receiver of the Huntingdonshire assessment for 1647.

3. Clement Spelman, Baron of the Exchequer.

the management of the House.[1]   But I do not think we can
safely meddle with it, at least I, unless I had time to look after it
myself – but the thing is very ingenious and Laudable.

Thence to my Lady Sandwiches, where my wife all this day,
having kept Good friday very strict with fasting. Here we
supped and talked very merry – my Lady alone with me, very
earnest about Sir G Carterets son, with whom I perceive they
do desire my Lady Jemimah may be matched.   Thence home
and to my office, and then to bed.

25.   *Lady day.*   Up betimes and to my office, where all the
morning.   At noon dined alone with Sir W Batten, where great
discourse of Sir W. Penn – Sir W. Batten being I perceive quite
out of love with him, thinking him too great and too high – and
beginning to talk that the world doth Question his courage; upon
which, I told him plainly I have been told that he was articled
against for it, and that Sir H. Vane was his great friend therein.[2]
This he was, I perceive, glad to hear.   Thence to the office and
there till very late very busy, to my great content.

This afternoon of a sudden is come home Sir W. Penn from
the fleet, upon what score I know not.

Late home to supper and to bed.

26.   *Lords day – and[a] Easter day.*   Up (and with my wife, who
hath not been at church a month or two) to church.   At noon
home to dinner, my wife and I (Mercer staying to the Sacrament)
alone.

This is the day, seven years, which, by the blessing of God, I
《Health》 have survived of my being cut of the stone.   And am
now in very perfect good health and have long been.
And though the last winter[b] hath been as hard a winter as any

          a repl. 'rose and with'   *b* repl. 'y'—

1. This appears to have been a
scheme for the manufacture of textile
supplies for Tangier at the house of
correction known as the New Bridewell, in Clerkenwell, of which
Francis Poyntz was master. He
already sold sails and flags to the navy:
cf. above, v. 289 & n. 2. In 1667 he
was making tapestries there: Bodl.,

Clar. 85, ff. 55–6. The act was that
of 1662 (14 Car. II c. 12) under which
the New Bridewell had been built.
Nothing came of the proposal. Cf.
Z. C. von Uffenbach, *London in 1710*
(ed. Quarrell and Mare), pp. 53–5;
W. J. Pinks, *Hist. Clerkenwell*, p. 125.
    2. See above, iv. 376 & n. 1.

hath been these many years,[1] yet I never was better in my life, nor have not, these ten years, gone cooler in the Summer then I have done all this winter – wearing only a doublet and a waistcoat cut open on the back – abroad, a cloak; and within doors, a coat I slipped on. Now I am at a loss to know whether it be my Hares-foot[2] which is my preservative against wind, for I never had a fit of the Collique since I wore it – and nothing but wind brings me pain; and the carrying away of wind takes away my pain – or my keeping my back cool; for when I do lie longer then ordinary upon my back in bed, my water[a] the next morning is very hot – or whether it be my taking of a pill of Turpentine every morning, which keeps me alway loose – or all together. But this I know, with thanks to God Almighty, that I am now as well as ever I can wish or desire to be – having now and then little grudgeings of wind that brings me a little pain, but it is over presently. Only, I do find that my backe grows very weak, that I cannot stoop to write or tell money without sitting but I have pain for a good while after it.

Yet a week or two ago I had one day's great pain, but it was upon my getting[b] a bruise on one of my testicles; and then I did void two small stones, without pain though, and upon my[c] going to bed and bearing up of my testicles, I was well the[d] next. But I did observe that my sitting with my back to the fire at the office did then, as it doth at all times, make my back ake and my water hot, and brings me some pain.[3]

I sent yesterday an invitation to Mrs. Turner and her family to come to keep this day with me; which she granted – but afterward sent me word, that it being Sunday and Easter-day, she desired to choose another and put off this. Which I was willing enough to do, and so put it off as to this day, and will leave it to my own convenience when to choose another – and perhaps shall escape a feast by it.[4] At my office all the afternoon, drawing up my agreement with Mr. Povy, for me to sign to him tomorrow morning.

a repl. 'heat'   *b* repl. 'g'-   *c* repl. 'the'   *d* repl. 'present'

1. Dr D. J. Schove writes: 'It was the hardest since that of 1657-8.'
2. See above, v. 359 & n. 1.
3. Cf. above, p. 51 & n. 4.
4. But see below, p. 124. At Pepys's 'stone-feast' Mrs Turner was always an honoured guest since it was in her house that the operation had been performed.

In the evening spent an hour in the garden walking with Sir J. Mennes, talking of the Chest business, wherein Sir W. Batten deals so unfairly;[1] wherein the old man is very hot for the present, but that zeal will not last nor is to be trusted.

So home to supper, prayers, and to bed.

27. Up betimes to Mr. Povy's, and there did sign and seal my agreement with him about my place of being Treasurer for Tanger – it being, the greatest part of it, drawn out of a draft of his own drawing up; only, I have added something here and there in favour of myself.[2]

Thence to the Duke of Albemarle, the first time that we officers of the Navy have waited upon him since the Duke of York's going, who hath deputed him to be Admirall in his absence.[3] And I find him a quiet, heavy man, that will help business when he can and hinder nothing – and am very well pleased with our attendance on him.

I did afterward, alone, give him thanks for his favour to me about my Tanger business, which he received kindly and did speak*a* much of*b* his esteem of me.

Thence and did the same to Sir H Bennet, who did the like to me very fully.   And did give me all his letters lately come from thence, for me to read – which I returned in the afternoon to him.

Thence to Mrs. Martin, who though her husband is gone away, as he writes, like a fool into France, yet is as simple and wanton as ever she was – with which*c* I made myself merry – and away.

So to my Lord Peterburgh's, where Povy, Creed, Williamson, Auditor Beale, and myself, and mighty merry to see how plainly

a MS. 'speech'   *b* repl. 'in'   *c* MS. 'much'

---

1. By keeping reserves in his own hands: cf. above, v. 301; below, p. 183.

2. Dated this day; holograph copy (in Povey's hand) in Rawl. A 172, ff. 102–3; another copy (? Pepys's counterpart) in Houghton Lib., Harvard, MS. Eng. 991. Povey was to receive half of Pepys's profits. Interpretation of the agreement led to several later disputes – when Povey's accounts were declared at the Exchequer in 1673 (Rawl., ib., ff. 90–111), and in 1686 when Povey attempted to extract a moiety from Pepys's successor (Rawl. A 179, ff. 38–40).

3. In the previous year a committee of council had been appointed for this purpose, but that method had not worked well.

my Lord and Povy did abuse one another about their account,[1] each thinking the other a fool, and I thinking they were not, either of them, in that point much in the wrong, though in everything, and even in this manner of reproaching one another, very witty and pleasant.

Among other things, we had here the genteelest dinner and the neatest house that I have seen many a day; and the latter beyond anything I ever saw in a nobleman's house.[2]

Thence visited my Lord Barkely and did sit discoursing with him in his chamber a good while – and mighty friendly to me about the same business of Tanger. From that to other discourse of the times, and the want of money, and he said that the parliament must be called again soon and more money raised; not by tax, for he said he believed the people could not pay it, but he would have either a general excise upon everything, or else that every City-incorporate should pay a toll into the King's revenue, as he says it is in all the cities in the world.[3] For here, a citizen[a] hath no more laid on them then their neighbours in the country; whereas, as a city, it ought to pay considerably to the King for their Charter. But I fear this will breed ill-blood.

Thence to Povy; and after a little talk, home to my office late. Then to supper and to bed.

28. Up betimes and to the office, where we sat all the morning, and I did most of the business there, God wot. Then to the Change, and thence to the Coffee-house with Sir W Warren, where much good discourse for us both till 4 a-clock, with great pleasure and content. And then parted, and I home to dinner, having eat nothing; and so to my office. At night supped with my wife at Sir W Pen, who is to go back for good and all to the fleet tomorrow. Took leave, and to my office, where till past 12 at night, and then home to bed.

29. Up betimes, and to Povys, where a good while talking

a MS. 'citiens'

1. See above, iv. 94; v. 48 & nn.

2. Pepys had earlier admired Peterborough's collection of engravings and bows and arrows: above, iv. 270. The house was in Long Acre.

3. For the excise, see above, v. 69,

n. 1. The small annual payments made by municipal corporations to the state survived longer on the continent than in England, but were not so valuable as Berkeley seems to suggest.

about our business. Thence abroad into the City, but upon his tally could not get any money in Lombardstreete, through the disrepute which he suffers, I perceive, upon his giving up his place; which people think was not choice but necessity, as endeed it was. So back to his house, after*a* we had been at my house to taste my wine; but my wife being abroad, nobody could come at it – and so we were defeated. To his house; and before dinner he and I did discourse of the business of Freight,*b* wherein I am so much concerned[1] – above 100*l* for myself, and in my over-hasty making a bill out for the rest for him; but he resolves to move Creed in it – which troubled me much; and Creed by and by comes, and after dinner he did, but in the most cunning ingenious manner, do his business with Creed by bringing it in by the by, that the most subtle man in the world could never have done it better; and I must say that he is a most witty, cunning man, and one that I [am] most afeared of in my conversation, though in all serious matters of business, the veriest fool that ever I met with. The bill was produced and a copy given Creed; whereupon he writ his *intratur*[2] upon the originall, and I hope it will pass; at least, I am now put to it that I must stand by it and justify it – but I pray God it may never come to the test.

Thence, between vexed and joyed, not knowing what yet to make of it, home, calling for my Lord's Cookes three volumes at my bookseller's;[3] and so home, where I find a new ⟨cook⟩-mayd, her name is   ,[4] that promises very little. So to my office, where late about drawing up a proposal for Captain Taylor for him to deliver to the City, about his building the new ship;[5] which I have done well, and I hope will do the business; and so home to supper and to bed.

30. Up, and to my Lord Ashly, but did nothing, and to Sir Ph. Warwicke and spoke with him about business; and so back to the office, where all the morning. At noon home to dinner, and thence to the Tanger Committee; where, Lord, to see how

a repl. 'and my'   *b* repl. 'Freighted'

---

1. See above, v. 340 & n. 2.
2. The treasurer's authorisation of payment by the Exchequer.
3. Sir Edward Coke's *Institutes of the laws of England* (3 vols, 1660–4); PL 2150–2. The bookseller was Kirton.

4. Supply 'Alice': below, p. 313.
5. He had built the original *London*, and now built her successor at Deptford. Cf. above, pp. 52, 53.

they did run into the giving of Sir J Lawson (who is come to town today to get this business done) 4000*l* about his Molle business, and were going to give him 4*s* per yard more, which arises in the whole Molle to 36000*l* – is a strange thing. But the latter by chance was stopped – the former was given.[1]

Thence to see Mrs. Martin, whose husband being it seems gone away, and as she is informed he hath another woman whom he uses, and hath long done, as a wife, she is mighty reserved, and resolved to keep herself so till the return of her husband – which is a pleasant thing to think of her.

Thence home and to my office, where late, and to bed.

31. Up betimes, and walked to my Lord Ashly, and there with Creed, after long waiting, spoke with him and was civilly used by him. Thence to Sir Ph. Warwicke, and then to visit my Lord of Falmouth, who did also receive me pretty civilly – but not as I expected; he, I perceive, believing that I had undertaken to justify Povys accounts, taking them upon myself. But I rectified him therein. So to my Lady Sandwiches to dinner, and up to her chamber after dinner and there discoursed about Sir G Carteret's son, in proposition between us two for my Lady Jemimah. So to Povy, and with him spent the afternoon very busy, till I was weary of fallowing this and neglecting my Navy business;[a] so at night called my wife at my Lady's, and so home – to my office, and there made up my month's accounts; which, God be praised, rise to 1300*l* – which I bless God for. So after 12 a-clock, home to supper and to bed.

I find Creed mightily transported by my Lord of Falmouth's kind words to him and saying that he hath a place in his intention for him, which he believes will be considerable.[2] A witty man he is in every respect – but of no good nature, nor a man ordinarily to be dealt with. My Lady Castlemayne is sick again – people think, slipping her filly.[3]

a MS. 'busy'

1. The contract price (1663) was 13*s*. per cubic yard: above, iv. 45. In the end the mole cost £340,000: Routh, p. 377. Cf. PRO, AO 1/310/1220.

2. The hope was belied by events. The Earl of Falmouth (previously Viscount Fitzhardinge, Keeper of the Privy Purse and a prime favourite of the King) was killed in battle in the following June.

3. But she gave birth to a boy on the following 28 December.

APRILL.

1. All the morning very busy at the office, preparing a last half-year's accounts for my Lord Treasurer:[1] at noon eat a bit and stepped to Sir Ph. Warwicke; by coach to my Lord Treasurer's, and after some private conference and examining of my papers with him – I did return into the City, and to Sir G Carteret, whom I find with the Comissioners of Prizes, dining at Captain Cocke's in Broadestreete, very merry. Among other tricks, there did come a blind fiddler to the door, and Sir G. Carteret did go to the door and lead the blind fiddler by the hand in. Thence with Sir G. Carteret to my Lord Treasurers, and by and by come Sir W. Batten and Sir J. Mennes and anon[a] we come to my Lord and there did lay open the expense for the six months past, and an estimate of the seven months to come, to November next – the first arising to above 500000*l*; and the latter will, as we judge, come to above a Million.

But to see how my Lord Treasurer did bless himself, crying he could do no more then he could, nor give more money then he had, if the occasion and expense were never so great, which is but a sad story; and then to hear how like a passionate and ignorant[b] asse Sir G. Carteret did harangue upon the abuse of Tickets, did make me mad almost, and yet was fain to hold my tongue. Thence home, vexed mightily to see how simply our greatest ministers do content themselfs to understand and do things, while the King's service in the meantime lies a-bleeding.

At my office late, writing letters, till ready to drop down asleep with my late sitting up late and running up and down a-days. So to bed.

2. *Lords day.* At my office all the morning, renewing my

a repl. 'alone'   b MS. 'ignorance'

---

1. Copy in PRO, Adm. 106/3520, f. 24r. The Board was making a special appeal to the government for funds: below, pp. 75, 78. On the 15th Pepys sent detailed figures to Coventry: *Further Corr.*, p. 42. Cf. ib., pp. 38, 39.

vowes in writing. And then home to dinner. All the afternoon Mr. Tasborough, one of Mr. Povy's clerks, with me about his maister's accounts; in the evening Mr. Andrews and Hill sung – but supped not with me. Then after supper to bed.

3. Up, and to the Duke of Albemarle and White-hall, where much business; thence home and to dinner; and then with Creed, my wife, and Mercer to a play at the Dukes of my Lord Orerey's, called *Mustapha* – which being not good, made Baterton's part and Ianthes but ordinary too, so that we were not contented with it at all.[1] Thence home and to the office a while; and then home to supper and to bed. All the pleasure of the play was, the King and my Lady Castlemaine was there – and pretty witty Nell at the King's house, and the younger Marshall,[2] sat next us; which pleased me mightily.

4. All the morning at the office busy. At noon to the Change, and then went up to the Change to buy a pair of cotton stockings, which I did at the husband's shop of the most pretty woman[3] there, who*a* did also invite me to buy some linen of her; and I was glad of the occasion and bespoke some bands of her, entending to make her my seamstress – she being one of the prettiest and most modest-looked women that ever I did see. Dined at home; and to the office, where very late, till I was ready to fall down asleep, and did several times nod in the middle of my letters.

5. This day was kept publicly, by the King's command, as a Fast-day against the Duch war.[4] And I betimes with Mr.

---

a repl. 'of'

---

1. *Mustapha, the son of Solyman the Magnificent*, a tragedy by Roger Boyle, Earl of Orrery, published in 1668; now performed at the LIF. This is the first reference to a performance. The cast listed by Downes (pp. 25–6) includes Harris as Mustapha and Smith as Zanger. Betterton played Solyman, and 'Ianthe' (Mrs Betterton) Roxalana. (A).

2. Nell Gwyn, who had recently become an actress at the Theatre Royal, and Rebecca, the younger sister of Anne Marshall. Both were popular actresses at the TR, Drury Lane. (A).

3. Presumably Mary Batelier (cf. below, p. 170). The 'husband' was probably her brother Joseph.

4. By a proclamation of 6 March; Steele, no. 3410.

Tooker, whom I have brought into the Navy* to serve us as a husband to see goods timely shipped off from hence to the fleet and other places,¹ and took him with me to Woolwich and Deptford, where by business I have been hindered a great while of going.   Did a very great deal of business.   And then home, and there by promise find Creed, and he and my wife, Mercer and I, by coach to take the ayre; and where we have formerly been, at Hackny,² did there eat some pullets we carried with us and some other things of the house; and after a game or two at shuffleboard, home; and Creed lay with me but being sleepy, he had no mind to talk about business, which endeed I intended by inviting him to lie with me.   But I would not force it on him, and so to bed, he and I, and to sleep – being the first time I have been so much at my ease and taken so much fresh ayre these many weeks or*ᵃ* months.

6.   At the office, sat all the morning – where in the absence of Sir W. Batten, Sir G. Carteret, being angry about the business of tickets, spoke of Sir W. Batten for speaking some words about the signing of tickets, and called Sir W. Batten in his discourse at the table to us (the clerks being withdrawn) " shitten fellow" – which vexed me.

At noon to the Change and there set my business, of Lighters buying for the King, to Sir W. Warren, and I think he will do it for me to very good advantage – at which I am mightily rejoiced.³   Home; and after a mouthful of dinner, to the office, where till 6 a-clock; and then to White-hall and there with Sir G. Carteret and my Lord Brunkerd attended the Duke of Albemarle about the business of money.

I also went to Jervas's my barber for my periwig that was mending there.   And there do hear that Jane is quite undone – taking that idle fellow⁴ for her husband, yet not married, and lay

a repl. a full stop (∴)

---

1. The warrant appointing John Tooker as a Thames river agent is dated 9 May: PRO, Adm. 106/3520, f. 25r.
2. See above, v. 175.
3. On the 4th Coventry had

written to Pepys from Harwich about the need for lighters: CSPD *1664-5*, p. 292. On the 8th Pepys lent £100 for the purchase of one: *Further Corr.*, p. 40.

4. The fiddler, Harbing.

with him several weeks that had another wife and child – and she is now going into Ireland.

So called my wife at the Change, and home and at my office, writing letters till one a-clock in the morning, that I was ready to fall down asleep again.   Great talks of a new Comett – and it is certain one doth now appear, as bright as the late one at the best; but I have not seen it myself.[1]

7.   Up betimes to the Duke of Albemarle about money to be got for the Navy, or else we must shut up shop.[2]   Thence to Westminster-hall and up and down, doing not much; then to London, but to prevent Povys dining with me (who I see is at the Change) I went back again and to Herberts at Westminster; there sent for a bit of meat and dined, and then to my Lord Treasurers and there with Sir Ph. Warwicke; and thence to White-hall, in my Lord Treasurer's chamber with Sir Philip till dark night, about four hours talking of the business of the Navy charge and how Sir G. Carteret doth order business, keeping us in ignorance what he doth with his money.   And also, Sir Philip did show me nakedly the King's condition for money for the Navy; and he doth assure me, unless the King can get some noblemen or rich money-gentlemen to lend him money – or to get the City to do it – it is impossible to find money. We having already, as he says, spent one year's share of the three-years' tax, which comes to 2500000*l*.[3]   Being very glad of this day's discourse, in all but that I fear I shall quite lose Sir G. Carteret, who knows that I have been privately here all this day with Sir Ph. Warwicke.   However, I will order it so as to give him as little offence as I can.   So home to my office, and then to supper and to bed.

1. Dr D. J. Schove writes: 'This comet was not nearly as bright as the great comet of 1664-5. The perihelion passage was on 14 April (by the English calendar); the orbit quite distinct from that of its predecessor. See Mundy, v. 168-9; *Diary Sam. Newton* (ed. Foster), p. 12. For continental accounts, see *Philos. Trans.* i. (for 1665-6), 17 +, 36+; Philipp Carl, *Repert. der cometen-* *astronomie*, pp. 76-7. For the previous comet, see above, v. 346 & n. 3.'

2. Hemp merchants were asking £50 a ton, and refusing to deliver new supplies until their old bills were paid. See Pepys to Coventry, 8 April: *Further Corr.*, p. 40.

3. The Royal Aid yielded c. £69,000 per month for three years from 25 December 1664.

8. Up, and all the morning full of business at the office. At noon dined with Mr. Povy and then to the getting some business looked over of his. And then I to my Lord Chancellors, where to have spoke with the Duke of Albemarle; but the King and Council busy, I could not; then to the Old Exchange and there of my new pretty seamstress bought four bands. And so home, where I found my house mighty neat and clean; then to my office late, till past 12, and so home to bed.

The French Embassadors are come incognito before their train, which will hereafter be very pompous. It is thought they come to get our King to joyne with the King of France in helping him against Flanders, and they to do the like to us against Holland.[1] We have lain a good while with a good fleet at Harwich. The Dutch not said yet to be out. We, as high as we make our show, I am sure are unable to set out another small fleet, if this should be worsted. Wherefore, God send us peace I cry.

9. *Lords day.* To church with my wife in the morning, in her new light-coloured silk gown, which is, with her new point, very noble. Dined at home, and in the afternoon to Fan=Church, the little church in the middle of Fanchurch-street[2] – where a very few people, and few of any rank. Thence after sermon, home; and in the evening, walking in the garden, my Lady Pen and her daughter walked with my wife and I; and so to my house to eat with us, and very merry – and so broke up and to bed.

10. Up, and to the Duke of Albemarle's; and thence to

1. They came in fact to prevent the English fleet from sailing against the Dutch, and to mediate in the dispute. They were in a hurry because war had already been declared. Louis, however, was still hoping to prevent a conflict since neither side had withdrawn its representatives. He sent one of the royal princes (Henri de Bourbon, Duc de Verneuil, natural son of Henri IV and uncle of Charles II), together with a professional diplomat, Honoré Courtin, who with the ambassador, de Cominges, constituted what became known as the *célèbre ambassade.* They stayed until December. Verneuil went to see both the King and the Queen Mother on the 9th, and paid many visits to court before the state entry on 6 May: *Rec. des instructions, Angleterre* (ed. Jusserand), i. 345+; *CSPVen. 1664–6*, pp. 94, 95, 110, 115, 121, 125; J. J. Jusserand, *French Ambassador*, pp. 233–4; Feiling, p. 142.

2. St Gabriel's, Fenchurch, which stood in the centre of the roadway. (R).

White-hall to a Committee for Tanger, where new disorder about Mr. Povy's accounts, that I think I shall never be settled in my business of Treasurer for him. Here Captain Cooke met me and did seem discontented about my boy Tom's having no time to mind his singing nor Lute; which I answered him fully in, that he desired me that I would baste his coate. So home and to the Change, and thence to the Old James to dine with Sir W Rider, Cutler, and Mr. Deering, upon the business of hemp.[1] And so thence to White-hall to have attended the King and Lord Chancellor about the debts of the Navy and to get some money; but the meeting failed. So my Lord Brunkard took me and Sir Tho. Harvy in his coach to the park – which is very troublesome with the Dust – and ne'er a great beauty there today but Mrs. Middleton. And so home to my office, where Mr. Warren proposed my getting of 100*l* to get him a protection for a ship to go out;[2] which I think I shall do. So home to supper and to bed.

11. Up, and betimes to Alderman Cheverton to treat with him about hemp, and so back to the office. At noon dined at the Sun behind the Change, with Sir Edw. Deering and his brother and Comissioner Pett, we having made a contract with Sir Edw. this day about Timber.[3] Thence to the office, where late very busy; but with some trouble, have also some hopes[a] of profit too. So home to supper and to bed.

12. Up, and to White-hall to a Committee of Tanger; where contrary to all expectation, my Lord Ashly, being vexed with Poveys accounts, did propose it as necessary that Povy should be still continued Treasurer of Tanger till he had made up his

a repl. 'home'

---

1. Cf. above, p. 75, n. 2.
2. Thomas Warren, brother of the timber merchant Sir William, traded to both the Baltic and the Mediterranean. The protection was a warrant giving exemption to the seamen from impressment.
3. For the supply of 400 oaks;

Pett had negotiated it: Rawl. A 174, f. 83r; *CSPD 1664–5*, pp. 274, 298, 336. Sir Edward Dering (politician and parliamentary diarist) was a landowner of Kent, and half-brother of Edward ('Red-Ned') Dering (here mentioned), Baltic agent for the navy.

account – and with such arguments as I confess I was not prepared to answer – but by putting off of that discourse; and so I think brought it right again, but it troubled me so all the day after, and night too, that I was not quiet, though I think it is doubtful whether*ª* I shall be much the worse for it or no, if it should come to be so.

Dined at home; and thence to White-hall again (where I lose most of my time nowadays, to my great trouble, charge, and loss of time and benefit) and there, after the Council rose, Sir G Carteret, my Lord Brunkard, Sir Tho. Harvy, and myself down to my Lord Treasurer's chamber to him and the Chancellor and the Duke of Albemarle. And there I did give them a large account of the charge of the Navy, and want of money.[1] But strange, to see how they held up their hands, crying, "What shall we do?" Says my Lord Treasurer, "Why, what means all this, Mr. Pepys? This is true, you say, but what would you have me to do? I have given all*ᵇ* I can for my life. Why will not people lend their money? Why will they not trust the King as well as Oliver? Why do our prizes come to nothing, that yielded so much heretofore?" And this was all we could get, and went away without other answer. Which is one of the saddest things, that at such a time as this, with the greatest action on foot that ever was in England, nothing should*ᶜ* be minded, but let things go on of themselfs – do as well as they can.

So home, vexed. And going to my Lady Battens, there found a great many women with her in her chamber, merry – my Lady Pen and her daughter, among others; where my Lady Pen flung me down upon the bed, and herself and others, one after another, upon me, and very merry we were; and thence I home and called my wife with my Lady Pen to supper, and very merry as I could be, being vexed as I was.

So home to bed.

13. Lay long in bed, troubled a little with wind, but not much. So to the office and there all the morning. At noon to

a repl. 'which'   *b* repl. 'alone'   *c* repl. 'so'

---

1. Pepys described this interview in a letter of 15 April to Coventry: *Further Corr.*, p. 42. He proposed to the Board 'a solemn hearing before the King, or whom his majesty should refer us to'.

Sheriffe Watermans to dinner, all of us men of the office in town –
and our wifes, my Lady Carteret and daughters, and Lady Batten,
Pen, and my wife, &c.; and very good cheer we had and merry.
Musique at and after dinner, and a fellow danced a jigg; but
when the company begin to dance, I came away, lest I should be
taken out; and God knows how my wife carried herself, but I left
her to try her fortune.

So home, and late at the office; then home to supper and to bed.

14. Up, and betimes to Mr. Povy, being desirous to have an
end of my trouble of mind touching my Tanger business, whether
he hath any desire of accepting what my Lord Ashly offered,
of his becoming Treasurer again. And there I did, with a seeming most generous spirit, offer him to take it back again upon his
own terms; but he did swear to me that he would not, above all
things in the world – at which I was for the present satisfied;
but going away thence and speaking with Creed, he puts me
in doubt that the very nature of the thing will require that he be
put in again, and did give me the reasons of the Auditors,[1] which
I confess are so plain, that I know not how to withstand them.
But he did give me most ingenious advice what to do in it. And
anon, my Lord Berkely and some of the Commissioners coming
together, though not in a meeting, I did procure that they should
order Povys payment of his remain of account to me; which
order, if it doth pass, will put a good step to the fastening of the
thing upon me.

At noon Creed and I to a cook's shop at Charing-cross, and
there dined and had much discourse, and his very good upon my
business – and upon other things; among the rest, upon Will
Howe's dissembling with us, we discovering one to another his
carriage to us, present and absent – being a very false fellow.
Thence to White-hall again and there spent the afternoon. And
then home to fetch a letter for the Council, and so back to
White-hall, where walked an hour with Mr. Wren, of my Lord
Chancellors and Mr. Ager;[2] and then to*a* Unthankes and called

a repl. 'off'

---

1. The Auditors of the Exchequer,
before whom Povey's accounts had
still to be declared.

2. I.e. Matthew Wren, Remem-
brancer, and Thomas Agar, Clerk of
Appeals, in Chancery.

my wife, and with her through the City to Mile end greene and eat some cream and cakes; and so back home, and I a little at the office and so home to supper and to bed.

This morning I was saluted with newes that the Fleetes, ours and the Dutch, were engaged, and that the guns were heard at Walthamstow to play all yesterday – and that Captain Tiddiman's legs were shot off in the *Royall Katherine*. But before night I hear the contrary, both by letters of my own and messengers thence, that they were all well of our side, and no enemy appear yet, and that the *Royall Katherine* is come to the fleet, and likely to prove as good a ship as any the King hath – of which I am heartily glad, both for Chr. Pett's sake and Captain Teddiman that is in her.[1]

15. Up, and to White-hall about several businesses, but chiefly to see the progress of my warrants about Tanger under Creed; but to my trouble, found them not finished. So back to the office, where all the morning busy. Then home to dinner; and then all the afternoon, till very late, at my office; and then home to supper and to bed, weary.

16. *Lords day.* Lay long in bed. Then up and to my chamber and my office, looking over some plats, which I find necessary for me to understand pretty well, because of the Duch warr. Then home to dinner, where Creed dined with us. And so after dinner he and I walked to the Rolls chapel, expecting to hear the great Stillingfleete[2] preach; but he did not, but a very sorry fellow, which vexed me. The sermon done, we parted, and I home – where I find Mr. Andrews; and by and by comes Captain Taylor,[3] my old acquaintance at Westminster that understands Musique very well and composes mighty bravely; he brought us some things of two parts to sing, very hard. But

---

1. The English battle fleet now lay off the Gunfleet, and Thomas Teddeman (an old friend both of Pepys and Sandwich) had joined it from the river on the 10th: Sandwich, p. 178. His ship, the *Catherine*, had been newly built by Christopher Pett.

2. Edward Stillingfleet. See below, p. 87 & nn.

3. Silas Taylor (alias Domville), antiquary and amateur musician; the friend of John Playford, the elder Purcell, and Matthew Locke. (E).

that that is the worst, he is very conceited of them; and that, though they are good, makes them troublesome to one, to see him every note commend and admire them. He supped with me, and a good understanding man he is and a good Scholler – and among other things, a great Antiquary. And among other things, he can, as he says, show the very Originall Charter to Worcester of King Edgars, wherein he styles himself *Rex Marium Brittaniæ* &c.; which is the great text that Mr. Selden and others do quote, but imperfectly and upon trust.[1] But he hath the very originall, which he says he will show me.

He gone, we to bed.

This night I am told that news is come of our taking of three Duch men-of-war, with the loss of one of our Captains.

17. Up, and to the Duke of Albemarles, where he showed me Mr. Coventry's letters; how three Dutch privateers are taken, in

1. The 10th-century King Edgar became in the 17th century a symbol of British maritime aspirations. He is featured in the decorations of the greatest warship of the time (the *Royal Sovereign*, finished in 1637) which in fact it was proposed to call the *Edgar*: J. Howell, *Epist. Ho-Elianæ* (ed. Jacobs), i. 338. In 1667 the Lord Admiral, the Duke of York, named his fourth son after him. The reference here is to a spurious charter allegedly of 28 December 964, printed e.g. in W. de G. Birch, *Cart. Saxon.*, iii, no. 1135. Taylor's MS. was probably the 12th-century copy now in BM, Harl. 7513. The phrase *Marium Brit. Domini* occurs on the box in which it was contained, not in the charter itself, and is of course much later: *Cat. Harl. MSS* (1808), iii. 533. Selden cited the charter with some circumspection in *Mare Clausum* (trans. 1652, pp. 273+), and Pepys several times refers to it in *Naval Minutes* (pp. 58, 290, 302). Cf. T. W. Fulton, *Sovereignty of sea*, pp. 27–8. Taylor had laid hands on the MS. during the Interregnum, when he was a sequestrator in Herefordshire. He showed it to several people, including Aubrey, who wrote (ii. 254–5): 'Taylor garbled the library of the church of Worcester, and evidences, where he had the originall grant of King Edgar Θαλασσιαρχης, whence the Kings of England derive the right to the sovereignty of the sea. 'Tis printed in Mr. Seldon's *Mare Clausum*. I have seen it many times, & it is as legible as but lately written (Roman character). He offered it to the king for 120 *li.* but his majesty would not give so much. Since his death, I acquainted the Secretary of Estate . . . & his creditors seized on his goods & papers. He told me that it did of right belong to Worcester Church. I told one of their prebends, & they cared not for such things. I beleeve it haz wrapt herings by this time.'

one whereof Everson's son is Captaine.[1] But they have killed
poor Captain Golding in the *Diamond*. Two of them, one of
32 and the other of 20 odd guns, did stand stoutly up against her,
which hath 46,[a] and the *Yarmouth*, that hath 52[b] guns, and as
many more men as they – so that they did more then we could
expect, not yielding till many of their men were killed. And
Everson, when he was brought before the Duke of Yorke and
was observed to be shot through the hat, answered that he wished
it had gone through his head, rather then been taken.[2] One
thing more is written: that two of our ships the other day appearing upon the coast of Holland, they presently fired their Beacons
round the country, to give notice.[3] And news is brought the
King that the Dutch Smirna fleet is seen upon the back of
Scottland; and thereupon, the King hath wrote to the Duke that
he doth appoint a fleet to go to the Northward to try to meet
them coming home round – which God send.[4]

Thence to White-hall; where the King seeing me, did come
to me, and calling me by name, did discourse with me about the
ships in the River; and this is the first time that ever I knew the
King did know me[c] personally, so that hereafter I must not go
thither but with expectation to be Questioned, and to be ready to
give good answers.

So home, and thence with Creed, who came to dine with me,

a repl. '52'   b repl. '46'   c repl. 'or'

---

1. The actions had taken place on
the 15th. The frigate *Mermaid* had
captured an armed merchantman, and
the *Diamond* and *Yarmouth* had taken
two 'direction' (reconnaissance)
vessels. For Coventry's letter to
Williamson (15 April), see *CSPD
1664–5*, p. 310; cf. *CSPVen. 1664–6*,
pp. 115–16, 120. Cornelis Evertsen,
jun., was the son of the Dutch admiral
of the same name.

2. This story also appears in a news-
letter (27 April) in HMC, *Rawdon
Hastings*, ii. 151. Evertsen was
released in June: *CSPD 1664–5*,
p. 407.

3. 'Two English ships have appeared off these coasts where they
have taken a small bark of Maeslant,
which makes us think that the body
of their fleet is not far away, and perhaps today we shall see them because
the wind . . . may cause them to
approach our coasts' (report from
The Hague, 13/23 April): *CSPVen.
1664–6*, p. 113.

4. No such order has been traced.
There were several alarms of this
sort.

to the Old James, where we dined with Sir W Rider and Cutler; and by and by, being called by my wife, we all to a play, *The Ghosts*,[1] at the Dukes house; but a very simple play.

Thence up and down, with my wife with me, to look Sir Ph. Warwicke (Mr. Creed going from me), but missed of him; and so home, and late and busy at my office. So home to supper and to bed.

This day was left at my house a very neat Silver watch, by one Briggs, a Scrivener and Sollicitor;[2] at which I was angry with my wife for receiving, or at least for opening the box wherein it was, and so far witnessing our receipt of it as to give the messenger 5s for bringing it. But it can't[a] be helped, and I will endeavour to do the man a kindness – he being a friend of my uncle Wights.

18. Up, and to Sir Ph. Warwicke and walked with him an hour with great delight in the park, about Sir G Carterets accounts and the endeavours that he hath made to bring Sir G. Carteret to show his accounts and let the world see what he receives and what he pays.

Thence home to the office – where I find Sir J. Mennes come home from Chatham and Sir W. Batten both this morning from Harwich, where they have been these seven or eight days.

At noon with my wife and Mr. Moore by water to Chelsy, about my privy-Seale for Tanger, but my Lord Privy Seale was gone abroad; and so we, without going out of the boat, forced to return; and find him not at White-hall. So I to Sir Ph. Warwicke and with him to my Lord Treasurer, who signed my

a MS. 'can'

---

1. 'By Mr. John Holden': Downes, p. 26; not printed; the first record of its being performed. (A).
2. The watch (a second-hand one) proved to be worth £14: below, p. 100. A 'neat' watch was likely to be one of the undecorated variety now known as 'puritan'. See *Comp.*: 'Clothes'; G. H. Baillie, *Watches, their history*, etc., passim and pl. 29. Timothy Brigg(s) was a notary-public who did some business with the Navy Office and Admiral's office, e.g. in obtaining ships' passes to the Mediterranean during the war.

Comission for Tanger=Treasurer and the Docquet of my privy Seale for the monies to be paid to me.[1]

Thence to White-hall to Mr. Moore again; and not finding my Lord, I home, taking my wife and woman up at Unthankes. Late at my office; then to supper and bed.

19. Up by 5 a-clock, and by water to White-hall; and there took coach and with Mr. Moore to Chelsy, where after all my fears what doubts and difficulties my Lord Privy Seale would make at my Tanger privy-seal, he did pass it at first reading, without my speaking with him – and then called me in and was very civil to me. I passed my time in contemplating (before I was called in) the picture of my Lord's son's lady, a most beautiful woman,[2] and most like to Mrs. Butler.[3] Thence, very much joyed, to London back again, and found out Mr. Povy, told him this, and then went and left my privy-seal at my Lord Treasurer's; and so to the Change and thence to Trinity-house, where a great dinner of Captain Crisp, who is made an Elder Brother. And so, being very pleasant at dinner, away home, Creed with me, and there met Povy; and we to Gresham College – where we saw some experiments up[on] a hen, a dog, and a cat of the Florence poyson.[4] The first it made for a time drunk, but it came to itself again quickly. The second it made vomitt mightily, but no other hurt. The third I did not stay to see the effect of it – being taken out by Povy; and he and I walked below[5] together, he giving me most exceeding discouragements in the getting of money (whether by design or no I know not, for I am now come to think him a most cunning fellow in most things he doth but his

1. Dated 18 April, this authorised payment (in quarterly instalments) of £70,000 p.a. to Pepys: PRO, Index 6752. But it did not cover payments in the current quarter: see below, p. 92 & n. 1.

2. Sarah (*née* Bodvile), wife of Lord Robartes's son, Robert Robartes. Pepys's opinion of her beauty was confirmed when he met her on 27 April 1668. The portrait has not been traced.

3. See above, v. 286 & n. 1.

4. A decoction of tobacco. There was at this time some controversy about whether tobacco produced paralysis: Birch, ii. 9, 41. A phial of the poison had been procured by the King from Florence 'on purpose to have those experiments related of the efficacy thereof, tried by the society'. The hen was stupefied rather than drunk, the kitten merely drowsy. Birch, ii. 31. See also below, pp. 95–6.

5. See illust., above, iv, opp. p. 151.

accounts) and made it plain to me that money will be hard to get –
and that it is to be feared Backewell[1] hath a design in it – to get
the thing forced upon himself. This put me into a cruel melancholy, to think I may lose what I have had so near my hand;
but yet something may be hoped for, which tomorrow will show.
He gone, Creed and I together a great while, consulting what to
do in this case; and after all, I left him to do what he thought fit
in his discourse tomorrow with my Lord Ashly. So home, and
in*a* my way met with Mr. Warren, from whom my hopes, I fear,
will fail of what I hoped for by my getting him a protection.[2]
But all these troubles will, if not be over, yet we shall see the
worst of them in a day or two. So to my office and thence to
supper; and my head akeing, betimes, that is by 10 ⟨or 11⟩
a-clock, to bed.

20. Up, and all the morning busy at the office. At noon
dined, and Mr. Povy by agreement with me (where his boldness
with Mercer, poor innocent wench, did make both her and me
blush to think how he were able to debauch a poor girl if he had
opportunity) at a dish or two of plain meat of his own choice.
After dinner comes Creed and then Andrews; where want of
money to Andrews[3] the main discourse; and at last, in confidence of Creeds judgment, I am resolved to spare him 4 or 500*l*
of what lies by me, upon the security of some Tallys. This
went against my heart to begin; but which, obtaining Mr. Creed
to join with me, we do resolve to assist Mr. Andrews. Then
anon we parted, and I to my office, where late, and then home to
supper and to bed. This night, I am told, the first play is played
in Whitehall=hall,[4] which is now turned to a house of Playing.
I had a great mind, but could not go to see it.

a repl. 'there'

---

1. Edward Backwell, goldsmith-
banker. Cf. below, pp. 109, 274.
2. See above, p. 77 & n. 2.
3. Thomas Andrews supplied victuals for Tangier. On 7 March he
and his partners asked for £2400:
Rawl. A 174, f.96r.
4. The Great Hall at the palace of
Whitehall, situated between the
Banqueting House and the Thames.
Previously used for occasional per-
formances of plays (see above, iv.
56; v. 299), in 1665 it was converted
into a permanent theatre and equipped
with scenery under the supervision
of John Webb, son-in-law of Inigo
Jones. See E. Boswell, *Restoration
court stage*, pp. 27–41. (A).

21. Up, and to my office about business. Anon comes Creed and Povy, and we treat about the business of our lending money, Creed and I, upon a Tally, for the satisfying of Andrews; and did conclude it as in papers is expressed. And as I am glad to have an opportunity of having 10 per cent for my money, so I am as glad that the sum I begin this trade with is no more then 350*l.*[1]

We all dined, at Andrews charge, at the Sun behind the Change; a good dinner, the worst dressed that ever I eat any; then home and there find Kate Joyce and Harman come to see us: with them, after long talk, abroad by coach, a Tour in the fields, and drunk at Islington, it being very pleasant, the dust being laid by a little rain; and so home, very well pleased with this day's work; and so, after a while at my office, to supper and to bed.

This day we hear that the Duke and the fleet are sailed yesterday: pray God go along with them – that they have good speed in the beginning of their work.

22. Up, and Mr. Cæsar, my boy's lute-Maister, being come betimes to teach him, I did speak with him seriously about the boy, what my mind was if he did not look after his lute and singing, that I would turn him away – which I hope will do some good upon the boy.

All the morning busy at the office. At noon dined at home; and then to the office again, very busy till very late; and so home to supper and to bed – my wife making great preparation to go to Court to chapel to-morrow.

This day I have news from Mr. Coventry that the fleet is sailed yesterday from Harwich to the coast of Holland, to see what the Duch will do. God go along with them.[2]

1. Writing on 20 June to Lanyon (who had paid him handsomely for the Tangier victualling contract and whom he wanted to impress) Pepys inflated this loan to £800 and invented another of like amount to Lawson: Rawl. A 193, f. 210r. He had recently been indignant that Creed should charge 10% interest: above, v. 399 & n. 1.

2. Coventry to Pepys, the *Charles*, 'under saile', 21 April: Rawl. A 174, f. 458r–v. It ends: 'God send mee a good journey. God send us a good meeting . . .'. The fleet had been delayed for a day by fog: Sandwich, p. 198. Pepys's reply (22 April) in which he looks forward to Coventry's return 'which God graunt may be with Victory', is in NMM, LBK/8, p. 197 (copy in Hayter's hand); partially printed in *Further Corr.*, p. 43.

23. *Lords day.* Mr. Povy, according to promise, sent his coach betimes, and I carried my wife and her woman to Whitehall chapel and set them in the Organ loft. And I, having list to untruss, went to the Harp-and-ball, and there drank also, and entertained myself in talk with the maid of the house, a pretty maid and very modest. Thence to the chapel and heard the famous young Stillingfleete, who I knew at Cambridge and is now newly admitted one of the King's chaplains – and was presented, they say, to my Lord Treasurer for St. Andrews Holborne, where he is now minister, with these words: that they (the Bishops of Canterbury, London, and another) believed he is the ablest young man to preach the gospel of any since the Apostles.[1] He did make the most plain, honest, good, grave sermon, in the most unconcerned and easy yet substantial manner, that ever I heard in my life – upon the words of Samuell to the people – "Fear the Lord in truth with all your heart, and remember the great things that he hath done for you"[2] – it being proper to this day, the day of the King's Coronation.

Thence to Mr. Povy's, where mightily treated, and Creed with us. But Lord, to see how Povy overdoes everything in commending it*ª* doth make it nauseous to me, and was not (by reason of my large praise of his house) over-acceptable to my wife. Thence after dinner Creed and we by coach; took the ayre in the fields beyond St. Pancras, it raining now and then; which it seems is most welcome weather. And then all to my house –

a MS. 'in'

---

1. Stillingfleet (now just thirty, two years younger than Pepys) had been at St John's College, Cambridge, 1649–53. He was preacher at the Rolls Chapel, and had recently achieved new fame by his *Rational account of the grounds of the Protestant religion* (1664), written to refute the Jesuits' propaganda. He had been presented by Southampton to the living of St Andrew's in January 1665, and was instituted on 21 March, holding it until 1689.

His appointment as chaplain-in-ordinary to the King dated from 4 April 1665: PRO, LC 3/173, p. 78. He later became Dean of St Paul's (1678) and Bishop of Worcester (1689).

2. A loose recollection of 1 Sam., xii. 24. Stillingfleet was, like South, Tillotson and Barrow, one of the greatest preachers of the age, and like them favoured a 'plain' style. See W. Fraser Mitchell, *Engl. pulpit oratory*, pp. 305+.

where comes Mr. Hill, Andrews, and Captain Taylor, and good Musique; but at supper, to hear the arguments we had against Taylor concerning a Corant – he saying that the law of a dancing Corant is to have every barr to end in a pricked Crochet[1] and quaver – which I did deny,*a* was very strange. It proceeded till I vexed him; but all parted friends, for Creed and I to laugh at when he was gone. After supper Creed and I together to bed in Mercer's bed – and so to sleep.

24. Up, and with Creed in Sir W. Batten's coach to Whitehall. Sir W. Batten and I to the Duke of Albemarle, where very busy. Then I to Creeds chamber – where I received with much ado my two orders about receiving of Povys monies and answering his Creditts; and it is strange how he will preserve his constant humour, of delaying all business that comes before him.

Thence he and I to London to my office, and back again to my Lady Sandwiches to dinner, where my wife by agreement.

After dinner alone, my Lady told me (with the prettiest kind of doubtfullness whether*b* it would be fit for her with respect to Creed to do it, that is in the world) that Creed had broke his desire to her of being a servant to Mrs. Betty Pickering, and placed it upon encouragement which he had from some discourse of her Ladyships, commending*c* of her virtues to him – which, poor lady, she meant most innocently. She did give him a cold answer, but not so severe as it ought to have been. And it seems, as the lady since to my Lady confesses, he had wrote a letter to her; which she answered slightly, and was resolved to contemn any motion of his therein. My Lady takes the thing very ill, as it is fit she should. But I advise her to stop all future occasions of the world's taking notice of his coming thither so often as of late he hath done. But to think that he should have this devilish presumption, to aim at a lady so near to my Lord, is strange, both for his modesty and discretion.[2]

Thence to the Cockepitt, and there walked an hour with my Lord Duke of Albemarle alone in his garden, where he expressed

a MS. 'denied'   *b* repl. 'which'   *c* repl. 'coming'

---

1. A dotted crotchet. Pepys was right. (E).   2. Nevertheless Creed married her in October 1668.

in great words his opinion of me: that I was the right hand of
the Navy here, nobody but I taking any care of anything therein –
so that he should not know what could be done without me – at
which I was (from him) not a little proud.   Thence to a Committee of Tanger – where, because not a Quorum,[1] little was done.
And so away to my wife (Creed with me) to my wife at Mrs.
Pierces; who continues very pretty and is now great with child.
I had not seen her a great while.   Thence by coach to my Lord
Treasurer's, but could not speak with Sir Ph. Warwicke.   So
by coach with my wife and Mercer to the park; but the King
being there, and I nowadays being doubtful of being seen in any
pleasure, did part from the Tour,[2] and away out of the park to
Knightsbridge and there eat and drank in the coach, and so
home; and I, after a while at my office, home to supper and to
bed – having got a great Cold,*a* I think by my pulling off my
periwigg so often.

25.   At the office all the morning, and the like after dinner;
at home all the afternoon till very late; and then to bed, being
very hoarse with a cold I did lately get with leaving off my
periwigg.
    This afternoon W. Pen, lately come from his father in the
Fleete, did give me an account how the fleet did sail: about 100
and 3 in all, besides small ketches – they being in sight of six or
seven Duch scouts, and sent ships in chase of them.[3]

26.   Up very betimes, my cold continuing and my stomach
sick with the butterd ale that I did drink the last night in bed,
which did lie upon me till I did this morning vomit it up.
    So walked to Povy's, where Creed met me, and there I did
receive the first parcel of money as Treasurer of Tanger and did
give him my receipt for it, which was about 2800*l* value in
Tallys; we did also examine and settle several other things, and
then I away to White-hall, talking with Povy alone about my
opinion of Creeds indiscretion in looking after Mrs. Pickering,

a   word blotted

---

1. The quorum was five: below,
vii. 156.
    2. See above, iv. 95, n. 3.
    3. The names of the English ships
are in Sandwich, pp. 195-8. For the
fleet's movements, see *CSPD 1664-5*,
p. 170.

desiring him to make no more a sport of it, but to correct him if he finds that he continues to own any such thing. This I did by my Lady's desire, and do entend to pursue the stop of it.

So to the Carriers by Cripplegate*a*,[1] to see whether my mother be come to town or no, I expecting her today; but she is not come. So to dinner to my Lady Sandwiches; and there, after dinner above in the dining-room, did spend an hour or two with her, talking again about Creeds folly; but strange it is, that he should dare to propose this business himself of Mrs. Pickering to my Lady – and to tell my Lady that he did it for her virtue sake, not minding her money, for he could have a wife with more; but for that, he did entend to depend upon her Ladyshipp to get as much of her father and mother for her as she could. And that what he did was by encouragement from discourse of her Ladyshipp's. He also had wrote to Mrs. Pickering, but she did give him a slighting answer back again. But I do*b* very much fear that her honour, if the world comes to take notice of it, may*c* be wronged by it.

Thence home, and all the afternoon till night at my office. Then home to supper and to bed.

27. Up, and to my office, where all the morning. At noon Creed dined with me; and after dinner walked in the garden, he telling me that my Lord Treasurer now begins to be scrupulous, and will know what becomes of the 26000*l* saved by my Lord Peterborough[2] before he parts with any more money – which puts us into new doubts, and me into a great fear that all my cake will be doe still; but I am well prepared for it to bear it, being not clear whether it will be more for my profit to have it or go without it, as my profits of the Navy are likely now to be.

All the afternoon till late, hard at the office. Then to supper and to bed.

This night Wm. Hewer is returned from Harwich, where he hath been paying off of some ships this fortnight, – and went to sea a good way with the fleet – which was 96 in company then, men-of-war, besides some come in and fallowing them since. Which makes now above 100 – whom God bless.

a repl. 'Ct'-   *b* repl. 'did'   *c* repl. 'be'

1. See below, p. 95, n. 4.   2. See above, p. 15.

28. Up by 5 a-clock; and by appointment, with Creed by 6 at his chamber, expecting Povy, who came not. Thence he and I out to Sir Phill.*ᵃ* Warwickes; but being not up, we took a turn in the garden hard by, and thither comes Povy to us. After some discourse of the reason of the difficulty that Sir Ph. Warwicke makes in issuing a warrant for my striking of tallies; namely, the having a clear account of the 26000*l* saved by my Lord of Peterborough – we parted; and I to Sir P. Warwicke, who did give me an account of his demurr – which I applied myself to remove, by taking Creed with me to my Lord Ashly. From whom, contrary to all expectation, I received a very kind answer, just as we could have wished it: that he would satisfy my Lord Treasurer.

Thence, very well satisfied, I home and down the River to visit the victualling-ships, where I find all out of order. And come home to dinner, and then to write a letter to the Duke of Albemarle about the victualling-ships;[1] and carried it myself to the council-chamber, where it was read; and when they rise, my Lord Chancellor, passing by, stroked me on the head, and told me that the Board had read my letter and taken order for the punishing of the watermen for not appearing on board the ships.[2] And so did the King afterward, who doth now know me so well, that he never sees me but he speaks to me about our Navy business.

Thence got my Lord Ashly to my Lord Treasurer below in his chamber, and there removed the scruple; and by and by brought

a repl. 'W'-

---

1. Pepys to Sir William Clarke (Secretary at War), 28 April: copy in NMM, LBK/8, p. 199. The Duke of York had on the 25th written a strong protest to Albemarle about the victualling: *Mem. (naval)*, pp. 44+. Cf. Pepys's note (22 April) on the difficulty of getting beer delivered to the ships: NWB, p. 112.

2. On 22 April Thomas Lewis of the Victualling Office wrote to the Navy Board reporting that the watermen pressed into service on the victualling ships had proved refractory, and were complaining that married

men had been taken while bachelors had been left. Some had deserted. Meanwhile, the fleet was held up for lack of beer and water – always the last commodities to be put on board. *CSPD 1664-5*, pp. 323, 335. The Rulers of the Watermen's Company had been summoned to discuss the situation with the Privy Council on the 26th (NMM, LBK/8, p. 199), and at this day's meeting on the 28th the Council had ordered Albemarle to see to the impressment of the watermen (PRO, PC 2/58, f. 59*v*).

Mr. Sherwin to Sir P. Warwicke and did the like. And so home; and after a while at my office, to bed.

29. All the morning busy at the office. In the afternoon to my Lord Treasurers and there got my Lord Treasurer to sign the warrant for my striking of tallies.[1] And so doing many Jobbs in my way. Home, and there late writing letters – being troubled in my mind to hear that Sir W. Batten and Sir J. Mennes do take notice that I am nowadays much from the office, upon no office business – which vexes me, and will make me mind my business the better, I hope in God. But what troubles me more, is that I do omit to write, as I should do, to Mr. Coventry; which I must not do, though this night I minded it so little as to sleep in the middle of my letter to him, and committed forty* blotts and blurrs in my letter to him.[2] But of this I hope never more to be guilty – if I have not already given him sufficient offence. So late home, and to bed.

30. *Lords day.* Up, and to my office alone all the morning, making up my monthly accounts; which though it hath been very intricate, and very great disbursements and receipts and odd reckonings, yet I differed not from the truth – *viz.*, between my first computing what my profit ought to be, and then what my cash and debts do really make me worth, not above 10*s* – which is very much, and I do much value myself upon that account. And herein, I with great joy find myself to have gained this month above 100*l* clear; and in the whole, to be worth above 1400*l* – the greatest sum I ever yet was worth.

Thence home to dinner and there find poor Mr. Spong walking at my door; where he had knocked, and being told I was at the office, stood modestly there walking, because of disturbing me; which methinks was one of the most modest acts (of a man that hath no need of being so to me) that ever I knew in my life.

He dined with me; and then after dinner, to my closet, where abundance of mighty pretty discourse; wherein, in a word,*a* I

a repl. same symbol badly formed

---

1. The tallies amounted to £17,500 to cover the current quarter: *CTB*, i. 659. See above, p. 84, n. 1; below, pp. 95, 100.

2. Copy in Hewer's hand in NMM, LBK/8, pp. 201–3; mostly about supplies.

find him the man of the world that hath of his own ingenuity obtained the most in most things, being withal no scholler.[1] He gone, I took boat and down to Woolwich and Deptford; and made it late home, and so to supper and to bed.

Thus I end this month:[a] in great content as to my estate and gettings. In much trouble as to the pains I have taken and the rubs I expect yet to meet with about the business of Tanger. The fleet, with about 106 ships, upon the coast of Holland, in sight of the Dutch within the Texell. Great fears of the Sickenesse here in the City, it being said that two or three houses are already shut up. God preserve us all.[2]

a repl. 'much'

1. John Spong in 1660 had been a Chancery clerk; now he was a mathematical practitioner and instrument maker.

2. This entry marks the beginning of Pepys's notices of the attack of plague in London – the most serious since that of 1625 – which has become known as the Great Plague. His account affords some of the best contemporary evidence. In its commonest form plague in England at this time was a bubonic infection caused by a bacillus carried by rat fleas. (The pneumonic variety spread by droplet infection was much less common.) It was endemic in Asia and parts of Africa, and according to most authorities came to W. Europe only as epidemics (though some believe that it was endemic here too), spread at intervals from the Mediterranean and Middle East by the rats which infested the trading ships. (Cf. the outbreak in Holland, 1663–4: above, iv. 340 & n. 2.) The outbreaks always abated in the winter when the fleas hibernated. They ceased altogether in England after 1671 for reasons which are still a matter of dispute. Possibly both rats and humans had developed an immunity. The illness took the form of a high fever, with swellings ('buboes') of the lymphatic glands, and sometimes spots ('tokens') on the skin. Contemporary medicine was unable to discover the cause or to prescribe any effective treatment. Whole households – the healthy with the sick – were isolated, sometimes virtually immured. Patients were bled, sweated and blistered, but usually died within a few days. The present outbreak was the most famous attack, as well as the last on a large scale in England, though that of 1561 in London is held to have caused more deaths in proportion to population. About 100,000 now died in London before November 1665 – between one-quarter and one-third of the total population. By then, apart from outbreaks in the provinces in 1666, it was virtually over. See J. F. D. Shrewsbury, *Hist. bubonic plague in Brit. Isles* (cf. C. Morris in *Camb. Hist. Journ.*, xiv. 205 +); Bell, *Plague*; Comp.: 'The Plague'.

MAY.

1. Up, and to Mr. Povy's, and by his bedside talked a good while. Among other things, he doth much insist, I perceive, upon the difficulty of getting of money, and would fain have me to concur in the thinking[a] of some other way[b] of disposing of the place of Treasurer to one Mr. Ball.[1] But I did seem slight of it, and resolved to try to do the best or to give it up. Thence to the Duke of Albemarle, where I was sorry to find myself to come a little late. And so home, and at noon, going to the Change, met my Lord Brunkerd, Sir Robert Murry, ⟨Deane Wilkins⟩, and Mr. Hooke, going by coach to Collonell Blunt's to dinner.[2] So they stopped and took me with them. Landed at the Tower-wharf and thence by water to Greenwich, and there coaches met us and to his house, a very stately seat for situation and brave plantations; and among[c] others, a Vineyard, the first that ever I did see.[3] No extraordinary dinner, nor any other entertainment good – but only, after dinner to the tryall of some experiments about making of coaches easy. And several we tried, but one did prove mighty easy (not here for me to describe, but the whole body of that coach lies upon one long spring) and we all, one after another, rid in it; and it is very fine and likely to take. These experiments were the intent of their coming, and pretty they are. Thence back by coach to Greenwich and in his pleasure-boat to Deptford; and there stopped, and in to Mr.

a repl. blotted symbol   b repl. 'p'-   c repl. 'above'

---

1. Probably John Ball, cashier to the Excise Commissioners for London.

2. Col. Thomas Blount, of Wricklemarsh, south of Blackheath, Kent, was a Fellow of the Royal Society. His guests were members, with him, of the society's 'mechanical committee' which had been directed to inspect and report on his new design of coach springs: Birch, ii. 45; ib., pp. 32, 41, 53, 56, 59.

3. For the house, see E. Hasted, *Hist. Kent* (ed. Drake), pp. 123–5, and, for the vineyard, *Garden book of Sir T. Hanmer* (ed. Rohde), pp. 163–4. The mansion was rebuilt in the 18th century; the house and grounds have now been destroyed and built over. Pepys had seen the vineyard at Hatfield in 1661: above, ii. 138–9.

Evelings, which is a most beautiful place,[1] but it being dark and late, I stayed not; but Dean Wilkins and Mr. Hooke and I walked to Redriffe, and noble discourse all day long did please me. And it being late, did take them to my house to drink, and did give them some sweetmeats – and thence sent them with a lanthorn home – two worthy persons as are in England, I think, or the world.[2] So to my Lady Batten, where my wife is tonight; and so after some merry talk, home to bed.

2. Up, and to the office all day – where sat late; and then to the office again. And by and by Sir W. Batten and my Lady and my wife and I, by appointment yesterday (my Lady Pen failing us, who ought to have been with us) to the Renish-wine-house at the Steelyard, and there eat a couple of lobsters and some prawns, and pretty merry – especially to see us four together, while my wife and my Lady did never entend ever to be together again, after a year's distance between one another. Hither by and by came Sir Rd. Ford and also Mrs. Esther, that lived formerly with my Lady Batten, now well married to a priest – come to see my Lady.

Thence, toward evening, home and to my office, where late; and then home to supper and to bed.

3. Up betimes, and walked to Sir Ph. Warwickes, where a long time with him in his chamber alone, talking of Sir G. Carteret's business and the abuses he puts on the nation by his bad payments – to both our vexations; but no hope of remedy for aught I see. Thence to my Lord Ashly to a Committee of Tanger for my Lord Rutherfords accounts.[3] And that done, we to my Lord Treasurer's, where I did receive my Lord's warrant to Sir R. Long for drawing a warrant for my striking of tallies. So to the Inn again by Criple-gate,[4] expecting my mother's coming to town; but she is not come this week neither, the coach being too full. So to the Change and thence home to dinner; and so out to Gresham College and saw a cat killed with the

1. Sayes Court, Deptford. John Evelyn had owned it since 1653. For an account of the house, see Evelyn, ii. 537, n. 6; iii. 59, n. 1. See also below, p. 97 & n. 1.

2. For Wilkins and Hooke, see above, p. 34, n. 2; p. 37, n. 1.
3. See below, p. 221, n. 2.
4. ? the White Hind.

Duke of Florence's poison.   And saw it proved that the oyle of
Tobacco, drawn by one of the Society, doth the same effect, and
is judged to be the same thing with the poison, both in colour
and smell and effect.[1]   ⟨(I saw also an abortive child, preserved
fresh in spirit of salt).⟩   Thence parted, and to White-hall to the
council-chamber about an order touching*a* the Navy (our being
impowered to commit seamen or maisters that do not, being
hired or pressed, fallow their work), but they could give us none.
So, a little vexed at that, because I put in the memorial to the
Duke of Albemarle alone, under my own hand[2] – home; and
after some time at the office, home to bed.

My Lord-Chief-Justice Hide did die suddenly this week, a day
or two ago, of an Apoplexy.[3]

4.   Up, and to the office, where we sat busy all the morning.
At noon home to dinner; and then to the office again all day, till
almost midnight; and then, weary, home to supper and to bed.

5.   Up betimes, and by water to Westminster, there to speak
the first time with Sir Robt. Long,[4] to give him my privy-seal
and my Lord Treasurers order for Tanger=Tallys.   He received
me kindly enough.   Thence home by water; and presently down
to Woolwige and back to Blackewall, and there viewed the
Breach, in order to a mast-Docke;[5] and so to Deptford to the
Globe, where my Lord Brunkard, Sir J. Mennes, Sir W. Batten,
and Comissioner Pett were at dinner, having been at the Breach
also – but they find it will be of too great charge to make use of

a repl. 'for'

---

1. See above, p. 84, & n. 4.
The fellow of the society referred to
was Daniel Coxe: Birch, ii. 42. The
experiment was reported in several
places at the time: see *Harl. Misc.*
(ed. Park, 1808–13), i. 535 & nn.

2. See above, p. 91 & n. 1.

3. Sir Robert Hyde (Chief Justice
of the King's Bench) had died of an
apoplectic fit at Serjeants' Inn on 1
May.

4. Auditor of the Receipt in the
Exchequer.

5. In the previous October two
estimates had been prepared for con-
verting the Upper and Lower
Breaches (harbours) into mast-docks
(*CSPD 1664–5*, pp. 29, 31), and on
22 March the Duke of York had
ordered the work to go forward
(*Mem. (naval)*, p. 53).

it. After dinner to Mr. Evelings; he being abroad, we walked in his garden, and a lovely noble ground he hath endeed.[1] And among other rarities, a hive of Bees; so, as being hived in glass, you may see the Bees making their honey and Combs mighty pleasantly.[2] Thence home, and I by and by to Mr. Povy's to see him, who is yet in his chamber, not well. And thence by his advice to one Lovetts, a Varnisher, to see his manner of new varnish,[3] but found not him at home; but his wife a[a] very beautiful woman, who showed me much variety of admirable work; and is in order to my having of some papers fitted with lines, for my use for Tables and the like.[4] I know not whether I was more pleased with the thing, or that I was showed it by her. But resolved I am to have some made. So home to my office late, and then to supper and to bed. My wife tells me that she hears that my poor aunt James hath had her breast cut off here in town – her breast having long been out of order.[5]

This day, after I had suffered my own hayre to grow long, in order to wearing it, I find the convenience of Perrywiggs is so great, that I have cut off all short again, and will keep to periwigs.

6. Up, and all day at the office but a little at dinner; and there late till past 12. So home to bed, pleased as I always am after I have rid a great deal of work, it being very satisfactory to me.

7. *Lords day.* Up, and to church with my wife. Home and dined. After dinner came Mr. Andrews, and spent the afternoon

a MS. 'and'

---

1. The extent of the estate is defined in Evelyn, iii. 80, n. 1; see also *Illust. London News*, 30 August 1952, pp. 348–9. Evelyn had been busy planting the grounds and laying out the gardens ever since he settled there in 1653. Much work had been done in 1664: Evelyn, iii. 370, 393. See below, p. 253 & n. 3.

2. A transparent apiary was given to Evelyn in 1654 by Dr John Wilkins, Warden of Wadham College, who owned several. It was adorned with

'variety of *Dials, little Statues, Vanes* etc.'; the King admired it on his visit to Sayes Court on 30 April 1663: Evelyn, iii. 110.

3. Cf. above, iv. 153 & n. 2.

4. See below, vii. 120, n.1.

5. Amputation of the breasts (to remove cancer) had long been practised. The method used in Pepys's time is described by Sir D'Arcy Power in *Liverpool Medico-Chirurg. Journ.*, 42/29+.

with me about our Tanger business of the victuals and then parted. And after sermon comes Mr. Hill and a gentleman, aᵃ friend of his, one Mr. Scott, that sings well also; and then comes Mr. Andrews, and we all sung and supped; and then to sing again, and passed the Sunday very pleasantly and soberly; and so I to my office a little, and then home to prayers and to bed.

Yesterday begun my wife to learn to Limb of one Browne,[1] which Mr. Hill helps her to. And by her beginning, upon some eyes,[2] I think she will [do] very fine things – and I shall take great delight in it.

8. Up very betimes, and did much business before I went out with several persons; among others, Captain Taylor, who would leave the management of most of his business, now he is going to Harwich, upon me. And if I can get money by it, which I believe it will, I shall take some of it upon me.[3]

Thence with Sir W. Batten to the Duke of Albemarls, and there did much business, and then to the Change, and thence off with Sir W Warren to an ordinary, where we dined and sat talking of most useful discourse till 5 in the afternoon, and then home and very busy till late, and so home and to bed.

9. Up betimes, and to my business at the office, where all the morning. At noon comes Mrs. The Turner and dines with us. And my wife's painting-maister stayed and dined, and I take great pleasure in thinking that my wife will really come to something in that business. Here dined also Luellin. So afterᵇ dinner to

---

a repl. 'of'   *b* repl. 'home'

---

1. Alexander Browne, printseller, teacher of drawing ('limning') and author of *Ars pictoria* . . . (1669). Pepys became dissatisfied with his wife's progress and came to resent both her neglect of domestic duties and Browne's presence at his table: below, vii. 116, 117. Later, however, he was delighted with his wife's pictures: below, vii. 232, 262. Browne appears to have given lessons also to Peg Penn: below, p. 210. (OM).

2. This was usually the pupil's first exercise. (OM).

3. John Taylor, shipbuilder, was now going to Harwich as Navy Commissioner. At 23 and 27 October 1665 Pepys records the receipt of over £120 from him for services rendered.

the office and there very busy till almost midnight, and so home to supper and to bed.

This day we have news of eight ships being taken by some of ours, going into the Texell, their two men of war that convoyed [them] running in.[1]   They came from about Ireland, round to the North.

10.   Up betimes, and abroad to the Cockepitt, where the Duke[2] did give Sir W. Batten and me an*a* account of the late taking of eight ships and of his[3] intent to come back to the Gunfleete with the fleet presently – which creates us much work and haste therein, against the fleet comes.   So to Mr. Povy; and after discourse with him, home and thence to the Guard in Southworke,[4] there to get some soldiers, by the Duke's order, to go keep press-men on board our ships.[5]   So to the Change and did much business; and then home to dinner and there find my poor mother come out of the country today, in good health; and I am glad to see her, but my business, which I am sorry for, keeps me from paying the respect I ought to her at her first coming – she being grown very weak in her judgment, and doting again in her discourse, through age and some trouble in her family.   Left her and my wife to go abroad to buy something, and then I to my office.   In the evening, by appointment to Sir W Warren and Mr. Deering at a tavern hard by, with intent to do some good upon their agreement in a great bargain of plank.[6]   So home to my office again, and then to supper and to bed, my mother being in bed already.

11.   Up betimes, and at the office all the morning.   At home dined, and then to the office all day till late at night; and then home to supper, weary with business, and to bed.

a   MS. 'and'

---

1. I.e. running into harbour.   The action took place on 4–5 May; see Sandwich, pp. 204–5.   Capt. Hyde of the *Sapphire* was reprimanded for letting the men-of-war escape.

2. Albemarle.

3. The Duke of York's.

4. Probably the Artillery House and Ground in Horsleydown.

5. A platoon of men was sent by the following day: *CSPD 1664–5*, p. 361.

6. Dering sent in a tender in July and a contract was agreed in September.

12.   Up betimes, and find myself disappointed in my receiving presently of my 50*l*, hoped for more, of Mr. Warren upon the benefit of my press warrant;[1] but he promises to make it good. So by water to the Exchequer, and there up and down through all the offices to strike*a* my tallies for 17500*l*[2] – which methinks is so great a testimony of the goodness of God to me; that I, from a mean clerk there, should come to strike tallies myself for that sum, and in the authority that I do now, is a very stupendous mercy to me. I shall have them struck tomorrow. But to see how every little fellow looks after his fees, and to get what he can for everything, is a strange consideration – the King's Fees, that he must pay himself for this 17500*l*, coming to above 100*l*.[3]

Thence, called my wife at Unthankes, to the New Exchange and elsewhere to buy a lace-band for me, but we did not buy. But I find it so necessary to have some handsome clothes, that I cannot but lay out some money*b* thereupon.

To the Change, and thence to my Wachmaker, where he has put it in order; and a good and brave piece it is, and he tells me worth 14*l* – which is a greater present then I valued it.[4]   So home to dinner, and after dinner comes several people; among others, my Cosen Tho Pepys of Hacham – to receive some money of my Lord Sandwiches; and then I paid him what was due to him upon my uncles Score;[5] but contrary to my expectation, did get him to sign and seal to my sale of lands for payment of debts:[6] so that now I reckon myself in better condition by 100*l* in my content then I was before – when I was liable to be called to an account, and others after me, by my uncle Tho. or his children, for every foot of land we had sold before.   This I reckon a great good fortune in the getting of this done.

He gone, came Mr. Povy,[7] Dr. Twisden and Mr. Lawson,

a repl. 'pass'   *b* repl. 'thing'

---

1. See above, p. 77 & n. 2.
2. *CTB*, i. 659; see above, p. 92 & n. 1.
3. Exchequer fees were usually paid on a percentage basis. For details, see S. B. Baxter, *Devel. of Treasury 1660–1702*, App. III; G. E. Aylmer, *King's Servants*, pp. 201–2.

4. See above, p. 83; below, p. 101.
5. See above, iv. 379.
6. See above, v. 211 & n. 2.
7. Povey appears as a witness to Thomas Pepys's signature on the agreement mentioned earlier in this entry.

about settling my security in the paying of the 4000*l* ordered to Sir J Lawson.[1]

So a little abroad, and then home and late at my office and closet, settling this day's disordering of my papers; then to supper and to bed.

13. Up, and all day in some little grutchings of pain, as I use to have – from Winde – arising, I think, from my fasting so long and want of exercise – and I think, going so hot in clothes, the weather being hot and I in the same clothes I wore all winter.

To the Change after office, and received my Wach from the watch-maker; and a very fine [one] it is – given me by Briggs the Scrivener.

Home to dinner; and then I abroad to the Atturny Generall about advice upon the act for Land Carriage[2] – which he desired not to give me before I had received the King's and Council's order therein. Going home, bespoke the King's *works*;[3] will cost me 50*s* I believe. So home, and late at my office. But Lord, to see how much of my old folly and childishnesse hangs upon me still, that I cannot forbear carrying my watch in my hand in the coach all this afternoon, and seeing what a-clock it is 100 times. And am apt to think with myself: how could I be so long without one – though I remember since, I had one and found it a trouble, and resolved to carry one no more about me while I lived.[4]

So home to supper and to bed – being troubled at a letter from Mr. Cholmly from Tanger, wherein he doth advise me how

1. Sir John Lawson was (like Sir Hugh Cholmley) one of the contractors for the Tangier mole: above, p. 71. His attorney was probably his cousin John Lawson, later overseer of his will. Dr John Twysden (a physician) acted for Cholmley, his uncle.

2. The act of 1662 which provided land transport for the navy's timber: cf. above, iii. 169, n. 4.

3. ΒΑΣΙΛΙΚΑ; *The workes of Charles I* (1662; PL 2577); cf. above, iii. 106 & n. 1. It was a secondhand

copy, and has the words 'Bridgett —— [illegible] Her Booke' written (but struck through) on the flyleaf. In 1700 Pepys collated this copy with another in the Lambeth Library which had been seized in Spain and expurgated by the Inquisition: *Priv. Corr.*, ii. 77.

4. Watches did not fully establish themselves until after the invention of the balance-spring (c. 1675). They were then equipped with minute- as well as hour-hands. Cf. below, p. 221 & n. 3.

people are at work to overthrow our victualling business; by which I shall lose 300*l* per annum.[1] I am much obliged to him for this secret kindness, and concerned to repay it him in his own concernments and look after this.

14. ⟨*Lords day.*⟩ Up, and with my wife to church, it being Whitsunday. My wife very fine in a new yellow birds-eye Hood, as the fashion is now.[2] We had a most sorry sermon. So home to dinner, my mother having her new suit brought home, which makes her very fine. After dinner my wife and she and Mercer to Tho. Pepys's[3] wife's christening of his first child. And I took a coach and to Wanstead, the house where Sir H. Mildmay did [live] and now Sir Rob. Brookes lives, having bought it of the Duke of Yorke, it being forfeited to him.[4] A fine seat, but a old-fashion house;[5] and being not full of people, looks desolately. Thence to Walthamstow, where (failing at the other place)[6] Sir W. Batten by and by came home, I walking up and down the house and garden with my Lady, very pleasant.[7] Then to supper, very merry; and then back by coach by dark night – I, all the afternoon in the coach, reading the treasonous book of the Court of King James, printed a great while ago and worth reading, though ill intended.[8] As soon as came home, upon a letter from Duke of Albemarle, I took boat, at about

1. See below, p. 105 & n. 2.
2. For women's hoods at this period, see Cunnington, pp. 108+, 179+. Birdseye was 'a spotted fabric of muslin or silk': ib., p. 194.
3. Probably the turner.
4. This was Old Wanstead House, Essex (replaced c. 1715 by another house pulled down in 1823; on the site of what is now Wanstead golf course). Sir Henry Mildmay, Brookes's father-in-law (d. ?1664), a regicide, had, with others of his family, possessed it since 1619. Sir Robert Brooke (M.P. for Aldeburgh, Suff.) lived there 1662-7. The house was sold to Josiah Child in 1673. P. Morant, *Essex* (1768), i. 30; D. Lysons, *Environs of London* (1792-1811), iv. 232-5; E. Walford, *Greater London*,

i. 476; O. S. Dawson, *Story of Wanstead Park.*
5. It had been extensively rebuilt under Edward VI and again under Elizabeth. According to Lysons (op. cit., iv. 235), a small print of the house was published by Stent in 1649.
6. Penn's house at Walthamstow.
7. For Batten's house, see above, i. 279, n. 2.
8. Sir Anthony Weldon's *Court and character of King James . . .* (q.v. above, p. 33 & n 3.) was the work of an embittered man who had in 1617 been dismissed from his post at court. It had first appeared in 1650 as part of the anti-Stuart propaganda campaign which followed the execution of Charles I.

12 at night, and down the River in a galley, my boy and I, down
to the Hope, and so up again, sleeping and waking with great
pleasure; my business, to call upon every one of our victualling-
《15.》 ships to set them a-going. And so home; and after
dinner, to the King's playhouse all alone, and saw *Loves
Maistresse.*[1] Some pretty things and good variety in it, but no
or little fancy in it. Thence to the Duke of Albemarle to give
him account of my day's works – where he showed me letters
from Sir G Downing, of four days' date, that the Duch are come
out and joyned – well-manned and resolved to board our best
ships; and fight for certain they will.[2]

Thence to the Swan at Herberts, and there the company of
Sarah a little while; and so away and called at the Harp-and*a*-Ball,
where the maid, Mary, is very formosa; but Lord, to see in what
readiness I am, upon the expiring of my vowes this day,[3] to begin
to run into all my pleasures and neglect of business.

Thence home; and being sleepy, to bed.

16. Up betimes, and to the Duke of Albemarle with an
account of my yesterday's action in writing.[4] So back to the
office, where all the morning very busy. After dinner by coach
to see and speak with Mr. Povy; and after little discourse, back
again home, where busy upon letters till past 12 at night; and so
home to supper and to bed, weary.

17. Up, and by appointment to a meeting of Sir John Lawson
and Mr. Cholmlys atturneys and Mr. Povy at the Swan tavern
at Westminster, to settle their business about my being secured in
the payment of money to Sir J Lawson in the other's absence.

a repl. 'an

---

1. An allegorical drama by Thomas
Heywood (see above, ii. 48 & n. 2);
now at the TR, Drury Lane. (A).
2. Cf. the letters Downing wrote
to Clarendon and to Arlington on
12/22 May: Bodl., Clar. 108, ff.
297+ (summarised in *CSPClar.*, v.
485–6); PRO, SP 84/176, ff. 25+.

3. Cf. above, p. 20, n. 2.
4. PRO, SP 29/121, no. 62; partly
in Pepys's hand; 15 May. Cf. the
correspondence in *CSPD 1664–5*,
pp. 365–7, arranging for a supply of
victuals to last until the end of August.

Thence at Langfords,[1] where I never was since my brother died there – I find my wife and Mercer, having with him agreed[a] upon two rich silk suits for me; which is fit for me to have, but yet the money is too much, I doubt, to lay out altogether; but it is done, and so let it be – it being the expense of the world that I can best bear with and the worst spare.

Thence home, and after dinner to the office, where late; and so home to supper and to bed.   Sir J. Mennes and I had an angry bout this afternoon with Comissioner Pett about his neglecting his duty and absenting himself, unknown to us, from his place at Chatham.[2]   But a most false man I every day find him, more and more; and in this, very full of equivocation.

The Fleete, we doubt not, come to Harwich by this time.[3] Sir W. Batten is gone down this day thither, and the Duchesse of Yorke went down yesterday to meet the Duke.

18.   Up, and with Sir J. Mennes to the Duke of Albemarle – where we did much business, and I with good content to myself. Among other things, we did examine Nixon and Stanesby about their late running from two Duchmen, for which they are committed to a vessel to carry them to the fleet to be tried – a most foule, unhandsome thing as ever was heard for plain cowardize, on Nixon's part.[4]   Thence with the Duke of Albemarle in his coach to my Lord Treasurer, and there was before the King

a   repl. 'above'

---

1. The tailor who had taken over Tom Pepys's house and business in Salisbury Court.
2. Mennes's account of the difficulties caused by Pett's absence in London is given in a letter to the Navy Board of 10 May: *CSPD 1664-5*, p. 358.
3. It arrived there on the 15th: Sandwich, p. 212.
4. The engagement had occurred in the Soundings (southwest of the Lizard), when two Dutch capers gave chase to the *Eagle* (Capt. John Stanesby) and the *Elizabeth* (Capt.

Edward Nixon). Stanesby, being wounded, asked Nixon to continue the fight, but Nixon refused.   At the court-martials, over which Sandwich presided, Nixon was condemned to be shot, and Stanesby cleared.   Sandwich, pp. 214-16; Rawl. A 174, ff. 460-1. Nixon's reputation for bravery stood high: Coventry wrote to Pepys (19 May) that Nixon had been recommended for a commission by Albemarle – one 'who hates a Coward as much as you love musicke': ib., f. 460r.

(who ever now calls me by my name) and Lord Chancellor and many other great Lords, discoursing about insuring of some of the King's goods,[1] wherein the King accepted of my motion that we should; and so away, well pleased.

To the office and dined; and then to the office again and abroad to speak with Sir G. Carteret. But Lord, to see how frail a man I am, subject to my vanities, that can hardly forbear, though pressed with never so much business, my pursuing of pleasure; but home I got, and there very busy very late – among other things, consulting with Mr. Andrews about our Tanger business, wherein we are like to meet with some[a] trouble and my Lord Bellases endeavour to supplant us[2] – which vexes my mind; but however, our undertaking is[b] so honourable, that we shall stand a tug for it I think. So home to supper and to bed.

19. Up, and to White-hall, where the Committee for Tanger met; and there, though the case as to the merit of it was most plain, and most of the company favourable to our business, yet it was with much ado that I got the business not carried fully against us, but put off to another day – my Lord Arlington being the great man in it, and I was sorry to be found arguing so greatly against him. The business,[c] I believe, will in the end be carried against us, and the whole business fall; I must therefore endeavour, the most I can, to get money another way. It vexed me to see Creed so[d] hot against it; but I cannot much blame him, having never declared to him my[e] being concerned in it.

But that that troubles me most, is my Lord Arlington calls to me privately and asks me whether I had ever said to anybody that I desired to leave this imployment, having not time to look after it. I told him no, for that the thing being settled, it will not require much time to look after it. He told me then he would do me right to the King, for he had been told so. Which I desired him to do. And by and by he called me to him again and asked me whether I had no friend about the Duke, asking me

a repl. 'good'	*b* repl. 'in'	
c repl. symbol rendered illegible	*d* repl. 'to'	*e* repl. 'by'

---

1. Naval stores on their way from Hamburg: below, p. 112.
2. In the proposals for the victual-

ling of Tangier; cf. Povey to Pepys, 19 May: PRO, CO 279/4, f. 90r.

(I making a stand) whether Mr. Coventry was not my friend; I told him I had received many friendships from him. He then advised me to procure that the Duke would, in his next letter, write to him to continue me in that place, and remove any obstruction; which I told him I would, and thanked him.

So parted, vexed at the first, and amazed at this business of my Lord Arlington's. Thence to the Exchequer and there got my tallies for 17500*l*, the first payment I ever had out of the Exchequer. And at the Legg spent 14*s* upon my old acquaintance, some of them the clerks. And away home with my tallies in a coach – fearful every step of having one of them fall out or snatched from me.

Being come home, I, much troubled, out again by coach (for company, taking Sir W Warren with me), entending to have spoke to my Lord Arlington to have known the bottom of it – but missed him; and afterward, discoursing the thing as a confidant to Sir W. Warren, he did give me several good hints and principally not to do anything suddenly, but consult my pillow upon that and every great thing in my life, before I resolve anything in it. Away back home; and not being fit for business, I took my wife and Mercer down by water to Greenwich at 8*ᵃ* at night, it being very fine and cool, and moonshine afterward – mighty pleasant passage it was. There eat a cake or two, and so home by 10 or 11 at night, and then to bed – my mind not settled what to think.

20. Up, and to my office, where busy all the morning. At noon dined at home; and to my office, very busy – till past 《21.》 one, Lords day, in the morning, writing letters to the fleet and elsewhere. And my mind eased of much business, home to bed and slept till 8. So up; and this day is brought home one of my new silk suits, the plain one, but very rich Camlott, and noble. I tried it, and pleases me – but did not wear it before: I would not go out today to church – so laid it by, and my mind changed, thinking to go see my Lady Sandwich; and did go a little way, but stopped and returned home to dinner. After dinner, up to my chamber to settle my Tanger accounts, and then to*ᵇ* my office, there to do the like with other papers. In the evening home to supper and to bed.

a repl. '9'   *b* repl. 'home'

22. Up, and down to the ships, which now are hindered from going to the fleet (to our great sorrow and shame) with their provisions, the wind being against them. So to the Duke of Albemarle – and thence down by water to Deptford, it being Trinity Monday and so the day of choosing the Master of Trinity-house for the next year – where, to my great content, I find that contrary to the practice and design of Sir W. Batten to break the rule and custom of the Company in choosing their Masters by succession, he would have brought in Sir W Rider or Sir W Pen over the head of Hurleston (who is a knave too besides, I believe): the Younger Brothers did all oppose it against the Elder, and with great heat*ª* did carry it for Hurleston – which I know will vex him to the heart.[1]

Thence, the election being over, to church; where an idle sermon from that conceited fellow Dr. Britton, saving that his advice to unity and laying aside all envy and enmity among them was very apposite.[2]

Thence walked to Redriffe, and so to the Trinity-house; and a great dinner, as is usual. And so to my office, where busy all the afternoon till late; and then home to bed – being much troubled in mind for several things. First, for the condition of the fleet for lack of provisions. The blame this office lies under, and the shame that they deserve to have brought upon them for the ships not being gone out of the River. And then for my business of Tanger, which is not settled; and lastly, for fear that I am not observed to have attended the office business of late as much as I ought to do, though there hath been nothing but my attendance on Tanger that hath occasioned my absence, and that of late not much.

23. Up, and at the office, busy all the morning. At noon dined alone, my*ᵇ* wife and mother being gone by invitation to

a repl. same symbol badly formed   *b* repl. 'and'

---

1. Pepys was a Younger Brother. Nicholas Hurlestone died in the following November, and Batten obtained the election of a compliant successor: below, p. 298.

2. The preacher was Dr Robert Breton, Vicar of Deptford, Rector of St Martin's Ludgate and Prebendary of St Paul's. Evelyn (who had a high regard for him) reported this sermon: 'our Doctor preached on 2: *Chro*: 15. 2. Admonitorie to union & Concord.'

dine with my mother's old servant, Mr. Cordery – who made
them very welcome. So to Mr. Povys, where after a little discourse about his business, I home again and late at the office, busy.

Late, comes Sir Arthur Ingram[1] to my office, to tell me that
by letters from Amsterdam of the 28th of this month, their style,[2]
the Duch fleet, being about 100 men-of-war, besides fire-ships
&c., did set out upon the 23 and 24 instant – being divided into
7 Squadrons – *viz.*, 1. Generall Opdam. 2. Cottenar of Rotter-
dam. 3. Trump. 4. Schram of Horne. 5. Stillingworth of
Freezland. 6. Everson. 7. One other, not named, of Zeeland.[3]

24. Up by 4 a-clock in the morning; and with W Hewer
there till 12 without intermission, putting some papers in order.
Thence to the coffee-house with Creed, where I have not been
a great while – where all the news is of the Dutch being gone
out – and of the plague growing upon us in this town and of
remedies against it; some saying one thing, some another.

So home to dinner; and after dinner Creed and I to Colvells,[4]
thinking to show him all the respect we could, by obliging him
in carrying him five tallies of 5000*l*, to secure him for so much
credit he hath formerly given Povy to Tanger. But he, like a
impertinent fool, cavills at it, the most ignorantly that ever I
heard man in my life. At last Mr. Viner[5] by chance comes, who
I find a very moderate man, but could not persuade the fool to
reason; but I brought away the tallies again, and so, vexed, to
my office, where late, and then home to my supper and to bed.

25. Up, and to the office, where all the morning. At noon
dined at home; and then to the office all the afternoon, busy till
almost 12 at night; and then home to supper and to bed.

1. Merchant; member of the
Council of Trade.
2. By English style, the 18th.
3. Cf. the lists given in Sandwich,
pp. 216–20. There were 103 men-
of-war (not counting yachts, fire-
ships and galliots) according to one
official Dutch list: *Hollantdse Mer-
curius* (Haarlem, 1670), pp. 69–70.
Obdam was in supreme command.
The other admirals mentioned here
were Lt-Adm. Egbert Meüssen
Cortenaer, Lt-Adm. Cornelis Tromp,
Vice-Adm. Volkert Schram, Lt-Adm.
Augustus Stellingwerf, Lt-Adm. Jan
Evertsen (commanding the Zeeland
squadron). The unnamed admiral
was D. Kerkhoven of the Maas (not
Zeeland) squadron.
4. John Colvill, goldsmith-banker;
he lived in Great Lombard St.
5. Robert Vyner, goldsmith-
banker.

26. Up at 4 a-clock, and all the morning in my office with W. Hewer, finishing my papers that were so long out of order. And at noon to my bookseller's and there bespoke a book or two; and so home to dinner, where Creed dined with me; and he and I afterward to Alderman Backewell's to try him about supplying us with money – which he denied at first, and last also, saving that he spoke a little fairer at the end then before. But the truth is, I do fear I shall have a great deal of trouble in getting of money. Thence home; and in the evening by water to the Duke of Albemarle, whom I found mightily off the hooks that the ships are not gone out of the River; which vexed me to see, insomuch that I am afeared that we must expect some change or addition of new officers[1] brought upon us, so that I must from this time forward resolve to make myself appear eminently serviceable in attending at my office duly, and nowhere else; which makes me wish with all my heart that I had never anything to do with this business of Tanger. After a while at my office, home to supper, vexed, and to bed.

27. Up, and to the office, where all the morning; at noon dined at home, and then to my office again, where late; and so to bed – with my mind full of care for the business of this office – and troubled with that of Tanger – concerning which Mr. Povy was with me; but doth give me little help but more reason of being troubled. So that were it not for our Plymouth business,[2] I would be glad to be rid of it.

28. *Lords day.* By water to the Duke of Albemarle – where I hear that Nixon is condemned to be shot to death for his Cowardize by a council of war.[3] Went to chapel and heard a little Musique and there met with Creed, and with him a little while walking and to Wilkinsons for me to drink, being troubled with Winde; and at noon to Sir Ph. Warwicke's to dinner, where abundance of company came in unexpectedly. And here I saw one pretty piece of household stuff; as the company encreaseth, to put a larger leaf upon an Ovall table.[4] After dinner much

1. Officers of the Navy Board.
2. The victualling contract for Tangier: cf. above, v. 210 & n. 3.
3. See above, p. 104 & n. 4.

4. ? a draw-leaf table, various forms of which date from the later 16th century.

good discourse with Sir Phillip, who I find, I think, a most
pious good man, and a professor of a philosiphicall manner of life
and principles like Epictetus, whom he cites in many things.[1]
Thence to my Lady Sandwiches, where to my shame I had not
been a great while before. Here, upon my telling her a story
of my Lord of Rochester's running away on Friday night last with
Mrs. Mallet, the great beauty and fortune of the North,[2] who had
supped at White-hall with Mrs. Stewart and was going home to
her lodgings with her grandfather, my Lord Haly, by coach,
and was at Charing-cross seized on by both horse and foot-men
and forcibly taken from him, and put into a coach with six
horses and two women provided to receive her, and carried
away. Upon immediate pursuit, my Lord of Rochester (for
whom the King had spoke to the lady often, but with no success)
was taken at Uxbridge; but the lady is not yet heard of, and the
King mighty angry and the Lord sent to the Tower.[3] Hereupon,
my Lady did confess to me, as a great secret, her being concerned
in this story – for if this match breaks between my Lord Rochester
and her, then, by the consent of all her friends,* my Lord Hinchingbrooke stands fair, and is invited for her.[4] She is worth, and will
be at her mother's death (who keeps but a little from her), 2500*l*
per annum. Pray God give a good success to it. But my poor

1. For Pepys's acquaintance with
Epictetus, see above, iii. 194, 231.
2. *Recte*, the West. Elizabeth
Malet, only child and heiress of the
wealthy John Malet, of Enmore,
Som. (d. 1656), and granddaughter of
Lord Hawley. She had many suitors
but in the end married Rochester in
early 1667. Rochester was now only
17 and she too was a minor.
3. A warrant for his conditional
discharge was issued on 19 June, but
he was never prosecuted for the
abduction: *CSPD 1664–5*, pp. 389,
435. On 6 July the King commanded
Sandwich to take Rochester to sea as
a volunteer: Sandwich MSS, Letters
from Ministers, i. f. 41r. The girl
was brought back to London about a
week after her abduction.

4. On 5 December 1664 Sandwich
had written to Secretary Bennet about
this heiress, but had been told in
reply that Rochester's suit was supported by the King, Lady Castlemaine
and the Chancellor: Sandwich MSS,
Letters from Ministers, i. f. 39r–*v*.
That the King encouraged Rochester
is confirmed by Henry Savile's letter
of 28 May 1665: *Savile Corr.* (ed.
W. D. Cooper), p. 5. Negotiations
on behalf of Hinchingbrooke continued for about a year, but by September 1666 the match was off. The
parties had been allowed to meet, had
liked each other's persons, but found
'a disagreement in their genius'
(Henry Moore to Sandwich, 11
September 1666): Carte 75, f.
477r–*v*; see also ib., 74, f. 343r.

Lady, who is afeared of the sickness and resolved to be gone into
the country, is forced to stay in town a day or two or three
about it, to see the event of it. Thence home, and to see my
Lady Pen – where my wife and I were shown a fine rarity: of
fishes kept in a glass*ᵃ* of water, that will live so for ever; and
finely marked they are, being foreign.[1] So to supper at home
and to bed – after many people being with me about business –
among others, the two Bellamys about their old debt due to
them from the King for their victualling business[2] – out of which
I hope to get some money.

29. Lay long in bed, being in some little pain of the wind,
Collique. Then up and to the Duke of Albemarle, and so to the
Swan and there drank at Herberts; and so by coach home, it
being kept a great holiday through the City, for the birth and
restoration of the King.[3] To my office, where I stood by and saw
Symson the Joyner[4] do several things, little Jobbs, to the rendering
of my closet handsome and the setting up of some neat plats
that Burston hath for my money made me.[5] And so home to
dinner; and then, with my wife, mother, and Mercer in one
boat, and I in another, down to Woolwich, I walking from
Greenwich, the others going to and fro upon the water till my
coming back, having done but little business. So home and to
supper, and weary to bed. We have everywhere taken some
prizes. Our merchants have good luck to come home safe:
Colliers from the North, and some Streights-men just now – and
our Hambrough ships, of whom we were so much afeared, are
safe in Hambrough.[6] Our Fleete resolved to sail out again from
Harwich in a day or two.

30. Lay long, and very busy all the*ᵇ* morning. At noon to the

a repl. 'vessel'   *b* repl. 'day'

---

1. Probably paradise fish. Goldfish
do not appear to have been introduced
into England until c. 1705: G. F.
Hervey and J. Hems, *The Goldfish*,
pp. 58–9.
2. See above, iv. 374 & n. 2.
3. Cf. above, i. 66, n. 2.
4. Thomas Simpson, Master-
joiner at Deptford and Woolwich
yards.
5. In September 1665 the Navy
Treasurer paid £4 15s. for a plate of
Deptford yard to hang in the Navy
Office: PRO, Adm. 20/6, p. 159. For
Burston, see above, p. 38, n.3.
6. A mistake: see below, p. 112.

Change, and thence to dinner to Sir G Carter[e]ts to talk upon the business of insuring our goods upon the Hambrough ships. Here, a very fine neat French dinner[1] without much cost – we being all alone with my Lady, and one of the house with her.

Thence home and wrote letters; and then in the evening by coach with my wife and mother and Mercer, our usual tour by coach, and eat at the old house at Islington.[2] But Lord, to see how my mother found herself talk, upon every object to think of old stories.[3] Here I met with one that tells me that Jacke Cole,[4] my old Schoolefellow, is dead and buried lately, of a consumption – who was a great crony of mine.

So back again home, and there to my closet – to write letters. Hear, to my great trouble, that our Hambrough ships, valued of the King's goods and the merchants' (though but little of the former) to 200000*l*, [are lost].[5] By and by, about 11 at night, called into the Guarden by my Lady Pen and daughter, and there walked with them and my wife till almost 12; and so in and closed my letters, and home to bed.

31. Up, and to my office ⟨and to Westminster⟩ doing business – till noon; and then to the Change, where great the noise and trouble of having our Hambrough ships lost – and that very much placed upon Mr. Coventry's forgetting to give notice to them of the going away of our fleet from the coast of Holland. But all without reason, for he did; but the merchants, not being ready, stayed longer then the time ordered the convoy to stay, which was ten days.   Thence home with Creed and Mr. Moore to dinner. Anon we broke up, and Creed and I to discourse about our Tanger matters of money, which vex me. So to Gresham College, stayed a very little while, and away; and I home busy, and busy late at the end of the month, about my

---

1. Soup was included and the courses served separately.

2. The King's Head: see above, ii. 125 & n. 2.

3. This was her native region. Cf. also above, v. 132.

4. A tradesman in the city.

5. On the evening of 20 May, eight merchantmen sailing from Hamburg with naval stores mistook the Dutch for the English fleet and sailed right into it. All were taken, together with the escort vessel, the *Good Hope*. Pepys probably heard by letter from Coventry. *CSPD 1664–5*, p. 393; Sandwich, p. 221; Clowes, ii. 258.

month's accounts; but by the addition of Tanger, it is rendered more intricate, and so (which I have not done these 12 months, nor would willingly have done now) failed of having it done; but I will do it as soon as I can. So, weary and sleepy, to bed. I endeavoured, but missed, of seeing Sir Tho Ingram at Westminster; so went to Housemans*a* the painter, who I entend shall draw my wife, but he was not within;[1] but I saw several very good pictures.

a followed by blot

---

1. Huysmans does not appear to have drawn Mrs Pepys. (OM).

JUNE.

1. Up, and to the office, where sat all the morning. At noon to the Change and there did*a* some business; and home to dinner, whither Creed comes. And after dinner I put on my new silk Camelott Sute, the best that ever I wore in my life, the suit costing me above 24*l*. In this I went with him to Goldsmiths hall to the burial of Sir Tho. Viner; which hall, and Haberdashers also, was so full of people, that we were fain for ease and coolness to go forth to Paternoster row to choose a silk to make me a plain ordinary suit. That done, we walked to Cornehill, and there at Mr. Cades stood in the Balcon*b* and saw all the funerals, which was with the Blue-coat*c* boys and old men[1] – all the Aldermen, and Lord Mayor, &c., and the number of the company very great – the greatest I ever did see for a Taverne. Hither came up to us Dr. Allen – and then Mr. Povy and Mr. Fox. The show being over, and my discourse with Mr. Povy – I took coach and to Westminster-hall, where I took the fairest flower[2] and by coach to Tothill-fields for the ayre, till it was dark. I light, and in with the fairest flower to eat a cake, and there did do*d* as much as was*e* safe with my flower, and that was enough on my part. Broke up, and away without any notice; and after delivering the rose where it should be, I to the Temple and light; and came to the middle door[3] and there took another coach, and so home – to write letters; but very few, God knows, being (by my pleasure) made to forget every-

a repl. 'met with Mr. Moore' *b* l. h. repl. l. h. 'Blac'- *c* repl. 'singing'
d repl. 'did'   *e* repl. 'is'

---

1. Vyner (a goldsmith-banker) had been President of Christ's Hospital. Old men or women were often a feature of funeral processions, their number corresponding to the years of the deceased. They preceded the corpse. Cf. HMC, *Le Fleming*, p. 69.

2. ? Betty Lane, or (as is suggested by a reference later in this entry) a girl at the Rose Tavern. Or possibly Mary of the Harp and Ball (Rosemary): cf. below, p. 115. Cf. Sir George Etherege's letter (2 February 1688; qu. *Dramatic Works*, ed. Brett-Smith, ii. 305n.): 'Remember me to all my friends at the Rose and do not forget the Lilly at the Bar'.

3. ? the door of the Middle Temple, or the middle door of Temple Bar.

thing that is. The coachman that carried [us] cannot know me^a
again, nor the people at the house where we were.

Home to bed, certain news being come that our fleet is in
sight of the Dutch ships.¹

2. Lay, troubled in mind, abed a good while, thinking of
my Tanger and victualling business, which I doubt will fall.
Up, and to the Duke of Albemarle, but missed him. Thence
to the Harp^b-and-Ball and to Westminster hall, where I visited
the flowers in each place; and so met with Mr. Creed, and he
and I to Mrs. Crofts's to drink; and did, but saw not her daughter
Borroughs. I away home, and there dined and did business.
In the afternoon went with my Tallys; made a fair end with
Colvile and Viner, delivering them 5000*l* tallies to each – and
very quietly had credit given me upon other tallies of Mr.
Colvill, for 2000*l* – and good words for more, and of Mr. Viner
too. Thence to visit the Duke of Albemarle; and thence, my
Lady Sandwich and Lord Crew. Thence home, and there met
an express from Sir W. Batten at Harwich, that the fleet is all
sailed from Solebay, having spied the Dutch Fleete at sea – and
that if the Calmes hinder not, they must needs be now engaged
with them.²

Another letter also came to me from Mr. Hater, committed
by the Council this afternoon to the Gatehouse, upon the misfortune of having his name used by one, without his knowledge
or privity, for the receiving of some powder that he had bought.³

Up to Court about these two. And for the former, was led
up to my Lady Castlemaynes lodgings,^c where the King and

---

a repl. 'him'   b repl. same symbol badly formed
c MS. 'longings'

---

1. See Coventry to Arlington, Southwold Bay, 1 June, 1.30 p.m.: *CSPD 1664–5*, p. 402.

2. Batten to Navy Board, Harwich, 2 June: PRO, SP 29/123, no. 21; summary in *CSPD 1664–5*, p. 403.

3. The charge was one of embezzl-ing powder from the King's stores. On the payment of bonds, Hayter was released on the 3rd, and five others on the 25th. Those involved were Philip Jones, of Winchester, grocer; Nathaniel Whitfield of London, gent.; Hugh Salisbury and Thomas Browne, of Portsmouth, gentlemen; and Joan Daniels, of Portsmouth, widow. PRO, PC 2/58, ff. 81*v*, 88*v*, 93*r*.

she and others were at supper – and there I read the letter and
returned.   And then to Sir G. Carteret about Hater, and shall
have him released tomorrow, upon my giving bail for his appearance – which I have promised to do.   Sir G. Carteret did go on
purpose to the King to ask this, and it was granted.   So home at
past 12, almost one a-clock in the morning.

To my office till past 2, and then home to supper and to bed.

3.   Up, and to White-hall, where Sir G Carteret did go with
me to Secretary Morris and prevailed with him to let Mr. Hater
be released, upon bail for his appearance.   So I at a loss how to
get another besides myself, and got Mr. Hunt, who did patiently
stay with me all the morning at Secretary Morris's chamber all
the morning, Mr. Hater being sent for with his keeper; and at
noon comes in the Secretary, and upon entering recognizances,
he for 200*l* and Mr. Hunt and I for 100*l* each, for his appearance
upon demand – he was released – it costing him, I think, above 3*l*.
I thence home, vexed to be kept from the office all the morning,
which I had not been in many months before, if not some years.
At home to dinner; and all the afternoon at the office, where
late at night and much business done; then home to supper and
to bed.

All this day, by all people upon the River and almost everywhere else hereabout, were heard the Guns, our two fleets for
certain being engaged; which was confirmed by letters from
Harwich, but nothing perticular;[1] and all our hearts full of
concernment for the Duke, and I perticularly for my Lord
Sandwich and Mr. Coventry after his Royal Highness.

4.   *Sunday.*   Up, and at my chamber all the forenoon at
evening my accounts, which I could not do sooner, for the last
month.   And blessed be God, am worth 1400*l* odd money –

---

1. The letters are probably those
from Batten (2, 3 June) summarised
in *CSPD 1664–5*, pp. 403, 405.   For
the battle (of Lowestoft), see below,
pp. 122 +.   The sound of the gunfire
was probably reflected by the stratos-
phere: hence it was possible for guns
firing in a s.–w. gale 120 miles to the
n.e. to be heard in London.   Cf.
Dryden's account: *Essays* (ed. Ker),
p. 28.   For reports of guns heard at
Cambridge and The Hague, see
Diary Sam. Newton (ed. Foster), pp.
12–13; BM, Harl. 7010, f. 284*r*.   For
the view that the noise was thunder,
see *N. & Q.*, 12 May 1951, pp. 204 +.

something more then ever I was yet in the world. Dined very
well at noon; and then to my office, and there and in the garden
discoursed with several people about business; among others,
Mr. Howell the Turner, who did give me so good a discourse
about the practices of the Paymaster, J. Fenn, that I thought fit to
recollect all when he was gone, and have entered it down to be
for ever remembered.*[a]* [1]

Thence to my chamber again, to settle my Tanger accounts
against tomorrow and some other things, and with great joy
ended them; and so to supper, where a good fowl and tansy,
and so to bed – news being come that our fleet is pursuing the
Duch, who, either by cunning or by being worsted, do give
ground; but nothing more for certain. Late to bed, upon my
papers being quite finished.

5. Up very betimes to look some other papers. And then
to White-hall to a Committee of Tanger, where I offered my
accounts with great acceptation, and so had some good words
and honour by it and one or two things done to my content in
my business of Treasurer; but I do clearly see that we shall lose
our business of victualling, Sir Tho. Ingram undertaking that it
shall be done by persons there, as cheap as we do it and give
the seamen their full allowance, and themselfs give good security
here for performance of contract – upon which terms, there is
no opposing it. This would trouble me but that I hope, when
that fails, to spend my time to some good advantage otherways.
And so shall submit all to God Almighty's pleasure.

Thence home to dinner, after Change, where great talk of the
Dutch being fled,*[b]* and we in pursuit of them. And that our
ship *Charity* is lost, upon our Captain's ⟨Wilkinson⟩ and
Lieutenant's yielding. But of this there is no certainty – save
the report of some of the sick men of the *Charity*, turned adrift

---

a repl. symbol rendered illegible   *b* MS. 'fleet' or 'flet'

---

1. NWB, pp. 95–7. Howell
reckoned Fenn's profits at £12,000
p.a., not counting those from the
the victualling. He thought that
Carteret knew of the malpractices,
but condoned them with the intention
of having one of his sons later appointed to the place. All who held
it at this period made great profits:
cf. the memorandum of about this
date in *CSPClar.*, v. 523.

in a boat out of the *Charity* and taken up and brought on shore yesterday to Sold Bay; and the news hereof brought by Sir Henery Felton.[1]

Home to dinner, and Creed with me. Then he and I down to Deptford, did some business, and back again at night – he home, and I to my office. And so to supper and to bed.

This morning I had great discourse with my Lord Berkely about Mr. Hater – towards whom, from a great passion reproaching him with being a fanatic and dangerous for me to keep[2] – I did bring him to be mighty calme and to ask me pardons for what he had thought of him, and to desire me to ask his pardon of Hater himself for the ill words he did give him the other day alone at White-hall (which was, that he had alway thought him a man that was no good friend to the King, but did never think it would break out in a thing of this nature) and did advise him to declare his*a* innocence to the Council and pray for his examination and vindication – of which I shall consider, and say no more; but remember one compliment that in great kindness to me he did give me, extolling my care and diligence – that he did love me heartily for my own sake, and, more, that he did will me whatsomever I thought for Mr. Coventry's sake. For though the world did think them enemies, and to have an ill aspect one to another, yet he did love him with all his heart – which was a strange manner of noble compliment, confessing his*b* owning me as a confidant and favourite of Mr. Coventry's.

6. Waked in the morning at 4 a-clock with great pain to piss and great pain in pissing, by having, I think, drank too great a draught of cold drink before going to bed – but by and by to sleep again; and then rose and to the office, where very

a MS. 'is'   *b* repl. 'is'

---

1. The *Great Charity*, a pressed merchantman, had been taken as prize by the *Stad en Landen*. Sandwich (p. 224) imputes nothing more than mistaken judgement to her captain (Robert Wilkinson), who with his lieutenant (Sandys Temple) was taken prisoner. The ship was small and had difficulty in keeping up with the rest of the fleet. She had been badly battered in a running fight against superior odds before being taken, and about 90 had escaped in boats. Edward Barlow, *Journal* (ed. Lubbock), i. 106; Clowes, ii. 263.

2. Cf. above, iv. 129 & n.

busy all the morning. And at noon to dinner with Sir G.
Carteret to his house, with all our Board, where a good pasty
and brave discourse. But our great fears was some fresh news of
the fleet, but not from the fleet, all being said to be well and
beaten the Dutch; but I do not give much belief to it, and endeed,*ᵃ* the news came from Sir W Batten at Harwich, and writ
so simply that we all made good mirth of it.¹ Thence to the
office, where upon Sir G Carteret's accounts, to my great
vexation, there being nothing done by the Controller to right
the King therein. I then to my office and wrote letters all the
afternoon; and in the evening by coach to Sir P Warwickes
about my Tanger business, to get money; and so to my Lady
Sandwiches, who, poor lady, expects every hour to hear of my
Lord; but in the best temper, neither confident nor troubled
with fear, that I ever did see in my life. She tells me my Lord
Rochester is now declaredly out of hopes of Mrs. Mallett,² and
now she is to receive notice in a day or two how the King stands
enclined to the giving leave for my Lord Hinchingbrooke to look
after her; and that being done, to bring it to an end shortly.
Thence by coach home, and to my office a little; and so, before
12 a-clock, home to bed.

7. This morning my wife and mother rose about 2 a-clock,
and with Mercer, Mary, the boy and W Hewer, as they had
designed, took boat and down to refresh themselfs on the water
to Gravesend. I lay till 7 a-clock; then up, and to the office
upon Sir*ᵇ* G Carteret's accounts again – where very busy.
Thence abroad and to the Change, no news of certainty being yet
come from the Fleete. Thence to the Dolphin Taverne, where
Sir J. Mennes, Lord Brunkard, Sir Tho Harvy and myself dined
upon Sir G Careteret's charge – and very merry we were, Sir
Tho Harvy being a very drolle. Thence to the office; and
meeting Creed, away with him to my Lord Treasurer's, there
thinking to have met the goldsmiths, or at White-hall; but did

a MS. 'in endeed'   *b* repl. 'a'

---

1. Batten to Navy Board, 6 June:
PRO, SP 29/123, no. 62; summary
in *CSPD 1664–5*, p. 411; a laconic
note reporting the destruction of
20–30 of the enemy fleet and the
pursuit of the rest.

2. Cf. above, p. 110 & n. 2.

not, and so appointed another time for my Lord to speak to them to advance us some money. Thence, it being the hottest day that ever I felt in my life, and it is confessed so by all other people the hottest they ever knew in England in the beginning of June – we to the New Exchange and there drunk whey; with much entreaty, getting it for our money, and would not be entreated to let us have one glasse more. So took water, and to Fox hall to the Spring-garden and there walked an hour or two with great pleasure, saving our minds ill at ease concerning the fleet and my Lord Sandwich, that we have no news of them, and ill reports run up and down of his being killed, but without ground. Here stayed, pleasantly walking and spending but 6*d*, till 9 at night; and then by water to White-hall, and there I stopped to hear news of the fleet, but none come, which is strange; and so by water home – where, weary with walking and with the mighty heat of *a* the weather, and for my wife's not coming home – I staying walking in the garden till 12 at night, when it begun to Lighten exceedingly through the greatness of the heat. Then, despairing of her coming home, I to bed.

This day, much against my Will, I did in Drury-lane see two or three houses marked with a red cross upon the doors, and "Lord have mercy upon us" writ there[1] – which was a sad sight to me, being the first of that kind that to my remembrance I ever saw. It put me into an ill conception of myself and my smell, so that I was forced *b* to buy some roll=tobacco to smell to and chaw – which took away the apprehension.[2]

8.   About 5 a-clock my wife came home, it having lightened all night hard, and one great shower of rain. She came and

a blot below symbol   *b* preceded by blot

---

1. This proved to be a heavily infected area. The red cross had, by a city regulation, to be one foot high and the houses so marked were shut up (often with the victims inside) for 40 days.
2. In the Plague tobacco was highly valued. Thomas Hearne (writing in 1721) has the story that no tobac-conist in London died of the Great Plague. He adds that at Eton one boy was flogged for being discovered not smoking: *Remains and collections* (1885-1921 ed.), vii. 208. For the medicinal value of tobacco, see above, ii. 128 & n. 1, and (for horses) below, viii. 390.

lay upon the bed. I up, and to the office, where all the morning. I alone at home to dinner, my wife, mother, and Mercer dining at W. Joyces, I giving her a caution to go round by the Half-Moone to his house, because of the plague.*a* I to my Lord Treasurer's, by appointment of Sir Tho. Ingram's, to meet the goldsmiths – where I met with the great news, at last newly come, brought by Bab May from the Duke of Yorke, that we have totally routed the Dutch. That the Duke himself, the Prince, my Lord Sandwich, and Mr. Coventry are all well. Which did put me into such a joy, that I forgot almost all other thoughts. The perticulars I shall set down by and by. By and by comes Alderman Maynell and Mr. Viner, and there my Lord Treasurer did intreat them to furnish me with money upon my tallies – Sir Ph. Warwicke, before my Lord, declaring the King's changing of the hand from Mr. Povy to me, whom he called a very sober person and one whom the Lord Treasurer would own in all things that I should concern myself with them in the business of money. They did at present declare they could not part with money at present. My Lord did press them very hard – and I hope, upon their considering, we shall get some of them.

Thence with great Joy to the Cockepitt – where the Duke of Albemarle, like a man out of himself with content, new told me all; and by and by comes a letter from Mr. Coventry's own hand to him;[1] which he never opened (which was a strange thing), but did give it me to open and read, and consider what was fit for our office to do in it and leave the letter with Sir W Clerke – which, upon such a time and occasion, was a strange piece of indifference, hardly pardonable. I copied out the letter, and did also take minutes out of Sir W Clerkes other letters;[2] and the sum of the news is:

a blot above symbol

---

1. Coventry to Albemarle, 4 June, printed in Smith, i. 85+ (from Pepys's copy in Rawl. A 195a, ff. 225–6); cf. Coventry to Arlington, 4 June, in *CSPD 1664–5*, pp. 407–8.

2. Pepys's copy and his notes of the rest of the information (all in s.h.) are in Rawl. A 195a, ff. 225–6. Clarke was Secretary at War and Albemarle's right-hand man. One of the official accounts appears to be based on the same information: L'Estrange's *Second narrative of the signal victory* . . . (10 June; printed in Penn, ii. 325–33). Cf. the earlier government account (8 June) in Penn, ii. 322–5; and the newspapers (e.g. *The Intelligencer*, 12 June, pp. 439–40).

Victory over the Dutch. June. 3. 1665./[1]

This day they engaged – the Dutch neglecting greatly the opportunity of the wind they had of us – by which they lost the benefit of their fire-ships.

The Earl of Falmouth, Muskery, and Mr. Rd. Boyle killed[a] on board the Dukes ship, the *Royall Charles*, with one shot.[2] Their blood and brains flying in the Duke's face – and the head of Mr. Boyle striking down the Duke, as some say.[3]

Earle of Marlbrough, Portland, Rere-[A]dmirall Sansum (to Prince Rupert) killed, and Captain Kirby and Ableson. Sir Jo. Lawson wounded on the knee – hath had some bones taken out, and is likely to be well again.[4] Upon receiving the hurt, he sent to the Duke for another to command the *Royall Oake*. The Duke sent Jordan out of the *St. George*, who did brave things in her. Captain Jer. Smith of the *Mary* was second to the Duke, and stepped between him and Captain Seaton of the *Urania* (76 guns and 400 men),[5] who had sworn to board the Duke. Killed him, 200 men, and took the ship. Himself losing 99 men, and never an officer saved but himself and Lieutenant.[b] His maister endeed is saved, with his leg cut off.

Admirall Opdam blown up. Trump killed, and said by Holmes. All the rest of their Admiralls, as they say, but Everson (whom they dare not trust for his affection to the Prince of Orange) are killed.[6] We have taken and sunk, as is believed, about 24 of their best ships. Killed and taken near 8 or 10000

a repl. 'shot'   *b* repl. 'bosun'

---

1. Usually known as the Battle of Lowestoft; the principal encounter of this year's campaign.
2. A chain-shot.
3. Of Falmouth's death, Marvell wrote: 'His shatter'd head the fearless Duke distains,/And gave the last first proof that he had Brains' (*Second advice to a painter*, 1667, ll. 187–8).
4. Gangrene, however, set in and he died at Greenwich on 25 June.

5. Bastiaan Centen of the *Oranje* (of 75 guns and 450 men according to Sandwich, p. 220).
6. Obdam, Cortenaer and Stellingwerf were killed, but no other flag-officers. Tromp survived to cover the retreat. Jan Evertsen was suspect because hostile to de Witt's republican party, then in power. He was soon afterwards dismissed: *CSPClar.*, v. 491, 495.

men; and lost, we think, not above 700.[1]   A great victory, never known in the world.   They are all fled; some 43 got into the Texell and others elsewhere, and we in pursuit of the rest.

Thence, with my heart full of Joy, home, and to my office a little; then to my Lady Pen's, where they are all joyed and not a little puffed up at the good success of their father; and good service endeed is said to have been done by him.

Had a great bonefire at the gate; and I with my Lady Pens people and others to Mrs. Turner's great room, and then down into the street.   I did give the boys 4*s* among them – and mighty merry; so home to bed – with my heart at great rest and quiet, saving that the consideration of the victory is too great for me presently to comprehend.

9.   Lay long in bed, my head akeing with too much thoughts, I think, last night.   Up, and to White-hall and my Lord Treasurer's to Sir Ph. Warwicke about Tanger business; and in my way met with Mr. Moore, who eases me in one point wherein I was troubled – which was, that I heard of nothing said or done by my Lord Sandwich.   But he tells me that Mr. Cowling, my Lord Chamberlain's Secretary, did hear the King say that my Lord Sandwich had done nobly and worthily.[2]

The King, it seems, is much troubled at the fall of my Lord of Falmouth.[3]   But I do not meet with any man else that so much as wishes him alive again, the world conceiving him a man of

1. Dr Anderson (Sandwich, p. lvi) calculates the Dutch losses at 17 ships and c. 5000 men. Clowes (ii. 264) suggests that English losses in killed were c. 250 and in prisoners not more than 200. Pepys's 'facts' and figures here are the same as those printed in the official accounts, being derived from the same sources. He gives Coventry's much better version below, pp. 129-30.

2. On this day the King wrote a letter of thanks to Sandwich; printed in Sir Henry Ellis (ed.), *Orig. Corr.* (ser. 1), iii. 328; Whitear, p. 124. See also below, pp. 127, 135. It seems possible that Sandwich should

be given the credit of having broken the Dutch line – a decisive turn in the battle, as the Dutch themselves acknowledged. His part in the engagement is fully discussed in Harris, i, App. C. The informant here, Richard Cooling, was secretary to the Earl of Manchester (Lord Chamberlain and Sandwich's cousin).

3. 'I have had as great a loss as 'tis possible in a good friend, poor Charles Berkeley. It troubles me so much as I hope you will excuse the shortness of this letter . . .': Charles to his sister, the Duchess of Orleans, 6 June (C. H. Hartmann, *The King my brother*, p. 166).

too much pleasure to do the King any good or offer any good office to him. But I hear of all hands, that he is confessed to have been a man of great Honour, that did show it in this his going with the Duke, the most that ever any man did.

Home, where my people busy to make ready*a* a supper against night for some guests, in lieu of my Stonefeast.[1]

At noon eat a small dinner at home; and so abroad to buy several things; and among others, with my Taylor to buy a silk suit; which, though I made one lately, yet I do for joy of the good news we have lately had of our victory over the Dutch, which makes me willing to spare myself something extraordinary in clothes; and after long resolution of having nothing but black, I did buy a coloured silk Ferrandin. So to the Old Exchange, and there at my pretty seamstress's[2] bought a pair of stockings of her husband; and so home, where by and by comes Mr. Honiwood and Mrs. Wilde[3] and Roger Pepys – and after long time spent, Mrs. Turner, The, and Joyce. We had a very good venison pasty – this being, endeed, instead of my Stonefeast the last March – and very merry we were; and the more I know, the more I like Mr. Honiwoods conversation. So after a good supper, they parted, walking to the Change for a coach, and I with them to see them there. So home and to bed – glad*b* it was over.

10. Lay long in bed; and then up and at the office all the morning. At noon dined at home, and then to the office, busy all the afternoon. In*c* the evening home to supper, and there to my great trouble hear that the plague is come into the City (though it hath these three or four weeks since its beginning been wholly out of the City);[4] but where should it begin but in my good friend and neighbour's, Dr. Burnett in Fanchurch-street – which in both points troubles me mightily.

a repl. 'what'   *b* repl. 'now'   *c* repl. 'at'

---

1. Postponed from 26 March (Easter Day); held in commemoration of his operation for the stone.
2. See above, p. 73, n. 3.
3. Peter Honywood, with his brothers, lodged at Pepys's old home in Salisbury Court. 'Mrs. Wilde' was probably Elizabeth Wiles (Wyld), kinswoman of the Honywoods, mentioned at viii. 365 – 'an ugly old maid but good housewife'.
4. In the crowded out-parishes.

To the office to finish my letters, and then home to bed – being troubled at the sickness, and my head filled also with other business enough, and perticularly how to put my things and estate in order, in case it should please God to call me away – which God dispose of to his own glory.

11. *Lords day.* Up, and expected long a new suit; but coming not, dressed myself in my late new black silk camelot suit; and when full ready, comes my new one of Colour'd Farrinden, which my wife puts me out of love with; which vexes [me], but I think it is only my not being used to wear Colours, which makes it look a little unusual upon me. To my chamber, and there spent the morning reading. At noon by invitation comes my two cousin Joyces and their wifes – my aunt James, and he-cousin Harman – his wife being ill. I had a good dinner for them, and as merry as I could be in such company. They being gone, I out of doors a little to show forsooth my new suit, and back again; and in going, saw poor Dr. Burnets door shut. But he hath, I hear, gained great goodwill among his neighbours; for he discovered it himself first, and caused himself to be shut up of his own accord – which was very handsome.

In the evening comes Mr. Andrews and his wife and Mr. Hill, and stayed and played and sung and supped – most excellent pretty company; so pleasant, ingenious, and harmless, I cannot desire better. They gone, we to bed – my mind in great present ease.

12. Up, and in my yesterday's new suit to the Duke of Albe-marle. And after a turn in White-hall and thence in West-minster Hall – returned, and with my Taylor bought some gold lace for my sleeve-hands at paternoster Row. So home to dinner, and then to the office and down the River to Deptford; and then back again and to my Lord Treasurer's, and up and down to look after my Tanger business; and so home to my office, then to supper and to bed.

The Duke of Yorke is sent for last night, and expected to be here tomorrow.

13. Up, and to the office, where all the morning doing business. At noon with Sir G. Carteret to my Lord Mayors to
dinner, where much company in a little room – and though a
good, yet no extraordinary Table. His name, Sir John Lawrence
– whose father, a very ordinary old man, sat there at table – but
it seems a very rich man. Here was at Table three Sir Rd.
Brownes – *viz.* he of the Councell a clerk – and the Alderman
and his son – and there was a little grandson, also Richard, who
will hereafter be Sir Rd. Browne.[1] The Alderman did here
openly tell in boasting, how he had, only upon suspicion of dis-
turbances (if there had been any bad news from sea), clapped up
several persons that he was afeared of. And that he had several
times done the like and would do, and take no bail where he saw
it unsafe for the King. But by and by he said that he was now
sued in the Exchequer by a man, for false imprisonment, that he
had upon the same score imprisoned while[a] he was Mayor, four
years ago – and asked advice about it. I told him I believed
there was none, and told my story of Field;[2] at which he was
troubled and said that it was then unsafe for any man to serve
the King – and I believed knows not what to do therein, but that
Sir Rd. Browne of the Council advised him to speak with my
Lord Chancellor about it.

My Lord Mayor very respectful to me. And so I after dinner
away, and found Sir J. Mennes ready with his coach and four
horses at our office-gate, for him and me to go out of town to
meet the Duke of Yorke, coming from Harwich tonight. And so
as far as Illford, and there light. By and by comes to us Sir Jo.
Shaw and Mr. Neale that married the rich widow Gold, upon
the same errand. After eating a dish of Creame, we took coach
again, hearing nothing of the Duke; and away home, a most
pleasant evening and road. And so to my office; where after

a repl. 'for'

---

1. Sir Richard Browne, Clerk to
the Privy Council, was John Evelyn's
father-in-law. The alderman, Sir
Richard Browne Bt, had been Lord
Mayor 1660–1; his son had been
knighted in 1660. The alderman's

grandson succeeded to the baronetcy
in 1684.
2. Field had similarly prosecuted
Pepys: see above, iii. 23 & n. 2.
The cases concerning Browne have
not been traced.

my letters writ, to supper and to bed. All our discourse in*ᵃ* our way was Sir J. Mennes's telling me passages of the late King's and his father's;[1] which I was mightily pleased to hear for information, though the pride of some persons and vice of most was but a sad story to tell how that brought the whole kingdom and King to ruine.

14. Up, and to Sir Ph. Warwickes and other places about Tanger business, but to little purpose. Among others, to my Lord Treasurers, there to speak with him; and waited in the lobby three long hours for to speak*ᵇ* with him, to the trial of my utmost patience, but missed him at last, and forced to go home without it – which may teach me how I make others wait. Home to dinner, and stayed Mr. Hater with me, and after dinner drew up a petition for Mr. Hater to present to the Council about his troublesome business of powder – desiring a trial, that his absence may be vindicated. And so to White-hall, but it was not proper to present it today.[2] Here I met with Mr. Cowling, who observed to me how he finds everybody silent in the praise of my Lord of Sandwich, to set up the Duke and the Prince. But that the Duke did, both to the King and my Lord Chancellor, write abundantly of my Lord's courage and service. And I this day met with a letter of Captain Ferrers, where he tells us my Lord was with his ship in all the heat of the day, and did most worthily. Met with Creed, and he and I to Westminster and there saw my Lord Marlborough brought to be buried – several Lords of the Council carrying him, and with the heralds in some state.[3] Thence, vexed in my mind to think that I do so little in my Tanger business, and so home, and after supper to bed.

15. Up, and put on my new stuff suit with close knees, which

a repl. same symbol badly formed   *b* repl. 'opening a door to'

---

1. Mennes had served as a naval officer under James I as well as under Charles I.

2. For the case, see above, p. 115 & n. 3. The petitions of certain others involved were this day examined and a committee appointed to examine and report: PRO, PC 2/58, f. 88*v*.

3. The 3rd Earl of Marlborough (commander of the expedition to Bombay in 1662) had been killed in the naval battle of 3 June. He was buried in the Abbey.

becomes me most nobly as my wife says. At the office all day. At noon put on my first laced-band, all lace, and to*a* Kate Joyce's to dinner; where my mother, wife, and abundance of their friends, and good usage. Thence wife and Mercer and I to the Old Exchange and there bought two lace-bands more, one of my Semstresse,[1] whom my wife concurs with me to be a pretty woman. So down to Deptford and Woolwich, my boy and I. At Woolwich discoursed with Mr. Shelden about my bringing my wife down for a month or two to his house; which he approves of, and I think will be very convenient.[2] So late back and to the office, wrote letters, and so home to supper and to bed.

This day the News-book (upon Mr Moores showing Lestrange Captain Ferrers letter) did do my Lord Sandwich great right as to the late victory.[3]

The Duke of Yorke not yet come to town. The town grows very sickly, and people to be afeared of it – there dying this last week of the plague 112, from 43 the week before – whereof, one in Fanchurch-street and one in Broadstreete by the Treasurer's office.[4]

16. Up, and to the office, where I set hard to business – but was informed that the Duke of Yorke is come, and hath appointed us to attend him this afternoon. So after dinner and doing some business at the office, I to White-hall, where the Court is full of

a repl. 'off to K'-

---

1. See above, p. 73, n. 3.

2. William Sheldon was Clerk of the Cheque at Woolwich. Mrs Pepys, with two of her three maids, went there on 5 July and returned to her London home on 2 December.

3. *The Newes*, 15 June (p. 449), has the following (from Norwich, 12 June): 'Upon *Friday* last there came a Person of Quality to this Town from abord the *Right Honourable* the *Earl* of *Sandwich* (the *Prince*) who gave us Intelligence . . . whereupon our *Loyal Mayor* sent the *Sword bearer* to invite him to dinner. . . . It seems

the Earl of *Sandwich* his vessel . . . was much damnified in the *Battle* . . . this *Lordship* shewing himself aloft all the while, as unconcerned, as if he had been in his own *Parlour.*' But the same issue continued to heap praise on Rupert (p. 442). Roger L'Estrange was the editor.

4. The Navy Treasurer's. The figures given are from the weekly bills of mortality (q.v. above, iii. 292, n. 1), which run from Tuesday to Tuesday (in this case 6–13 June). See the collection in GL, A.1.5, no. 96.

the Duke and his Courtiers, returned from sea – all fat and lusty,
and ruddy by being in the sun.   I kissed his hands, and we waited
all the afternoon.   By and by saw Mr. Coventry, which rejoiced
my very heart.   Anon he and I from all the rest of the company
walked into the matted-gallery – where after many expressions
of love, we fell to talk of business.   Among other things, how
my Lord Sandwich, both in his counsels and personal service,
hath done most honorably and serviceably.   Sir J Lawson is come
to Greenwich, but his wound in his knee yet very bad.   Jonas
Poole in the *Vantguard* did basely, so as to be, or will be, turned
out of his ship.[1]   Captain Holmes, expecting upon Sansums
death to be made Rere admirall to the Prince (but Harman is
put in), hath delivered up to the Duke his commission, which
the Duke took and tore.[2]   He, it seems, had bid the Prince, who
first told him of Holmes's intention,[a] that he should dissuade
him from it, for that he was resolved to take it if he offered it.
Yet Holmes would do it, like a rash, proud coxcomb – but he is
rich, and hath it seems sought an occasion of leaving the service.[3]
Several of our Captains have done ill.   The great Shipps are the
ships do the business, they[b] quite deadening the enemy – they
run away upon sight of the *Prince*.[4]   It is strange, to see how
people do already slight Sir Wm. Berkely, my Lord Fitzharding's
brother, who three months since was the delight of the Court.[5]
Captain Smith of the *Mary*, the Duke talks mightily of, and
some great thing will be done for him.[6]   Strange, to hear how
the Dutch do relate, as the Duke says, that they are the conquerors
– and bonefires are made in Dunkirke in their behalf – though a
clearer victory can never be expected.   Mr. Coventry thinks

a repl. 'his'   *b* MS. 'that'

1. He held no commission after
1665.

2. Sandwich (p. 234) says that
Rupert had promised Holmes the appointment, but makes no mention of
the tearing of the commission.

3. In 1666 he was knighted and
made rear-admiral. He also served
in 1667 and 1672.

4. Sandwich's ship: she mounted
more guns (86) than any other in the
fleet.

5. Berkeley, Rear-Admiral of the
Duke's squadron, in the *Swiftsure*
(54–64 guns), was alleged, probably
wrongly, to have sheered away from
the battle after the death of his brother,
Lord Falmouth ('Fitzharding'). Cf.
Marvell, *Second Advice*, ll. 190–6.

6. Jeremy Smith was knighted
later this month.

they cannot have lost less then 6000 men; and we not dead above
200, and wounded about 400; in all, about 600.[1]   Thence home,
and to my office till past 12 and then home to supper and to bed –
my wife and mother not being yet come home from W Hewres
chamber, who treats my mother tonight.

⟨Captain Grove, the Duke told us this day, hath done the
basest thing at Lastoffe, in hearing of the guns and could not
(as others) be got out, but stayed there – for which he will be
tried; and is reckoned a prating coxcombe, and of no courage.⟩[a][2]

17.   My wife came to bed about one in the morning.
I up, and abroad about Tanger business; then back to the
office, where we sat.   And at noon home to dinner, and then
abroad to Mr. Povys – after I and Mr. Andrews had been with
Mr. Ball and one Major Strange, who looks after the getting of
money for Tallys and is helping Mr. Andrews.[3]   I had much
discourse with Ball, and it may be he may prove a necessary man
for our turns.   With Mr. Povy, I spoke very freely my indifference as to my place of Treasurer, being so much troubled
in it;   which he took with much seeming trouble – that I should
think of letting go so lightly the place.   But if the place can be
held, I will.   So hearing that my Lord Treasurer was gone out
of town with his family because of the sickness, I returned home
without staying there.   And at the office find Sir W Pen come
home, who looks very well;[4] and I am gladder to see him then
otherwise I should be, because of my hearing so well of him for
his serviceableness in this late great action.   To the office late,
and then home to bed.

It stroke me very deep this afternoon, going with a Hackny-

a   addition crowded in at bottom of page and preceded by '17' struck through
and smudged in margin

---

1. Cf. above, p. 123 & n. 1.
2. Edward Grove commanded the
Success (28–32 guns) in the Duke of
York's squadron.   He held no commission after this year.   Although
ordered to sail from Lowestoft, 'he
lay drinking many hours': Longleat,
Coventry MSS 96, f. 99r.
3. Both John Ball and Edward

Strange were officers of the Excise
Commission, and it was on excise
revenue that Pepys's Tangier tallies
had been drawn.   Thomas Andrews
was a merchant engaged in the
victualling of Tangier.
4. He had recently been ill: Pepys
to Coventry, 10 June 1665 (NMM,
LBK/8, p. 221).

coach from my Lord Treasurer's down Holborne – the coachman I found to drive easily and easily*; at last stood still, and came down hardly able to stand; and told me that he was suddenly stroke very sick and almost blind, he could not see. So I light and went into another coach, with a sad heart for the poor man and trouble for myself, lest he should have been stroke with the plague – being at that end of the town that I took him up. But God have mercy upon us all.

Sir Jo. Lawson, I hear, is worse then yesterday – the King went to see him today, most kindly. It seems his wound is not very bad, but he hath a fever – a thrush and a Hickup, all three together; which are, it seems, very bad symptoms.

18. *Lords Day.* Up, and to church, where Sir W Pen was the first time come from sea after the battle. Mr Mills made a sorry sermon, to prove that there was a world to come after this. Home and dined. And then to my chamber, where all the afternoon. Anon comes Mr. Andrews to see and sing with me; but Mr. Hill not coming, and having business, we soon parted – there coming Mr. Povy and Creed to discourse about our Tanger business of money. They gone, I hear Sir W. Batten and my Lady are returned from Harwich. I went to see them, and it is pretty to see how we appear kind one to another, though neither of us care 2*d* one for another. Home to supper; and there coming a hasty letter from Comissioner Pett, for pressing of some calkers (as I would ever on his Majesty's service) with all speed, I made a warrant presently, and issued it.[1] So to my office a little, and then home to bed.

19. Up; to White-hall with Sir W. Batten (calling at Lord Ashlys, but to no purpose, by the way, he being not up) and there had our usual meeting before the Duke, with the officers of the Ordinance with us; which in some respects I think will be the better for us – for despatch sake. Thence home to the Change and dined alone (my wife gone to her mother's); after dinner to my little new goldsmith's,[2] whose wife endeed is one

---

1. Peter Pett to Pepys, 18 June: CSPD *1664–5*, p. 433. Thirty-one were pressed by the 19th: ib., p. 435.
2. John Colvill, Lombard St.

of the prettiest modest black* women that ever I saw.   I paid for a
dozen of silver salts, 6*l*-14*s*-6*d*.   Thence with Sir W. Penn from
the office, down to Greenwich to see Sir J. Lawson; who is
better, but continues ill.   His Hickup not being yet gone – could
have little discourse with him.   So thence home and to supper.
A while to the office, my head and mind mightily vexed to see
the multitude of papers and business before [me] and so little
time to do it in.   So to bed.

20.   *Thanksgiving day for Victory over the Dutch.*[1]   Up, and
to the office, where very busy alone all the morning till church
time; and there heard a mean sorry sermon of Mr. Mills.   Then
to the Dolphin Taverne, where all we officers of the Navy met
with the Comissioners of the Ordnance by agreement and
dined – where good Musique, at my direction.   Our club came
to 34*s* a man – nine of us.

Thence after dinner I to White-hall with Sir W Berkely in
his coach.   And so I walked to Herberts and there spent a little
time avec la mosa,[2] sin hazer algo con ella que kiss and tocar ses
mamelles, que me haza hazer*ᵃ* la cosa a mi mismo con gran
plaisir.   Thence by water to Fox hall, and there walked an hour
alone, observing the several humours of the citizens that were
there this holiday, pulling of cherries[3] and God knows what.
And so home to my office, where late, my wife not being come
home with my mother, who have been this day all abroad upon
the water, my mother being to go out of town speedily.   So I
home and to supper and to bed.   ⟨My wife came home when I
came from the office.⟩

This day I informed myself that there died four or five at
Westminster of the plague, in one alley in several houses upon
Sunday last – Bell Alley, over against the Palace-gate.   Yet

a repl. same symbol badly formed

---

1. The celebration was ordered by
a proclamation of 14 June to take
place this day in London and Westminster; in other places on 4 July:
Steele, no. 3421. The service is
given in *A form of common prayer*
with thanksgiving for the late victory
. . . (1665).
2. Sarah Udall. Herbert kept the
Swan in New Palace Yard.
3. I.e. playing at the game of
bob-cherry.

people do think that the number will be fewer in the town then it was the last week.[1]

The Dutch are come out again, with 20 sail under Banker – supposed gone to the Norward to meet their East India fleet.[2]

21. Up, and very busy all the morning. At noon with Creede[a] to the Excize Office, where I find our Tallys will not be money in less then sixteen months;[3] which is a sad thing, for the King to pay all that interest for every penny he spends – and which is strange[b], the goldsmiths with whom I spoke do declare that they will not be moved to part with money upon the encrease of their consideration of 10 per cent[4] which they have; and therefore desire I would not move in it. And endeed, the consequence would be very ill to the King, and have its ill consequences fallow us through all the King's revenue.

Home, and my uncle Wight and aunt James dined with me – my mother being to go away tomorrow.

So to White-hall and there, before and after Council, discoursed with Sir Tho. Ingram about our ill case as to Tanger for money. He hath got the King to appoint a meeting on Friday, which I hope will put an end one way or other to my pain.

So homewards, and to the Crosse Keys at Cripplegate, where I find all the town almost going out of town, the coaches and waggons being all full of people going into the country. Here I had some of the company of the tapster's wife a while; and so home to my office, and then home to supper and to bed.

22. Up pretty betimes, and in great pain whether to send my mother into the country today or no, I hearing by my people that she, poor wretch, hath a mind to stay a little longer; and I cannot blame her, considering what a life she will, through her own

a l.h. repl. l.h. 'Creditt'   b MS. 'the strange'

---

1. The figures were, in fact, 112 deaths from the plague during 13–20 June, and 168 during 20–27 June (GL, A.1.5, no. 96).

2. Rear-Adm. Adriaen Banckert returned on 1 July without having sighted the E. India ships or having met a single English ship. See below,

p. 146; *CSPVen. 1664–6*, pp. 149, 161, 166.

3. In the event, over two years: below, vii. 407.

4. This was the normal rate paid by the government. To the legal maximum of 6% was added, by special warrant, a 'gratuity' of 4%.

folly, lead when she comes home again; unlike the pleasure and
liberty she hath had here.   At last I resolved to put it to her,
and she agreed to go, so I would not oppose it because of the
sickness in the town, and my intentions of removing my wife.
So I did give her money and took a kind leave of her – she, poor
wretch, desiring that I would forgive my brother John,[1] but I
refused it to her; which troubled her, poor soul, but I did it in
kind words and so let the discourse go off, she leaving me,
though, in a great deal of sorrow.   So I to my office and left
my wife and people to see her out of town, and I at the office
all the morning.   At noon my wife tells me that she is with
much ado gone, and I pray God bless her.   But it seems she was
to the last unwilling to go; but would not say so, but put it off
till she lost her place in the coach and was fain to ride in the
waggon part.[2]

After dinner to the office again till night, very busy; and so
home, not very late, to supper and to bed.

23.   Up, and to Whitehall to a Committee for Tanger, where
his Royal Highness was.   Our great design was to state to them
the true condition of this commission for want of money, the
want whereof was so great as to need some sudden help; and it
was with some content resolved to see it supplied, and means
proposed toward the doing of it.[3]

At this Committee, unknown to me, comes my Lord of Sandwich, who it seems came to town last night.   After the Committee was up, my Lord Sandwich did take me aside, and we
walked an hour alone together in the robe-chamber, the door
shut – telling me how much the Duke and Mr. Coventry did,
both in the fleet and here, make of him, and that in some opposi-
tion to the Prince;[a][4] and as a more private passage, he told

a   repl. 'Duke'

---

1. For their quarrel, see above, v.
91.
2. In the open section behind.
For the structure of coaches, see Joan
Parkes, *Travel in Engl. in 17th cent.*,
p. 90;   R. Straus, *Carriages and
coaches.*

3. Cf. the undated memorandum
on this subject in PRO, CO 279/4,
ff. 102–3, which may well be connected with this meeting.

4. Rupert.

me that he hath been with them both when they have made sport of the Prince and laughed at him. Yet that all the discourse of the town, and the printed relation, should not give him one word of honour, my Lord thinks mighty strange[1] – he assuring me that though by accident the Prince[a] was in the Van the beginning of the fight for the first pass, yet all the rest of the day my Lord was in the Van, and continued so. That notwithstanding all this noise of the Prince, he hath hardly a shot in his side, nor a man killed – whereas he hath above 30 in her hull, and not one mast whole nor yard – but the most battered ship of the fleet, and lost most men, saving Captain Smith of the *Mary.* That the most the Duke did was almost out of gun-shot. But that endeed, the Duke did come up to my Lord's rescue, after he had a great while fought with four of them. How poorly Sir John Lawson performed, notwithstanding all that that was said of him; and how his ship turned out of the way, while Sir J. Lawson himself was upon the deck, to the endangering of the whole fleet.[2] It therefore troubles my Lord that Mr. Coventry should not mention a word of him in his relation.[3] I did in answer offer that I was sure the relation was not compiled by Mr. Coventry, but by Lestrange out of several letters, as I could witness. And that Mr. Coventry's letter that he did give the Duke of Albimarle did give him as much right as the Prince – for I myself read it first and then copied it out, which I have promised to show my Lord[4] – with which he was something satisfied.

From that discourse, my Lord did begin to tell me how much

a repl. 'Duke'

---

1. Neither of the two printed official accounts gave Sandwich more than one mention, and that in a passage which described his squadron as being at the rear of the English line: Penn, ii. 327. Cf. Marvell, *Second advice to a painter,* ll. 106–7: 'Hence by the gazetteer he was mistook,/As unconcern'd as if at Hinchingbrooke'.

2. In his journal Sandwich was by no means so harsh on Lawson. He there stated that 'disorder for want of government' broke out on board Lawson's ship, but only after Lawson had been wounded: Sandwich, p. 226.

3. *The second narrative . . .*: cf. above, p. 123 & n. 1.

4. Cf. above, p. 129. Pepys had already, in a letter of the 17th, assured Sandwich that Coventry's account was different from the official printed version: *Further Corr.,* p. 47.

he was concerned to dispose of his children, and would have my advice and help; and propounded to match my Lady Jemimah to Sir G Careterets eldest son*a*1 – which I approved of, and did undertake the speaking with him about it as from myself; which my Lord liked. So parted, with my head full of care about this business.

Thence home to the Change, and so to dinner. And thence by coach to Mr. Povys; whence by appointment with him and Creed to one Mr. Finch, one of the Comissioners for the Excize, to be informed about some things of the Excize, in order to our settling matters therein better for us for our Tanger matters.2 I find him a very discreet, grave person. Thence, well satisfied, I and Creed to Mr. Fox3 at Whitehall to speak with him about the same matter; and having some pretty satisfaction from him also, he and I took boat and to Fox hall, where we spent two or three hours, talking of several matters very soberly, and contentfully to me – which, with the ayre and pleasure of the garden, was a great refreshment to me, and methinks that which we ought to Joy ourselfs in. Thence back to White hall, where we parted; and I to find my Lord to receive his further direction about his proposal this morning – wherein I did [agree] that I should first, by another hand, break my intentions to Sir G Carteret. I pitched upon Dr Clerke,4 which my Lord liked – and so I endeavoured, but in vain, to find him out tonight. So home by hackney-coach; which is become a very dangerous passage nowadays, the sickness encreasing mightily.5 And to bed.

a repl. 'some'

---

1. Philip Carteret; he and Lady Jemima Mountagu were married on 31 July 1665 after a fortnight's acquaintance, he being then 24 and she 17.

2. The commissioner was Francis Finch, ironmaster. The Tangier tallies were drawn on excise funds.

3. Stephen Fox, Paymaster-General.

4. Timothy Clarke, a physician-in-ordinary to the royal household, of which Carteret was Vice-Chamberlain.

5. The city regulations required any hackney-coach which had carried a plague victim to be aired afterwards for five to six days: *Orders . . . by the Lord Mayor* in *A collection of very valuable and scarce pieces relating to the Plague* (1721), p. 9 (no date). Special pest-coaches were sometimes employed: below, p. 181.

24. *Midsummer Day.* Up very betimes, by 6, and at Dr. Clerkes at Westminster by 7 of the clock, having over-night by a note acquainted him with my intention of coming. And there I, in the best manner I could, broke my errand about a match between Sir G Carter[e]ts eldest son and my Lord Sandwiches eldest daughter – which he (as I knew he would) took with great content; and we both agreed that my Lord and he, being both men relating to the sea – under a kind aspect of His Majesty – already good friends, and both virtuous and good families, their allyance might be of good use to us. And he did undertake to find out Sir George this morning, and put the business in execution. So being both well pleased with the proposition, I saw his neece[1] there and made her sing me two or three songs, very prettily; and so home to the office – where to my great trouble, I found Mr. Coventry and the board met before I came. I excused my late coming, by having been upon the River about office business. So to business all the morning. At noon Captain Ferrers and Mr. Moore dined with me; the former of them, the first time I saw him since his coming from sea – who doth give me the best account[a] in general, and as good an account of the perticular service of the Prince and my Lord of Sandwich in the late sea fight that I could desire. After dinner they parted. So I to Whitehall, where I with Creed and Povy attended my Lord Treasurer, and did prevail with him to let us have an assignment for 15 or 20000*l*, which I hope will do our business for Tanger.[2] So to Dr. Clerke, and there find that he hath broke the business to Sir[b] G Carteret and that he takes the thing mighty well. Thence I to Sir G. Carteret at his Chamber, and in the best manner I could, and most obligingly, moved that business; he received it with great respect and content and thanks to me, and promised that he would do what he could possibly for his son, to render him fit for my Lord's daughter. And showed great kindness to me, and sense of my kindness to him herein. Sir Wm. Pen told me this day that Mr. Coventry is to be sworn a Privy Counsellor – at which my soul is glad.[3] So home and to my letters by the post, and so home – to supper and bed.

a MS. 'evil'   *b* repl. 'Dr.'

---

1. Mrs Worship: below, p. 215.   3. See below, p. 141 & n. 2.
2. See below, p. 139 & n. 3.

25. *Lords day.* Up, and several people about business came to me by appointment, relating to the office; thence I to my closet about my Tanger papers. At noon dined. And then I abroad by water, it raining hard, thinking to have gone down to Woolwich; but I did not, but back through bridge to White-hall – where after I had again visited Sir G Carteret and received his (and now his Lady's) full content in my proposal, I went to my Lord Sandwich; and having told him how Sir G. Carteret received it, he did direct me to return to Sir G. Carteret and give him thanks for his kind reception of this offer, and that he would the next day be willing to enter discourse with him about that business. Which message I did presently do, and so left the business, with great joy to both sides.[a] My Lord, I perceive, entends to give 5000*l* with her, and expects about 800*l* per annum joynture.[1] So by water home and to supper and bed, being weary with long walking at Court. But had a psalm or two with my boy and Mercer before bed, which pleased me mightily. ⟨This night Sir G. Carteret told me with great kindness, that the order of the Council did run for the making of Hater and Whitfield uncapable of ever[b] serving the King again – but that he had stopped the entry of it;[2] which he told me with great kindness – but the thing troubles me.⟩

After dinner, before I went to White-hall, I went down to Greenwich by water, thinking to have visited Sir Jo Lawson; where when I came, I find that he is dead, and died this morning – at which I was much surprized. And endeed, the nation hath a great loss; though I cannot, with[out] dissembling, say that I am sorry for it, for he was a man never kind to me at all.

Being at White-hall, I visited Mr. Coventry – who, among other talk, entered about the great Question now in the House,[3] about the[c] Dukes going to sea again – about which the whole House is divided. He did concur with me, that for the Dukes honour and safety it were best, after so great a service and victory

a repl. 'wise'   b MS. 'every'   c l.h. repl. s.h. 'him'

---

1. This would accord with the prevailing rates: cf. above, iii. 231 & n. 1. In 1693 Evelyn's daughter received £500 p.a. from a marriage portion of £4000: Evelyn, v. 138.

2. See above, p. 115 & n. 3. No such order is entered in the Privy Council register.

3. The royal household: parliament was not in session.

and danger, not to go again;[1] and above all, that the fall of the
Duke cannot be*a* a security to the Crowne – if he were away,
it being more easy to attempt anything upon the King. But
how the fleet will be governed without him, the Prince being a
man of no government, and severe in council, that no ordinary
man can offer any advice against his – saying truly, that it had
been better he had gone to Guinny. And that were he away,
it were easy to say how things might be ordered, my Lord
Sandwich being a man of temper* and justice, as much as any
he ever knew – and that up[on] good observation he said this –
and that his temper must correct the Princes. But I perceive
he is much troubled what will be the event of that Question.[2]
And so I left him.

26. Up; to White-hall with Sir J. Mennes and to the Committee of Tanger, where my Lord Treasurer was, the first and
only time he ever was there – and did promise us 15000*l* for
Tanger, and no more;[3] which will be short, but if I can pay Mr.
Andrews all his money, I care for no more[4] – and the bills of
exchange. Thence with Mr. Povy and Creed below to a new
chamber of Mr. Povys, very pretty, and there discourse about
his business; not to his content, but with the most advantage I
could to him; and Creed also did the like. Thence with Creed
to the Kings-head, and there dined with him at the ordinary;
and good sport with one Mr. Nicholls,[5] a prating coxcomb that

a MS. 'but be'

---

1. His ship had closely engaged
the enemy in the recent Battle of
Lowestoft: above, p. 122.
2. The Duke of York was sent to
York in late July to secure the north
against invasion, and to escape the
risks both of the Plague and of further
service in the navy. The fleet which
went to sea in early July was put
under Sandwich and Penn. Rupert
held no further command in this
year's campaign, and in 1666 Albemarle was made joint-commander
with him.

3. But a warrant for £17,500
(the amount originally promised)
was issued on 19 August after a letter
of direction on the subject had been
issued on 28 June: *CTB*, i. 659, 668,
678.
4. Cf. Pepys to Lanyon, 20 June,
'I . . . will take care the best I can
to support Mr. Andrewes, whose
case I am very sensible is at this time
to be pittied': Rawl. 193, f. 210r.
5. Unidentified. Possibly the
Henry Nicholl who published *Argu-
menta*, a broadside, in 1678.

would be thought a poet but would not be got to repeat any of his verses. Thence I home – and there find my wife's brother and his wife, a pretty little modest woman, where they dined with my wife. He did come to desire my assistance for a living; and upon his good promises of care, and that it should be no burden to me, I did say and promise I would think of finding something for him – and the rather, because his wife seems a pretty discreet young thing, and humble; and he, above all things desirous to do something to maintain her – telling me sad stories of what she endured with him in Holland.[1] And I hope it will not be burdensome.

So down by water to Woolwich, walking to and again from Greenwich, thither and back again – my business being to speak again with Shelden, who desires and expects my wife's coming thither to spend the summer. And upon second thoughts, I do agree that it will be a good place for her, and me too.[2]

So, weary, home and to my office a while, till almost midnight, and so to bed. The plague encreases mightily – I this day seeing a house, at a bittmakers over against St. Clements church in the open street, shut up; which is a sad sight.

27. Up, and to the office, where all the morning. At noon dined by chance at my Lady Battens, and they sent for my wife, and there was my Lady Pen and Pegg – very merry; and so I to my office again, where till 12 at night, and so home to supper and to bed.

28. Sir J Minnes carried me ⟨and my wife⟩ to White-hall; and thence, his coach along with my wife where she would. Thereafter attending the Duke to discourse of the Navy. We did not kiss his hand; nor do I think, for all their[3] pretence of going away tomorrow – yet I believe they will not go for good

---

1. Balty St Michel had served in the Dutch army since early 1664. Pepys had him made a naval muster-master later in the year.

2. See above, p. 128 & n. 1. Pepys himself spent most of the period from 28 August to 22 Septem-

ber there, but after 11 October until his return to London on 7 January 1666 took lodgings at Greenwich where the Navy Board had temporary accommodation. See below, p. 195, n. 1.

3. The court's.

and all.[1] But I did take my leave of Sir[a] Wm. Coventry, who it seems was knighted and sworn a Privy Councillor two days since[2] – who with his old kindness treated me, and I believe I shall ever find a noble friend.

Thence by water to Blackfriars, and so to Paul's churchyard and bespoke several books, and so home and there dined – my man William giving me a lobster, sent him by my old maid Sarah.

This morning I met with Sir G. Carteret, who tells me how all things proceed between my Lord Sandwich and himself to full content, and both sides depend upon having the match finished presently. And professed great kindness to me, and said that now we were something akinned. I am mightily, both with respect to myself and much more of my Lord's family, glad of this alliance.

After dinner to White-hall, thinking to speak with my Lord Ashly, but failed; and I whiled away some time in Westminster hall against he did come – in my way observing several plague-houses in Kings-street and the Palace. Here I hear Mrs. Martin is gone out of town, and that her husband, an idle fellow, is since come out of France, as he pretends; but I believe not that he hath been. I was fearful of going to any house, but I did to the Swan; and thence to White-hall, giving the waterman a shilling, because a young fellow and belonging to the *Plymouth*.

Thence by coach to several places, and so home and all the evening with Sir J. Minnes and all the women of the house (excepting my Lady Batten[b]) late in the garden, chatting. At 12 a-clock home to supper and to bed.

My Lord Sandwich is gone toward the sea today, it being a sudden resolution – I having taken no leave[c] of him.

29. Up, and by water to White-hall, where the Court full of

a l.h. repl. s.h. 'Mr.' *b* l.h. repl. s.h. 'Bet'-
c repl. 'notice of him at his coming'

1. But see below, p. 142.
2. This entry (confirmed by *The Newes*, 29 June, p. 520) corrects the date for the knighthood (3 March) given in W. A. Shaw, *Knights of*

Engl., ii. 240, and in *CSPD 1664–5*, p. 239, n. For Coventry's admission to the Privy Council, see Longleat, Coventry MSS 64, f. 183r; ib., 98, f. 162r.

waggons and people ready to go out of town.[1]   To the Harp and
Ball and there drank and talked with Mary – she telling me in
discourse that she lived lately at my neighbour's, Mr. Knightly –
which made me forbear further discourse.   This end of the town
every day grows very bad of the plague.   The Mortality bill is
come to 267[a] – which is about 90 more[b] then the last; and of
these, but 4 in the City – which is a great blessing to us.[2]   Thence
to Creed, and with him up and down about Tanger business, to
no purpose.   Took leave again of Mr. Coventry, though I hope
the Duke is not gone to stay – and so do others too.   So home,
calling[c] at Somersett-house, where all are packing up too; the
Queene-mother setting out for France this day to drink Bourbon
waters this year, she being in a consumption – and entends not to
come till winter come twelvemonths.[3]

So by coach home, where at the office all the morning.   And
at noon Mrs. Hunt dined with us – very merry, and she a very
good woman.   To the office, where busy a while, putting some
things in my office in order, and then to letters till night.   About
10 a-clock home – the days being sensibly shorter: before, I
have once kept a summer's day by shutting up office by daylight,
but my life hath been still as it was in winter almost.   But I will
for a month try what I can do by daylight.   So home to supper
and to bed.

30.   Up, and to White-hall to the Duke of Albemarle, who I
find at Secretary Bennets, there being now no other great statesman, I think, but my Lord Chancellor in town.   I received
several commands from them; among others, to provide some

---

a repl. '297'   *b* repl. 'ever'   *c* repl. same symbol badly formed

---

1. The court now moved to Syon
House, Isleworth;   on 9 July to
Hampton Court, and at the end of
July to Salisbury, arriving there on
1 August.   From 23 September to the
following 27 January it was at
Oxford, which remained immune to
the plague.   It then moved back to
Hampton Court and on 1 February
returned to Whitehall.

2. The 267 were plague victims
only, out of a total of 684 burials:
GL, A.1.5, no. 96.

3. Henrietta-Maria never returned
to England, but died (aged almost 60)
at her château at Colombes, near
Paris, on 21/31 August, after a long
illness.   Bourbon-l'Archambault, near
Vichy, was one of the most fashion-
able French spas.

bread and cheese for the garrison at Guernsy; which they promised to see me paid for.

So to the Change, and home to dinner. In the afternoon, I down to Woolwich and after me, my wife and Mercer, whom I led to Mr. Sheldens to see his house; and I find it a very pretty place for them to be at. So I back again, walking both forward and backward, and left my wife to come by water. I straight to Whitehall late, to Secretary Bennets to give him an account of the business I received from him today; and there stayed, weary and sleepy, till past 12 at night. Then writ my mind to him; and so back by water, and in the dark and against tide shot the bridge, groping with their pole for the way; which troubled me before I got through. So home about one or two a-clock in the morning – my family at a great loss what was become of me. To supper and to bed.

Thus this book of two years ends. Myself and family in good health, consisting of myself and wife – Mercer, her woman – Mary, Alce and Su, our maids; and Tom, my boy. In a sickly time, of the plague growing on. Having upon my hands the troublesome care of the Treasury of Tanger, with great sums drawn upon me and nothing to pay them with. Also, the business of the office great. Consideration of removing my wife to Woolwich. She lately busy in learning to paint, with great pleasure and successe. All other things well; especially a new interest I am making, by a match in hand between the eldest son of Sir G Carteret and my Lady Jemimah Mountagu. The Duke of York gone down to the fleet; but, all*a* suppose, not with intent to stay there – as it is not fit, all men conceive, he should.

FINIS.*b*

a repl. 'also'   *b* end of third volume of MS.

1. Called up betimes, though weary and sleepy, by appointment by Mr. Povy and Collonell Norwood, to discourse about some payments of Tanger. They gone, I to the office and there sat all the morning. At noon dined at home, and then to the Duke of Albemarles by appointment to give him an account of some disorder in the yard at Portsmouth, by workmen's going away of their own accord for lack of money, to get work of haymaking or anything else to earn themselfs bread.[1]

Thence I to Westminster, where I hear the sickness encreases greatly. And to the Harp and Ball with Mary, talking, who tells me simply her losing of her first love in the country in Wales and coming up hither unknown to her friends. And it seems Dr. Williams doth pretend love to her, and I have found him there several times.

Thence by coach, and late at the office and so to bed – sad at the news that seven or eight houses in Bazing-hall street are shut up of the plague.

2. *Sunday.* Up, and all the morning dressing my closet at the office with my plat very neatly, and a fine place now it is – and will be a pleasure to sit in – though I thank God I needed none before.[2] At noon dined at home, and after dinner to my accounts and cast them up, and find that though I have spent above 90*l* this month, yet I have saved 17*l* and am worth in all above 1450*l*, for which the Lord be praised.

In the evening my Lady Pen and daughter came to see and supped with us. Then a messenger about business of the office from Sir G. Carteret at Chatham – and by word*a* of mouth did

a repl. 'and by'

1. See two letters from Commissioner Middleton of Portsmouth to Pepys, 29 June, in *CSPD 1664–5*, p. 453. The ropemakers had gone haymaking; blockmakers and joiners had also left. Pepys sent these letters to Coventry on 1 July: *Further Corr.*, pp. 47–8. Many workers were pressed men; for a summary of their wages, etc., see Ehrman, pp. 89+; D. C. Coleman in *Econ. Hist. Rev.* (ser. 2), 6/134+, esp. 145.

2. For the construction of this closet, and for the plate, see above, p. 111 & n. 5.

send me word that the business between my Lord and him[1] is fully agreed on and is mightily liked of by the King and the Duke of Yorke, and that he sent me this word with great joy. They gone, we to bed.

I hear this night that Sir J Lawson was buried late last night at St. Dunstans by us,[2] without any company at all – and that the condition of his family is but very poor,[3] which I could be contented to be sorry for, though he never was the man that ever obliged me by word or deed.

3. Up, and by water with Sir W. Batten and Sir J. Mennes by water to Whitehall to the Duke of Albemarles, where, after a little business – we parted, and I to the Harp and Ball and there stayed a while talking with Mary, and so home to dinner; after dinner to the Duke of Albemarles again, and so to the Swan and there demeurais un peu de temps con la fille. And so to the Harp and Ball and alone demeurais un peu de temps besándola; and so away home and late at the office about letters; and so home, resolving from this night forward to close all my letters if possible and end all my business at the office by daylight, and I shall go near to do it and put all my affairs in the world in good order, the season growing so sickly that it is much to be feared how a man can scape having a share with others in it – for which the good Lord God bless me or to be fitted to receive it.

So after supper to bed, and mightily troubled in my sleep all night with dreams of Jacke Cole my old school-fellow, lately dead, who was born at the same time with me, and we reckoned our fortunes pretty equal. God fit me for his condition.

4. Up, and sat at the office all the morning. At noon to the Change, and thence to the Dolphin, where a good dinner at the cost of one Mr. Osbaston, who lost a wager to Sir W. Batten, Sir W Rider, and Sir R Ford a good while since, and now it is spent. The wager was that ten of our ships should not have a fight with ten of the enemy's before Michaelmas. Here was other very good company and merry, and at last in comes Mr. Buckeworth, a very fine gentleman and proves to be a Huntingtonshire

---

1. The marriage alliance between the families.

2. St Dunstan-in-the-East.

3. An exaggeration: see *Comp.*

man.[1] Thence to my office and there all the afternoon till night, and so home to settle some accounts of Tanger and other papers. I hear this day the Duke and Prince Robert are both come back from sea, and neither of them go back again. The latter I much wonder at, but it seems the town reports so and I am very glad of it.

This morning I did a good piece of work with Sir W Warren, ending the business of my lighters, wherein honestly I think I shall get above 100*l*.[2]

Bankert it seems is come home with the little[a] fleet he hath been abroad with, without doing anything, so that there is nobody of an enemy at sea.[3] We are in great hopes of meeting with the Dutch East India fleet, which is mighty rich, or with De Ruyter, who is so also.

Sir Rd. Ford told me this day at table a fine account how the Dutch were like to have been mastered by the present Prince of Orange his father, to be besieged in Amsterdam – having drawn an army of foot into the town and horse[b] near to the town by night, within three miles of the town, and they never knew of it; but by chance the Hambrough post in the night fell among the horse and heard their design; and knowing the way, it being very dark and rainy, better then they, went from them and did give notice to the town before the others could reach the town; and so were saved.[4] It seems this De Witt and another family,

a repl. same symbol badly formed   *b* repl. 'foot'

---

1. John Buckworth, merchant; knighted 1681; alderman of London, 1683–6; Commissioner of the Customs, 1684–5, 1685–7; Deputy-Governor of the Levant Company, 1672–87. He was a son of Everard Buckworth of Wisbech, Cambs.

2. These were boats for use in Tangier roadstead, for which Warren had provided the timber. For Pepys's profit, see below, p. 286.

3. According to a report from The Hague, Banckert re-entered the Texel on 28 June/8 July 'because he did not know what to do, not having met a single Englishman at sea': *CSPVen.*

1664–6, p. 166. See above, p. 133 & n. 2.

4. Cf. a similar account in A.L. Pontalis, *John de Witt* (trans.), i. 48. The incident occurred in July 1650 during the struggle between William II of Orange and the republican (States) party (led by the de Witt brothers and supported by the estates of Holland and the city of Amsterdam), who opposed the Orangists' plans for a war with Spain. William's death shortly afterwards led to the collapse of his cause: the republicans controlled the United Provinces until the accession of his son William III in 1672.

the Beckarts,[1] were among the chief of the families that was enemies to the Prince, and were afterward suppressed by the Prince – and continued so till he was (as they say) poisoned;[2] and then they turned all again, as it was, against the young Prince, and have so carried it to this day, it being about twelve or fourteen years – and De Witt[3] in the head of them.

5. Up, and advised about[a] sending of my wife's bedding and things today to Woolwich, in order to her removal thither. So to the office, where all the morning till noon; and so to the Change and thence home to dinner. In the afternoon I abroad to St. James,[b] and there with Mr. Coventry a good while and understand how matters are ordered in the fleet; that is, my Lord Sandwich goes Admiral – under him, Sir G Ascu and Sir T Teddiman – Vice=admirall, Sir W Pen; and under him, Sir W Berkeley and Sir Jos. Jordan – Reere-admirall, Sir Tho. Allen; and under him, Sir Christopher Mings and Captain Harman.[4] We talked in general of business of the Navy – among others, how he had lately spoken to Sir G. Carteret and professed great resolution of friendship with him and reconciliation, and resolves to make it good as well as he can, though it troubles him (he tells me) that some things will come before him wherein he must give him offence. I do find upon the whole that Mr. Coventry doth not listen to these complaints of money with that readiness and resolvedness to remedy that he used to do. And I think if he begins to draw in, it is high time for me to do so too.

From thence walked round to Whitehall, the park being quite locked up. And I observed a house shut up this day in the Pell

a repl. 'up'   *b* repl. 'Westminster and'

---

1. Andries Bicker was burgomaster from 1627. He and his brothers (all wealthy merchants and shipowners) belonged to one of the most important regent families of Amsterdam.

2. William II died at the age of 24 on 25 October/6 November 1650 of a fever caught after hunting. His death came so opportunely for the States party that these rumours of his

having been poisoned were quickly put about. His son was not born until a week later.

3. Jan de Witt, Grand Pensionary of Holland, 1653–72.

4. Cf. above, p. 139, n. 2. Sandwich commanded the Red; Penn (although senior) taking the inferior command, that of the White. Penn, ii. 361–2.

Mell, where heretofore in Cromwells time we young men used to keep our weekly clubs.[1]   And so to Whitehall to Sir G. Carteret, who is come this day from Chatham; and mighty glad he is to see me, and begun to talk of our great business of the match – which goes on as fast as possible.   But for convenience, we took water and over to his coach to Lambeth, by which we went to Deptford, all the way talking – first, how matters are quite concluded with all possible content between my Lord and him, and signed and sealed – so that my Lady Sandwich is to come thither tomorrow or next day, and the young lady is sent for – and all likely to be ended between them in a very little while – with mighty joy on both sides, and the King, Duke, Lord Chancellor, and all mightily pleased.

Thence to news, wherein I find that Sir G. Carteret doth now take all my Lord Sandwichs business to heart, and makes it the same with his own.

He tells me how at Chatham it was proposed to my Lord Sandwich to be joined with the Prince in the command of the fleet, which he was most willing to.   But when it came to the Prince, he was quite against it, saying there could be no government, but that it would be better to have two fleets and neither under the command of the other – which he[2] would not agree to; so the King was not pleased, but without any unkindness did order the fleet to be ordered as above, as to the admirals – and commands.   So the Prince is come up, and Sir G. Carteret, I[a] remember, had this word once: that, says he, "By this means, though the King told him that it would be but for this expedition, yet I believe we shall keep him out for altogether."   He tells me how my Lord was much troubled at Sir W Pen's being ordered forth (as it seems he is, to go to Soldbay and with the best fleet he can to go forth) and no notice taken of my Lord Sandwiches going after him and having the command over him.[3]   But after

---

a repl. 'r'-

---

1. At Wood's: cf. above, i. 208 & n. 4.   These clubs were a common feature of tavern life in London.

2. Sandwich. For Sandwich's account of these decisions (which were taken on 2 July), see Sandwich, pp. 236–7.

3. Cf. Coventry to Penn, Chatham, 4 July: Sandwich, p. 238. The fleet had been hastened away under Penn in order to catch the Dutch E. India fleet now on its way back.

some discourse, Mr. Coventry did satisfy, as he says, my Lord, so as they parted friends both in that point and upon the other wherein I know my Lord was troubled; and which Mr. Coventry did speak to him of first, thinking that my*a* Lord might justly take offence at his not being mentioned in the relation of the fight in the news-book[1] – and did clear all to my Lord how little he was concerned in it; and therewith my Lord also satisfied, which I am mightily glad of, because*b* I should take it a very great misfortune to me to have them two to differ, above all the persons in the world.

Being come to Deptford, my Lady not being within, we parted; and I by water to Woolwich, where I found my wife come and her two maids, and very prettily accommodated they will be.[2] And I left them going to supper, grieved in my heart to part with my wife, being worse by much without her, though some trouble there is in having the care of a family at home in this plague time. And so took leave, and I in one boat and W. Hewer in another, home very late, first against tide – we having walked in the dark to Greenwich.

Late home and to bed – very alonely.

6. Up, and forth to give order at my pretty grocer's wife's[3] house, who, her husband tells*c* me, is going this day for the summer into the country. I bespoke some sugar &c. for my father,*d* and so home to the office, where all the morning. At noon dined at home, and then by water to Whitehall to Sir G. Carteret about money for the office; a sad thought,*e* for in a little time all must go to wrack, winter coming on apace, when a great sum must be ready to pay part of the fleet. And so far we are from it, that we have not enough to stop the mouths of poor people and their hands from falling about our eares here, almost in the office. God give a good end to it. Sir G. Carteret told me one considerable thing. Alderman Backewell is ordered abroad upon some private* score with a great sum of money – wherein I was instrumental the other day in shipping him away. It seems some of his Creditors have taken notice of it, and he was

a repl. 'might' *b* repl. 'but' *c* repl. 'is' *d* repl. 'b'- *e* followed by blot

---

1. See above, p. 135 & n. 3.   3. Mrs Beversham: below, p. 298.
2. See above, p. 128, n. 2.

like to be broke yesterday in his absence – Sir G. Carteret telling me that the King and the Kingdom must as good as fall with that man at this time; and that he was forced to get 4000*l* himself to answer Backewells people's occasions, or he must have broke; but committed this to me as a great secret – and which I am heartily sorry to hear.[1]

Thence, after a little merry discourse of our marrying business, I parted; and by coach to several places, among others to see my Lord Brunkerd, who is not well but was at rest when I came. I could not see him, nor had much mind, one of the great houses within two doors of him being shut up;[2] and Lord, the number of houses visited which this day I observed through the town, quite round in my way by Long Lane and London Wall.

So home to the office; and thence to Sir W. Batten and spent the evening at supper; and among other discourse, the rashness of Sir. Jo Lawson for breeding up his daughter so high and proud – refusing a man of great interest, Sir W Berkely, to match her with a melancholy fellow, Collonell Nortons son, of no interest nor good-nature nor generosity at all – giving her 6000*l*, when the other would have taken her with two.[3] When he himself knew that he was not worth the money himself in all the world, he did give her that portion – and is sence dead, and left his wife and two daughters beggars, and the other gone away with 6000*l* and no content in it, through the ill qualities of her father-in-law and husband, who it seems, though a pretty woman, contracted for her as if he had been buying a horse. And worst of all, is now of no use to serve the mother and two little sisters in any stead at Court; whereas the other might have done what

1. Backwell (the goldsmith–banker) was in Flanders until December, arranging the payment of subsidies to the King's allies. A warrant for £1750 from the secret-service moneys was issued to him on 27 June: *CSPD 1664–5*, p. 447. The run on his bank was stopped by grants from the Exchequer: *CTB*, i. 677. He well knew that his bankruptcy would have been disastrous to the government: see e.g. his remarks below, vii. 214–15. See also below, pp. 163, 165, 171; *CSPD 1664–5*, pp. 508, 509, 580; *CTB*, i. 677, 678, 684–5, 688; Sir A. E. Feavearyear, *Pound Sterling*, p. 103.

2. Brouncker lived in the Piazza, Covent Garden.

3. She had married Daniel Norton, of Southwick, Hants., who died in August 1666 leaving his widow a jointure of £800 p.a.: see below, vii. 264. Sir William Berkeley was brother of the late Earl of Falmouth, who had been Keeper of the Privy Purse and one of the King's closest friends.

he would for her. So here is an end of this family's pride –
which with good care might have been what they would, and
done well.

Thence, weary of this discourse as the act of the greatest rashness that ever I heard of in all my little conversation, we parted,
and I home to bed.

Sir W Pen, it seems, sailed last night from Soldbay with *a* about
60 sail of ships, and my Lord Sandwich in the *Prince*, and some
others it seems *b* going after them to overtake them, for I am sure
my Lord Sandwich will do all possible to overtake them, and will
be troubled to the heart if he do it not.

7. Up, and having set my neighbour Mr. Hudson, wine
cooper, at work drawing out a tierce of wine for the sending
of some of it to my wife – I abroad, only taking notice to what a
condition it hath pleased God to bring me, that at this time I have
two tierces of claret – two quarter-cask of canary, and a smaller
vessel of sack – a vessel of tent, another of Malaga, and another of
white wine, all in my wine-cellar together – which I believe
none of my friends* ⟨of my name⟩ now alive ever had of his own
at one time.

To Westminster, and there with Mr. Povy and Creed talking
of our Tanger business. And by and by I drow Creed aside,
and acquainted him with what Sir G. Carteret did tell me about
Backewell the other day – because he hath money of his in his
hands. So home, taking some new books, 5*l* worth, home, to
my great content. At home all the day after, busy. Some
excellent discourse and advice of Sir W Warrens in the afternoon; at night home to look over my new books, and so late
to bed.

8. All day very diligent at the office. Ended my letters by
9 at night, and then fitted myself to go down to Woolwich to
my wife; which I did, calling at Sir G. Carteret's at Deptford[1]
and there hear that my Lady Sandwich is come but not very well.
By 12 a-clock to Woolwich; found my wife asleep in bed.
But strange, to think what a fine night I had down, but before

a MS. 'without' *b* repl. 'some'

---

1. An official residence in the royal dockyard.

I had been one minute on shore, the mightiest storm came of wind and rain that almost could be for a quarter of an hour, and so left. I to bed, being the first time I came to her lodgings – and there lodged well.

9. *Lords day*. Very pleasant with her and among my people while she made her ready; and about 10[a] a-clock by water to Sir G. Carteret, and there find my Lady in her chamber; not very well, but looks the worst almost that ever I did see her in my life – it seems her drinking of the water at Tunbridge did almost kill her before she could with most violent physic get it out of her body again. We are received with most extraordinary kindness by my Lady Carteret and her children, and dined most nobly; Sir G. Carteret went to Court this morning; after dinner I took occasion to have much discourse with Mr. Ph. Carteret, and find him a very modest man, and I think verily of mighty good nature – and pretty understanding. He did give me a good account of the fight with the Dutch. My Lady Sandwich dined in her chamber.

About 3 a-clock I, leaving my wife there, took boat and home, and there shifted myself into my black silk suit; and having promised Harman yesterday, I to his house, which I find very mean, and mean company.[1] His wife very ill; I could not see her. Here I, with her father and Kate Joyce, who was also very ill, were godfathers and godmother to his boy, and was christened Will. Mr. Meriton[2] christened it. The most observable thing I found there, to my content, was to hear him and his clerk tell me that in this parish of Michells Cornhill, one of the middlemost parishes and a great one of the town, there hath, notwithstanding this sickliness, been buried of any disease, man, woman, or child, not one for thirteen months last past; which very strange.[3] And

a repl. '10'

---

1. Philip Harman, upholsterer, had married Mary Bromfield, cousin of the Joyces. Though in Cornhill, one of the richest wards in the city, his house had only four hearths, Thomas Harman, next door, having only three. (R).

2. John Meriton, Rector of St

Michael's, Cornhill. The mother was buried on 18 July: *Harl. Soc. Reg.*, vii. 254.

3. There had been several burials, presumably from natural causes: GL, A.1.5, no. 96. The clerk in 1662 was Daniel Hinson: GL, MS. 10942/1.

the like in a good degree in most other parishes, I hear, saving only of the plague in them. But in this, neither the plague nor any other disease.

So back again home, and reshifted myself and so down to my Lady Carterets, where mighty merry and great pleasantness*a* between my Lady Sandwich and the young ladies and me; and all of us mighty merry, there never*b* having been in the whole world, sure, a greater business of general content then this match proposed between Mr. Carter[e]t and my Lady Jemimah. But withal, it is mighty pretty to think how my poor Lady Sandwich, between her and me, is doubtful whether her daughter will like of it or no, and how troubled she is for fear of it; which I do not fear at all and desire her not to do it. But her fear is the most discreet and pretty that ever I did see.

Late here; and then my wife and I, with most hearty kindness from my Lady Carteret*c*, by boat to Woolwich; came thither about 12 at night, and so to bed.

10. Up, and with great pleasure looking over a nest of puppies of Mr. Sheldens,[1] with which my wife is most extraordinarily pleased, and one of them is promised her. Anon I took my leave, and away by water to the Duke of Albemarles, where he tells me that I must be at Hampton Court anon.[2] So I home to look over my Tanger papers; and having a coach of Mr. Povy's attending me by appointment, in order to my coming to dine at his country house at Branford,[3] where he and his family is, I went, and Mr. Tasbrough[4] with me, therein, it being a pretty chariot but most inconvenient as to the horses*d* throwing dirt and dust into one's eyes and upon one's clothes. There I stayed a quarter of an hour, Creed being there, and being able to do little business (but the less the better); Creed rode before, and Mr. Povy and I after him in the chariot. And I was set down by

a repl. 'discourse'   *b* repl. 'being'   *c* repl. 'Sandwich'
d l.h. repl. s.h. 'd'-

---

1. Clerk of the Cheque, Woolwich, with whom Mrs Pepys was lodging.

2. The court had gone there on the 9th.

3. The Priory, Hounslow, near Brentford, Mdx. Thomas Povey's father, Justinian, Auditor of the Exchequer, had bought it in 1625; he himself sold it in 1671: D. Lysons, *Environs of London* (1792–1811), ii. 38.

4. One of Povey's clerks.

him at the parke pale, where one of his saddle-horses was[a] ready for me – he himself not daring to come into the house or be seen, because that a servant of his, out of his house, happened to be sick; but is not yet dead but was never suffered to come into his house after he was ill. But this opportunity was taken to injure Povy; and most horribly he is abused by some persons hereupon, and his fortune I believe quite broke, but that he hath a good heart to bear, or a cunning one to conceal his evil. There I met with Sir Wm. Coventry, and by and by was heard by my Lord Chancellor and Treasurer about our Tanger money; and my Lord Treasurer had ordered me to forbear meddling with the 15000*l* he offered me the other day,[1] but upon opening the case to them, they did offer it again, and so I think I shall have it; but my Lord Generall must give his consent in it, this money having been promised to him – and he very angry at the proposal.[b]

Here, though I have not been in many years, yet I lack time to stay, besides that it is, I perceive, an unpleasing thing to be at Court, everybody being fearful one of another; and all so sad, enquiring after the plague – so that I stole away by my horse to Kingston, and there with much trouble was forced to press two sturdy rogues to carry me to London; and met at the waterside with Mr. Charnocke, Sir[c] Phillip Warwicke's clerk, who had been with company and was quite foxed. I took him with me in my boat, and so away to Richmond and there by night walked with him to Moreclack, a very pretty walk; and there stayed a good while,[2] now and then talking and sporting with Nan the servant, who says she is a seaman's wife; and at last bade good-night.

11. And so all night down by water, a most pleasant passage, and came thither by 2 a-clock; and so walked from the Old Swan home, and there to bed to my Will – being very weary, and he lodging at my desire in my house.

At 6[d] a-clock up, and to Westminster (where, and all the town besides I hear, the plague encreases); and it being too soon to go

---

a repl. 'stayed'   *b* followed by two blank pages   *c* repl. 'Mr.'   *d* repl. '7'

1. See above, p. 137 & n. 2.   (built 1662), or one on the site of the
2. Sc. at an inn, which may have present Ship Hotel.
been the White Hart, Mortlake

to the Duke of Albemarle, I to the Harp and Ball and there made a bargain with Mary to go forth with me in the afternoon, which she with much ado consented to. So I to the Duke of Albemarle, and there with much ado did get his consent in part to my having the money promised for Tanger; and the other part did not concur.[1] So being displeased with this, I back to the office and there sat alone a while doing business; and then by a solemn invitation, to the Trinity-house, where a great dinner and company; Captain Dobbins's feast for Elder Brother. But I broke up before the dinner half-over, and by agreement by water to the Harp and Ball; and thence had Mary meet me at the New Exchange, and there took coach and I with great pleasure took the ayre to Highgate and thence to Hamsted. Much pleased with her company, pretty and innocent, and had what pleasure almost I would with her; and so at night, weary and sweaty, it being very hot beyond bearing, we back again and I set her down in St. Martins Lane; and so I to the evening Change and there hear, all the town full, that Ostend is delivered to us, and that Alderman Backewell did go with 50000*l* to that purpose.[2] But the truth of it I do not know; but something I believe there is extraordinary in his going. So to the office, where I did what I could as to letters; and so away to bed, shifting myself and taking some Venice Treakle,[3] feeling myself out of order, and there to bed to sleep.

12. After doing what business I could in the morning, it being a solemn fast-day for the plague growing upon us,[4] I took boat and down to Deptford, where I stood with great pleasure an hour or two by my Lady Sandwiches bedside, talking to her (she lying prettily in bed) of my Lady Jemimah's being from my Lady Pickerings when our letters came to that place, she being at my Lord Montagu's at Boughton. The truth is, I had received

1. It was a question of allocating certain excise revenues; Albemarle still claimed some for the army. Cf. *CTB*, i. 682 (warrant, 7 September).

2. A canard; for Backwell's journey, see above, p. 150 & n. 1.

3. A panacea: see above, iv. 39, n. 2.

4. A proclamation of 6 July appointed 12 July and every first Wednesday in each month a fast day in London, Westminster and the places adjacent: Steele, no. 3426. Service in *A form of common prayer for the averting of Gods heavy visitation* . . . (1665).

letters of it two days ago, but had dropped them and was in a very extraordinary strait what to do for them, or what account to give my Lady.   But sent to every place; I sent to Moreclacke, where I had been the night*a* before, and there they were found, which with mighty joy came safe to me.   But all ending with satisfaction to my Lady and me, though I find my Lady Carteret not much pleased with this delay, and principally because of the plague, which renders it unsafe to stay long at Deptford; I eat a bit (my Lady Carteret being the most kind lady in the world) and so took boat, and a fresh boat at the Tower, and so up the River, against tide all the way, I having lost it by staying prating to and with my Lady.   And from before*b* one, made it 7 ere we got to Hampton Court; and when I came there, all business was over, saving my finding Mr. Coventry at his Chamber; and with him a good while about several businesses at his chamber, and so took leave and away to my boat; and all night upon the water, staying a while with Nan*c* at Moreclack, very much pleased and merry with her; and so on homeward and came home by 2 a-clock (shooting the bridge at that time of night) and so to bed – where I find Will is not, he staying at Woolwich to*d* come with my wife to dinner tomorrow to my Lady Carterets.   ⟨I heard Mr. Williamson repeat at Hampton Court today how the King of France hath lately set out a most high arrest against the Pope, which is reckoned very lofty and high.⟩*e1*

13. Lay long, being sleepy; and then up to the office, my Lord Brunker (after his sickness) being come to the office, and did what business there was; and so I by water, at night late, to Sir G Carterets.   But there being no oares to carry me, I was fain to call a Sculler that had a gentleman already in it; and he proved a man of love to Musique and he and I sung together the way down – with great pleasure, and an accident extraordinary to be met with.   There came to Dinner, they having dined, but

---

a repl. 'two nights'   *b* repl. same symbol badly formed   *c* repl. 'Mary'
  d repl. 'he coming'   *e* addition crowded in between entries

---

1. Probably the *arrêt* of the Parlement (not the King), 13/23 June, forbidding the clergy to receive the anti-Jansenist papal bull of 5/15 February: see C. Gérin, *Louis XIV et le Saint-Siège*, ii, esp. pp. 7–8. Joseph Williamson was secretary to Arlington.

my Lady caused*ᵃ* something to be brought for me and I dined well, and mighty merry, especially my Lady Slany and I about eating of Creame and brown bread – which she loves as much as I. Thence, after long discourse with them and my Lady alone, I and wife, who by agreement met me here, took leave; and I saw my wife a little way down (it troubling me that this absence makes us a little strange instead of more fond) and so parted, and I home to some letters and then home to bed. Above 700*ᵇ* dead of the plague this week.[1]

14. Up, and all the morning at the Exchequer endeavouring to strike tallies for money for Tanger; and mightily vexed to see how people attend there, some out of town and others drowsy; and to others it was late, so that the King's business suffers ten times more then all their service is worth – so I am put off to tomorrow. Thence to the Old Exchange by water and there bespoke two fine shirts of my pretty seamstress, who, she tells me, serves Jacke Fenn.[2] Upon the Change, all the news is that guns have been heard, and that news is come by a Dane that my Lord was in view of De Ruter, and that since his parting from my Lord of Sandwich he hath hear[d] guns. But little of it do I think true. So home to dinner, where Povy by agreement; and after dinner we to talk of our Tanger matters – about keeping our profit at*ᶜ* the pay and victualling of the garrison, if the present undertakers[3] should leave it – wherein I did nor will do anything unworthy me and any just man; but they being resolved to quit it, it is fit I should suffer Mr. Povy to do what he can with Mr. Gawden about it to our profit. Thence to the discoursing of putting some sums of money in order and tallies, which we did pretty well. So he in the evening gone, I by water to Sir G. Carteret, and there find my Lady Sandwich and her buying things for my Lady Jem's wedding. And my Lady Jem is

a repl. 'understood'   *b* repl. '700*l*'   *c* MS. 'at to'

1. 725 in the week 4–11 July: GL, A.1.5, no. 96.

2. Fenn was the son of the paymaster to the Navy Treasurer; the sempstress was Mary Batelier.

3. John Lanyon and partners: see above, v. 226.

beyond expectation come to Dagenhams,[1] where Mr. Carteret is to go to visit her tomorrow; and my proposal of waiting on him, he being to go alone to all persons strangers to him, was well accepted and so I go with him.[2] But Lord, to see how kind my Lady Carteret is to her – sends her most rich Jewells, and provides bedding and things of all sorts most richly for her – which makes my Lady and me out of our wits almost, to see the kindness she treats us all with – as if they would buy the young lady.

Thence away home; and foreseeing my being abroad two days, did sit up late, making of letters ready against tomorrow and other things; and so to bed – to be up betimes by the help of a larum-wach, which by chance I borrowed of my watchmaker today while my own is mending.[3]

15. Up, and after all business done at the office, though late, I to Deptford. But before I went out of the office, saw there young Bagwells wife returned; but could not stay to speak to her, though I had a great mind to it. And also another great lady, as to fine clothes, did attend there to have a ticket signed; which I did do, taking her through the garden to my office, where I signed it and had a salute of her; and so I away by boat to Redriffe, and thence walked; and after dinner, at Sir G. Carteret, where they stayed till almost 3 a-clock for me; and anon took boat, Mr. Carteret and I, to the ferry-place at Greenwich[4] and there stayed an hour, after crossing the water to and again to get our coach and horses over, and by and by set out and so toward Dagenham. But Lord, what silly discourse we had by the way

1. Dagnams, Essex, the home of Lady Wright, widow of Sir Henry Wright (d. 1663) and Lady Jemima Mountagu's aunt. The house (pulled down and rebuilt in the late 18th century; now demolished) had been built by Sir Henry: P. Morant, *Essex* (1768), i. 62. It stood about three miles from the village of Dagenham, on part of what is now the Harold Hill Estate.

2. It was common, in days when marriages were arranged between families, for courtship to be super-vised by a family adviser in this way. John Locke saw Shaftesbury's son through his courtship in 1669, just as Pepys now helped Lady Jemima: K. H. D. Haley, *Shaftesbury*, p. 223.

3. Alarm-watches are almost as old as watches themselves.

4. A ferry from Greenwich to the Isle of Dogs, capable of taking horses or vehicles, had existed at least since 1592. Another, from Deptford to the Isle of Dogs, is mentioned by Pepys at 20, 24 and 31 July. (R).

as to matter of love-matters, he being the most awkerd man I
ever I met withal in my life as to that business. Thither we came
by time it begin to be dark, and were kindly received by my Lady
Wright and my Lord Crew; and to discourse they went, my
Lord discoursing with him, asking of him questions of Travell,
which he answered well enough in a few words. But nothing
to the lady from him at all. To supper, and after supper to talk
again, he yet taking no notice of the lady. My Lord would have
had me have consented to leaving the young people together
tonight to begin their amours, his staying being but to be little.
But I advised against it, lest the lady might be too much surprized.[1]
So they led him up to his chamber, where I stayed a little to
know how he liked the lady; which he told me he did mightily,
but Lord, in the dullest insipid manner that ever lover did. So I
bid him good-night, and down to prayers with my Lord Crew's
family. And after prayers, my Lord and Lady Wright and I to
consult what to do; and it was agreed at last to have them go to
church together as*a* the family used to do, though his lameness
was a great objection against it; but at last my Lady Jem sent
me word by my Lady Wright that it would be better to do
just as they used to do before his coming, and therefore she
desired to go to church – which was yielded then to.

16. *Lords day.* I up, having lain with Mr. Moore in the
Chaplins chamber. And having trimmed myself, down to Mr.
Carteret; and he being ready, we down and walked in the
gallery an hour or two, it being a most noble and pretty house that
ever for the bigness I saw.[2] Here I taught him what to do; to
take the lady alway by the hand to lead her; and telling him that
I would find opportunity to leave them two together, he should
make these and these compliments, and also take a time to do the
like to my Lord Crew and Lady Wright. After I had instructed
him, which he thanked me for, owning that he needed my
teaching him, my Lord Crew came down and family, the young
lady among the rest; and so by coaches to church, four mile off –
where a pretty good sermon – and a declaration of penitence of a

a repl. 'as they used'

1. The shyness of both lovers was
perhaps due to poor health: Philip
Carteret was lame, and Lady Jemima

had suffered from a deformation of
the neck. He was 24; she 17.
2. See above, p. 158, n. 1.

man that had undergone the Church censure for his wicked life.[1]

Thence back again by coach – Mr. Carteret having not had the confidence to take his lady once by the hand, coming or going; which I told him of when we came home, and he will hereafter do it. So to dinner. My Lord excellent discourse. Then to walk in the gallery and to sit down. By and by my Lady Wright and I go out (and then my Lord Crew, he not by design); and lastly my Lady Crew came out and left the young people together. And a little pretty daughter of my Lady Wright's most innocently came out afterward, and shut the door to, as if she had done it, poor child, by inspiration – which made us without have good sport to laugh at.

They together an hour; and by and by church-time, whither he led her into the coach and into the church; and so at church all the afternoon. Several handsome ladies at church – but it was most extraordinary hot that ever I knew it.

So home again and to walk in the gardens, where we left the young couple a second time; and my Lady Wright and I to walk together, who to my trouble tells me that my Lady Jem must have something done to her body by Scott before she can be married, and therefore care must be had to send him – also, that some more new clothes must of necessity be made her, which, and other things, I took care of.

Anon to supper, and excellent discourse and dispute between my Lord Crew and the Chaplin,[2] who is a good Scholler but a nonconformist.

Here this[a] evening I spoke with Mrs. Carter, my old acquaintance that hath lived with my Lady these twelve or thirteen years, the sum of all whose discourse, and others for her, is that I would get her [a] good husband; which I have promised, but know not when I shall perform.

After Mr. Carteret carried to his chamber, we to prayers again and then to bed.

17. Up, all of us, and to Billiards – my Lady Wright, Mr. Carter[e]t, myself and everybody. By and by the young couple

a repl. 'in'

---

1. Public penance was still imposed by church courts, usually for sexual offences. It was occasionally com- muted. The church was St Peter's, South Weald.

2. Unidentified.

left together. Anon to dinner, and after dinner Mr. Carteret took my advice about giving to the servants, and I led him to give 10*l* among them, which he did by leaving it to the chief man-servant, Mr. Medows, to do for him. Before we went, I took my Lady Jem apart and would know how she liked this gentleman and whether she was under any difficulty concerning him. She blushed and hid her face awhile, but at last I forced her to tell me; she answered that she could readily obey what her father and mother had done – which was all she could say or I expect.

So anon took leave and for London. But Lord, to see, among other things, how all these great people here are afeared of London, being doubtful of anything that comes from thence or that hath lately been there, that I was forced to say that I lived wholly at Woolwich.

In our way Mr. Carteret did give me mighty thanks for my care and pains for him, and is mightily pleased – though the truth is, my Lady Jem hath carried herself with mighty discretion and gravity, not being forward at all in any degree but mighty serious in her answers to him, as by what he says and I observed, I collect.*

To London to my office and there took letters from the office, where all well; and so to the bridge, and there he and I took boat and to Deptford, where mighty welcome, and brought the good news of all being pleased to them.

Mighty mirth at my giving them an account of all; but the young man could not be got to say one word before me or my Lady Sandwich of his adventures; but by what he afterward related to his father and mother and sisters, he gives an account that pleases them mightily.

Here Sir G. Carteret would have me lie all night, which I did most nobly, better then ever I did in my life – Sir G. Carteret being mighty kind to me, leading me to my chamber; and all their care now is to have the business ended; and they have reason, because the sickness puts all out of order and they cannot safely stay where they are.

18. Up, and to the office, where all the morning. And so to my house and eat a bit of victuals; and so to the Change, where a little business, and a very thin Exchange; and so walked through London to the Temple, where I took water for Westminster to

the Duke of Albemarle to wait on him; and so to Westminster hall and there paid for my news-books and did give Mrs. Michell (who is going out of town because of the sickness) and her husband a pint of wine. And so Sir W Warren coming to me by appointment, we away by water home, by the way discoursing about the project I have of getting some money, and doing the King good service too, about the mast-dock at Woolwich, which I fear will never be done if I do not go about it.[1]

After despatching letters at the office, I by water down to Deptford, where I stayed a little while; and by water to my wife, whom I have not seen six or five days. And there supped with her and mighty pleasant, and saw with content her drawings and so to bed mighty merry. I was much troubled this day to hear at Westminster how the officers do bury the dead in the open Tuttle-fields, pretending want of room elsewhere; whereas the New-Chapel church-yard was walled in at the public charge in the last plague-time[2] merely for want of room, and now none but such as are able to pay dear for it can be buried there.

19. Up, and to the office; and thence presently to the Exchequer and there with much trouble got my tallies; and afterward took Mr. Falconbr[idge], Spicer, and another or two to the Leg and there gave them a dinner; and so with my tallies and about 30 dozen of bags, which it seems are my due, having paid the fees as if I had received the money – I away home; and after a little stay, down by water to Deptford, where I find all full of joy, and preparing to go to Dagenham tomorrow. To supper, and after supper to talk without end. Very late, I went away, it raining, but I had un design pour aller à la femme de Bagwell;[a] and did so, mais ne savais obtener algún cosa de ella como jo quisiere sino tocarla. So away about 12; and it raining hard, I back to Sir G. Carteret, and there called up the page and to bed there – being all in a most violent sweat.

---

a s.h.

---

1. A creek was now being used there for masts. In 1669 a mast-house was built (PRO, Adm. 20/7/1, p. 94; ib., 20/12, no. 12); a mast-dock was not constructed until 1784 (E. Hasted, *Hist. Kent*, ed. Drake, i. 154).

2. In 1647, when 3597 victims died: Bell, *Plague*, p. 5. The New Chapel was in Orchard St, Westminster.

20. Up in a boat, among other people, to the Tower, and there to the office, where we sat all the morning. So down to Deptford and there dined; and after dinner saw my Lady Sand-wich and Mr. Carteret and his two sisters over the water, going to Dagenhams, and my Lady Carteret toward Cranburne.¹ So all the company broke up in most extraordinary joy – wherein I am mighty contented that I have had the good fortune to be so instrumental, and I think it will be of good use to me. So walked to Redriffe, where I hear the sickness is, and endeed is scattered almost everywhere – there dying 1089 of the plague this week.² My Lady Carteret did this day give me a bottle of plague-water³ [to take] home with me. So home to write letters late, and then home to bed, where I have not lain these three or four nights. I received yesterday a letter from my Lord Sandwich, giving me thanks for my care about their marriage business and desiring it to be despatched, that no disappointment may happen therein – which I will help on all I can. This afternoon I waited on the Duke of Albemarle; and so*ᵃ* to Mrs. Crofts, where I found and saluted Mrs. Burrows, who is a very pretty woman for a mother of so many children. But Lord, to see how the plague spreads; it being now all over Kings-street, at the Axe and the next door to it, and in other places.

21. Up, and abroad to the goldsmiths to see what money I could get upon my present tallies upon the advance of the Excize, and I hope I shall get 10000*l*. I went also and had them entered at the Excize Office. Alderman Backewell is at sea. Sir R Viner came to town but this morning – so Covill was the only man I could yet speak withal to get any money of. Met with Mr. Povy, and I with him and dined at the Custome-house tavern, there to talk of our Tanger business, and Stockedale and Hewet with us.⁴ So abroad to several places; among others, to Anth. Joyces and there broke to him my desire to have Pall

a repl. 'there'

---

1. Carteret (appointed Keeper of Windsor Forest in October 1664) had an official residence at Cranbourne Lodge, Berks.
2. In the week 11–18 July.

3. Probably a distillation of herbs. There is a recipe in HMC, *Rawdon Hastings*, iv. 346.
4. Robert Stockdale and Simon Hewitt were London merchants.

married to Harman (whose wife, poor woman, is lately dead, to my trouble, I loving her very much), and he will consider it.[1]

So home, and late at my Chamber, setting some papers in order, the plague growing very raging and my apprehensions of it great. So very late, to bed.

22. As soon as*[a]* up, I among my goldsmiths, Sir Rob. Viner and Colvill, and there got 10000*l* of my new tallies accepted; and so I made it my work to find out Mr. Mervin,[2] and sent for others to come with their bills of exchange, as Captain Hewett, &c; and sent for Mr. Jackson but he was not in town. So all the morning at the office; and after dinner, which was very late, I to Sir R Viner's (by his invitation in the morning) and got near 5000*l* more accepted. And so from this day, the whole, or near 15000*l*, lies upon interest. Thence I by water to Westminster; and the Duke of Albemarle being gone to dinner to my Lord of Canterburys, I thither and there walked and viewed the new Hall, a new old-fashion Hall, as much as possible – begun, and means left for the ending of it, by Bishop Juxon.[3] Not coming prepare[d] to speak with him, I to Fox-hall, where to the Spring-garden, but I do not see one guest there – the town being so empty of anybody to come thither – only, while I was there, a poor woman came to scold with the maister of the house that a kinswoman, I think, of hers, that was newly dead of the plague,

---

a repl. 'soon'

---

1. Pepys pursued this plan for almost a year, but nothing came of it. Philip Harman's wife had died in childbed and had been buried only three days before: above, p. 152 & n. 1.

2. John Mervin, now paid £400 for supplies to Tangier: PRO, Ao1/310/1220.

3. Lambeth Palace had suffered much during the Interregnum: the house being divided into tenements, the High Commission Court made into a dancing-school, and part of the chapel into a dining hall. The Great Hall itself (dating largely from the 13th century) had been de-

stroyed. It was now rebuilt at a cost of over £10,000 by money provided by Archbishop Juxon (d. 1663), on the original site and in the original style – Pepys's 'new old-fashion' – 'nor could all the Persuasions of Men versed in Architecture and his Friends, induce him to rebuild it in the modern way, and unite it to the Library, though it would have cost less money': Aubrey, *Nat. hist. and antiq. Surrey* (1719, 1718), v. 273. In his will Juxon required his heir to complete it. See *CSPD 1670*, p. 685; D. Gardiner, *Story of Lambeth Palace*, pp. 174–5.

might be buried in the churchyard; for, for her part, she should not be buried in the Commons[1] as they said she should.

Back to Whitehall; and by and by comes the Duke of Albemarle, and there, after a little discourse, I by coach home, not meeting with but two coaches and but two carts from Whitehall to my own house – that I could observe – and the streets mighty thin of people.

I met this noon with Dr Burnett, who told me, and I find in the news-book this week that he posted upon the Change, that whoever did spread[a] that report that instead of the plague, his servant was by him killed, it was forgery; and showed me the acknowledgment of the maister of the Pest-house that his servant died of a Bubo on his right groine, and two Spots on his right thigh, which is[b] the plague.[2]

To my office, where late writing letters and getting myself prepared with business for Hampton Court tomorrow. And so, having caused a good pullet to be got for my supper all alone, I very late to bed.

All the news is great that we must of necessity fall out with France, for he will side with the Dutch against us. That Alderman Backewell is gone over (which endeed he is) with money, and that Oastend is in our present possession.[3] But it is strange to see how poor Alderman Backewell is like to be put to it in his absence – Mr. Shaw his right-hand being ill. And the Aldermans absence gives doubts to people, and I perceive they are in great straits for money, besides what Sir G. Carteret told me about fourteen days ago.[4]

Our fleet under my Lord Sandwich being about the Latitude $55\frac{1}{2}$ (which is a great secret) to the Northward of the Texell.

So to bed very late. In my way I called upon Sir W Turner and at Mr. Shelcrosses (but he was not at home, having left his

---

a symbol blotted   *b* repl. 's'-

---

1. For burials in common ground ('plague pits'), see Bell, *Plague*, pp. 36, 39.

2. *The Intelligencer*, 17 July, pp. 593–4. The servant, William Pas-

son, was one of the first victims of the plague in the city itself. Cf. above, p. 124.

3. Cf. above, p. 155 & n. 2.

4. See above, p. 150.

bill with Sir W Turner),[1] that so I may prove I did what I could as soon as I had money to answer all bills.

23. *Lord's day.* Up very betimes, called by Mr. Cutler by appointment, and with him in his coach ⟨and four horses⟩ over London Bridge to Kingston, a very pleasant Journy, and at Hampton Court by 9 a-clock. In our way, very good and various discourse, as he is a man that though I think he be a knave, as the world thinks him, yet a man of great experience and worthy-to-be-heard discourse.[2] When we came there, we to Sir W Coventrys chamber and there discoursed long*a* with him, he and I alone, the other being gone away. And so walked together through the garden to the house, where we parted, I observing with a little trouble that he is too great now to expect too much familiarity with, and he I find doth not mind me as he used to do; but when I reflect upon him and his business, I cannot think much of it –*b* for I do not observe anything but the same great kindness from him. I fallowed the King to chapel, and there hear a good sermon; and after sermon, with my Lord Arlington, Sir Tho. Ingram and others, spoke to the Duke about Tanger, but not to much purpose. I was not invited anywhither to dinner, though a stranger, which did also trouble me; but yet I must remember it is a Court, and endeed where most are strangers; but however, Cutler carried me to Mr. Marriotts the house-keeper, and there we had a very good dinner and good company; among others, Lilly the painter.

Thence to the Councell Chamber, where in a back room I sat all the afternoon; but the Council begun late to sit, and spent most of the time upon Morisco's Tarr=business.[3] They sat long, and

a followed by blot   *b* followed by blot

---

1. John Shalcross was a West-minster draper; Sir William Turner (an alderman of the city and a relative of Pepys by marriage) was a cloth merchant.

2. William Cutler was a much-travelled merchant and had served as a navy victualler. For what appears to be a reference to his sharp practice, see above, v. 52.

3. Presumably a committee meeting not recorded in the Council register. The dispute has not been identified with certainty. Morisco monopolised the importation of Stockholm tar and had once attempted to overcharge the Navy Board: see Pepys's notes (16 June 1664, 8 February 1665) in NWB, pp. 50, 79.

I forced to fallow Sir T. Ingram, the Duke, and others, so that when I got free and came to look for Cutler, he was gone with his coach, without leaving any word with anybody to tell me so – so that I was forced with great trouble to walk up*ᵃ* and down looking of him, and at last forced to get a boat to carry me to Kingston; and there, after eating a bit at a neat Inne, which pleased me well, I took*ᵇ* boat, and slept all the way without intermission from thence to Queenhive; where it being about 2 a-clock, too late and too soon to go home to bed, I lay*ᶜ* and ⟪24.⟫ slept till about 4. And then up*ᵈ* and home; and there dressed myself and by appointment to Deptford to Sir G. Carteret between 6 and 7 a-clock, where I found him and my Lady almost ready; and by and by went over to the Ferry and took coach and six horses nobly for Dagenhams, himself and Lady and their little daughter Louisonne[1] and myself in the coach – where when we came, we were bravely entertained and spent the day most pleasantly with the young ladies, and I so merry as never more. Only, for want of sleep, and drinking of strange beer, had a rheum in one of my eyes which troubled me much. Here with great content all the day, as I think I ever passed a day in my life, because of the contentfulness of our errand – and the nobleness of the company and our manner of going. But I find Mr. Carteret yet as backward almost in his caresses as he was the first day. At night, about 7 a-clock, took coach again; but Lord, to see in what a pleasant humour Sir G. Carteret hath been, both coming and going; so light, so fond, so merry, so boyish (so much content he takes in this business), it is one of the greatest wonders I ever saw in my mind. But once, in serious discourse, he did say that if he knew his son to be a debauch, as many and most are nowadays about the Court, he would tell it, and my Lady Jem should not have him. And so enlarged, both he and she, about the baseness and looseness of the Court, and told several stories of the Duke of MonMouth and Richmond. And some great person ⟨my Lord of Ormonds second son⟩ married to a lady of extraordinary Quality (fit and that might have made a wife for the King himself) about six

---

a repl. 'upon'   *b* repl. 'boat'   *c* repl. 'sl'-   *d* repl. 'having'

---

1. Louisa-Margaretta.

months since, that this great person hath given the pox to.[1]   And
discoursed how much this would oblige the Kingdom if the
King would banish some of these great persons publicly from the
Court – and wished it with all their hearts.

We set out so late that it grew dark, so as we doubted the
losing of our way; and a long time it was or seemed before we
could get to the waterside, and that about 11 at night; where
when we come, all merry (only, my eye troubled me as I said),
we find no ferry-boat was there nor no Oares to carry us to
Deptford.   However[a], afterward oares was called from the other
side at Greenwich; but when it came, a frolic, being mighty
merry, took us, and there we would sleep all night in the Coach
in the Isle of Doggs; so we did, there being now with us my Lady
Scott[2] – and with great pleasure drew up the glasses and slept
till daylight; and then some victuals and wine being brought us –
we eat a bit, and so up and took boat, merry as might be; and
when come to Sir G. Carteret, there all to bed – our good
《25.》 humour in everybody continuing; and there I slept till
7 a-clock, then up, and to the office well refreshed, my eye only
troubling me, which by keeping a little covered with my hanker-
cher and washing now and then with cold water grew better by
night.   At noon to the Change, which was very thin; and thence
homeward and was called in by Mr. Rawlinson, with whom I
dined, and some good company, very harmlessly merry.   But
sad the story of the plague in the City, it growing mightily.   This
day my Lord Bruncker did give me Mr. Grant's book upon the
Bills of Mortality, new-printed and enlarged.[3]

Thence to my office awhile, full of business; and thence by
coach to the Duke of Albemarle's, not meeting one coach going
nor coming from my house thither and back again, which is very

---

a repl. 'so'

---

1. Lord Richard Butler, second sur-
viving son of Ormond, had married
Mary, sister and heiress of Esmé, 2nd
Duke of Richmond (of the Lennox
branch of the Stuart family). Pepys's
allusion here helps to determine the
date of this marriage which GEC
fixes at 'before 16 March 1666/7'.
Gramont (pp. 99–100) speaks of him
as a 'lover who had met with tolerable success'.

2. Carteret's daughter.

3. See above, iii. 52, n. 1. This
was the 3rd edition issued by order
of the Royal Society, of which
Brouncker, Pepys and the author
were fellows. A 4th edition appeared later in the year.

strange. One of my chief errands was to speak to Sir W. Clerke[1] about my wife's brother, who importunes me, and I doubt he doth want me. But I can do little for him there as to imployment in the army, and out of my purse I dare not, for fear of a precedent, and let[ting] him come often to me is troublesome, and dangerous too, he living in the dangerous part of the town.[2] But I will do what I can possibly for him, and as soon as I can.

Mightily troubled all this afternoon with people's coming to me about bills of Exchange and my assigning them upon my goldsmith; but I did send for them all, and hope to ease myself this week of all that clamour.

These two or three days, Mr. Shaw at Alderman Backewell's hath lain sick, like*a* to die, and is feared will not live a day to an end.

At night home and to bed – my head full of business. And among others this day, came a letter to me from Paris from my Lord Hinchingbrooke about his coming over; and I have sent this night an order from the Duke of Albemarle for a ship of 36 guns to [go] to Calais to fetch him.[3]

26. **Up**; and after doing a little business, down to Deptford with Sir W. Batten – and there left him, and I to Greenwich to the park, where I hear the King and Duke are come by water this morn from Hampton Court. They asked me several Questions. The King mightily pleased with his new buildings there.[4] I fallowed them to Castles ship in building[5] and there met Sir W. Batten; and thence to Sir G. Carteret, where all the morning with them – they not having any but the Duke of Monmouth and Sir W. Killigrew, and one gentleman and a page more. Great variety of talk – and was often led to speak to the King and Duke. By and by they to dinner; and all to dinner and sat down to the King saving myself, which though I could not

a repl. 'more'

---

1. Secretary at War.

2. Balty St Michel lived in one of the crowded western out-parishes: Bell, *Plague*, p. 65.

3. He had been abroad since August 1661 and had written to Pepys on 15/25 July. Pepys replied on this day, addressing the letter to

Calais and giving him notice of these arrangements: BM, Harl. 7001, f. 258*r* (printed Smith, i. 94–5; and Braybrooke, 1879, vi. 99–100). He sailed on 3/13 August: Smith, i. 97.

4. At Greenwich: see above, v. 75 & n. 3.

5. See above, p. 7 & n. 2.

in modesty expect, yet God forgive my pride, I was sorry I was there, that Sir W. Batten should say that he could sit down where I could not – though he had twenty times more reason then I. But this was my pride and folly.

I down and walked with Mr. Castle, who told me the design of Ford and Rider to oppose and do all the hurt they can to Captain Taylor in his new ship, the *London*[1] – and how it comes; and that they are a couple of false persons – which I believe; and with all that, he himself is a knave too.

He and I by and by to dinner, mighty nobly; and the King having dined, he came down, and I went in the barge with him, I sitting at the door – down to Woolwich (and there I just saw and kissed my wife, and saw some of her painting, which is very curious,* and away again to the King) and back again with him in the barge, hearing him and the Duke talk and seeing and observing their manner of discourse; and God forgive me, though I adore them with all the duty possible, yet the more a man considers and observes them, the less he finds of difference between them and other men, though (blessed be God) they are both princes of great nobleness and spirits.

The Barge put me into another boat that came to our side, Mr. Holder[2] with a bag of gold to the Duke; and so they away, and I home to the office. The Duke of Monmouth is the most skittish, leaping gallant that ever I saw, alway in action, vaulting or leaping*a* or clambering.[3]

Thence, mighty full of the honour of this day – took coach and to Kate Joyce, but she not within; but*b* spoke with Anth, who tells me he likes well of my proposal for Pall to Harman; but I fear that less then 500*l* will not be taken, and that I shall not be able to give – though I did not say so to him. After a little other discourse, and the sad news of the death of so many in the parish of the plague, 40 last night – the bell alway going – I back to the Exchange, where I went up and sat talking with my beauty, Mrs. Batelier,[4] a great while, who is endeed one of the finest women I

a repl. 'laughing'   *b* repl. 'and'

1. See above, p. 53 & n. 4.

2. Thomas Holder, Auditor-General of the Duke's revenue.

3. For his athletic habits, see Gramont, p. 298; Evelyn, iv. 456.

He was now 16.

4. See above, p. 73, n. 3. She and her brother Will were soon on very friendly terms with Pepys and his wife.

ever saw in my life. After buying some small matter, I home, and there to the office – and saw Sir J. Mennes, now come from Portsmouth; I home to set my Journall for these four days in order, they being four days of as great content and honour and pleasure to me as ever I hope to live or desire or think anybody else can live. For methinks if a man could but reflect upon this, and think that all these things are*a* ordered by God Almighty to make me contented, and even*b* this very marriage now on foot is one of the things entended to find me content in in my life and matter of mirth, methinks it should make one mightily more satisfied in the world then he is. This day poor Robin Shaw at Backewells died[1] – and Backewell himself now in Flanders. The King himself asked about Shaw; and being told he was dead, said he was very sorry for it.

The Sickenesse is got into our parish this week; and is got endeed everywhere,[2] so that I begin to think of setting things in order, which I pray God enable me to put, both as to soul and body.

27. Called up at 4 a-clock. Up, and to my preparing some papers for Hampton Court; and so by water to Fox hall, and there Mr. Gaudens coach took me up; and by and by I took up him, and so both thither – a brave morning to ride in, and good discourse with him. Among others, he begun with me to speak of the Tanger Victuallers resigning their imployment, and his willingness to come on – of which I was glad, and took the opportunity to answer him with all kindness and promise of assistance. He told me, a while since my Lord Berkely did speak of it to him, and yesterday a message from Sir Tho. Ingram. When I come to Hampton Court, I find Sir T. Ingram and Creed ready with papers signed for the putting Mr. Gawden in, upon a resignation signed to by Lanyon and sent to Sir T Ingram. At this I was surprized but yet was glad; and so it passed, but

a MS. 'or'   *b* repl. 'en'-

---

1. Shaw had been a colleague of Pepys in the Exchequer before the Restoration. He had in fact died on the 25th and was buried at St Mary Woolnoth on the 26th, aged about 34.

2. In St Olave's there was one death from plague (out of a total of 1089) recorded in the bills of mortality for the week ending 25 July: GL, A.1.5, no. 96.

with respect enough to these that are in, at least without anything
ill taken from it.¹   I got another order signed about the boats,
which I think I shall get something by.²   So despatched all my
business, having assurance of continuance of all hearty love from
Sir W Coventry; and so we stayed and saw the King and
Queene set out toward Salsbury³ – and after them, the Duke and
Duchesse – whose hands I did kiss.   And it was the first time I
did ever or did see anybody else kiss her hand; and it was a most
fine white and fat hand.   But it was pretty to see the young
pretty ladies dressed like men; in velvet coats, caps with ribbands,
and with laced bands just like men – only, the Duchesse herself
it did not become.⁴   They gone, we with great content took
coach again, and hungry came to Clapham⁵ about one a-clock,
and Creed thereto before us – where a good dinner, the house
having dined; and so to walk up and down in the gardens –
mighty pleasant.   By and by comes, by promise to me, Sir G.
Carteret, and viewed the house above and below, and sat and
drank there.   And I had a little opportunity to kiss and spend
some time with the ladies above; his daughter,⁶ a buxom lass,

1. Gauden accepted the same terms
as his predecessors: Pepys to Yeabsley *et
al.*, 29 July (Rawl. A 193, ff. 211-13).
2. See above, p. 146 & n. 2.   This
was the second order this year; the
total cost was about £470: PRO, AO
1/310/1220. The boats (7-11 tons)
were used for loading and unloading.
For Pepys's gains by the transaction,
see below, p. 286.
3. The court stayed at Salisbury
until 23 September, when it moved to
Oxford.
4. This was a fashion set by the
Queen c. 1662: 'plush caps like mon-
teros, either full of ribbons or feathers
. . . and riding coats of a red colour
all bedaubed with lace which they
call vests' (Wood, *L. & T.*, i. 509-10).
See the description of her riding
habit (1664; scarlet coat, band and
ribbons), in HMC, *Heathcote*, p. 149.
Cf. D. de Repas to Sir R. Harley, 19
October 1665, Oxford: 'For news

from Court I shall tell you that one
cannot possibly know a woman from
a man, unless one hath the eyes of a
linx who can see through a wall; for
by the face and garbe they are like
men.   They do not weare any hood
but only men's perwick hatts and
coats . . .' (HMC, *Portland*, iii. 293).
Cf. also below, vii. 162; Evelyn, 13
September 1666. Von Uffenbach
(a German visitor in 1710) remarked
of the women attending a race meeting on horseback that they 'wore
men's clothes and feathered hats,
which is quite usual in England – they
may, indeed, be seen in companies of
ten or a dozen riding through the
streets at a prodigious speed': *London
in 1710* (ed. Quarrell and Mare), p.
106.
5. To Denis Gauden's house (q.v.
above, iv. 244 & n. 1); he kept his
office there this summer.
6. Gauden's.

and his sister Fissant, a serious lady – and a little daughter of hers that begins to sing prettily. Thence, with mighty pleasure, with Sir G. Carteret by coach, with great good discourse of kindness with him to my Lord Sandwich, and to me also; and I every day see more good by that alliance. Almost at Deptford, I light and walked over to Halfway-house; and so home, in my way being shown my cousin Pepys's[1] house,[2] which seems at distance a pretty house. At home met the weekly Bill, where above 1000 encreased in the Bill; and of them, in all, about 1700 of the plague[3] – which hath made the officers this day resolve of sitting at Deptford,[4] which puts me to some consideration what to do. Therefore, home to think and consider of everything about it; and without determining anything, eat a little supper and to bed, full of the pleasure of these six or seven last days.

28. Up betimes, and down to Deptford – where after a little discourse with Sir G. Carteret, who is much displeased with the order of our officers yesterday to remove the office to Deptford; pretending other things, but to be sure it is with regard to his own house (which is much because[a] his family is going away). I am glad I was not at the order-making, and so I will endeavour to alter it. Set out with my Lady all[b] alone with[c] her with six horses to Dagenhams, going by water to the Ferry. And a pleasant going and good discourse – and when there, very merry and the young couple now well acquainted. But Lord, to see in what fear all the people here do live would make one mad. They are afeared of us that come to them, insomuch that I am

---

         a repl. 'that'   *b* repl. 'alone'   *c* repl. 'in'

---

1. Here and at one other point in the diary (below, vii. 312.) Pepys writes his surname in s.h. The symbol in both places reads 'P-e-p-s'. This establishes that the word was monosyllabic, but does not define the vowel: it could be pronounced 'Peeps', 'Pepps' or 'Payps'. But writing his name in Greek letters on the flyleaf of one of his books (Xenophon's *De Cyri institutione libri octo*, Eton, 1613; PL 1304), he used the long 'e' ('eta'): 'Πῆπυς'. There is little room for doubt, therefore, that he pronounced his name 'Peeps'.

2. Thomas Pepys's house at Hatcham Barnes, Surrey.

3. There was an increase in burials of 1204; 1843 had died of the plague in the week 18–25 July: GL, A.1.5, no. 96.

4. On Tuesday and Thursday mornings: PRO, Adm. 106/3520, f. 26r.

troubled at it and wish myself away. But some cause they have, for the Chaplain, with whom but a week or two ago we were here mighty high disputing,[1] is since fallen into a fever and dead, being gone hence to a friend's a good way off – a sober and a healthful man. These considerations make us all hasten the marriage; and resolve it upon Monday next, which is three days before we entended it. Mighty merry all of us; and in the evening, with full content took coach again, and home by daylight with great pleasure. And thence I down to Woolwich, where find my wife well; and after drinking and talking a little, we to bed.

29. Up betimes. And after viewing some of wife's pictures, which now she is come to do very finely, to my great satisfaction, beyond what I could ever look for – I went away; and by water to the office, where nobody to meet me, but busy all the morning. At noon to dinner, where I hear that my Will is come in thither and laid down upon my bed, ill of the head-ake; which put me into extraordinary fear, and I studied all I could to get him out of the house, and set my people to work to do it without discouraging him. And myself went forth to the Old Exchange to pay my fair Batelier for some linen, and took leave of her, they breaking up shop for a while. And so by coach to Kate Joyces, and there used all the vehemence and Rhetorique I could to get her husband to let her go down to Brampton, but I could not prevail with him – he urging some simple reasons, but most that of profit,[2] minding the house – and the distance, if either of them should be ill. However, I did my best, and more then I had a mind to do, but that I saw him*a* so resolved against it – while she was mightily troubled at it. At last he yielded she should go to Winsor to some friends there. So I took my leave of them, believing that it is great odds that we ever all see one another again – for I dare not go any more to that end of the town.

So home, and to writing of letters hard; and*b* then at night home and fell to my Tanger Papers – till late; and then to bed – in

---

a repl. 'them'   *b* repl. 'very late'

---

1. Cf. above, p. 160.   2. Anthony and Kate Joyce kept a
tallow chandler's shop.

some ease of mind that Will is gone to his lodging and that he is likely to do well, it being only the head-ake.

30. *Lord's day.* Up, and in my nightgown, cap, and neck-cloth, undressed all day long; lost not a minute, but in my chamber setting my Tanger accounts to rights, which I did by night, to my very heart's content; not only that it is done, but I find everything right and even beyond what, after so long neglecting them, I did hope for. The Lord of Heaven be praised for it.

Will was with me today and is very well again. It was a sad noise to hear our Bell to toll and ring so often today, either for deaths or burials; I think five or six times.

At night, weary with the day's work but full of joy at my having done it – I to bed, being to rise betimes tomorrow to go to the wedding at Dagenhams.

So to bed – fearing I have got some cold sitting in my loose garment all this day.

31. Up, and very betimes, by 6 a-clock, at Deptford; and there find Sir G. Carteret and my Lady ready to go – I being in my new coloured-silk suit and coat, trimmed with gold buttons and gold broad lace round my hands, very rich and fine. By water to the Ferry, where, when we came, no coach there – and tide of ebb so far spent as the horse-boat could not get off on the other side the river to bring away the coach. So we were fain to stay there in the unlucky Isle of Doggs – in a chill place, the morning cool and wind fresh, above two if not three hours, to our great discontent. Yet being upon a pleasant errand, and seeing that could not be helped, we did bear it very patiently; and it was worth my observing, I thought as ever anything, to see how upon these two scores, Sir G. Carteret, the most passionate man in the world and that was in greatest haste to be gone, did bear with it, and very pleasant all the while, at least not troubled much*a* so as to fret and storm at it.

Anon the coach comes – in the meantime there coming a citizen thither with his horse to go over, that told us he did come from Islington this morning, and that Proctor the vintener of the Miter in Woodstreet, and his son, is dead this morning there – of

a repl. 'very'

the plague. He having laid out abundance of money there – and was the greatest vintener for some time in London for great entertainments.[1]

We fearing the canonicall hour would be past before we got thither, did with a great deal of unwillingness*a* send away the Licence and wedding-ring. So that when we came, though we drove hard with six horses, yet we found them gone from home; and going toward the church,[2] met them coming from church – which troubled us. But however, that trouble was soon over – hearing it was well done – they being both in their old Cloaths. My Lord Crew giving her – there being three coach-fulls of them. The young lady mighty sad, which troubled me; but yet I think it was only her gravity, in a little greater degree then usual. All saluted her, but I did not till my Lady ⟨Sandwich⟩ did ask me whether I had not saluted her or no. So to dinner, and very merry we were; but yet in such a Sober way as never almost any wedding was in so great families – but it was much better. After dinner, company divided, some to cards – others to talk. My Lady Sandwich and I up to settle accounts and pay her some money – and mighty*b* kind she is to me, and would fain have had me gone down for company with her to Hinchingbrooke – but for my life I cannot.

At night to supper, and so to talk and, which methought was the most extraordinary thing, all of us to prayers as usual, and the young Bride and bridegroom too. And so after prayers, Soberly to bed; only, I got into the bridegroom's chamber while he undressed himself, and there was very merry – till he was called to the bride's chamber and into bed they went. I kissed the bride in bed, and so the curtaines drawne with the greatest gravity that could be, and so good-night.

But the modesty and gravity of this business was so decent, that it was to me, endeed, ten times more delightful then if it had been twenty times more merry and Joviall.

Whereas I feared I must have sat up all night, we did here all get good beds – and I lay in the same I did before, with Mr.

---

a repl. 'trouble' *b* MS. 'my'

---

1. The father, William Proctor, was said to have died insolvent: Richard Smyth, *Obituary*, p. 64. Smyth gives 1 August as the date of his death.

2. Probably that of South Weald.

Brisband, who is a good scholar and sober man;[1] and we lay in bed, getting him to give me an account of Rome, which is the most delightful talk a man can have of any traveller. And so to sleep – my eyes much troubled already with the change of my drink.

Thus I ended this month with the greatest joy that ever I did any in my life, because I have spent the greatest part of it with abundance of joy and honour, and pleasant Journys and brave entertainments, and without cost of money. And at last live to see that business ended with great content on all sides.[2]

This evening with Mr. Brisband speaking of inchantments and spells, I telling him some of my Charmes,[3] he told me this of his own knowledge at Bourdeaux in France. The words these –

> *Voicy un Corps mort*
> *Royde comme un Baston*
> *Froid comme Marbre*
> *Leger comme un Esprit,*
> *Levons te au nom de Jesus Christ.*

He saw four little Girles, very young ones, all[a] kneeling, each of them upon one knee; and one begin the first line, whispering in the eare of the next, and the second to the third, and the third to the fourth, and she to the first. Then the first begun the second line, and so round quite through. And putting each one finger only to a boy that lay flat upon his back on the ground, as if he was dead. At the end of the words they did with their four fingers raise this boy as high as they could reach. And he being[b] there and wondering at it (as also being afeared to see it – for they would have had him to have bore a part in saying the words in the room of one of the little girls, that was so young that they could hardly make her learn to repeat the words), did, for fear

---

a MS. 'all that'   *b* repl. 'be'

---

1. John Brisbane, later Judge-Advocate of the fleet (1669), and Secretary to the Admiralty (1680–4). In the diary period he appears to have been in Carteret's service.

2. Cf. Pepys to Sandwich, 7 August, referring to the marriage as 'the only occurrence of my life I ever mett with begun, proceded on & finished with the same uninterrupted Excesse of Satisfaction to all partys'. He added that Sandwich would do well to 'quicken the settlement of the mony=matter on both sides': Carte 75, ff. 327–8.

3. See above, v. 361–2.

there might be some sleight used in it by the boy, or that the boy might be light, called the cook of the house, a very lusty fellow, as Sir G. Carteret's Cooke, who is very big, and they did raise him just in the same manner.[1]

This is one of the strangest things I ever heard, but he tells it me of his own knowledge and I do heartily believe it to be true. I enquired of him whether they were Protestant or Catholique girls, and he told me they were Protestant – which made it the more strange to me.

Thus we end this month, as I said, after the greatest glut of content that ever I had; only, under some difficulty[a] because of the plague, which grows mightily upon us, the last week being about 1700[b] or 1800 of the plague.[2]

My Lord Sandwich, at sea with a fleet of about 100 sail to the Norward, expect De Ruyter or the Duch East-India fleet.

My Lord Hinchingbrooke coming over from France, and will meet his sister[3] at Scott's hall.

Myself having obliged both these families in this business very much, as both my Lady and Sir G. Carteret and his Lady do confess exceedingly; and the latter two also now call me Cosen, which I am glad of.

So God preserve us all friends long, and continue[c] health among us.

a repl. 'deliver'   *b* repl. '1700l'   *c* repl. 'to'

1. For accounts (at second-hand) of similar experiments, see Sir David Brewster, *Letters on natural magic to Sir Walter Scott* (1834), pp. 255–7; N. & Q., 3 July 1852. It is said to be essential that all the people concerned shall breathe in simultaneously, and hold their breath.

2. See above, p. 173 & n. 3.

3. The bride, Lady Jemima: her sister-in-law Caroline Carteret had on 16 July 1665 married Sir Thomas Scott, of Scot's Hall, Smeeth, Kent. James R. Scott, *Memorials of Scott of Scot's Hall*, pp. 236–7.

AUGUST.

1.[a] Slept and lay long, then up; and my Lord and Sir G. Carteret being gone abroad, I first to see the bridegroom and bride, and found them both up, and he gone to dress himself. Both red in the face and well enough pleased this morning with their night's lodging.

Thence down, and Mr. Brisband and I to Billiards. Anon came my Lord and Sir G. Carteret in, who had been looking abroad and visiting some farms that Sir G. Carteret hath thereabouts – and among other things, report the greatest stories of the bigness[b] of the Calfes they find there ready to sell to the butchers; as big, as they say, as little Cowes. And that they do give them a piece of Chalke to lick, which they hold makes them white in the flesh within.[1]

Very merry at Dinner, and so to talk and laugh after dinner, and up and down, some to [one] place, some to another – full of content on all sides.

Anon, about 5 a-clock, Sir G. Carteret and his lady and I took coach, with the greatest joy and kindness that could be from the two families – or that ever I saw with so much appearance, and I believe reality, in all my life.

Drove hard home, and it was night ere we got to Deptford – where, with much kindness from them to me, I left them; and home to the office, where I find all well. And being weary and sleepy, it being very late, I to bed.

2. Up, it being a public fast, as being the first Wednesday of the month, for the plague.[2] I within-doors all day, and upon my month's accounts late[c] – and there to my great joy settled almost all my private matters of money in my books clearly; and allowing myself several sums which I had hitherto not reckoned myself sure of, because I would not be over-sure of anything, though

_a_ repl. '2' _b_ repl. same symbol badly formed _c_ MS. 'last'

1. There were good marshland pastures near Dagenhams: VCH, _Essex_, v. 282. The use of chalk does not appear to be among those recommended by contemporary writers on animal husbandry. It has no scientific basis.

2. See above, p. 155 & n. 4.

with reason enough I might do it, I did find myself really worth
1900*l* – for which the great God of heaven and earth be praised.
At night to the office to write a few letters, and so home to bed,
after fitting myself for tomorrow's Journy.

3.   Up, and betimes to Deptford to Sir G. Carteret's; where
not liking the horse which had been hired by Mr. Uthwayt for
me, I did desire Sir G. Carteret to let me ride his new 40*l* horse;[1]
which he did and so I left my hacquenee behind.   And so after
staying a good while in their bedchamber while they were dressing themselfs, discoursing merrily, I parted and to the Ferry,
where I was forced to stay a great while before I could get my
horse brought over.   And then mounted and rode very finely to
Dagenham's – all the way, people, Citizens, walking to and again
to enquire how the plague is in the City this week by the Bill –
which by chance at Greenwich I had heard was 2010 of the
plague, and 3000 and odd of all diseases;[2] but methought it was a
sad question to be so often asked me.   Coming to Dagenham's,
I there met our company coming out of the house, having stayed
as long as they could for me.   So I let them go a little before, and
went and took leave of my Lady Sandwich – good woman, who
seems very sensible of my service and this late business – and
having her directions in some things; among others, to get Sir G.
Carteret and my Lord to settle the portion and what Sir G.
Carteret is to settle into land as soon as may be; she not liking that
it should lie long undone, for fear of death on either side.[3]   So
took leave of her, and then down to the buttery and eat a piece of
cold venison-pie and drank and took some bread and cheese in my
hand; and so mounted after them, Mr. Marr[4] very kindly staying
to lead me the way.   By and by met my Lord Crew returning,
after having accompanied them a little way.   And so after them,

1. An expensive one: for prices,
see *Verney Mem.*, ii. 58, 277 etc.;
J. Parkes, *Travel in Engl. in 17th cent.*,
p. 60; and cf. below, ix. 391.

2. During 25 July–1 August: GL,
A.1.5, no. 96. There were 3014
burials altogether.

3. There are letters on this subject
from Carteret to Sandwich (2, 9

August) and from Pepys to Sandwich
(7 August) in Carte 75, ff. 323*v*, 350,
327–8.   Carteret increased the jointure beyond the original agreement
to £12,000, and by 9 August
c. £6,000 was in the hands of 'honest
Mr. Pepys' (to use his phrase).   Cf.
above, p. 158 & n. 2.

4. Unidentified.

Mr. Marr telling me by the way how a maid-servant of Mr. John Wrights (who lives thereabouts),[1] falling sick of the plague, she was removed to an out-house, and a nurse appointed to look to her – who being once absent, the maid got out of the house at the window and run away. The nurse coming and knocking, and having no answer, believed she was dead, and went and told[a] Mr. Wright so; who, and his lady, were in great strait what to do to get her buried. At last resolved to go to Burntwood hard by, being in that parish, and there get people to do it – but they would not; so he went home full of trouble, and in the way met the wench walking over the Common, which frighted him worse then before. And was forced to send people to take her; which he did, and they got one of the pest Coaches and put her into it to carry her to a pest-house. And passing in a narrow lane, Sir Anthony Browne,[2] with his brother and some friends in the coach, met this coach with the Curtains drawn close. The brother being a young man, and believing there might be some lady in it that would not be seen, and the way being narrow, he thrust his head out of his own into her coach to[b] look, and there saw somebody look very ill, and in a sick dress and stunk mightily; which the coachman also cried out upon. And presently they came up to some people that stood looking after it; and told our gallants that it was a maid of Mr. Wrights carried away sick of the plague – which put the young gentleman into a fright had almost cost him his life, but is now well again.

I, overtaking our young people, light and into the coach to them, where mighty merry all the way. And anon came to the Blockehouse over against Gravesend,[3] where we stayed a great while – in a little drinking-house – sent back our coaches to Dagenhams. I by and by, by boat to Gravesend, where no news of Sir G. Carteret come yet. So back again and fetched them all over but the two saddle[c]-horses that were to go with us, which could not be brought over in the horse-boat, the wind and tide being against us, without towing. So we had some difference with some watermen, who would not tow[d] them over under

a repl. 'did'   *b* MS. 'and to'   *c* repl. 'two'   *d* repl. 'bring'

---

1. Probably the John Wright who was a relative of Sandwich.
2. Of Weald Hall, nr Brentwood, Essex.
3. Tilbury fort.

20s – whereupon I swore to send one of them to sea, and will do it. Anon some others come to me and did it for ten.   By and by comes Sir G. Carteret, and so we set out for Chatham – in my way overtaking some company, wherein was a lady, very pretty, riding single, her husband in company with her.   We fell into talk, and I read a copy of verses which her husband showed me, and he discommended but the lady commended; and I read them so as to make the husband turn to commend them.   By and by he and I fall into acquaintance, having known me formerly at the Exchequer; his name is Nokes,¹ over against Bow Church; he was servant to Alderman Dashwood.   We promised to meet if ever we came both to London again.   And at parting I had a fair salute on horseback in Rochester streets of the lady – and so parted.

Came to Chatham mighty merry.   And anon to supper, it being near 9 a-clock ere we came thither.   My Lady Carteret came thither, in a coach by herself, before us.   Great mind they have to buy a little hacquenee that I rode on from Gravesend, for a woman's horse.   Mighty merry; and after supper, all being withdrawn, Sir G. Carteret did take an opportunity to speak with much value and kindness to me, which is of great joy to me.   So anon to bed – Mr. Brisband and I together, to my content.

4.   Up at 5 a-clock, and by 6 walked out alone with my Lady Slanning² to the Docke Yard, where walked up and down; and so to Mr. Petts, who led us into his garden, and there the lady, the best-humoured woman in the world, and a devout woman (I having spied her on her knees half an hour this morning in her chamber), clambered up to the top of the banqueting-house to gather nuts, and mighty merry; and so walked back again through the new rope-house,³ which is very useful, and so to the Hill-house to breakfast – and mighty merry; then they took coach, and Sir G. Carteret kiss[ed] me himself heartily, and my Lady several times – with great kindness; and then the young

---

1. Probably Nathaniel Nokes, silk-man. (R).

2. Carteret's eldest daughter, Anne, wife of Sir Nicholas Slaning of Maristow, Devon.

3. A wooden ropehouse and rope-way had been built earlier in the year: *CSPD 1664–5*, p. 162.

ladies; and so with much joy bade "God*ª* be with you". And an end I think it will be to my mirth for a great while, it having been the passage of my whole life the most pleasing for the time, considering the quality and nature of the business,*ᵇ* and my noble usage in the doing of it, and very many fine journys, entertainments, and great company.

I returned into the house for a while, to do business there with Comissioner Pett; and then with the Officers of the Chest, where I saw more of Sir W. Batten's baseness then ever I did before;[1] for whereas he did own once under his hand to them that he was accountable for 2200*l*, of which*ᶜ* he hath yet paid but 1600*l*, he writes them a letter lately that he hath but about 150*l* left that is due to the*ᵈ* Chest. But I will do something in it, and that speedily.

That being done, I took horse, and Mr. Barrow with me; bore me company to Gravesend, discoursing of his business,[2] wherein I vexed him, and he me, I seeing his frowardness, but yet that he is in my conscience a very honest man; and some good things he told me, which I shall remember to the King's advantage.

There I took boat alone (and the tide being against me), landed at Blackewall and walked it to Wapping, Captain Prowd,[3] whom I met with, talking with me all the way, who is a sober man. So home, and found all things well – and letters from Dover that my Lord Hinchingbrooke is arrived at Dover – and would*ᵉ* be at Scotts hall this*ᶠ* night, where the whole company will meet – I wish myself with them. After writing a few letters – I took boat, and down to Woolwich very late and there found my wife and her woman upon the Key, hearing a fellow in a barge that lay by fiddle. So I to them, and in, very merry, and to bed – I sleepy and weary. In the morning up, and my wife showed me several things of her doeing, especially one fine woman's persian head mighty finely done, beyond what I could expect of her. And so away by water, having ordered in the yard six or

《5.》

a repl. 'Good'	*b* repl. 'serv'-	*c* repl. 'where'
d repl. 'them'	*e* repl. 'will'	*f* repl. 'after'

---

1. Cf. above, p. 68 & n. 1.
2. Philip Barrow was Storekeeper of Chatham yard; his business was his dispute with his colleagues. See esp. above, v. 5 & n. 1.

3. John Prowd, an Elder Brother of Trinity House; employed by the Navy Board as a surveyor of ships.

eight barge men to be whipped, who had last night stolen some of the King's cordage from out of the yard.

I to Deptford, and there by agreement met with my Lord Bruncker, and there we kept our office, he and I, and did what there was to do and at noon parted – to meet at the office next week.   Sir W. Warren and I thence did walk through the rain to Halfway-house, and there I eat a piece of boiled beef, and he and I talk over several businesses; among others, our design upon the Mast Docke,[1] which I hope to compass and get 2 or 300*l* by.

Thence to Redriffe, where we parted; and I home, where busy all the afternoon.   Stepped to Colvills to set right a business of money, where he told me that for certain De Ruyter is come home with all his fleet;[a] which is very ill news – considering the charge we have been at in keeping a fleet to the Northward so long, besides the great expectation of snapping him; wherein my Lord Sandwich will I doubt suffer some dishonour.[2]

I am told also of a great Ryott upon Thursday last in Cheapeside, Collonell Danvers, a Delinquent, having been taken, and in his way to the Tower was rescued from the Captain of the Guard and carried away – one only of the Rescuers being taken.[3]

I am told also that the Duke of Buckingham is dead, but I know not of a certainty.[4]   So home, and very late at letters, and then home to supper and to bed.

a repl. same symbol badly formed

---

1. At Woolwich: see above, p. 162 & n. 1.

2. De Ruyter, hugging the coasts of Norway and Denmark, had slipped past the superior English battle-fleet, and reached Delfzijl, in the western Ems, on 26 July. His voyage (q.v. above, v. 121, n.2) had lasted 16 months; he had lost none of his 19 ships, and had brought home 30 prizes. G. Brandt, *Michel de Ruiter* (trans., Amsterdam, 1698), pp. 287–8; *CSPVen. 1664–6*, p. 183.

3. Cf. the brief account in the letter (10 August) to William Sancroft, Dean of St Paul's, in Sir Henry Ellis (ed.), *Orig. Letters* (1825–46), ser. 2, iv. 28. Henry Danvers, a millenarian Baptist, Governor of Stafford in the civil war, was now regarded as a dangerous leader of rebellion, and a warrant for his arrest had been out since 1662. Clarendon indirectly mentioned his escape in his speech to parliament in the following October: *LJ*, xi. 688. He was later arrested, and released in 1671. For his connection with the plots of 1665, see *CSPD 1664–5*, pp. 329, 555; ib., *1665–6*, p. 24. See also ib., *1662–3*, p. 51; *1664–5*, pp. 506, 542 (in the indexes to these volumes he is sometimes wrongly named Robert); and C. E. Whiting, *Studies in Engl. puritanism, 1660–88*, pp. 121+.

4. He did not die until 1687.

6. *Lords day*. And dressed and had my head combed by my little girle,[1] to whom I confess que je sum demasiado kind, nuper ponendo sæpe mes mains in su dos choses de son breast. Mais il faut que je leave it, lest it bring me to alguno major inconvenience. So to my business in my chamber – look[ing] over and settling more of my papers then I could do the two last days I have spent about them. In the evening, it raining hard, down to Woolwich, where after some little talk, to bed.

7. Up, and with great pleasure looking over my wife's pictures; and then to see my Lady Pen, whom I have not seen since her coming hither; and after being a little merry with her, she went forth and I stayed there, talking with Mrs. Pegg and looking over her pictures; and commended them, but Lord, so far short of my wife as no comparison. Thence to my wife, and there spent, talking till noon, when by appointment Mr. Andrews came out of the country to speak with me about their Tanger business. And so having done with him and dined, I home by water, where by[a] appointment I met Dr. Twisden, Mr. Povy, Mr. Lawson, and Stockdale about settling their business of money; but such confusion I never met with, nor could anything be agreed on, but parted like a company of fools – I vexed to lose so much time and pains to no purpose.

They gone, comes Rayner the boat-maker about some business, and brings a piece of plate with him, which I refused to take of him; thinking endeed that the poor man hath no reason nor incouragement from our dealings with him to give any of us any presents. He gone, there comes Lewellin about Mr. Deerings business of Planke, to have the contract perfected, and offers me twenty pieces in gold, as Deering had done some time[b] since himself; but I both then and now refused it, resolving not to be bribed to despatch business; but will have it done, however, out of hand forthwith.[2]

So he gone, I to supper and to bed.

8. Up, and to the office, where all the morning we sat. At

a MS. 'my'   *b* repl. 'tar'

---

1. Susan.
2. See below, p. 245 & n. 3. The tender had been submitted on 25 July: *CSPD 1665–6*, p. 130.

noon I home to dinner alone. And after dinner Bagwell's[a] wife waited at the door, and went with me to my office, en lequel jo haze todo which I had a corasón a hazer con ella. So parted, and I to Sir W. Batten's and there sat the most of the afternoon, talking and drinking too much with my Lord Bruncker, Sir G Smith, G Cocke, and others, very merry. I drunk a little, mixed, but yet more then I should do. So to my office a little, and then to the Duke of Albemarle's about some business. The streets mighty empty all the way now, even in London, which is a sad sight. And to Westminster hall, where talking, hearing very sad stories from Mrs. Mumford among others, of Mrs. Michell's son's family. And poor Will that used to sell us ale at the Hall-door[1] – his wife and three children dead, all I think in a day. So home through the City again, wishing I may have taken no ill in going; but I will go, I think, no more thither.

Late at the office; and then home to supper, having taken a pullet home with me. And then to bed.

The News of De Ruter's coming home is certain – and told to the great disadvantage of our fleet and the praise of De Ruyter; but it cannot be helped – nor do I know what to say to it.

9. Up betimes to my office, where Tom Hater to the writing of letters with me, which have for a good while been in arreare; and we close at it all day till night – only, made a little step out for half an hour in the morning, I to the Exchequer about striking of tallies; but no good done therein, people being most out of town. At noon T. Hater dined with me. And so at it all the afternoon. At night home and supped; and after reading a little in Cowly's poems,[2] my head being disturbed with overmuch business today, I to bed.

10. Up betimes, and called upon earely by my she-Cosen Porter, the Turners wife, to tell me that her husband was carried to the Tower for buying of some of the King's Powder[3] – and

a s.h.

---

1. Will Griffith, who kept an ale-house in Old Palace Yard. (R).

2. See above, iv. 386, n. 3.

3. It was an offence to sell or buy gunpowder from the royal stores, and the Crown enjoyed large privileges in its manufacture. The case has not been traced, nor has the identity of this 'cousin' been established with certainty, but he appears to be the same Porter whom Pepys befriended after the Fire: cf. *Further Corr.*, p. 321.

would have my help; but I could give her none, not daring any more to appear in that business – having too much trouble lately therein.¹ By and by to the office, where we sat all the morning, in great trouble to see the Bill this week rise so high, to above 4000 in all, and of them, about 3000 of the plague.² And an odd story of Alderman Bences stumbling at night over a dead Corps in the street; and going home and telling his wife, she at the fright, being with child, falls sick and died of the plague. We sat late; and then by invitation My*ᵃ* Lord Brouncker, Sir J. Mennes, Sir W. Batten, and I to Sir G Smith's to dinner, where very good company and good cheer. Captain Cocke was there, and Jacke Fenn – but to our great wonder, Alderman Bence; and tells us that not a word of all this is true, and others said so too. But by his own story, his wife hath been ill,*ᵇ* and he fain to leave his house and comes not to her – which continued a trouble to me all the time I was there.

Thence to the office; and after writing letters, home to draw over anew my Will,³ which I had bound myself by oath to de-spatch by tomorrow night, the town growing so unhealthy that a man cannot depend upon living two days to an end. So having done something of it, I to bed.

11. Up, and all day long finishing and writing over my will twice, for my father and my wife. Only in the morning a pleasant rancontre happened, in*ᶜ* having a young married woman brought me by her father, old Delkes, that carries pins alway in his mouth, to get her husband off, that he should not go to sea. Uno ombre pouvait avoir done any cosa cum ella, but I did natha sino besar her. After they were gone, my mind run upon having them called back again; and I sent a messenger to Blackewall but he failed, so I lost my expectation. I to the Exchequer about

a repl. 'Sir'   *b* repl. 'all'   *c* repl. 'after'

---

1. In Hayter's case: see above, p. 115 & n. 3.
2. The figures (for 1–8 August) were 4030 and 2817 respectively: GL, A.1.5, no. 96.

3. Untraced. For Pepys's wills, see above, i. 90, n. 1.

striking new tallies; and I find the Exchequer, by Proclamacion, removing to Nonesuch.[1]

Back again and at my papers, and putting up my books into chests, and settling my house and all things in the best and speediest order I can, lest it should please God to take me away or force me to leave my house.

《*Health*》 Late up at it, and weary and full of wind, finding perfectly that so long as I keep myself in company at meals and do there eat lustily, which I cannot do alone, having no love to eateing, but my mind runs upon my business, I am as well as can be; but when I come to be alone, I do not eat in time, nor enough, nor with any good heart, and I immediately begin[a] to be full of wind, which brings me pain, till I come to fill my belly a-days again; then am[b] presently well.

12.   The office now not sitting but only hereafter on Thursdays at the office, I within all the morning about my papers and setting things still in order; and also much time in settling matters with Dr Twisden.[2]   At noon am sent for by Sir G. Carteret to meet him and my Lord Hinchingbrooke at Deptford; but my Lord did not come thither, he having[c] crossed the River at Gravesend to Dagenhams – whither I dare not fallow him – they being afeared of me.   But Sir G. Carteret says he is a most sweet youth in every circumstance.   Sir G. Carteret being in haste of going to the Duke of Albemarle and the Archbishop, he was pettish, and so I would not fasten any discourse, but take another time.   So he gone, I down to Greenwich and sent away the *Bezan*,[3] thinking to go with my wife tonight, to come back again tomorrow night to the *Soveraigne* at the Bouy of the Nowre.   Coming back to Dept-

a MS. 'being'   *b* repl. 'am'   *c* MS. 'being'

---

1. Nonsuch House, near Epsom, Surrey. The proclamation (necessitated by the plague) was issued on 26 July, and the Receipt of Exchequer and the Tally Office stayed there until 20 January 1666. *CSPD 1664–5*, p. 492; *CTB*, i. 712; Steele, nos 3428, 3447.

2. This was to adjust accounts with Povey, whom Pepys had suc-ceeded as Treasurer to the Tangier Committee. Pepys now gave an acquittance for £692 to Dr Twysden (attorney for Sir Hugh Cholmley), payable to Povey. For Pepys's note on the transaction, and for Povey's receipt, see Rawl. A 172, f. 163r. Cf. above, pp. 100–01, 185.

3. A yacht much used by Pepys in his river journeys.

ford, old Bagwell walked a little way with me and would have me in to his daughter's; and there, he being gone dehors, ego had my volunté de su hija. Eat and drank, and away home; and after a little at the office, to my chamber to put more things still in order, and late to bed.

The people die so, that now it seems they are fain to carry the dead to be buried by daylight, the nights not sufficing to do it in. And my Lord Mayor commands people to be within at 9 at night, all (as they say) that the sick may have liberty[a] to go abroad for ayre.[1] There is one also dead out of one of our ships at Deptford, which troubles us mightily – the *Providence* fire-ship, which was just fitted to go to sea.[2] But they tell me today, no more sick on board. And this day W Bodham tells me that one is dead at Woolwich, not far from the Ropeyard. I am told too,[b] that a wife of one of the groomes at Court is dead at Salsbury, so that the King and Queene are speedily to be all gone to Milton.[3] God preserve us.

13. *Lords day.* Up betimes, and to my chamber (it being a very wet day all day, and glad I am that we did not go by water to see the *Soveraigne* today as I entended),[4] clearing all matters in packing up my papers and books – and giving instructions in writing to my Executors, thereby perfecting the whole business of my Will, to my very great joy. So that I shall be in much better state of soul, I hope, if it should please the Lord to call me away this sickly time. At night to read, being weary with this day's great work. And then after supper to bed, to rise betimes tomorrow. And to bed with a mind as free as to the business of the world as if I were not worth 100*l* in the whole world, everything

a repl. 'leave to'   *b* repl. 'so'

---

1. There appears to be no basis for this story: Bell, *Plague*, p. 176.

2. See Christopher Pett to Pepys, 15 August: *CSPD 1664–5*, p. 519.

3. *Recte* Wilton, the Earl of Pembroke's house, three miles from Salisbury. The project to go there was soon abandoned, and the court moved to Oxford on 23 September. The plague victim was the wife of a groom in the service of an equerry to the Queen: efforts were made to conceal the illness. Bell, *Plague*, p. 171.

4. For a later visit, see below, p. 194. The *Royal Sovereign* (largest ship in the navy) had been fitted out again for service this summer: *CSPD 1664–5*, pp. 366 etc.

being evened under my hand in my books and papers; and upon the whole, I find myself worth (besides Brampton estate) the sum of 2164*l* – for which the Lord be praised.

14. Up; and my mind being at mighty ease from the despatch of my business so much yesterday, I down to Deptford to Sir G. Carteret; where with him a great while, and a great deal of private talk concerning my Lord Sandwich's and his matters – and chiefly of the latter, I giving him great deal of advice about the necessity of his having caution concerning Fenn, and the many ways there are of his being abused by any man in his place.[1] And why he should not bring his son in to look after his business, and more, to be a Comissioner of the Navy; which he listened to and liked, and told me how much the King was his good maister, and was sure would not deny him that or anything else greater then that. And I find him a very cuning man, whatever at other times he seems to be. And among other things, he told me he was not for the Fanfarroons, to make a show with a great Title, as he might have had long since, but the main thing to get an estate; and another thing, speaking of minding of business, "By God," says he, "I will, and have already almost brought it to that pass, that the King shall not be able to whip a cat but I must be at the tayle of it" – meaning, so necessary he is, and the King and my Lord Treasurer and all do confess it. Which, while I mind my business, is my own case in this office of the Navy; and I hope shall be more, if God give me life and health.

Thence by agreement to Sir J Minnes's lodgings, where I find my Lord Bruncker; and so by water to the Ferry, and there took Sir W. Batten's coach that was sent for us and to Sir W Batten's, where very merry, good cheer, and up and down the garden, with great content to me. And after dinner beat Captain Cocke at Billiards; won about 8*s* of him and my Lord Bruncker. So in the evening, after much pleasure, back again – and I by water to Woolwich, where supped with my wife; and then to bed betimes, because of rising tomorrow at 4 of the clock, in order to the going out with Sir G. Carteret toward Cranborne to meet my Lord Hinchingbrooke in his way to Court. This night I did present my wife with the Dyamond ring a while since given me by

1. Cf. above, p. 117, n. 1.

Mr.   ,¹ Dicke Vines's brother, for helping him to be a
purser – valued at about 10*l* – the first thing of that nature I did
ever give her.   Great fears we have that the plague will be a great
Bill* this week.²

15.   Up by 4 a-clock and walked to Greenwich, where called
at Captain Cockes and to his chamber, he being in bed – where
something put my last night's dream into my head, which I think
is the best that ever was dreamed – which was, that I had my Lady
Castlemayne in my armes and was admitted to use all the dalliance
I desired with her, and then dreamed that this could not be awake
but that it was only a dream.   But that since it was a dream and
that I took so much real pleasure in it, what a happy thing it would
be, if when we are in our graves (as Shakespeere resembles it),³
we could dream, and dream but such dreams as this – that then
we should not need to be so fearful of death as we are this plague-
time.

Here I hear that news is brought Sir G. Carteret that my Lord
Hinchingbrooke is not well, and so cannot meet us at Cranborne
tonight.   So I to Sir G. Carteret, and there was sorry with him
for our disappointment – so we have put off our meeting there till
Saturday next.   Here I stayed talking with Sir G. Carteret, he
being mighty free with me in his business; and among other
things, hath Ordred Rider and Cutler to put into my hands Copper
to the value of 5000*l* (which Sir G. Carteret's share, it seems, came
to in it), which is to raise part of the money he is to lay out for a
purchase for my Lady Jemimah.⁴

Thence he and I to Sir J. Mennes by invitation, where Sir W.
Batten and my Lady and Lord Brouncker, and all of us dined –
upon a venison-pasty and other good meat, but nothing well-
dressed.   But my pleasure lay in getting some bills signed by Sir

1. ? Thomas Blayton, Vines's brother-in-law.

2. Deaths from plague during 8–15 August were 3880, an increase of almost 1000 over the previous week: GL, A.1.5, no. 96.

3. Cf. *Hamlet*, Act III, sc. 1.

4. The purchase was for her jointure: see above, p. 180, n. 3. The transaction may have been connected with the contracts made in 1664 by Rider and Cutler for the supply of tar, pitch and hemp: *CSPD 1664–5*, pp. 132–4, 494. Carteret, as Navy Treasurer, received 3*d.* in every pound.

G. Carteret, and promise of present payment from Mr. Fenn;
which doth rejoice my heart, it being one of the heaviest things I
had upon me, that so much of the little I have should lie (*viz.* near
1000*l*[a]) in the King's hands.   Here very merry, and (Sir G. Carteret being gone presently after dinner) to Captain Cockes and
there merry; and so broke up, and I by water to the Duke of
Albemarle, with whom I spoke a great deal in private with him,
they being designed to send a fleet of ships privately* to the
Streights.   No news yet from our Fleete, which is much wondered at; but the Duke says for certain, Guns have been heard to
the Norward very much.

It was dark before I could get home; and so land at church-
yard-stairs, where to my great trouble I met a dead Corps, of the
plague, in the narrow ally, just bringing down a little pair of
stairs – but I thank God I was not much disturbed at it. However,
I shall beware of being late abroad again.

16.   Up; and after doing some necessary business about my
accounts at home, to the office, and there with Mr. Hater wrote
letters.   And I did deliver to him my last Will, one part of it to
deliver to my wife when I am dead.

Thence to the Exchange, which I have not been a great while.
But Lord, how sad a sight it is to see the streets empty of people,
and very few upon the Change – jealous of every door that one
sees shut up, lest it should be the plague – and about us, two shops
in three, if not more, generally shut up.

From the Change to Sir G Smiths with Mr. Fenn, to whom I
am nowadays very complaisant, he being under payment of my
bills to me, and some other sums at my desire – which he readily
doth.[1]

Mighty merry with Captain Cocke and Fenn at Sir G Smiths,
and a brave dinner.   But I think Cocke is the greatest Epicure*
that is; eats and drinks with the greatest pleasure and Liberty that
ever man did.

a   repl. '700'

---

1. Sir George Smith was an   Street. Fenn was paymaster to the
Africa merchant, of Throgmorton   Navy Treasurer.

Very contrary news today upon the Change. Some, that our fleet hath taken some of the Dutch East India ships. Others, that we did attacque it at Bergen and were repulsed. Others, that our fleet is in great danger after this attacque, by meeting with the great body now gone out of Hollanders, almost 100 sail of men-of-war. Everybody is at a great loss, and nobody can tell.[1]

Thence among the Goldsmiths to get some money; and so home, settling some new money-matters; and to my great joy, have got home 500*l* more of the money due to me – and got some more money, to help Andrews with, advanced.

This day I had the ill news from Dagenhams that my poor Lord of Hinchingbrooke his indisposition is turned to the Small-pox. Poor gentleman, that should be come from France so soon to fall sick, and of that disease too, when he should be gone to see a fine lady, his Mistress.[2] I am most heartily sorry for it.

So late setting papers to rights, and so to bed.

17. Up, and to the office, where we sat all the morning; and at noon dined together upon some victuals I had prepared at Sir W. Batten's upon the King's charge. And after dinner, I having despatched some business and set things in order at home, we down to the water and by boat to Greenwich to the *Bezan* Yacht, where Sir W. Batten, Sir J. Mennes, my Lord Bruncker and myself, with some servants (among others, Mr. Carcasse, my Lord's Clerke, a very civil Gentleman) imbarked in the Yacht, and down we went most pleasantly – and noble discourse I had with my Lord Bruncker, who is a most excellent person. Short of Gravesend, it*a* grew calme, and so we came to an Anchor – and to supper mighty merry. And after, it being moonshine, we out

a repl. 'we'

---

1. For the engagement at Bergen, see below, p. 196 & n. 1.
2. Elizabeth Malet. Sandwich on 18 December abandoned negotiations for the match on hearing that the King had disposed her hand else-where (*CSPD 1664–5*, p. 116), and in 1667 Hinchingbrooke married Lady Anne Burlington. He had been abroad – with a tutor in Paris and travelling – for the past four years.

of the Cabbin to laugh and talk; and then, as we grew sleepy, went in, and upon ve[l]vet cushions of the King's that belong to the Yacht fell to sleep – which we all did pretty well till 3 or 4 of the clock – having risen in the night to look for a new Comet which is said to have lately shone.[1]   But we could see no such thing.

18.   Up about 5 a-clock and dressed ourselfs; and to sail again down to the *Soveraigne* at the buoy of the Noure – a noble ship, now rigged and fitted and manned.   We did not stay long, but to enquire after her readiness; and thence to Sheerenesse, where we walked up and down, laying out the ground to be taken in for a yard to lay provisions for cleaning and repairing of ships; and a most proper place it is for that purpose.[2]   Thence with great pleasure up the Meadeway, our yacht contending with Commissioner Pett's,[3] wherein he met us from Chatham; and he had the best of it.   Here I came by, but had not*a* tide enough to stop at Quinbrough.   With mighty pleasure spent the day in doing all*b* and seeing these places, which I had never done before.   So to the Hill house at Chatham,*c* and there dined; and after dinner spent some time discoursing of business – among others, arguing with the Comissioner about his proposing the laying-out so much money upon Sheerenesse, unless it be to the slighting of Chatham yard, for it is much a better place then Chatham;

a blot above word   *b* followed by symbol made illegible by blot
      c rest of paragraph crowded into bottom of page

---

1. Dr D. J. Schove writes: 'Possibly this was a meteor; no record of a comet has been traced.'

2. An estimate for this work at the mouth of the Medway was made immediately, and a warrant ordered for payment of the cost (almost £700) on 4 November: *CSPD 1664–5*, p. 546; ib., *1665–6*, p. 42.   Plan (1667) in BM, Add. 16370, f. 37r; plans and view (1698) in Ehrman, pl. v; details of establishment, ib., pp. 86–7, 104.   Its fortification in early 1667 was insufficient to prevent its capture in the Dutch raid on the Medway later that year. Thereafter it was strengthened and used as an advance base in the Third Dutch War (replacing Harwich), but for long remained the smallest of the royal yards, used for repair work etc., but not for shipbuilding.

3. The *Catherine*, a royal yacht built by Commissioner Pett.

which, however, the King is not at present in purse to do, though it were to be wished he were. Thence in Comissioner Pett's coach (leaving them there), I late in the dark to Gravesend, where great is the plague, and I troubled to stay there so long for the tide. At 10 at night, having supped, I took boat alone, and slept well all the way to the Tower docke, about 3 a-clock in the morning. So knocked up my people and to bed.

《19.》 Slept till 8 a-clock; and then up, and met with letters from the King and Lord Arlington for the removal of our office to Greenwich.[1]

I also wrote letters and made myself ready to go to Sir G. Carteret at Windsor; and having borrowed a horse of Mr. Blackbrough,[2] did send him to wait for me at the Duke of Albemarle's door – when on a sudden, a letter comes to us from the Duke of Albemarle, to tell us that the fleet is all come back to Solebay and are presently to be despatched back again.[3] Whereupon I presently by water to the Duke of Albemarle to know what news – and there I saw a letter from my Lord Sandwich to the Duke of Albemarle, and also from Sir W Coventry and Captain Teddiman,[4] how my Lord, having commanded Teddiman with 22

---

1. Pepys himself seems to have suggested this move in a letter to Coventry of 5 August: 'I have been a good while alone here. . . . The truth is, few but ticketeers and people of very ordinary errands now come hither, merchants and all persons of better rank with whom we have to deal for provisions and otherwise having left the town; so that I think it will be necessary with respect to them that we remove to some place to which they may be invited to come to us, such as Greenwich or the like' (*Further Corr.*, p. 49). The King ordered the transfer on 15 August, and rooms were prepared for the office in Greenwich Palace. Except on office-days, Pepys remained at first in Seething Lane. 'You, Sir,' he wrote to Coventry on 25 August, 'took your turn at the sword; I

must not therefore grudge to take mine at the pestilence' (ib., p. 53: Coventry had been at sea with the Duke of York in the summer). But within three days Pepys had moved first to Woolwich, then to Greenwich; see above, p. 140, n. 2.
2. Peter Blackbury, timber merchant.
3. Albemarle to Navy Board, Cockpit, 19 August: PRO, SP 29/129, no. 65; summary in *CSPD 1664–5*, p. 524.
4. Pepys's s.h. summaries of these letters are in Rawl. A 195a, ff. 218v–20r; his l.h. endorsement runs: 'August 19 1665. Abstract of letters come this day to the D. Albem. about the Action at Bergen.' The letters have not been traced.

ships (of which but 15 could get thither, and of those 15 but eight or nine could come up to play) to go to Bergen,[1] where after several messages to and fro from the Governor of the Castle, urging that Teddiman ought not to[a] come thither with more then five ships, and desiring time to think of it, all the while he suffering the Dutch ships to land their guns to their best advantage – Teddiman, on the second present,[2] begun to play at the Dutch ships (whereof ten East India-men) and in three hours' time (the town and Castle without any provocation playing on our ships) they did cut all our cables, so as the wind being off the land, did force us to go out – and rendered our fire-ships useless – without doing anything but what hurt, of course, our guns must have done them. We having lost five commanders – besides Mr. Edwd Mountagu and Mr. Windham.[3]

Our fleet is come home, to our great grief with not above five weeks dry and six days wet provision. However, must out again; and the Duke[b] hath ordered the *Souveraigne* and all other ships ready to go out to go to the fleet to strengthen them. This news

a repl. 'together'   *b* repl. 'Dutch'

---

1. Sandwich, riding with the battle fleet off Dogger, had detached a squadron under Teddeman to attack the Dutch E. Indiamen who were creeping home along the Norwegian coast. He relied on a secret understanding which the English envoy had made with Frederick III (King of Denmark and Norway), by which the Danes, in return for connivance with the attack, were to get a share of the booty. But the arrangement seems to have broken down a few days before the attack took place, and while Teddiman was on his way to Bergen where the ships lay. The governor of the town refused to co-operate when the English squadron appeared offshore on 1 August. Teddiman found the Danes to be neutral in favour of the Dutch, not of the English, and his attack on the

morning of 2 August was beaten off by the Dutch and their hosts. Sandwich's reputation suffered, unfairly, from this failure. Sandwich, pp. 261+; Pepys's l.h. copy of Sandwich's narrative (Rawl. A 468); *CSPD 1664–5*, p. 520; Lister, iii. 393+; J.C.M. Warnsinck, *De retourvloot van Pieter de Bitter*; Harris, i, ch. viii; Tedder, pp. 132 +; C. H. Hartmann, *Clifford*, ch. iii.

2. Sc. at the second time of aiming (presenting) his fire. The Governor was Johan Caspar von Cicignon.

3. Teddeman's report to Sandwich names six commanders lost. Edward Mountagu was Sandwich's second cousin. John Windham was a gentleman volunteer on Teddeman's ship: Sandwich, p. 263. No ships were lost.

troubles us all, but cannot be helped. Having read all this news, and received commands of the Duke with great content, he giving me the words which to my great joy he hath several times said to me, that his greatest reliance is upon me – and my Lord Craven[1] also did come out to talk with me, and told me that I am in mighty esteem with the Duke, for which I bless God.

Home; and having given my fellow-officers an account hereof to Chatham and wrote other letters, I by water to Charing-cross to the post-house;[2] and there the people tell me they are shut up, and so I went to the new post-house[3] and there got a guide and horses to Hounslow – where I was mightily taken with a little girl, the daughter of the maister of the House (Betty Gysby), which if she lives, will make a great beauty.

Here I met with a fine fellow, who, while I stayed for my horses, did enquire news; but I could not make him remember Bergen in Norway – in six or seven times telling – so ignorant he was.

So to Stanes, and there by this time it was dark night, and got a guide who lost his way in the forest, till by help of the Moone (which recompenses me for all the pains I ever took about studying of her motions) I led my guide into the way again back; and so we made a man rise that kept a gate,[a] and so he carried us to Cranborne –

where in the dark I perceive an old house new-building with a great deal of Rubbish, and was fain to go up a ladder to Sir G. Carteret's chamber.[4] And there in his bed I sat down and told him all my bad news, which troubled him mightily, but yet we were very merry and made the best of it; and being myself weary,

---

a repl. 'guide'

---

1. A distinguished soldier who acted as personal assistant to Albemarle.

2. The White Hart by the Inner Spring Garden and opposite the royal mews. (R).

3. Untraced; there were several. (R).

4. The house (Cranbourne Lodge, in Windsor Forest) was mostly Tudor, attached to a 15th-century tower which still survives. Carteret rebuilt most of it. The house was finally pulled down c. 1830. See G. M. Hughes, *Hist. Windsor Forest*, pp. 298+ (illust. opp. p. 298); VCH, *Berks.*, iii. 86. Descriptions in Evelyn, 23 October 1686; Celia Fiennes, *Journeys* ([c. 1701-3], ed. Morris), p. 360.

did take leave, and after having spoken with Mr. Fen in bed – I
to bed in my Lady's chamber that she uses to lie in, and where the
Duchesse of Yorke that now is was born.[1]   So to sleep – being
very well but weary, and the better by having carried with me a
bottle of strong water – whereof now and then a sip did me good.

20.   *Lords day.*   Sir G. Carteret came and walked by my bed's
side half an hour, talking and telling how my Lord is in this un-
blameable, in all this ill-success he having fallowed orders.   And
that all ought to be imputed to the falseness of the King of Denmarke, who[a] (he told me as a secret) had promised to deliver up
the Duch ships to us, and we expected no less.   And swears it will,
and will easily, be the ruine of him and his Kingdom if we fall out
with him – as we must in honour do.   But that all that can be,
must be to get the fleet out again to intercept De Witt, who
certainly will be coming home with the East India ships, he being
gone thither.[2]

He being gone, I up and with Fen, being ready to walk forth
to see that place; and I find it to be a very noble seat, in[b] a noble
forest, with the noblest prospect toward Windsor and round
about over many Countys that can be desired.   But otherwise a
very melancholy place and little variety save only Trees.

I had thoughts of going home by water and of seeing Windsor
Chapel and Castle; but finding at my coming in that Sir G.
Carteret did prevent me, in speaking for my sudden return to look
after business, I did presently eat a bit off the spit about 10 a-clock,
and so took horse for Staines, and thence for Brainford to Mr.
Povys,[3] the weather being very pleasant to ride in.   Mr. Povy not
being at home, I lost my labour; only, eat and drank there with

a repl. 'whom'   b repl. 'at'

---

1. The house was at the time of
the Duchess's birth (1637) occupied
by her maternal grandfather, Sir
Thomas Aylesbury, Bt, Master of
the Mint and a Master of Requests.
This room was spared in the rebuild-
ing: Evelyn, loc. cit.

2. The Dutch battle-fleet, over 100
strong, had left the Texel on 4 August

under the command of de Ruyter and
Tromp. Jan de Witt, the Grand
Pensionary of Holland, was one of the
three plenipotentiaries of the States-
General accompanying it: Colen-
brander, i. 292.   It brought the E.
India fleet safely back from Bergen:
see below, p. 218.

3. The Priory, Hounslow, Mdx.

his lady, and told my bad news and hear the plague is round about them there. So away – to Brainford; and there at the Inn that goes down to the water-side, I light and paid off my post-horses; and so slipped on my shoes and laid my things by, the tide not serving, and to church[1] – where a dull sermon and many Londoners. After church to my Inn and eat and drank; and so about 7 a-clock by water, and got between 9 and 10 to Queene hive, very dark – and I could not get my waterman to go elsewhere, for fear of the plague. Thence with a lanthorn, in great fear of meeting of dead corses carrying to be buried; but blessed be God, met none, but did see now and then a Linke (which is the mark of them) at a distance. So got safe home about 10 a-clock, my people not all a-bed; and after supper, I weary to bed.

21. Called up by message from Lord Bruncker and the rest of my fellows that they will meet me at the Duke of Albemarle this morning; so I up and weary; however, got thither before them and spoke with my Lord, and with him and other Gentlemen to walk in the parke, where I perceive he spends much of his time, having no*a*-whither else to go. And here I hear him speak of some presbyter-people that he caused to be apprehended yesterday at a private meeting in Covent garden, which he would have released upon paying 5*l* per man to the poor;[2] but it was answered they would not pay anything, so he ordered them to another prison from the guard.[3] By and by comes my fellow-officers, and the Duke walked in and to counsel with us; and that being done, we departed, and Sir W. Batten and I to the office, where after I had done a little business, I to his house to dinner; whither comes Captain Cocke, for whose*b* epicurisme a dish of Pa[r]triges was sent for, and still gives me reason to think him the greatest epicure in the world.

a repl. 'little'   *b* repl. 'his'

---

1. If the church Pepys attended was St Lawrence's, Brentford, the inn was probably the one (there no longer) near the ferry: cf. T. Faulkner, *Hist. Brentford* (1845), p. 163. But the situation of Povey's house suggests that the church may have been All Saints, Isleworth, and the inn the London Apprentice there: cf. *Home Counties Mag.*, 7/245.

2. The fine for first offenders under the Conventicle Act of 1664: only one-third of it was in fact supposed to go to the poor.

3. The guard-house, Whitehall.

Thence after dinner I by water to Sir W Warren's,[1] and with him two hours, talking of things to his and my profit – and perticularly, good advice from him what use to make of Sir G. Carteret's kindness to me and my interest in him, with exceeding good cautions for my not using it too much, nor obliging him too far by prying into his secrets, which it were easy for me to do.[2]

Thence to my Lord Bruncker at Greenwich, and Sir J. Mennes by appointment, to look after the lodgings appointed for us there for our office, which do by no means please me, they being in the heart of all the labourers and workmen there, which makes it as unsafe as to be I think at London.[3]   Mr. Hugh May,[4] who is a most ingenuous man, did show us the lodgings, and his acquaintance I am desirous of.   Thence walked, it being now dark, to Sir J. Mennes, and there stayed at the door, talking with him an hour while messengers went to get a boat for me to carry me to Woolwich, but all to no purpose.   So I was forced to walk it in the dark, at 10 a-clock at night, with Sir J. Mennes's George with me – being mightily troubled for fear of the Doggs at Coome farme,[5] and more for fear of rogues by way, and yet more because of the plague which is there (which is very strange, it being a single house, all alone from the town; but it seems they use to admit beggars [a] (for their own safety) to lie in their barns, and they brought it to them); but I bless God, I got about 11 of the clock well to my wife; and giving 4s in recompence to George, I to my wife; and having first viewed her last piece of drawing since I saw her (which is seven or eight days), which pleases me beyond anything in the world, I to bed with great content – but weary.

22.   Up; and after much pleasant talk, and being importuned by my wife and her two maids (which are both good wenches) for

a symbol blotted

---

1. At Rotherhithe.
2. As in the matter of his son's jointure: above, p. 180 & n. 3.
3. Greenwich Palace was now being partially rebuilt: see above, v. 75 & n. 3.   The Board met there for the first time on 26 August, and continued to hold meetings there until 9 January 1666.

4. Paymaster of the Works to the King; architect, courtier and friend of Lely and Evelyn.
5. 'Probably in the marshes, east of the palace': E. Hasted, *Hist. Kent* (ed. Drake), i. 43, n. 13.   There were several combes in this district.

me to buy a necklace of pearl for her, and I promising to give her one of 60*l* in two year at furthest, and in less if she pleases me in her*ᵃ* painting,[1] I went away and walked to Greenwich, in my way seeing a coffin with *ᵇ* a dead body therein, dead of the plague, lying in an open close belonging to Coome farme, which was carried out last night and the parish hath not appointed anybody to bury it – but only set a watch there day and night, that nobody should go thither or come thence, which is a most cruel thing – this disease making us more cruel to one another then we are [to] dogs.

So to the King's-house, and there met my Lord Brouncker and Sir J. Mennes, and to our lodgings again that are appointed for us, which do please me better today then last night, and are set a-doing. Thence I to Deptford, where by appointment I find Mr. Andrews come; and to the Globe, where we dined together and did much business as to our Plymouth Gentlemen.[2] And after a good dinner and good discourse, he being a very good man, I think verily – we parted, and I to the King's yard, walked up and down, and by and by out at the back gate and there saw the Bagwells wifes, mother and daughter, and went to them; and went in to the daughter's house without*ᶜ* the mother and faciebam*ᵈ* la cosa que ego tenebam a mind to con ella – and drinking and talking: by and by away, and so walked to Redriffe, troubled to go through the little lane where the plague is; but did, and took water and home – where all well; but Mr. Andrews not coming to even accounts as I expected, with relation to something of my own profit, I was vexed that I could not settle to business, but home to my viall; though in the evening he did come, to my satisfaction: so after supper (he being gone first), I to settle my Journall and to bed.

23. Up; and whereas I had appointed Mr. Hater and Will to come betimes to the office to meet me about business there – I was

a repl. 'his' *b* MS. 'of' *c* MS. 'with'
d strictly 'fasebam'

---

1. On 30 April 1666 she bought one costing £80.
2. Lanyon and Yeabsley, victual-lers (with Andrews) for Tangier. Denis Gauden was about to take over their contract.

called upon as soon as ready by Mr. Andrews, to my great content; and he and I to our Tanger accounts, where I settled, to my great joy, all my*a* accounts with him – and which is more, cleared for my service to the Contractors since the last sum I received of them, 222. 13. 00 profit to myself – and received the money actually in the afternoon.

After he was gone, comes, by a practice of mine yesterday, old Delkes the waterman with his daughter Robins, and several times to and again, he leaving her with me – about the getting of his son Robins off, who was pressed yesterday again. And jo haze ella mettre su mano upon my*b* pragma hasta hazerme hazer la cosa in su mano. Pero ella no voulut permettre que je ponebam meam manum a ella, but I do not doubt but ἄλλῳ χ[ρ]όνῳ de obtenir le.

All the afternoon at my office, mighty busy writing letters. And received a very kind and good one from my Lord Sandwich – of his arrival with the fleet at Sold bay – and the joy he hath at my last news he met with of the marriage of my Lady Jemimah.

And he tells me more, the good news that all our ships (which were in such danger that nobody would insure upon them) from the Eastland were all safe arrived[1] – which I am sure is a great piece of good luck – being in much more danger then those of Hambrough which were lost[2] – and their value much greater at this time to us.

At night home, much contented with this day's work; and being at home alone, looking over my papers, comes a neighbour of ours hard by to speak with me about business of the office – one Mr. Fuller, a great merchant but not my acquaintance.[3] But he came drunk, and would have had me gone and drunk with him at home or have let him send for wine hither; but I would do neither, nor offered him any. But after some sorry discourse, parted, and I up to chamber and to bed.

24. Up betimes to my office, where my clerks with me, and

a repl. 'our'   *b* MS. 'her'

---

1. The convoy of '14 sail laden with tar and cordage' which arrived in Bridlington Bay from the Baltic on the 18th: Sandwich, p. 266.

2. See above, p. 112 & n. 4.

3. Probably Richard Fuller, Mark Lane, of the Drapers' Company.

very busy all the morning writing letters. At noon down to Sir J Minnes and Lord Brunker to Grenwich to sign some of the Treasurer's books, and there dined very well; and thence to look upon our rooms again at the King's house, which are not yet ready for us. So home, and late writing letters; and so, weary with business, home to supper and to bed.

25. Up betimes to the office, and there, as well as all the afternoon (saving a little dinner time, all alone) till late at night, writing letters and doing business, that I may get beforehand with my business again, which hath run behind a great while; and then home to supper and to bed.

This day I am told that Dr. Burnett my physician is this morning dead of the plague – which is strange, his man dying so long ago, and his house this month open again. Now himself dead – poor unfortunate man.[1]

26. Up betimes, and prepared to my great Satisfaction an account for*a* the Board of my office disbursements, which I had suffered to run on to almost 120*l*.[2]

That done, I down by water to Greenwich, where we met the first day, my Lord Brouncker, Sir J. Mennes, and I, and I think we shall do well there. And begun very auspiciously to me, by having my account above-said passed and put into a way of having it presently* paid.[3]

When we rose, I find Mr. Andrews and Mr. Yeabsly, who is just come from Plymouth, at the door, and we walked together

---

a repl. 'to'

---

1. He died shortly after helping to perform an autopsy on the body of a plague victim, and others taking part in the operation were said to have died also: George Thomson, *Loimotomia* (1666), pp. 70–1; Sir Henry Ellis (ed.), *Orig. Letters* (1825–46), ser. 2, iv. 37. It has been suggested that a streptococcus was the cause of the deaths: J. F. D. Shrewsbury, *Hist. bubonic plague in Brit. Isles*, pp. 470–1.

But Burnet may well have died of the plague, since he was still living in the house in which his servant had died (cf. above, p. 124).

2. £119 10s. in prest- and conduct-money for seamen: PRO, Adm. 20/6, p. 170.

3. Will Hewer collected the money on this day: PRO, Adm. 20/6, loc. cit.

toward my Lord Brunker's – talking about their business,
Yeabsly being come up on purpose to discourse with me about it;
and finished all in quarter of an hour and is gone again. I perceive they have some inclination to be going on with their
victualling business for a while longer before they resign it to Mr.
Gawden; and I am well contented, for it brings me very good
profit, with certainty, yet with much care and some pains.

We parted at my Lord Brunckers door – where I went in
(having never been there before) – and there he made a noble
entertainment for Sir J. Mennes, myself, and Captain Cocke;
none else – saving some painted lady that dined there, I know not
who she is.[1] But very merry we were. And after dinner into
the garden and to see his and her Chamber, where some good
pictures, and a very handsome young woman for my lady's
woman.

Thence I by water home, in my way seeing a man taken up
dead out of the Hold of a small ketch that lay at Deptford; I doubt
it might be the plague, which, with the[a] thought of Dr. Burnett,
did something disturb me, so that I did not what I entended and
should have done at the office as to business. But home sooner
then ordinary; and after supper to read melancholy alone, and
then to bed.

27. *Lords day.* Very well in the morning; and up, and to my
chamber all the morning to put[b] my things and papers yet more
in order; and so to dinner. Thence all the afternoon at my office
till late, making up my papers and letters there into a good condition of order. And so home to supper; and after reading a good
while in the Kings *works*,[2] which is a noble book – to bed.

28. Up; and being ready, I out to Mr. Colvill the goldsmith's,
having not for some days ⟨been⟩ in the streets. But now, how
few people I see, and those walking like people that had taken

a repl. 'what'　　　*b* repl. 'make'

---

1. She was 'Madam' Williams,
Brouncker's mistress, once an actress
in the Duke of York's company.
Pepys disliked heavy make-up: cf.

below, 16 September, 5 October
1667.
　2. *The Workes* of Charles I; see
above, iii. 106, n. 1.

leave of the world. I there, and made even all accounts in the world between him and I in a very good condition. And would have done the like with Sir Rob. Viner, but he is out of town – the sickness being everywhere thereabouts. I to the Exchange, and I think there was not 50 people upon it and but few more like to be, as they told me, Sir G Smith and others. Thus, I think to take Adieu today of London streets, unless it be to go again to Viners.

Home to dinner, and there W. Hewer brings me 119*l* he hath received for my office disbursements, so that I think I have 1800*l* and more in the house; and blessed be God, no money out but what I can very well command, and that but very little – which is much the best posture I ever was in in my life, both as to the quantity and the certainty I have of the money I am worth, having most of it in my own hand. But then this is a trouble to me, what to do with it, being myself this day going to be wholly at Woolwich. But for the present I am resolved to venture it in an Iron Chest – at least, for a while.[1]

In the afternoon I sent down my boy to Woolwich with some things before me, in order to my lying there for good and all, and so I fallowed him.

Just now comes news that the Fleete is gone, or going this day, out again – for which God be praised; and my Lord Sandwich hath done himself great right in it in getting so soon out again.[2] Pray God he may meet the Enemy.

Towards the evening, just as I was fitting myself, comes W. Hewer and shows me a letter which Mercer had writ to her mother, about a great difference between my wife and her yesterday, and that my wife will have her go away presently. This, together with my natural jealousy that some bad thing or other may be in the way, did trouble me exceedingly, so as I was in a doubt whether to go thither or no. But having fitted myself and my things, I did go – and by night got thither – where I met my wife walking to the waterside with her painter, Mr. Browne,[3] and her maids. There I met Comissioner Pett and my Lord

1. For Pepys's banking methods, see above, v. 269, n. 1.

2. The fleet weighed anchor from Sole Bay on the 28th: Sandwich, p. 268. Both the King and the Duke of York had been anxious for Sand-wich to sail: *CSPD 1664–5*, p. 537. But he failed in his attempt to inter-cept the Dutch fleet sailing home from Bergen.

3. Alexander Browne, drawing master.

Brunker, and the lady at his house had been there today to see her.
Comissioner Pett stayed a very little while. And so I to supper
with my wife and Mr. Shelden, and so to bed – with great
pleasure.

29. In the morning waking, among[a] other discourse, my wife
begun to tell me the difference between her and Mercer, and that it
was only from restraining her to gad abroad to some Frenchmen
that were in the town; which I do not wholly, yet in part believe,
and for my quiet would not enquire into it. So rise and dressed
myself, and away by land, walking a good way; then remembered that I had promised Comissioner Pett to go with him in
his coach; and therefore I went back again to him, and so by his
coach to Greenwich and called at Sir The. Bidulph's, a sober
discreet man, to discourse of the preventing of the plague in
Grenwich and Woolwich and Deptford, where in every place it
begins to grow very great.[1]   We appointed another meeting,
and so walked together to Greenwich and there parted, and Pett
and I to the office, where all the morning. And after office done,
I to Sir J. Mennes and dined with him; and thence to Deptford,
thinking to have seen Bagwell, but did not, and so straight to
Redriffe and home, and late at my business to despatch away
letters. And then home to bed – which I did not entend, but to
have stayed for altogether at Woolwich. But I made a shift for a
bed for Tom, whose bed is gone to Woolwich, and so to bed.

30. Up betimes, and to my business of settling my house and
papers; and then abroad and met with Hadly our Clerke,[2] who
upon my asking how the plague goes, he told me it encreases

a   repl. 'a'

---

1. Sir Theophilus Biddulph was a
J.P. living at Westcombe Manor (a
house pulled down in the early 18th
century). Cf. John Evelyn to Lord
Cornbury, 9 September: 'Neare 30
houses are visited in this miserable
village, whereof one has beene the
very nearest to my dwelling . . . a
servant of mine now sick of a swelling

. . . behold me a living monument
of God Almighty's protection and
mercy' (Diary and corr., ed.
Wheatley, iii. 317). On 2 September
Evelyn sent his wife away from Deptford to Wotton: Evelyn, iii. 417, n. 4.
2. James Hadley, parish clerk of
St Olave's, Hart St.

much, and much in our parish: "For," says he, "there died nine
this week, though I have returned but six" – which is a very ill
practice, and makes me think it is so in other places, and therefore
the plague much greater then people take it to be.[1]

Thence, as I entended, to Sir R Viner's, and there found not Mr.
Lewes ready for me; so I went forth and walked toward Moore-
fields to see (God forgive my presumption) whether I could see
any dead Corps going to the grave;[2] but as God would have it, did
not. But Lord, how everybody's looks and discourse in the
street is of death and nothing else, and few people going up and
down, that the town is like a place distressed – and forsaken.
After one turn there, back to Viners and there found my business
ready for me and evened all reckonings with them to this day, to
my great content. So home; and all day, till very late at night,
setting my Tanger and private accounts in order, which I did in
both – and in the latter, to my great joy do find myself yet in the
much best condition that ever I was in – finding myself worth
2180*l* and odd, besides plate and goods which I value at 250*l* more
– which is a very great blessing to me. The Lord make me
thankful. ⟨And of this, at this*a* day above 1800*l* in cash in my
house, which speaks but little out of my hands in desperate condition. But this is very troublesome to have in my house at this
time.⟩*b*

So late to bed, well pleased with my accounts, but weary of
being so long at them.

31. Up, and after putting several things in order to my removal to Woolwich,*c* the plague having a great encrease this

---

a repl. 'one time'   *b* addition crowded in between paragraphs
      c repl. 'Dep'-

---

1. The bill of mortality for 22–9
August (GL, A.1.5, no. 96) gives
nine burials all told and six deaths
from the plague. The parish registers
(*Harl. Soc. Reg.*, 46/200) give eleven
deaths in the week without specifying
causes. Hadley's returns were made
to the Company of Parish Clerks:
cf. above, iii. 292, n. 1. Clarendon

refers to some of the reasons for the
unreliability of the figures given in
the bills of mortality: *Life*, iii. 35–6;
cf. also below, p. 283; J. F. D.
Shrewsbury, *Hist. bubonic plague in
Brit. Isles*, pp. 455+.

2. In the improvised plague-pits
there.

week beyond all expectation, of almost 2000 – making the general
Bill 7000, odd 100, and the plague above 6000 – I down by
appointment to Greenwich to our office, where I did some
business, and there dined with our company and Sir W Boreman
and Sir The Bidulph at Mr. Boreman's,[1] where a good venison
pasty.   And after a good merry dinner, I to[a] my office and there
late, writing letters; and then to Woolwich by water, where
pleasant with my wife and people; and after supper, to bed.

Thus this month ends, with great sadness upon the public
through the greatness of the plague, everywhere through the
Kingdom almost.   Every day sadder and sadder news of its encrease.   In the City died this week 7496; and of them, 6102 of
the plague.[2]   But it is feared that the true number of the dead this
week is near 10000 – partly from the poor that cannot be taken
notice of through the greatness of the number, and partly from
the Quakers and others that will not have any bell ring for them.

Our fleet gone out to find the Dutch, we having about 100 sail
in our fleet, and in them, the *Soveraigne* one; so that it is a better
fleet then the former with the Duke was.   All our fear is that the
Dutch should be got in before them – which would be a very
great sorrow to the public, and to me perticularly, for my Lord
Sandwichs sake.[3]   A great deal of money being spent, and the
Kingdom not in a condition to spare, nor a parliament, without
much difficulty, to meet to give more.   And to that, to have it
said "What hath been done by our late fleets?"

As to myself, I am very well; only, in fear of the plague, and as
much of an Ague, by being forced to go early and late to Woolwich, and my family to lie there continually.

My late gettings have been very great, to my great content, and
am likely to have yet a few more profitable jobbs in a little while –
for which,[b] Tanger and Sir W Warren I am wholly obliged to.

a repl. 'home'   *b* repl. symbol rendered illegible

---

1. George Boreman was Keeper of
the Wardrobe and Privy Lodgings at
Greenwich.   Batten and Mennes
lived in his house during the Plague.

2. The week was that of 22–9
August.   Burials were almost double

those of the previous week. GL,
A.1.5, no. 96.

3. See below, p. 218.   A list of the
Dutch ships (28 August), giving the
number of guns, is in Rawl. A 195a,
f. 217r.

SEPTEMBER.

1. Up, and to visit my Lady Pen and her daughter at the Rope-yard,[1] where*a* I did breakfast with them and sot chatting a good while. Then to my lodging to Mr. Sheldens, where I met Captain Cocke and eat a little bit of dinner; and with him to Greenwich by water, having good discourse with him by the way. After being at Greenwich a little while, I to London to my house; there put many more things in order for my Totall remove, sending away my girle Susan and other goods down to Woolwich, and I by water to the Duke of Albemarle – and thence home late by water.

At the Duke of Albemarle I overheard some examinations of the late plot that is discoursed of, and a great deal of do there is about it.[2] Among other discourses, I heard read, in the presence of the Duke, an examination and*b* discourse of Sir Ph. Howards[3] with one of the plotting party – in many places these words being then said:*c* Sir P. Howard, "If you will come over to the King and be faithful to him, you shall be maintained and be set up with a horse and armes and I know not what." And then said such a one: "Yes, I will be true to the King." "But, damn me!" said Sir Philip, "will you, so and so?" And thus, I believe, twelve times Sir P. Howard answered him a "Damn me!" – which was a fine way of Rhetorique to persuade a Quaker or anabaptist from his persuasion. And this was read, in the hearing of Sir P. Howard, before the Duke and twenty more officers, and they made sport of it only, without any reproach or he being anything shamed of it. But it ended, I remember, at last: "But such a one

a repl. 'which'   *b* repl. 'of'   *c* repl. 'such a one'

---

1. They were lodging during the Plague with William Bodham, Ropemaker to Woolwich Yard.

2. West-country fanatics were alleged to have planned to seize the Tower of London on 3 September – the anniversary of Dunbar, of the meeting of the first Protectorate parliament and of Oliver Cromwell's death. Albemarle had arrested several leaders: the examination of one (1 September) is given in *CSPD 1664–5*, p. 545. See also ib., pp. 538–44; ib., *1665–6*, p. 366; *Parl. Hist.*, iv. 325; *AHR*, 14/700–01.

3. Captain of Albemarle's troop of the King's Lifeguard.

(the plotter) did at last bid them remember that he had not told them what king he would be faithful to."

2. This morning I wrote letters to Mr. Hill and Andrews to come to dine with me tomorrow, and then I to the office, where busy, and thence to dine with Sir J. Mennes, where merry – but only that Sir J. Mennes, who hath lately lost two coach-horses,[a] dead in the stable, hath a third now a-dying. After dinner I to Deptford and there took occasion to andar a la casa de la gunaica de mi Minusier and did what I had a mind a hazer con⟨ella⟩, and volvió. To Greenwich, where wrote some letters; and home in pretty good time.

3. *Lords day.* Up, and put on my colourd silk suit, very fine, and my new periwigg, bought a good while since, but darst not wear it because the plague was in Westminster when[b] I bought it. And it is a wonder what will be the fashion after the plague is done as to periwigs, for nobody will dare to buy any haire for fear of the infection – that it had been cut off of the heads of people dead of the plague.

Before church-time comes Mr. Hill (Mr. Andrews failing because he was to receive the sacrament), and to church, where a sorry dull parson; and so home and most excellent company with Mr. Hill, and discourse of Musique. I took my Lady Pen home and her daughter Peg, and merry we were, and after dinner I made my wife show them her pictures, which did mad pegg Pen who learns of the same man[1] – and cannot do so well. After dinner left them, and I by water to Greenwich, where much ado to be suffered to come into the town because of the sickness, for fear I should come from[c] London – till I told them who I was. So up to the church, where at the door I find Captain Cocke in my Lord Brunkers coach, and he came out and walked with me in the churchyard till the church was done. Talking of the ill-government of our Kingdom, nobody setting to heart the business of the Kingdom, but everybody minding their perticular profit or pleasures, the King himself minding nothing but his ease – and so we let things go to wrack. This arose upon considering what we

a repl. 'coaches'   b repl. 'where'   c repl. 'to'

---

1. Alexander Browne, drawing master.

shall do for money when the fleet comes in, and more if the fleet should not meet with the Dutch, which will put a disgrace upon the King's actions, so as the Parliament and Kingdom will have the less mind to give more money. Besides, so bad an account of the last money, we fear, will be given; not half of it being spent, as it ought to be, upon the Navy.[1] Besides, it is said that at this day our Lord Treasurer cannot tell what the profits of Chimny money is; what it comes to per annum[2] – nor looks whether that or any other part of the Revenue be duly gathered as it ought – the very money that should pay the City the 200000*l* they lent the King[3] being all gathered and in the hands of the Receiver, and hath been long, and yet not brought up to pay the City, whereas*a* we are coming to borrow 4 or 500000*l* more of the City – which will never be lent as is to be feared.[4]

Church being done, my Lord Brouncker, Sir J. Mennes, and I up to the Vestry at the desire of the Justices of the Peace, Sir Th Bidolph and Sir W Boreman and Alderman Hooker – in order to the doing something for the keeping of the plague from growing; but Lord, to consider the madness of people of the town, who will (because they are forbid) come in Crowds along with the dead Corps to see*b* them buried. But we agreed on some orders for the prevention thereof.[5] Among other stories, one

a MS. 'when as' ('when' repl. 'but')   *b* repl. 'be'

1. Pepys here refers to a voluntary appropriation from the Royal Aid of 1665. There had been no statutory appropriation of these revenues to the navy such as was later provided for in the Additional Aid voted on 31 October: see below, p. 292 & n. 3.
2. The Hearth Tax of 1662, designed to produce £300,000 p.a., was valued in 1666 at £200,000 p.a.: below, vii. 326. Its proceeds were particularly difficult to calculate since, being paid into the Chamber of the city to cover the city's loans, they did not pass through the Exchequer.
3. In 1664: above, v. 307 & n. 2.
4. The city granted a loan of £100,000 in June 1666: below, vii. 174 & n. 4. There is no trace in the

city records of any discussion about the proposal here mentioned.
5. No vestry minutes survive. In London all funeral processions and gatherings were forbidden during the Plague, whatever the cause of death. The plague victims themselves were supposed to be buried only between sunset and sunrise, but the sheer numbers of deaths made nonsense of the law: *Orders by the Lord Maior* . . . (in *A collection of very valuable and scarce pieces relating to the Plague* . . . , 1721, pp. 6–7; J. Tillotson to Sancroft, 14 September 1665, in Sir Henry Ellis, ed., *Orig. Letters*, 1825–46, ser. 2, iv. 36). The Principal Officers of the Navy were *ex officio* magistrates for all counties in which royal dockyards were situated.

was very passionate methought – of a complaint brought against a man in the town for taking a child from London from an infected house.   Alderman Hooker told us it was the child of a very able citizen in Gracious-street, a saddler, who had buried all the rest of his children of the plague; and himself and wife now being shut up, and in despair of escaping, did desire only to save the life of this little child; and so prevailed to have it received stark-naked into the arms of a friend, who brought it (having put it into new fresh clothes) to Grenwich; where, upon hearing the story, we did agree it should be ⟨permitted to be⟩ received and kept in the town.[1]   Thence with my Lord Brouncker to Captain Cockes, where we mighty merry, and supped; and very late, I by water to Woolwich, in great apprehensions of an Ague.   Here was my Lord Brouncker's lady of pleasure, who I perceive goes everywhere with him, and he I find is obliged to carry her and make all the Courtship to her that can be.

4.   Writing letters all the morning.   Among others, to my Lady Carteret, the*a* first I have wrote her – telling her the state of the city as to health, and other sorrowful stories.[2]   And thence after dinner to Greenwich to Sir J. Mennes, where I find my Lord Brouncker; and having stayed our hour for the Justices by agreement, the time being past, we to walk into the Parke with Mrs. Hammond and Turner, and there eat some fruit out of the King's garden and walked in the park; and so back to Sir J. Mennes and thence *b* walked home, my Lord Brouncker giving me a very neat Cane to walk with.   But it troubled me to pass by Come Farme, where about 21 people have died of the plague – and three or four days since I saw a dead corpse in a Coffin lie in the close unburyed[3] – and a watch is constantly kept there, night and day, to keep the people in – the plague making us cruel as dogs one to another.

a repl. 'to'   *b* repl. 'there'

---

1. Pepys tells the story, in almost the same words, in a letter to Lady Carteret: below, n. 2.

2. Woolwich, 4 September; written in his most stately style. Copy (in Gibson's hand) in Rawl.

A 195a, ff. 199–200; printed in Braybrooke (1854), iv. 191–3; *Letters*, pp. 24–6.

3. See above, p. 201. For the farm's closes, see E. Hasted, *Hist. Kent* (ed. Drake), i. 43, n. 13.

5. Up, and walked, with some Captains and others talking to me, to Greenwich – they crying out upon Captain Teddiman's management of the business of Bergen;[1] that he stayed treating too long while he saw the Dutch fitting themselfs. And that at first he might have taken every ship and done what he would with them. How true I cannot tell.

Here we sat very late, and for want of money (which lies heavy upon us) did nothing of business almost. Thence home with my Lord Brouncker to dinner, where very merry with him and his Doxy. After dinner comes Collonell Blunt in his new Charriott made with Springs, as that was of Wicker wherein a while since we rode at his house.[2] And he hath rode, he says, now this Journy, many mile in it with one horse, and out-drives any coach and out-goes any horse, and so easy he says. So for Curiosity I went into it to try it; and up the hill to the Heath[3] and over the Cartrutts went to try it, and found it pretty well, but not so easy as he pretends; and so back again and took leave of my Lord and drove myself in the chariot to the office – and there ended my letters; and home pretty betimes, and there find W Pen, and he stayed supper with us, and mighty merry talking of his Travells and the French humours, &c;[4] and so parted and to bed.

6. Busy all the morning writing letters to several. So to dinner – to London to pack up more things thence; and there I looked into the street and saw Fires burning in the street, as it is through the whole City by the Lord Mayors order.[5] Thence by water to the Duke of Albemarle. All the way fires on each side the Thames; and strange to see in broad*a* daylight two or three Burialls upon the Bankeside, one at the very heels of another – doubtless all of the plague – and yet at least 40 or 50 people going*b*

a MS. 'brought'   *b* repl. 'at the h'-

1. See above, p. 196 & n. 1.
2. See above, p. 94 & n. 2.
3. Up Crooms Hill to Blackheath.
4. For young Penn's tour on the continent, see above, v. 255 & n. 1.
5. The fires were meant to clear the air of infection, and were perhaps the result of the city's recent appointment of physicians to advise on

measures against the plague: LRO, Repert. 70, ff. 144*v*–145*r*, 152*r*. For the distribution of the fires, see the map in J. F. D. Shrewsbury, *Hist. bubonic plague in Brit. Isles*, opp. p. 486. Expenditure on them is recorded in the City Cash Books for 1665 and 1666, but the order here referred to has not been traced.

along with every one of them.   The Duke mighty pleasant with me – telling me that he is certainly informed that the Dutch were not come home upon the first instant, and so he hopes our fleet may meet with them.   And here to my great joy I got him to sign bills for the several sums I have paid on Tanger business by his single letter, and so now I can get more hands to them.   This was a great joy to me.

Home to Woolwich late by water; found wife in bed – and yet, late as was, to write letters, in order to my rising betimes to go to Povy tomorrow.   So to bed, my wife asking me tonight about a letter of hers I should find, which endeed Mary[1] did the other day give me, as if she had found it in my bed, thinking it had been mine – wrote to her from a man without name, owning great kindness to her and I know not what.   But looking it over seriously, and seeing it bad sense and ill-wrote, I did believe it to be her brother's and so had flung it away; but finding her now concerned at it and vexed with Mary about it, it did trouble me; but I would take no notice of it tonight – but fell to sleep as if angry.

7.   Up by 5 of the clock, mighty full of fear of an Ague, but was obliged to go; and so by water, wrapping myself up warm, to the Tower; and there sent for the Weekely Bill and find 8252 dead in all, and of them, 6978[2] of the plague – which is a most dreadfull Number – and shows reason to fear that the plague hath got that hold that it will yet continue among us.   Thence to Brainford, reading *The Villaine* (a pretty good play)[3] all the way. There a coach of Mr. Povy's stood ready for me, and he at his house ready to come in; and so we together merrily to Swakely, Sir R Viner's[4] – a very pleasant place, bought by him of Sir James

---

1. Chambermaid.

2. *Recte* 6988: GL, A.1.5, no. 96 (29 August–5 September).

3. A tragedy by Thomas Porter; see above, iii. 229–30 & n. Pepys retained a copy of the first (1663) edition: PL 1075. (A).

4. Swakeleys, half a mile south-west of the church at Ickenham, Mdx. It had been bought by Sir Robert Vyner in this year, having been built in 1629–38 by Sir Edmund Wright on the H-plan, with cross wings at the n. and s. ends.   Wright had left it to his daughter, wife of Sir James Harrington (puritan politician and cousin of the author of *Oceana*), who occupied it 1643–60. Descriptions in W. H. Godfrey, *Swakeleys* (LCC, *Survey of London*, Monograph no. 13); and R. Comm. Hist. Mon. Engl., *Middlesex*, pp. 82+.

Harringtons lady. He took us up and down with great respect and showed us all his house and grounds; and is a place not very moderne in the gardens nor house, but the most uniforme in all that ever I saw – and some things to excess. Pretty to see over the Screene of the Hall (put up by Sir J Harrington, a Long Parliament-man) the King's head, and my Lord of Essex on one side and Fairfax on the other – and upon the other side of the Screene, the parson of the parish and the lord of the manor and his sisters.[1] The window-cases, door-cases, and Chimnys of all the house are Marble. He showed me a black boy that he had that died of a consumption; and being dead, he caused him to be dried in a Oven, and lies there entire in a box.

By and by to dinner, where his lady I find yet handsome, but hath been a very handsome woman – now is old – hath brought him near 100000*l*.[2] And now he lives no man in England in greater plenty, and commands both King and Council with his Creditt he gives them. Here was a fine lady, a merchant's wife, at dinner with us; and who should be here in the quality of a Woman but Mrs. Worships daughter, Dr.[a] Clerke's niece. And after dinner Sir Rob. led us up to his long gallery, very fine, above stairs (and better or such furniture I never did see), and there Mrs. Worship did give us three or four very good songs, and sings very neatly – to my great delight.

After all this, and ending the chief business to my content, about getting a promise of some money of him – we took leave, being exceeding well treated here. And a most pleasant Journy we had back, Povy and I; his company most excellent in anything but business – he here giving me an account of as many persons at Court as I had a mind or thought of enquiring after. He tells me,

a   repl. 'Captain'

---

1. The screen is described by Mrs K. A. Esdaile in LCC, *Survey*, op. cit., App. C, and ascribed to John Colt, jun., c. 1655, who probably made all the busts with the exception of that of the King, which appears to be by Peter Bennier (Besnier). See op. cit., pls 23–6. Two of the busts survive *in situ* – those of Charles and of Fairfax, the parliamentary general. That of Fairfax appears to be the only contemporary bust. The bust of Essex (another parliamentary general) is now in the mausoleum attached to the church at Ickenham. Those of the parson (Nathaniel Nicholas) and lord of the manor (Harrington) and his sisters have disappeared.

2. Mary, widow of Sir Thomas Hyde, of Albury, Hants. She was about 34.

by a letter he showed me, that the King is nor hath been of late very well, but quite out of humour and, as some think,[a] in a consumption* and weary of everything. He showed me my Lord Arlingtons house that he was born in, in a Towne called Harlington.[1] And so carried me through a most pleasant country to Brainford, and there put me into my boat and good[b]-night. So I wrapped myself warm, and by water got to Woolwich about one in the morning. My wife and all in bed.

8. Waked, and fell in talk with my wife about the Letter, and she satisfied me that she did not know from whence it came, but believed it might be from her Cosen Franke Moore, lately come out of France. The truth is, the thing I think cannot have much in it; and being unwilling (being in other things so much at ease) to vex myself in a strange place at a melancholy time – I passed all by, and were presently friends.

Up, and several with me about business. Anon comes my Lord Brouncker, as I expected, and we to the enquiring into the business of the late desertion of the Shipwrights from work, who had left us for three days together for want of money.[2] And upon this all the morning and brought it to a pretty good issue, that they, we[c] believe, will come tomorrow to work.

To dinner, having but a mean one, yet sufficient for him and he well enough pleased, besides that I do not desire to vye entertainments with him or any else. Here was Captain Cocke also, and Mr. Wayth. We stayed together talking upon one business or other all the afternoon. In the evening, my Lord Brouncker hearing that Mr. Ackeworths clerk, the Dutch-man who writes

---

a repl. same symbol badly formed   *b* repl. 'god'-   *c* repl. 'should'

---

1. Dawley House. Arlington's grandfather, Sir John Bennet (d. 1627), had bought the reversion of the manor in 1607, and it remained in the family until 1724. Arlington was not born there but at Little Saxham, Suff., where he was baptised on 6 September 1618. But he spent his youth at Harlington, where his father lived

after 1624. *DNB*; D. Lysons, *Hist. Middlesex parishes* (1780), pp. 127–8; V. Barbour, *Arlington*, pp. 1–5.

2. Possibly the dispute at Deptford referred to in *CSPD 1665–6*, p. 18 (J. Shish to Pepys, 17 October). For similar trouble at Portsmouth in the previous July, see above, p. 144 & n. 1.

and draws so well,[1] was transcribing*a* a book of Rates and our ships for Captain Millet,[2] a gallant of his Mistress's[3] – we sent for him for it.   He would not deliver it, but said it was his mistress's and had delivered it to her.   At last we were forced to send to her for it. She would come herself, and endeed, the book was a very neat one and worth keeping as a rarity.   But we did think fit, and though much against my will, to cancel all that he had finished of it, and did give her the rest – which vexed her; and she bore it discreetly enough, but with a cruel deal of malicious rancour in her looks.   I must confess I would have persuaded her to have let us had it to the office, and it may be the board would not have censured too hardly of it.   But my intent was to have had it for a Record for the office.   But she foresaw what*b* would be the end of it, and so desired it might rather be cancelled, which was a plaguy deal of spite.

My Lord Brouncker being gone, and company, and she also afterward – I took my wife and people and walked into the Fields about a while till night, and then home, and so to sing a little and then to bed.   I was in great trouble all this day for my boy Tom, who went to Greenwich yesterday by my order and came not home till tonight – for fear of the plague.*c*   But he did come home tonight, saying he stayed last night by Mr. Haters advice, hoping to have me called as I came home with my boat, to come along with me.

9.   Up, and walked to Greenwich;   and there we sat and despatched a good deal of business I had a mind to.   At noon by invitation to my Lord Brouncker's, all of us, to dinner, where a good venison pasty and mighty merry.   Here was Sir W Doyly, lately come from Ipswich about the sick and wounded – and Mr. Eveling and Captain Cocke.[4]   My wife also was sent for by my Lord Brouncker, by Cocke, and was here.   After dinner my Lord and his mistress would see her home again, it being a most cursed rainy afternoon, having had none a great while before.

a repl. 'copying'   *b* repl. 'it'   *c* '9' struck through in margin

1. Unidentified.   William Ackworth was the Storekeeper at Woolwich yard.

2. Probably Capt. Henry Millett of the *Mathias*.

3. Mrs ('Madam') Williams : see above, p. 204, n. 1.

4. Doyly, Evelyn and Cocke were Commissioners for the Sick and Wounded.

And I, forced to go to the office on foot through all the[a] rain, was almost wet to the skin, and spoiled my silk breeches almost.

Rained all the afternoon and evening, so as my letters being done, I was forced to get a bed at Captain Cockes – where I find Sir W Doyly and he and Eveling at supper; and I with them, full of discourse of the neglect of our masters, the great officers of State, about all businesses, and especially that of money – having now some thousands prisoners kept to no purpose, at a great charge, and no money provided almost for the doing of it. We fell to talk largely of the want of some persons understanding to look after businesses, but all goes to wrack. "For," says Captain Cocke, "My Lord Treasurer, he minds his ease and lets things go how they will;[1] if he can have his 8000*l* per annum and a game at Lombre, he is well. My Lord Chancellor, he minds getting of money and nothing else; and my Lord Ashly will rob the devil and the Alter[b] but he will get money if it be to be got." But that that put us into this great melancholy was news brought today, which Captain Cocke reports as a certain truth, that all the Dutch fleet, men-of-war and merchant East India ships, are got every one in from Bergen the 3rd of this month, Sunday last – which will make us all ridiculous.[2] The fleet came home with shame to require great deal of money, which is not to be had – to discharge many men, that must get the plague then or continue at greater charge on shipboard. Nothing done by them to encourage the Parliament to give money – nor the Kingdom able to spare any money if they would, at this time of the plague. So that as things look at present, the whole state must come to Ruine. Full of these melancholy thoughts, to bed – where though I lay the saftest I ever did in my life, with a down bed (after the Danish manner, upon me),[3] yet I slept very ill, chiefly through the

---

a repl. 'is'   *b* repl. 'spital'

---

1. Cf. the similar allegations below, vii. 313 etc. Southampton's administration of the office was slow and in many ways inefficient: see S. B. Baxter, *Devel. Treasury, 1660–1702*, pp. 9–11. He had in 1660 accepted a salary of £8000 p.a. in commutation of the traditional payment mainly by fees: H. Roseveare, *The Treasury*, p. 50 & n.

2. They got into the Texel on 7/17 September: G. Brandt, *Michel de Ruiter* (trans., Amsterdam, 1698), p. 312.

3. Pepys had been to Denmark briefly in the course of the naval expedition of 1659. Cocke's wife, his hostess, came from Danzig.

thoughts of my Lord Sandwiches concernment in all this ill-success at sea.

10. *Lords day.* Walked home, being forced thereto by one of my watermen falling sick yesterday; and it was God's great mercy I did not go by water with them yesterday, for he fell sick on Saturday night and it is to be feared of the plague. So I sent him away to London with his fellow.

But another boat came to me this morning, whom I sent to Blackewall for Mr. Andrews; I walked to Woolwich, and there find Mr. Hill, and he and I all the morning at Musique and a song[a] he hath set, of three parts; methinks very good. Anon comes Mr. Andrews,[b] though it be a very ill day. And so after dinner we to Musique and sang till about 4 or 5 a-clock, it blowing very hard, and now and then raining – and, wind and tide being against us, Andrews and I took leave and walked to Greenwich – my wife before I came out telling me the ill news that she hears, that her father is very ill; and then I told her I feared of the plague, for that the house is shut up. And so, she much troubled, she did[c] desire me to send them something, and I said I would, and will do so.

But before I came out, there happened news to come to me by an expresse from Mr. Coventry, telling me the most happy news of my Lord Sandwiches meeting with part of the Dutch; his taking two of their East India ships and six or seven others, and very good prize[1] – and that he is in search of the rest of the fleet, which he hopes to find upon the Well bancke[2] – with the loss only of the *Hector*, poor Captain Cuttle. This news doth so overjoy me, that I know not what to say enough to express it; but the better to do it, I did[d] walk to Greenwich; and there sending away Mr.

---

a repl. 'psalm'   *b* repl. 'Hill'   *c* repl. 'did'   *d* repl. 'am'

---

1. Coventry to Pepys, York, 8 September, enclosing copy of Sandwich to Albemarle, 5 September: Rawl. A 195a, ff. 183–7; partially printed in Braybrooke (1825). ii. 5–6. The engagement took place on the 3rd and 4th. The Dutch ships, on their way under convoy from Norway, had been dispersed by a storm. Sandwich also took four men-of-war: cf. Sandwich, p. 277. These prizes and those taken on the 9th were to cause untold trouble: see below, pp. 230+, esp. p. 231 & n. 1. The E. Indiamen were the *Golden Phoenix* and the *Slothany*.

2. The Well Bank, 18 miles w.n.w. of the Texel.

Andrews, I to Captain Cocke's, where I find my Lord Brouncker and his mistress and Sir J. Mennes – where we supped (there was also Sir W Doyly and Mr. Eveling); but the receipt of this news did put us all into such an extasy of joy, that it inspired into Sir J. Mennes and Mr. Eveling such*ᵃ* a spirit of mirth, that in all my life I never met with so merry a two hours as our company this night was.   Among other humours, Mr. Eveling's repeating of some verses made up of nothing but the various acceptations of May and Can, and doing it so aptly, upon occasion of something of that nature, and so fast, did make us all die almost with laughing, and did so stop the mouth of Sir J. Mennes in the middle of all his mirth (and in a thing agreeing with his own manner of Genius) that I never saw any man so out-done in all my life; and Sir J. Mennes's mirth too, to see himself out-done, was the crown of all our mirth.

In this humour we sat till about 10 at night; and so my Lord and his mistress home, and we to bed – it being one of the times of my life wherein I was the fullest of true sense of joy.

11.   Up, and walked to the office,*ᵇ* there to do some business till 10 of the clock; and then by agreement my Lord, Sir J. Mennes, Sir W. Doyly, and I took boat and over to the ferry, where Sir W. Batten's coach was ready for us, and to Waltham-stow¹ drove merrily.   Excellent merry discourse in the way, and most upon our last night's revells.   There come, we were very merry, and a good plain venison dinner.   After dinner to Billiards, where I won an angel.   And among other sports, we were merry with my pretending to have a warrant to Sir W Hickes (who was there, and was out of humour with Sir W Doyly's hav[ing] lately got a warrant for a lease of Buckes, of which we were now eating one), which vexed him.²   And at last would compound with me to give my Lord Bruncker half a buck now, and me a Dow for it a while hence when the season comes in,

a repl. 'into'   *b* repl. 'G'-

---

1. Batten had a country house there.

2. Warrants issued by a secretary of state were required for the grant of buck from royal forests. Hickes's jealousy arose perhaps from his being Ranger of Waltham (Epping) Forest and so having a prior claim to Doyly's. Hickes had been given a warrant for 'a leash [i.e. three] of fat bucks' from the forest on 17 July: PRO, SP 44/22, p. 226.

which we agreed to – and had held, but that we fear Sir W. Doyly did betray our design, which spoilt all. However, my Lady Batten invited herself to dine with him[1] this week, and she invited all us to dine with her there – which we agreed to only to vex him, he being the most niggardly fellow, it seems, in the world.

Full of good victuals and mirth, we set homeward in the evening, and very merry all the way. So to Greenwich, where when come, I find my Lord Rutherford and Creed come from Court, and among other things have brought me several orders for money to pay for Tanger; and among the rest, 7000*l* and more to this Lord – which is an excellent thing to consider; that though they can do nothing else, they can give away the King's money upon their progresse.[2] I did give them the best answer I could, to pay him with Tallys, and that is all they could get from me. I was not in humour to spend much time with them, but walked a little before Sir J. Mennes's door, and then took leave and I by water to Woolwich – where with my wife to a game at Tables, and to bed.

12. Up, and walked to the office, where we sat late. And thence to dinner home with Sir J. Mennes; and so to the office, where writing letters, and home in the evening – where my wife shows me a letter from her brother, speaking of their father's being ill, like to die, which (God forgive me) did not trouble me so much as it should, though I was endeed sorry for it. I did presently resolve to send him something in a letter from my wife – *viz*. 20*s*. So to bed.

13. Up, and walked to Greenwich,*a* taking pleasure to walk with my minute wach[3] in my hand, by which I am now come to see the distances of my way*b* from Woolwich*c* to Greenwich. And

a repl. 'Woolwich'   *c* l.h. repl. badly-written l.h.   *b* MS. 'wife'

1. Hickes. For his house, see below, p. 222, n. 1.
2. Treasurer's warrant, 7 September: *CTB*, i. 682. Rutherford was the heir of the late Governor of Tangier. The court was now at Salisbury: it moved to Oxford on the 23rd.
3. Probably a watch with two dials,

one recording the minutes; possibly the 'watch with many motions' which he exchanged in 1666: below, vii. 293. They were rare (and inaccurate) before the introduction of the balance-spring c. 1675. In the diary Pepys usually gives the time of day roughly by the hour.

do find myself to come within two minutes constantly to the same place at the end of each quarter of an hour.

Here we Rendezvoused at Captain Cocke's and there eat oysters; and so my Lord Brouncker, Sir J. Mennes and I took boat; and in my Lord's coach to Sir W Hickes's,[1] whither by and by my Lady Batten and Sir Wm. comes. It is a good seat – with a fair grove of trees by it, and the remains of a good garden. But so let to run to ruine, both house and everything in and about it – so ill furnished and miserably looked after, I never did see in all my life. Not so much as a latch to his dining-room door – which saved him nothing, for the wind blowing into the room for want thereof, flung down a great Bowpott that stood upon the side-table, and that fell upon some Venice-glasses and did him a crown's worth of hurt.

He did give us the meanest dinner – of beef – shoulder and umbles of venison which he takes away from the keeper of the Forest – and a few pigeons; and all in the meanest manner that ever I did see – to the basest degree.

After dinner we officers of the Navy stepped aside to read some letters and consider some business, and so in again. I was only pleased at a very fine picture of ⟨the⟩ Queene Mother – when she was young, by Van Dike;[2] a very good picture and a lovely sweet face.

Thence in the afternoon home; and landing at Greenwich, I saw Mr. Pen walking my way; so we walked together and for discourse I put him into talk of France, which he took delight to tell me of his observations, some good, some impertinent,* and all ill-told[3] – but it served for want of better; and so to my house,[4] where I find my wife abroad and hath been all this day, nobody

---

1. Ruckholts, Essex, residence of the Ranger of Waltham Forest; built under Elizabeth; taken down 1757. Hickes had another house, Beverston Castle, Glos. P. Morant, *Hist. Essex* (1768), i. 24; Thomas Wright, *Hist. Essex* (1835), ii. 498.

2. Henrietta-Maria had sat on many occasions to Van Dyck from the time of his arrival in London in the spring of 1632. None of his extant original portraits of the Queen is known to have been in private hands at this date, and Hickes may have owned a version of one of Van Dyck's earlier and smaller portraits of the Queen – e.g. G. Glück, *Van Dyck (Klassiker der Kunst,* Stuttgart, 1931), 376 or 393. A number of versions exist of both these patterns. (OM).

3. For William Penn's journey to France, see above, v. 255 & n. 1.

4. I.e. to his lodgings at Sheldon's house in Woolwich.

knew where; which troubled me, it being late and a cold evening. So (being invited to his mother's to supper) we took Mrs. Barbara,[1] who was mighty finely dressed, and in my Lady's coach (which we met going for my wife) we thither, and there after some discourse went to supper; by and by comes my wife and Mercer, and had been with Captain Cocke all day, he coming and taking her out to go see his boy at school at Brumly, and brought her home again with great respect. Here pretty merry, only I had no stomach (having dined late) to eat. After supper Mr. Pen and I fell to discourse about some words in a French song my wife was singing,[a] *D'un air tout interdict,*[2] wherein I laid twenty to one against him – which he would not agree with me, though I knew myself in the right as to the sense of the word. And almost angry we were, and were an hour and more upon the dispute – till at last broke up, not satisfied, and so home, it being late, in their coach. And so to bed.

H. Russell[3] did this day deliver my 20s to my wife's father or mother. But hath not yet told us how they do.

14. Up, and walked to Greenwich and there fitted myself in several businesses to go to London, where I have not been now a pretty while. But before I went from the office, news is brought by word of mouth that letters are now just now brought from the Fleete of our taking a great many more of the Dutch fleet – in which I did never more plainly see my command of my temper, in my not admitting myself to receive any kind of joy from it till I had heard the certainty of it. And therefore went by water directly to the Duke of Albemarle, where I find a letter of the 12th from Soldbay, from my Lord Sandwich,[4] of the fleet's meeting with about 18 more of the Dutch fleet and his taking of most of them; and the messenger says they had taken three after the letter was wrote and sealed; which being 21, and the 14 took the other day, is 45[5] sail – some of which are good, and others rich ships – which is so great a cause of joy in us all, that my Lord and every-

a MS. 'saying'

---

1. Barbara Sheldon, niece of the Pepyses' host.
2. Untraced. (E).
3. Waterman to the Navy Office.
4. Sandwich to the King: PRO,

SP29/132, no. 83; summary in *CSPD 1664–5*, p. 562. This action took place off the Dutch coast on the 9th.
5. *Sic*; the total was in fact lower: Sandwich, pp. 280–1; Penn, ii. 364.

body is highly joyed thereat. And having taken a copy of my Lord's letter,[1] I away back again to the Bear at the Bridge-foot, being full of wind and*ᵃ* out of order, and there called for a biscuit and a piece of cheese and gill of sack – being forced*ᵇ* to walk over the Bridge toward the Change, and the plague being all thereabouts. Here my news was highly welcome, and I did wonder to see the Change so full, I believe 200 people; but not a man or merchant of any fashion, but plain men all. And Lord, to see how I did endeavour all I could to talk with as few as I could, there being now no observation of shutting*ᶜ* up of houses infected, that to be sure we do converse and meet with people that have the plague upon them. I to Sir Rob. Viners, where my main business was about settling the business of Debusty's 5000*l* tallies – which I did for the present to enable me to have some money.[2] And so home, buying some things for my wife in the way. So home and put up several things to carry to Woolwich – and upon serious thoughts, I am advised by W Griffin to let my money and plate rest there, as being as safe as any place, nobody imagining that people would leave money in their houses now, when all their families are gone. So for the present, that being my opinion, I did leave them there still. But Lord, to see the trouble that it puts a man to to keep safe what with pain a*ᵈ* man hath been getting together; and there is good reason for it. Down to the office, and there wrote letters to and again about this good news of our victory, and so by water home late –

Where when I came home, I spent some thoughts upon the occurrences of this day, giving matter for as much content on one hand and melancholy on another as any day in all my life – for the first, the finding of my money and plate and all safe at London ⟨and speeding in my business of money this day⟩ – the hearing of this good news, to such excess after so great a despair of my Lord's doing anything this year – adding to that, the decrease of 500 and more, which is the first decrease we have yet had in the sickness since it begun – and great hopes that the next week it will be

---

a repl. 'of'   *b* repl. same symbol badly formed
       c repl. 'stopping'   *d* repl. 'we'

---

1. Rawl. A 195a, f. 221r (s.h.).

2. Lawrence Debusty (Debussy) was a provision merchant. This transaction (presumably relating to Tangier) has not been traced. In 1666 Debussy provided a letter of credit for Belasyse, Governor of Tangier: below, vii. 174.

greater.[1]   Then on[a] the other side – my finding that though the Bill* in general is abated, yet the City within[b] the walls is encreased and likely to continue so ⟨and is close to our house there⟩ – my meeting dead corps's of the plague, carried to be buried close to me at noonday through the City in Fanchurch-street – to see a person sick of the sores carried close by me by[c] Grace-church[2] in a hackney-coach[3] – my finding the Angell tavern at the lower end of Tower-hill shut up; and more then that, the alehouse at the Tower-stairs;[4] and more then that, that the person was then dying of the plague when I was last there, a little while ago at night, to write a short letter there, and I overheard[d] the mistress of the house sadly saying to her husband somebody was very ill, but did not think it was of the plague – to hear that poor Payne my water[man] hath buried a child and is dying himself – to hear that ⟨a labourer I sent but the other day to Dagenhams to know how they did there is dead of the plague; and that⟩ one of my own watermen, that carried me daily, fell sick as soon as he had landed me on Friday morning last, when I had been all night upon the water (and I believed he did get his infection that day at Brainford) is now dead of the plague – to hear ⟨that Captain Lambert and Cuttle are killed in the taking these ships and⟩ that Mr. Sidny Mountagu is sick of a desperate fever at my Lady Carteret's at Scott's hall – to hear that Mr. Lewes hath another daughter sick – and lastly, that both my servants, W Hewers and Tom Edwards, have lost their fathers, both in St. Sepulcher's parish, of the plague this week – doth put me into great apprehensions of melancholy, and with good reason.   But I put off the thoughts of sadness as much as I can; and the rather to keep my[e] wife in good heart, and family also.   After supper (having eat nothing all this day) upon a fine Tench of Mr. Sheldens taking, we to bed.[f]

a repl. 'other'   *b* MS. 'when'   *c* repl. 'in'
d repl. 'where'   *e* repl. 'it'
f The number and extent of the insertions in this paragraph suggests that Pepys revised it after it was entered – a procedure rather unusual in the diary.

---

1. In the week 5–12 September, 6544 died of the plague, as against 6988 in the previous week: GL, A.1.5, no. 96.

2. St Benet, Gracechurch St.

3. For regulations controlling this practice, see above, p. 136, n. 5.

4. Probably the Rose and Crown: c.f. Boyne, i. 775.

15. Up, it being a cold misling morning, and so by water to the office, where very busy upon several businesses. At noon got the messenger, Marlow, to get me a piece of bread and butter and cheese and a bottle*ᵃ* of beer and ale, and so I went not out of the office but dined off that, and my boy Tom, but the rest of my clarks went home to dinner. Then to my business again, and by and by sent my waterman to see how Sir W Warren doth, who is sick, and for which I have reason to be very sorry, he being the friend I have got most by of most friends in England but the King. Who returns me that he is pretty well again, his disease being an ague. I by water to Deptford, thinking to have seen my valentine,*¹* but I could*ᵇ* not and so come back again – and to the office, where a little business; and thence with Captain Cocke and there drank a cup of good drink (which I am fain to allow myself during this plague time, by advice of all and*ᶜ* not contrary to my oath, my physician being dead and Chyrurgeon out of the way whose advice I am obliged to take); and so by water home and eat my supper, and so to bed – being in much pain to think what I shall do this winter time; for, go every day to Woolwich I cannot, without endangering my life, and staying from my wife at*ᵈ* Greenwich is not handsome.

16. Up, and walked to Greenwich, reading a play, and to the office, where I find Sir J. Mennes gone to the fleet like a doting fool, to do no good but proclaim himself an asse – for*ᵉ* no service he can do there, nor inform my Lord (who is come in thither to the Buoy of the Nore) in anything worth his knowledge. At noon to dinner to my Lord Bruncker, where Sir W Batten and his Lady came by invitation, and very merry we are – only, that the discourse of the likelihood of the increase of the plague this week makes us a little sad. But then again, the thoughts of the late prizes make us glad. After dinner by appointment comes Mr. Andrews, and he and I walking·alone in the garden, talking of our Tanger business; and I endeavoured by the by to offer some encouragements for their continuing in that business,*²*

a repl. 'dr'-   *b* MS. 'did could'   *c* repl. 'that'
d repl. 'there'   *e* MS. 'asse for—'

1. Mrs Bagwell.
2. See Pepys to Yeabsley (Andrews's partner in the Tangier victualling), 16 September: Rawl. A 193, f. 213*v* (copy by Hayter).

which he seemed to take hold of; and the truth is, my profit is so much concerned, that I could wish they would, and would take pains to ease them in the business of money as much as was possible.

He being gone (after I had ordered him 2000*l* and he paid me my Quantum out of it), I also walked to the office; and there to my business, but find myself, through the unfitness of my place to write in, and my coming from great dinners and drinking wine, that I am not in that good temper of doing business nowadays that I used to be and ought still to be.

At night to Captain Cockes, meaning to lie there, it being late; and he not being at home, I walked to him to my Lord Bruncker's and there stayed a while, they being at tables;* and so by and by parted, and walked to his house, and after a mess of good broth, to bed in great pleasure, his company being most excellent.

17. *Lords day.* Up, and before I went out of my chamber, did draw a Musique*ª* Scale, in order to my having it at any time ready in my hand to turn to for exercise, for I have a great mind in this vacation to perfect myself in my Scale, in order to my practising of composition.[1] And so that being done, I downstairs and there find Captain Cocke under the barber's hands – the barber that did heretofore trim Comissioner Pett, and with whom I have been. He[2] offered to come this day after dinner with his violin, to play me a set of Lyra=ayres[3] upon it, which I was glad of, hoping to be merry thereby.

Being ready, we to church, where a company of fine people to church, and a fine church and very good sermon (Mr. Plume being a very excellent scholler and preacher)[4]; coming out of the

---

a repl. 'scheme of'

1. The existing system of naming the degrees of the scale (the gamut) was complex, and Pepys did not master it until 8–10 April 1668. (E).

2. The barber (Golding): cf. below, p. 263. (E).

3. He would play the melodies of lyra-viol pieces either solo, or accompanied by Pepys on the lyra-viol: cf. above, i. 295, n. 4; v. 18. Possibly Playford's *Musicks recreation: on*

the lyra viol (?1652), or his *Musicks recreation on the viol, lyra-way* (1661) was to be used. (E).

4. Thomas Plume was Vicar of Greenwich, 1658–1704; in 1679 he was made a Canon of Rochester. Evelyn heard him on the following Sunday. He was a bibliophile, and founder of the Plumian chair of astronomy at Cambridge.

church, I met Mrs. Pierce, whom I was shamed to see, having not been with her since my coming to town – but promised to visit her.

Thence with Captain Cocke (in his coach) home to dinner, whither comes by invitation My Lord Bruncker and his mistress,[1] and very good company we were. But in dinner-time comes Sir Jo. Minnes from the fleet like a simple weak man, having nothing to say of what he hath done there, but tells us of what value he imagines the prizes to be, and that my Lord Sandwich is well and mightily concerned to hear that I was well. But this did put me upon a desire of going thither; and moving of it to my Lord, we presently agreed upon it to go this very Tide, we two and Captain Cocke. So everybody prepared to fit himself for his Journy, and I walked to Woolwich to trim and shift myself; and by the time I was ready they came down in the *Bezan*[a] Yacht, and so I aboard and my boy Tom. And there very merrily we sailed to below Gravesend, and there came to Anchor for all night and supped and talked, and with much pleasure at last settled ourselfs to sleep – having very good lodging upon Cushions in the Cabbin.

18. By break of day we came to within sight of the fleet, which was a very fine thing to behold, being above 100 ships, great and small – with the flag-ships of each squadron distinguished by their several flags on their main, fore, or mizzen masts. Among others, the *Soveraigne*, *Charles*, and *Prince*, in the last of which my Lord Sandwich was. When we called by her side, his Lordship was not stirring; so we came to anchor a little below his ship, thinking to have rowed on board him; but the wind and tide was so strong against us that we could not get up to him; no, though rowed by a boat of the *Prince*'s that came to[b] us to tow us up; at last, however, he brought us within a little way, and then they flung out a rope to us from the *Prince*, and so came on board, but with great trouble and time and patience, it being very cold. We find my Lord newly up in his night-gown, very well. He received us kindly, telling us the state of the fleet; lacking provisions, having no beer at all, nor have had most of them these three weeks or month, and but few days' dry provisions. And

a repl. 'pr'-   *b* repl. 'up'

1. See above, p. 204, n. 1.

endeed, he tells us that he believes no fleet was ever set to sea in so ill condition of provision as this was when it went out last.   He did inform us in the business of Bergen,[1] so as to let us see how the judgment of the world is not to be depended on in things they know not; it being a place just wide enough, and not so much hardly, for ships to go through to it, the yard-arms sticking in the very rocks.   He doth not, upon his best enquiry, find reason to except against any part of the management of that business by Teddiman, he having stayed treating no longer then during the night whiles he was fitting himself to fight, bringing his ship abreast, and not a quarter of an hour longer (as is said); nor could more ships have been brought to play, as is thought – nor could men be landed, there being 10000 men effectively alway in armes of the Danes; nor, says he, could we expect more from the Dane then he did, it being impossible to set fire on the ships but it must burn the Towne.   But that wherein the Dane did amisse[a] is that he did assist them, the Duch, all the while while he was treating with us, while he should have been newtrall to us both.   But however, he did demand but the treaty of us; which is, that we should not come with more then five ships.   A flag of Truce is set, and confessed by my Lord that he believes it was hung out; but while they did hang it out, they did shoot at us, so that it was not (either seen perhaps or) fit to cease upon sight of it, while they continued actually in action against us.   But the main thing my Lord wonders at, and condemns the Dane for, is that that blockhead,[2] who is so much in debt to the Hollanders, having now a treasure more by much then all his Crowne was worth, and that which would for ever have beggared the Hollander, should not take this time to break with the Hollanders, and thereby paid his debt, which must have been forgiven him, and got the greatest treasure into his hands that ever was together in the world.

By and by my Lord took me aside to discourse of his private matters; who was very free with me touching the ill condition of the fleet that it hath been in, and the good fortune that he hath

a repl. illegible symbol and 'us'

1. See above, p. 196 & n. 1.   2. The King – Frederick III, King
of Denmark and Norway.

had, and nothing else that these prizes are to be imputed to.   He also talked with me about Mr. Coventry's dealing with him, in sending Sir W Pen away before him,[1] which was not fair nor kind; but that he hath mastered and cajolled Sir W. Penn that he hath been able to do nothing in the fleet, but been obedient to him; but withal, tells me he is a man that is but*a* of very mean parts, and a fellow not to be lived with, so false and base he is; which I know well enough to be very true, and did, as I have formerly done, give my Lord my knowledge of him.

By and by was called a council of warr on board, when came Sir W Pen there – and Sir Chr. Mings, Sir Edwd Spragg, Sir Jos. Jordan, Sir Tho. Teddiman, and Sir Rogr. Cuttance.   And so the necessities of the fleet for victuals, clothes, and money was discoursed, but by the discourse there of all but my Lord – that is to say, the counterfeit grave nonsense of Sir W Pen and the poor mean discourse of the rest, methinks I see how the government and management of the greatest business of the three nations is committed to very ordinary heads, saving my Lord; and in effect, is only upon him, who is able to do what he please with them, they not having the meanest degree of reason to be able to oppose anything that he says.   And so I fear it is ⟨ordered⟩ but like all the rest of the King's public affayres.

The council being up, they most of them went away, only Sir W. Penn, who stayed to dine there, and did so; but the wind being high, the ship (though the motion of it was hardly discernible to the eye) did make me sick, so as I could not eat anything almost.

After dinner Cocke did pray me to help him to 500*l* of W How, who is Deputy-Treasurer, wherein my Lord Bruncker and I am to be concerned; and I did ask it my Lord, and he did consent to have us furnished with 500*l*, and I did get it paid to Sir Rogr Cuttance and Mr. Pierce in part for above 1000*l*-worth of goods, Mace, Nuttmeggs, Cynamon, and Cloves.   And he tells us we may hope*b* to get 500*l* by it – which God send.   Great spoil, I hear, there hath been of the two East India ships, and that yet they will

a repl. 'a'   *b* repl. same symbol badly formed

---

1. See above, p. 148 & n. 3.

come in to the King very rich[1] – so that I hope this journy will be worth 100*l* to me. After having paid this money, we took leave of my Lord, and so to our Yacht again, having seen many of my friends there. Among others, I hear that W Howe will grow very rich by this last business and grows very proud and insolent by it – but it is what I ever expected.

I hear by everybody how much my poor Lord of Sandwich was concerned for me during my silence awhile, lest I had been dead of the plague in this sickly time.

No sooner come into the Yacht, though overjoyed with the good work we have done today, but I,*a* was overcome with sea-

a repl. 'we'

---

1. The two E. Indiamen (the *Phoenix* and the *Slothany*) had been captured by Sandwich, along with 11 other ships, on 3 September. Most imprudently, he had allowed his commanders and seamen to take their accustomed share (all that lay between decks) before it was legally judged to be prize. This, together with his failure to put out against the Dutch in early October, was to lead to his removal to the Madrid embassy in the following December. Penn and Cuttance had been his principal advisers, and he seems to have received more than £4000 from sales. See his own account of the affair in Sandwich MSS, Journals, x. 22–33, 38–54, 64–8, 208–10, 230–2. Cf. also PRO, HCA 32/11, nos 303, 304 (examinations of the ships); PRO, SP 29/149, nos 89, 90 (report of prize officers); Penn, ii. 477+; Harris, vol. ii, ch. ix; *Occ. papers Pepys Club*, ii, no. ix; Bryant, i. 266+. Pepys recounts his own part more fully in the diary than in the brief journal he kept of the affair itself (Rawl. A 174, f. 299*r–v*, covering 17 September–13 November 1665; printed in *Tangier Papers*, App. iv; incorrectly in Smith, i. 104–8).

With Cocke, Pepys agreed to purchase some of the flag-officers' share, but on 13 November, for fear of implication in what was growing into a national scandal, prudently sold out to his partner for £500. Cocke was the merchant most deeply implicated. No public enquiry was held, but the matter was investigated by the Brooke House Committee which in 1668 examined the war finances: copy in BM, Harl. 7170, ff. 73+. ('The Report of the Commissioners of Accounts to the Parliament touching the East India=Prizes', 10 April 1668; copy by Hayter and Hewer.) Penn was impeached, and Sandwich escaped only because of his status as ambassador: Milward, pp. 268–9. Two important letters from Pepys to the committee in self-exculpation are supported by the evidence of the diary: Rawl. A 174, f. 301*r*; *Further Corr.*, pp. 192+. He had acted only after receiving Sandwich's authority. For some of his letters to Sandwich, see *Shorthand Letters*, pp. 60+. The custom governing the division of prize-goods (made statutory in 1692) is summarised in Ehrman, p. 130.

sickness, so that I begun to spew soundly – and so continued a good while – till at last I went into the Cabbin, and shutting*ᵃ* my eys, my trouble did cease, that I fell asleep; which continued till we came into Chatham River, where the water was smooth, and then I rose and was very well. And the tide coming to be against*ᵇ* us, we did land before we came to Chatham and walked a mile – having very good discourse by the way – it being dark and it beginning to rain just as we got thither.

At Comissioner Petts we did eat and drink very well, and very merry we were. And about 10 at night, it being moonshine and very cold, we set out, his coach*ᶜ* carrying us, and so all night travelled to Greenwich – we sometimes sleeping a little, and then talking and laughing by the way; and with much pleasure, but that it was very horrible cold, that I was afeared of an ague.

A pretty passage was that the coach stood of a sudden, and the coachman came down, and the horses stirring, he cried "Hold!" which waked me; and the coach[man] standing at the boot to[do] something or other, and crying "Hold!," I did wake of a sudden; and not knowing who he was nor thinking of the coachman, between sleeping and waking I did take up the heart to take him by the shoulder, thinking verily he had been a thief. But when I waked, I found my cowardly heart to discover a fear within me, and that I should never have done it if I had been awake.

19. About 4 ⟨or 5⟩ of the clock we came to Greenwich; and having first set down my Lord Bruncker, Cocke and I went to his house, it being light. And there to our great trouble, we being sleepy and cold, we met with the ill news that his boy Jacke was gone to bed sick, which put Captain Cocke, and me also, into much trouble – the boy, as they told us, complaining of his head most, which is a bad sign it seems. So they presently betook themselfs to consult whether and how to remove him. However, I thought it not fit for me to discover too much fear to go away, nor had I any place to go to; so to bed I went and slept till 10 of the clock, and then comes Captain Cocke to wake me and tell me that his boy was well again – with great joy I heard the news and he told it; so I up,*ᵈ* and to the office, where we did a little, and but a little, business.

At noon by invitation to my Lord Bruncker's, where we

a repl. 'slept'   *b* repl. 'again'   *c* repl. 'ch'-   *d* repl. 'hope' stayed till 4 of the clock for my Lady Batten; and she not then coming, we to dinner, and pretty merry but disordered by her making us stay so long.

After dinner I to the office and there wrote letters and did business till night. And then to Sir Jo Minnes, where I find my Lady Batten come, and she and my Lord Brouncker and his mistress and the whole houseful there at Cards. But by and by my Lord Brouncker goes away, and others of the company, and when I expected Sir J. Mennes and his sister should have stayed to have made Sir W. Batten and Lady supped, I find they go up in snuffe to bed, without taking any manner of leave of them, but left them with Mr. Boreman.[1] The reason of this I could not presently learn, but anon I hear it is that Sir J. Mennes did expect and intend them a supper, but they, without respect to him, did first apply themselfs to Boreman; which makes all this great fewd. However, I stayed and there supped – all of us being in great disorder from this, and more from Cockes boy's being ill, where my Lady Batten and Sir W. Batten did come to town with an intent to lodge, and I was forced to go seek a lodging; which ⟨my⟩ W. Hewer did get me, *viz.*, his own chamber in the towne, whither I went, and find it a very fine room and there lay most excellently.

20. Called up by Captain Cocke (who was last night put into great trouble upon his boy's being rather worse then better, upon which he removed him out of his house to his stable), who told me that to my comfort his boy was now as well as ever he was in his life.

So I up; and after being trimmed (the first time I have been touched by a barber these 12 months I think and more),[2] went to Sir J. Mennes, where I find all out of order still, they having not seen one another; till by and by Sir J. Mennes and Sir W. Batten met to go into my Lord Brouncker's coach, and so we four to Lambeth, and thence to the Duke of Albemarle to inform him what we have done as to the fleet, which is very little, and to receive his direction. But Lord, what a sad time it is, to see no boats upon the River – and grass grow all up and down Whitehall-court – and nobody but poor wretches in the streets. And which

1. George Boreman, Mennes's   2. Cf. above, v. 6 & n. 3.
host: see above, p. 208, n. 1.

is worst of all, the*a* Duke showed us the number of the plague this week, brought in the last night from the Lord Mayor – that it is encreased about 600 more then the last, which is quite contrary to all our hopes*b* and expectations from the coldness of the late season: for the whole general number is 8297; and of them, the plague 7165 – which is more in the whole, by above 50, then the biggest Bill* yet[1] – which is very grievous to us all.

I found here a design in my Lord Brouncker and Captain Cocke to have had my Lord Brouncker chosen as one of us, to have been sent aboard one of the East India men – and Captain Cocke, as a merchant, to be joined with him – and Sir J. Mennes for the other, and Sir G Smith to be joined with him. But I did order it so that my*c* Lord Brouncker and Sir J. Mennes were ordered; but I did stop the merchants to be added, which would have been a most pernicious thing to the King I am sure.[2] In this, I did I think a very good office, though I cannot acquit myself from some envy of mine in the business, to have that profitable business done by another hand, while I lay wholly imployed in the trouble*d* of the office.

Thence back again by my Lord's coach to my Lord Brouncker's house, where I find my Lady Batten (who is become very great with Mrs. Williams, my Lord Brouncker's whore), and there we dined and were mighty merry.

After dinner I to the office, there to write letters to fit myself for a journy tomorrow to Nonsuch to the Exchequer by appointment.

That being done, I to Sir J. Mennes, where I find Sir W. Batten and his Lady gone home to Walthamstow, in great snuffe as to Sir J. Mennes, but yet with some necessity, hearing that a maidservant of theirs is taken ill. Here I stayed, and resolved of my going in my Lord Bruncker's coach, which he would have me to

---

a repl. 'as'   *b* repl. 'fears'   *c* repl. 'our'   *d* repl. 'world'

---

1. The week 12–19 September was to prove the worst of the whole plague period: J. F. D. Shrewsbury, *Hist. bubonic plague in Brit. Isles*, pp. 473–5. During the previous week plague deaths had been 6544 out of a total of 7690: GL, A.1.5, no. 96.
2. They were to go aboard the

E. Indiamen and supervise the unloading of the prize goods: below, p. 242; *CSPD 1664–5*, p. 570. On 6 October, they were reinforced by two government servants, Charles Bennett and Richard Kingdon: BM, Harl. 1509, f. 192*v*.

take (though himself cannot go with me as he intended); and so to my last night's lodging to bed, very well.

21. Up between 5 and 6 a-clock, and by the time I was ready, my Lord's coach comes for me; and taking Will Hewers with me (who is all in mourning for his father, who is lately*a* dead of the plague, as my boy Tom's is also), I set out, and took about 100*l* with me to pay the Fees there – and so I rode in some fear of robbing. When I come thither, I find only Mr. Ward, who led me to Burges's bedside and Spicer's (who watching of the house, as*b* it is their turns every night,*c* did lie long in bed today), and I find nothing at all done in my business, which vexed me. But not seeing how to help it, I did walk up and down with Mr. Ward to see the house; and by and by Spicer ⟨and Mr. Falconbrige⟩ came to me, and he and I to a town near by, Yowell, and there drink and set up my horses, and also bespoke a dinner. And while that is dressing, went with Spicer and walked up and down the house and park; and a fine place it hath heretofore been, and a fine prospect about the house[1] – a great walk of a Elme and a Walnutt set one after another in order[2] – and all the house on the outside filled with figures of story, and good painting of Rubens or Holben's doing.[3] And one great thing is that most of the house is covered, I mean the posts and quarters in the walls, covered with Lead and gilded. I walked into the ruined garden, and there found a plain little girl, kinswoman of Mr. Falconbrige, to sing very finely, by the eare only but a fine way of singing – and if I come ever to lack a girl again, I shall think of getting her.[4]

Thence to the towne, and there Spicer, Woodruffe and W Bowyer and I dined together, and a friend of Spicers, and a good dinner I had for them – Falconbrige dined somewhere else by

---

a repl. 'little' *b* repl. 'by' *c* followed by bracket struck through

1. See *Comp.*: 'Nonsuch House'.
2. The park had suffered some tree-felling during the Interregnum, but the avenue had been spared.
3. Evelyn (2 January 1666) has a description of the figures. They consisted of a series of statues, bas-reliefs and mezzo-reliefs 'of the heathen gods', and appeared to him to be 'the work of some excellent *Italian*'. There is no evidence for Pepys's statement about Holbein and Rubens.
4. Her name was Barker, and she came to serve the Pepyses on 12 October 1666.

appointment. Strange, to see how young W Bowyer looks at 41 years – one would not take him for 24 or more – and is one of the greatest wonders I ever did see.

After dinner, about 4 of the clock, we broke up, and I took coach and home (in fear for the money I had with me, but that this friend of Spicers, one of the Duke's guard, did ride along the best part of the way with us); I got to my Lord Brunckers before night, and there I sat and supped with him and his mistress and Cocke, whose boy is yet ill.

Thence, after losing a Crowne betting at tables, we walked home, Cocke seeing me at my new lodging,[1] where I went to bed. ⟨All my work this day in the coach, going and coming, was to refresh myself in my Musique Scale,[2] which I would fain have perfecter then ever I had yet.⟩[a]

22. Up betimes, and to the office, meaning to have entered my last five or six days' journall, but was called away by my Lord Bruncker and Sir J. Mennes; and to Blackewall,[3] there to look after the store-houses, in order to the laying of goods out of the East India ships when they shall be unloaden. That being done, we into Johnsons house[4] and were much made of – eating and drinking. But here it is observable what he tells us; that digging his late Docke, he did 12-foot under ground find perfect trees over-Covered with earth – nut-trees, with the branches and the very nuts upon them – some[b] of whose nuts he showed us – their shells black with age and their Kernell, upon opening, decayed; but their shell perfectly hard as ever.[5] And an Ewe-tree he showed us (upon which he says the very Ivy was taken up whole about it), which upon cutting with an addes, we found to be rather harder then the living tree usually is – they say very much; but I do not know how hard a yew-tree naturally is. The armes, they say,

---

a addition crowded in between entries   *b* repl. 'such'

1. Mrs Clerke's: see below, p. 261 & n. 3.

2. See above, p. 227, n. 1. (E).

3. The dockyard owned by Henry Johnson, shipbuilder, and used by the E. India Company.

4. At the entrance to the yard; built by the E. India Company in 1612, rebuilt by Johnson in 1678: Sir W. Foster, *John Company*, p. 150.

5. For the dock, see above, ii. 14 & n. 2. For a similar discovery made during the excavation of the Brunswick Dock, Blackwall, in 1789, see *N. & Q.*, 17 September 1853, p. 263. A note on oak-trees found preserved below the surface of marsh-land is in *Phil. Trans.*, i (for 1665–6), p. 323.

were taken up at first, whole about the body – which is very strange.

Thence away by water; and I walked with my Lord Brouncker home, and there at dinner comes a letter from my Lord Sandwich to tell me that he would this day be at Woolwich and desired me to meet him – which, fearing [it] might have lain in Sir J. Mennes's pocket a while, he sending it me, did give my Lord Brouncker and his mistress and I occasion to talk of him as the most unfit man for business in the world – though at last afterward I found he was not in this faulty. But hereby I have got a clear evidence of my Lord Brouncker's opinion of him. My Lord Brouncker presently ordered his coach to be ready, and we to Woolwich; and my Lord not being come, we took a boat, and about a mile off I met him in his ketch, and boarded him and came up with him. And after making a little halt at my house, which I ordered to have my wife see him, we all together by coach to Mr. Boreman's,[1] where Sir J. Mennes did receive him very handsomely; and there he is to lie. And Sir J. Mennes did give him on the sudden a very handsome supper, and brave discourse – my Lord Brouncker and Captain Cocke and Captain Herbert being there – with myself.

Here my Lord did witness great respect to me, and very kind expressions. And by other occasions, from one thing to another, did take notice how I was overjoyed at first to see the King's letter to his Lordshipp at first; and told them how I did kiss it, and that whatever he was, I did alway love the King.[2] This my Lord Brouncker did take such notice [of], as that he could not forbear kissing me before my Lord, professing his finding occasion every day more and more to love me. And Captain Cocke hath since of himself taken notice of that speech of my Lord's then concerning me; and may be of good use to me.

Among other discourse concerning long life, Sir J. Mennes saying that his great-grandfather was alive in Edward the 5th.'s time[3] – my Lord Sandwich did tell us how few there have been of

1. At Greenwich: see above, p. 208, n. 1.

2. This was probably the letter of 4/14 April 1660 enclosing the Declaration of Breda, which Pepys refers to at 3 May 1660. He does not there mention having kissed it.

3. This was probably Andrew Mennes (the first of the family recorded in the Heralds' pedigree of 1619) who was Mayor of Sandwich, 1533–4: *Harl. Soc. Reg.*, 42/107.

his family since King Harry the 8th.   That is to say – the then
Chiefe Justice, and his son the Lord Mountague, who was father to
Sir Sidny, who was his father.¹   And yet, what is more wonderful, he did assure us from the mouth of my Lord Mountagu
himself² – that in King James's time had a mind to get the King to
cut off the entayle of some land which was given in Harry the 8th's
time to*ᵃ* that family, with the*ᵇ* remainder in the Crowne, he did, to
answer the King in showing how unlikely it was that ever it could*ᶜ*
revert to the Crown, but that it would be a present convenience to
him – did show that at that time there was 4000 persons derived
from the very body of the Chiefe Justice.   It seems the number of
daughters in the family having been very great, and they too have
most of them many children and grandchildren and great-grand-
children.   This he tells as a most known and certain truth.

After supper my Lord Brouncker took his leave.   And I also
did mine, taking Captain Herbert home to my lodging to lie with
me – who did mighty seriously enquire after who was that in the
black dress*ᵈ* with my wife yesterday, and would not believe that
it was my wife's maid Mercer; but it was she.³

23.   Up, and to my Lord Sandwich – who did advise alone
with me how far he might trust Captain Cocke in the business of
the prize goods – my Lord telling me that he hath taken into his
hands 2 or 3000*l* value of them.⁴   It being a good way, he says, to
get money, and afterward to get the King's allowance thereof – it
being easier, he observes, to keep money when got of the King,
then to get it when it is too late.⁵   I advised him not to trust
Cocke too far.   And did thereupon offer him ready money for a

a repl. 'with the'   *b* repl. 'a'   *c* repl. 'could'   *d* MS. 'drest'

---

1. The succession ran: Sir Edward
Mountagu, C. J. (d. 1557); his son
Sir Edward (d. 1602); and his grand-
son Sir Sidney (d. 1644). Pepys is
mistaken in calling the second Sir
Edward 'Lord'.

2. Presumably   the   1st   Lord
Mountagu   of   Boughton,   eldest
brother of Sir Sidney.

3. Even lowlier servants than Mercer, such as chambermaids, wore
no distinctive uniform.   Defoe was
put to the blush by kissing one by
mistake when saluting the ladies of
his host's household: *Everybody's
Business* . . . (1725), p. 15.

4. See below, p. 334.

5. When Pepys lost his office in
1689 he alleged that the Crown owed
him over £28,000: *Priv. Corr.*, ii.
310 & n. It was never paid.

thousand pound or two, which he listens to and doth agree to – which is great joy to me, hoping thereby to get something.

Thence by coaches to Lambeth, his Lordshipp and all our office, and Mr. Eveling, to the Duke of Albemarle – where after the compliment with my Lord, very kind, we sat down to consult of the disposing and supporting of the fleet with victuals and money, and for the sick men and prisoners. And I did propose the taking out some goods out of the prizes, to the value of 10000*l*; which was accorded to, and an order drawn up and signed by the Duke and my Lord, done in the best manner I can and referred to my Lord Brouncker and Sir J. Mennes.[1] But what inconveniences may arise from it I do not yet see, but fear there may be many.

Here wc dined, and I did hear my Lord Craven whisper (as he is mightily possessed with a good opinion of me) much to my advantage, which my good Lord did second; and anon my Lord Craven did speak publicly of me to the Duke, in the hearing of all the rest, and the Duke did say something of the like advantage to me; I believe, not much to the satisfaction of my brethren – but I was mightily joyed at it.

Thence took leave, leaving my Lord Sandwich to go visit the Bishop of Canterbury, and I and Sir W. Batten down to the tower, where he went further by water, and I home; and among other things, took out all my gold to carry along with me tonight with Captain Cocke down to the fleet – being 180*l*[a] and more – hoping to lay out that and a great deal more to good advantage.

Thence down to Greenwich to the office, and there wrote several letters; and so to my Lord Sandwich and mighty merry, and he mighty kind to me in the face of all, saying much in my favour; and after supper I took leave and with Captain Cocke set out in the Yacht about 10 a-clock at night. And after some discourse and drinking a little – my mind full of what we are going about, and jealous of Cocke's out-doing me – so to sleep upon beds brought by Cocke on board, mighty handsome, and never slept better then upon this bed upon the floor in the Cabbin.

---

a repl. '130*l*'

1. A warrant for the payment of £10,000 was issued on 27 September: *CSPD 1664–5*, p. 574. For this transaction, see Evelyn, 23, 29 September, 11 October 1665; BM, Harl. 1509, f. 193*r*; *CSPD 1664–5*, p. 570; ib., *1665–6*, p. 12; Evelyn, *Diary and corr.* (ed. Wheatley), iii. 169–73.

24. *Lords day.* Waked, and up and drank and then to discourse. And then, being about Grayes and a very calme curious*
morning – we took our wherry, and to the Fishermen and bought
a great deal of fine fish – and to Gravesend to Whites and had part
of it dressed. And in the meantime, we to walk about a mile
from the town, and so back again. And there, after breakfast,
one of our watermen told us he had heard of a bargain of Cloves
for us. And we went to a blind*a* alehouse at the further end of the
town, to a couple of wretched, dirty seamen, who, poor wretches,
had got together about 37 *lb* of Cloves and 10 *lb* of Nuttmeggs.
And we bought them of them – the first at 5s-6d per *lb.*, and the
latter at 4s*1* – and paid them in gold; but Lord, to see how silly
these men are in the selling of it, and easily to be persuaded almost
to anything – offering a bag to us, to pass as 20 *lb* of cloves, which
upon weighing proved 25 *lb.* But it would never have been*b*
allowed by my conscience to have wronged the poor wretches,
who told us how dangerously they had got some and dearly paid
for the rest of these goods.

This being done, we, with great content herein, on board again;
and there Captain Cocke and I to discourse of our business, but he
will not yet be open to me, nor am I to him till I hear what he will
say and do with Sir Rogr. Cuttance.*2* However, this discourse*c*
did do me good and got me a Copy of the agreement made the
other day on board for the parcel of Mr. Pierce and Sir Rogr.
Cuttance, but this great parcel is of my Lord Sandwiches'.

By and by to dinner about 3 a-clock. And then I in the cabin
to writing down my journall for these last seven days, to my great
content – it having pleased God that in this sad time of the plague,
everything else hath conspired to my happiness and pleasure, more
for these last three months then in all my life before in so little
time. God long preserve it, and make me thankful for it. After
finishing my Journall, then to discourse and to read, and then to
supper and to bed, my mind not being at full ease, having not fully
satisfied myself how Captain Cocke will deal with me as to the
share of the profits.

a repl.'fl'-   *b* repl. 'given'   *c* repl. 'did'

---

1. The Lord Steward's department
was this year paying 13*s.* 4*d.* a lb. for
cloves and 8*s.* for nutmegs: Sir W.

Beveridge *et al., Prices and wages,* i.
429.

2. Captain of the *Prince.*

25. Found ourselfs come to the fleet; and so aboard the *Prince*, and there, after a good while in discourse, we did agree a bargain of 5000*l* with Sir Rog. Cuttance for my Lord Sandwich, for silk, cinnamon, nutmegs and Indico.[1]   And I was near signing to an undertaking for the payment of the whole sum, but I did by chance escape it, having since, upon second thoughts, great cause to be glad of it, reflecting upon the craft and not good condition, it*ª* may be, of Captain Cocke.

I could get no trifles for my wife.   Anon to dinner, and thence in great haste to make a short visit to Sir W Pen, where I found them, and his lady and daughter and many commanders at dinner – among others, Sir G Askue, of whom, whatever the matter is, the world is silent altogether.[2]   But a very pretty dinner there was; and after dinner Sir W. Penn made a bargain with Cocke for ten bales of Silke at 16*s* per *lb* – which, as Cocke says, will be a good pennorth.   And so away to the *Prince*, and presently comes my Lord on board from Greenwich, with whom, after a little discourse about his trusting of Cocke, we parted and to our Yacht; but it being calme, we, to make haste, took our Wherry toward Chatham; but it growing dark, we were put to great difficultys, our simple yet confident waterman not knowing a step of the way; and we found ourselfs to go backward and forward, which, in that dark night and a wild place, did vex us mightily.   At last we got a fisher-boy by chance and took him into the boat; and being an odd kind of boy, did vex us too, for he would not answer us aloud when we spoke to him; but did carry us safe thither, though with a mistake or two, but I wonder they were not more. In our way I was [surprised], and so we were all, at the strange nature of the Sea-water in a dark night; that it seemed like fire upon every stroke of the Oare – and they say is a sign of Winde.[3] We went to the Crowne Inne at Rochester,[4] and there to supper and made ourselfs merry with our poor fisher-boy, who told us he

a repl. 'of'

1. Their total value, when sold (excluding those sent to Hinchingbrooke), was £4786 9*s*. 0*d*., of which Sandwich gave £600 to Cuttance: PRO, SP 29/149, no. 90 (Pepys's note).

2. He was still in command of the *Henry*, in which he had served as Vice-Admiral of the Blue (Sandwich's squadron) in the summer campaign: Sandwich, p. 271.

3. Dr D. J. Schove writes: 'This phenomenon is caused by the oxidation of living organisms. Several gales were reported about this date.'

4. See above, iii. 153, n. 2.

had not been in a bed in the whole seven year since he came to prentice, and hath two or three year more to serve. After eating something, we in our clothes to bed.

26. Up by 5 a-clock and got post-horses and so set out for Greenwich, calling and drinking at Dartford. Being come to Greenwich, and shifting myself, I to the office; from whence by and by my Lord Bruncker and Sir Jo Minnes set out toward Erith to take charge of the two East India Shipps which I had a hand in contriving for the King's service, and may do myself a good office too thereby. I to dinner with Mr. Waight to his father-in-law's in Greenwich[1] – one of the most silly, harmless, prating old men that ever I heard in my life. Creed dined with me; and among other discourses, got of me a promise of half that he could get my Lord Rutherford to give me upon clearing his business,[2] which should*a* not be less, he said, then 50*l* for my half – which is a good thing, though cunningly got of him. By and by Luellin comes, and I hope to get something of Deering shortly. They being gone, Mr. Waight and I went into the garden to discourse with much trouble, for fear of losing all the profit and principal of what we have laid out in buying of prize-goods – and therefore puts me upon thoughts of flinging up my interest; but yet I shall take good advice first. Thence to the office; and after some letters, down to Woolwich, where I have not lain with my wife these eight days I think, or more. After supper, and telling her my mind about my trouble in what I have done as to buying of these goods – we to bed.

27. Up, and saw and admired my wife's picture of Our Saviour, now finished, which is very pretty.[3] So by water to Greenwich, where with Creed and Lord Rutherford; and there my Lord told me that he would give me 100*l* for my pains – which pleased me well, though Creed, like a cunning rogue, hath got a promise of half of it from me. We to the King's-head, the great Musique-house,[4] the first time I was ever there – and had a

a repl. 'he'

---

1. Robert Waith, paymaster to the Navy Treasurer, had married Elizabeth Lowe of Greenwich.

2. In the payment of his Tangier accounts: above, p. 221 & n. 2;

below, p. 250.

3. She later painted the Virgin: below, vii. 241.

4. A tavern by the dockside: E. Hasted, *Hist. Kent* (ed. Drake), i. 79 n.

good breakfast. And thence parted, I being much troubled to hear from Creed that he was told at Salsbury[1] that I am come to be a great swearer and drinker – though I know the contrary; but Lord, to see how my late little drinking of wine is taken notice of by envious men to my disadvantage.*a* I thence to Captain Cockes (he not yet come to town), to Mr. Evelins, where much company, and thence in his coach with him to the Duke of Albemarle by Lambeth, who was in a mighty pleasant humour. There the Duke tells us that the Dutch do stay abroad, and our fleet must go out again, or to be ready to do so. Here we got several things ordered as we desired, for the relief of the prisoners and sick and wounded men.[2] Here I saw this week's Bill of Mortality, wherein, blessed be God, there is above 1800 decrease, being the first considerable decrease we have had.[3]

Back again the same way, and had most excellent discourse of Mr. Eveling touching all manner of learning; wherein I find him a very fine gentleman, and perticularly of Paynting, in which he tells me the beautiful Mrs. Middleton is rare, and his own wife doth brave things.[4] He brought me to the office, whither comes unexpectedly Captain Cocke, who hath brought one parcel of our goods by waggons. And at first resolved to have lodged them at our office; but then the thoughts of its being the King's house altered our resolution, and so put them at his friend's, Mr. Glanvill's,[5] and there they are safe: would the rest of them were so too. In discourse we came to mention my profit, and he offers me 500*l* profit clear, and I demand 600*l* for my certain profit. We part tonight, and I lie there at Mr. Glanvill's house, there being none there but a mayd-servant and a young man – being *b* in some pain, partly from not knowing what to do in this business, having

a l.h. repl. badly-formed s.h.   *b* repl. 'partly'

1. At court. See above, p. 142, n. 1.

2. A secretary of state's warrant was this day issued for the payment (from prize-money) of £10,000 for prisoners and wounded seamen: *CSPD 1664–5*, p. 574. Evelyn was a Commissioner for the Sick and Wounded.

3. 5533 deaths from the plague occurred in the week 19–26 September; 7615 in the previous week: GL, A.1.5, no. 96.

4. For Jane, wife of Charles Myddleton, see above, p. 64, n. 2. No paintings by either her or Mrs Evelyn have been traced. (OM).

5. Probably William Glanville, Evelyn's brother-in-law.

a mind to be at a certainty in my profit, and partly through his having Jacke sick still, and his Blackemore now also fallen sick. So he being gone, I to bed.

28. Up, and being mightily pleased with my night's lodging, drank a cup of beer and went out to my office and there did some business; and so took boat and down to Woolwich (having first made a visit to Madam Williams, who is going down to my Lord Bruncker) and there dined, and then fitted my paper and money and everything else for a Journy to Nonsuch tomorrow. That being done, I walked to Greenwich; and there to the office pretty late, expecting Captain Cocke's coming, which he did; and so with me to my new Lodgeing¹ (and there I chose rather to lie, because of my interest in the goods*a* that we have brought there to lie); but the people were abed, so we knocked them up. And so I to bed, and in the night was mightily troubled with a looseness (I suppose from some fresh damp Linnen that I put on this night); and feeling for a chamber pott, there was none, I having called the maid up out of her bed, she had forgot I suppose to put one there; so I was forced in this strange house to rise and shit in the Chimny twice; and so to bed and was very well again, and to sleep till
《29.》 5 a-clock, when it is now very dark; and then rose, being called up by order by Mr. Marlow; and so up and dressed myself, and by and by comes Lashmore² on horseback, and I had my horse (I borrowed of Mr. Gilsthropp, Sir W Batten's Clerke) brought to me, and so we set out, and rode hard and was at Nonsuch by about 8 a-clock, a very fine journy and fine day. There I came just about Chappell-time, and so I went to Chappell with them, and thence to the several offices about my tallies; which I find done, but struck*b* for sums not to my purpose, and so was forced to get them to promise me to have them cut into other Summs; but Lord, what a do I had to persuade the dull fellows to it (especially Mr. Warder, Master of the Pells), and yet without any manner of reason for their scruple. But at last I did, and so left my tallies there against another day; and so walked to Yowell and there did spend a peece upon them, having a whole house-full, and much mirth by a sister of the mistress of the house,

---

a repl. same symbol badly formed   *b* MS. 'string'

1. Mrs Clarke's, in Greenwich: 2. Navy Office messenger.
see below, p. 261, n. 3.

an old mayd lately married to a Lieutenant of a company that Quarters there. And much pleasant discourse we had; and dinner being done, we to horse again and came to Greenwich before night; and so to my lodging, and there, being a little weary, sat down and fell to order some of my pocket-papers; and then comes Captain Cocke, and after a great deal of discourse with him seriously, upon the disorders of our state through lack of men to mind the public business and to understand it, we broke up, sitting up talking very late. We spoke a little of my late business propounded, of taking profit for my money laid out for these goods, but he finds I rise in my demand, he offering me still 500*l* certain – so we did give it over, and I to bed. ⟨I hear for certain this night upon the road, that Sir Martin Noell[1] is this day dead of the plague in London, where he hath lain sick of it these eight days.⟩

30. Up, and to the office, where busy all the morning; and at noon with Sir W Batten to Collonell Cleggat[a][2] to dinner, being invited – where a very pretty dinner to my full content, and very merry. The great burden we have upon us at this time at the office is the providing for prisoners and sick men that are recovered, they lying before our office-doors all night and all day, poor wretches. Having been on shore, the Captains won't receive them on board, and other[b] ships we have not to put them on, nor money to pay them off or provide for them. God remove this difficulty. This made us fallowed all the way to this gentleman's house, and there are waited for our coming out after dinner. Hither came Luellin to[c] me, and would force me to take Mr. Deerings 20 pieces in gold he did offer me a good while since;[3] which I did, yet really and sincerely against my will and content, I seeing him a man not likely to do well in his business, nor I to reap any comfort in having to do, and be beholden to a man that minds more his pleasure and company then his business.

Thence, mighty merry and much pleased with the dinner and company, and they with me, I parted; and there was set upon by

a repl. 'L'-   *b* repl. 'serve'   *c* repl. 'came'

1. Financier: see below, p. 258 & n. 1.
2. Of Greenwich.
3. See above, p. 185. Edward Dering, timber merchant, had now contracted to supply plank from Hamburg. See his letter to the Navy Board (17 August): *CSPD 1664–5*, pp. 521–2.

the poor wretches, whom I did give good words and some little money to; and the poor people went away like lambs, and in good earnest are not to be censured if their necessities drive them to bad Courses of stealing or the like, while they lack wherewith to live.   Thence to the office, and there wrote a letter or two and despatched a little business; and then to Captain Cocke's, where I find Mr. Temple, the fat blade, Sir Rob. Viner's chief man, and we three, and two companions of his, in the evening by agreement took ship in the *Bezan*, and the tide carried us no further then Woolwich, about 8 at night.   And so I on shore to my wife, and there to my great trouble find my wife out of order; and she took me downstairs, and there alone did tell me her falling out with both her maids, and perticularly Mary, and how Mary had to her teeth told her she could tell me of something that should stop her mouth, and words of that sense – which I suspect may be about Browne;[1] but my wife prays me to call it to examination, and this, I being of myself jealous, doth make me mightily out of temper; and seeing it not fit to enter into the dispute, did passionately go away, thinking to go on board again.   But when I came to the stairs, I considered the *Bezan* could not go till the next ebb, and it was best to lie in a good bed, and it may be get myself into a better humour by being with my wife; so I back again and to bed; and having otherwise so many occasions to rejoyce, and hopes of good profit besides, considering the ill that trouble of mind and melancholly may in this sickly time bring a family into, and that if the difference were never so great, it is not a time to put away servants, I was resolved to salve up the business rather then stir in it; and so became pleasant*a* with my wife,*b* and to bed, minding nothing of this difference.   So to sleep with a good deal of content.   And saving only this night, and a day or two about the same business about a month or six weeks ago,[2] I do end this month with the greatest content, and may say that these last three months, for joy, health and profit, have been much the greatest that ever I received in all my life in any twelve months almost in my life – having nothing upon me but the consideration of the sickliness of the season during this great plague to mortify mee. For all which, the Lord God be praised.

a   repl. 'mighty'   *b*   repl. 'people'

1. Mrs Pepys's painting-master.   quarrel between Mrs Pepys and
2. This appears to have been a   Mercer: above, pp. 205, 206.

OCTOBER.

1. *Lords day.* Called up about 4 of the clock, and so dressed myself; and so on board the *Bezan*, and there finding all my company asleep, I would not wake them; but it beginning to be break of day, I did stay upon the Decke walking and then into the Maisters Cabbin and there leaned* and slept a little; and so at last was wakened by Captain Cockes calling of me, and so I turned out, and then to chat and talk and laugh, and mighty merry. We spent most of the morning talking, and reading of *The Seige of Rhodes*,[1] which is certainly (the more I read it the more I think so) the best poem that ever was wrote. We breakfasted betimes and came to the fleet about 2 of the clock in the afternoon, having a fine day and a fine winde. My Lord received us mighty kindly; and after discourse with us in general, left us to our business, and he to his officers, having called a council of Warr. We in the meantime settling of papers with Mr. Pierce[2] and everybody else, and by and by with Captain Cuttance. Anon*a* called down to my Lord, and there with him till supper, talking and discourse. Among other things, to my great joy he did assure me that he had wrote to the King and Duke about these prize-goods, and told me that they did approve of what he had done and that he would own*b* what he had done, and would have me to tell all the world so; and did under his hand give Cocke and me his Certificate of our bargains,*c* and giving us full power of disposal of what we have so bought.[3] This doth ease my mind of all my fear, and makes

a repl. 'And on my com'-   *b* repl. 'open on'   *c* repl. 'bus'-

---

1. An opera by Sir William Davenant: see above, v. 278 & n. 4. Pepys kept a copy of the 1663 edition, which contained both parts of the work. (A).

2. The papers concerned the prize-goods. Andrew Pearse was purser of the *Royal Charles*.

3. Pepys's certificate (in his own hand; signed by Sandwich; dated this day) is in Rawl. A 174, f. 305r. He had bought 'severall parcells of Spices, Silkes and other Goods', and was to dispose of them as he liked, having paid customs dues. They were worth over £1000. In Carteret's letter of 28 September, which gave Sandwich the authority to sell his share of the goods, he was warned to await the King's warrant, which was not issued until 17 October: Sandwich MSS, Letters from Ministers, i, f. 49r–v; Harris, ii. 7, 10.

my heart lighter by 100*lb* then it was before.   He did discourse to
us of the Dutch fleet being abroad, 85 of them still, and are now at
the Texell he believes, in expectation of our Eastland ships coming
home with masts and hemp, and our loaden Hambrough ships
going to Hambrough.   He discoursed against them that would
have us yield to no conditions but conquest over the Dutch, and
seems to believe that the Dutch will call for the protection of the
King of France and come under his *a* power – which were to be
wished they might be brought to do under ours, by fair means;
and to that end would have all Dutchmen and families that would
come hither and settled, to be declared Denizens.   And my Lord
did whisper to me alone, that things here must break in pieces,
nobody minding anything, but every man his own business of
profit or pleasure, and the King some little designs of his own;
and that certainly the Kingdom could not stand in this condition
long – which I fear and believe is very true.

So to supper, and there my Lord the kindest man to me before
all the table, talking of me to my advantage, and with tenderness
too, that it overjoyed me.   So after supper Captain Cocke and I
and Temple on board the *Bezan*, and there to Cards for a while,
and then to read again in *Rhodes* and so to sleep.   But Lord, the
mirth which it caused to me to be waked in the night by their
Snoaring round about me – I did laugh till I was ready to burst,
and waked one of the two companions of Temple, who could not
a good while tell where he was, that he heard one laugh so, till he
recollected himself and I told him what it was at;   and so to sleep
again, they still Snoaring.

2.   We having sailed all night (and I do wonder how they in
the dark could find the way), we got by morning to Gillingham;
and thence all walked to Chatham, and there with Comissioner
Pett viewed the Yard;   and among other things, a Teame of four
horses came close by us, he being with me, drawing a piece of
timber that I am confident one man would easily have carried
upon his back;   I made the horses be taken away and a man or two
take the timber away with their hands.   This the Comis-

a   repl. 'power'

sioner did see, but said nothing; but I think had cause to be ashamed of.

We walked, he and I and Cocke, to the Hill house, where we find Sir Wm. Pen in bed, and there much talk and much dissembling of kindness from him; but he is a false rogue and I shall not trust him. But my being there did procure his consent to have his silk carried away before the money^a received, which he would not have done for Cocke I am sure. Thence to Rochester;^b walked to the Crowne,¹ and while dinner was getting ready, I did there walk to visit the old Castle ruines, which hath been a noble place;² and there going up, I did upon the stairs overtake three pretty maids^c or women and took them up with me, and I did besarlas muchas vezes et tocar leur mains and necks, to my great pleasure: but Lord, to see what a dreadful thing it is to look down præcipices,³ for it did fright me mightily and hinder me of much pleasure which I would have made to myself in the company of these three if it had not been for that. The place hath been very noble, and great and strong in former ages. So to walk up and down the Cathedrall, and thence to the Crowne, whither Mr. Fowler, the Mayor of the towne, was come in^d his gowne, and is a very Reverend Magistrate. After I had eat a bit, not staying to eat with them, I went away; and so took horses and to Gravesend, and there stayed not, but got a boat (the sickness being very much in the Towne still) and so called on board my Lord Bruncker and Sir Jo. Minnes, on board one of the East India-men at Erith, and there do find them full of envious complaints for the pillageing of the ships. But I did pacify them and discoursed about making money of some^e of the goods, and do hope to be the better by it honestly. So took leave (Madam Williams being here also with my Lord) and about 8 a-clock got to Woolwich;

a repl. 'receive'-   *b* repl. 'Chatham'   *c* repl. 'g'-
      d repl. 'his'   *e* repl. 'them'

1. See above, iii. 153, n. 2.
2. Mostly Norman, it stood on an eminence just above the bridge. Engraving (1735) reproduced in Frederick F. Smith, *Hist. Rochester*, opp. p. 32.
3. Gundulph's Tower is 112 ft

above ground: [W. Shrubsole and S. Denne,] *Hist. . . . Rochester* (1772), p. 32. View (c. 1662, by W. Schellinks) in *Drawings of Engl. in 17th cent.* (ed. P. H. Hulton), ii, pl. 13(*b*).

and there supped and mighty pleasant with my wife, who is, for aught I see, all friends with her maids; and so in great joy and content to bed.

3. Up, and to my great content visited betimes by Mr. Woolly,[1] my uncle Wights cosen, who comes to see what work I have for him about these East India goods; and I do find that this fellow might have been of great use, and hereafter may be of very great use to me in this trade of prize-goods, and glad I am fully of his coming hither. While I dressed myself, and afterward in walking to Greenwich, we did discourse over all the business of the prize-goods; and he puts me in hopes I may get some money in what I have done, but not so much as I expected – but that I may hereafter do more. We have laid a design of getting more, and are to talk again of it a few days hence.

To the office, where nobody to meet me, Sir W. Batten being the only man, and he gone this day to meet to adjourne the Parliament to Oxford.[2]

Anon by appointment comes one to tell me my Lord Rutherford is come;[3] so I to the Kings-head to him, where I find his Lady, a fine young Scotch lady,[4] pretty handsome and plain*– my wife also and Mercer by and by comes, Creed bringing them; and so presently to dinner and very merry, and after dinner to even our accounts and I to give him tallies, where he doth[a] allow me 100*l*, of which to my grief that rogue Creed hath trapanned me out of 50*l*.[5]   But I do foresee a way how it may be I may get a greater Sum of my Lord, to his content – by getting him allowance of Interest upon his tallies.

That being done, and some Musique and other diversions, at last away goes my Lord and Lady, and I sent my wife to visit Mrs. Pierce and so I to my office, where wrote important letters to the Court; and at night (Creed having clownishly left my wife)

a repl. 'did he'

---

1. Robert Woolley, a city broker.
2. *CJ*, viii. 613. Parliament sat at Oxford from 9 to 31 October.
3. Rutherford was now settling some Tangier accounts, as heir of the 1st Baron, lately Governor there.

4. Christian Urquhart, niece of Sir Thomas Urquhart, the translator of Rabelais. She survived her husband to marry twice again.
5. Cf. above, p. 242.

I to Mrs. Pierce's to her, and brought her and Mrs. Pierce to the King's-head and there spent a piece upon a supper for her; and mighty merry and pretty discourse – she being as pretty as ever – most of our mirth being upon "my Cosen" (meaning my Lord Bruncker's ugly mistress, whom he calls Cosen); and to my trouble, she tells me that the fine Mrs. Middleton[1] is noted for carrying about her body a continued soure base Smell*a* that is very offensive, especially if she be a little hot. Here some bad Musique to close the night; and so away, and all of us saw Mrs. Belle Pierce (as pretty as ever she was almost) home; and so walked to Will's lodging, where I used to lie, and there made shift for a bed for Mercer, and mighty pleasantly to bed.

This night I hear that of our two watermen that used to carry our letters, and were well on Saturday last, one is dead and the other dying, sick of the plague – the plague, though decreasing elsewhere, yet being greater about the Tower and thereabouts.[2]

4. Up, and to my*b* office, where Mr. Andrews comes; and reckoning with him, I get 64*l* of him. By and by comes Mr. Gawden; and reckoning with him, he gives me 60*l* in his account – which is a great mercy to me.*c* Then both of them met and discoursed the business of the first man's resigning and the other's taking up the business of the victualling of Tanger, and I do not think but I shall be able to do as well under Mr. Gawden as under these men, or within a little as to profit, and less care upon me.

Thence to the King's-head to dinner, where we three, and Creed and my wife and her woman, dined mighty merry – and sat long talking; and so in*d* the afternoon broke up, and I led my wife to our lodging again and I to the office, where did much business, and so to my wife.

This night comes Sir George Smith*e* to see me at the office, and tells me how the plague is decreased this week 740, for which God be praised – but that it encreases at our end of the town still.[3]

---

a l.h. repl. s.h. 'sm'-   *b* MS. 'the my'
c followed by 'at this time' struck through   *d* repl. 'to'   *e* repl. 'G.C.'

1. See above, p. 64, n. 2.
2. See below, n. 3.
3. Plague burials during 19–26 September had decreased from the previous week by 604; 740 was the

decrease in deaths from all causes. Plague burials in St Olave's, Hart St, had gone up from 11 to 19. GL, A.1.5, no. 96.

And says how all the town is full of Captain Cocke's being in some ill condition about prize-goods, his goods being taken from him and I know not what; but though this troubles me to have it said, and that it was likely to be a business in Parliament, yet I am not much concerned at it, because yet I believe this news is all false, for he would have wrote to me, sure, about it.

Being come to my wife at our lodging, I*ª* did go to bed, and left my wife with her people to laugh and dance, and I to sleep.

5. Lay long in bed, talking; among other things, talking of my sister Pall, and my wife of herself is very willing that I should give her 400*l* to her portion – and would have her married as soon as we could; but this great sickness-time doth make it unfit to send for her up.

I abroad to the office, and thence to the Duke of Albemarle, all my way reading a book of Mr. Evelins translating, and sending me as a present, about directions of gathering a Library, but the book is above my reach, but his epistle to my Lord Chancellor is a very fine piece.[1] When I came to the Duke, it was about the

a repl. 'we'

---

1. *Instructions concerning erecting of a library . . . by Gabriel Naudeus . . . and now interpreted by Jo. Evelyn, Esquire* (1661); a translation of *Advis pour dresser une bibliothèque* (first published 1627); retained in the PL (PL 789) and inscribed: 'Be pleasd to accept this trifle from yr most humble ser[van]t. J.E.', and containing a few corrections in Evelyn's hand. The dedicatory letter is by Evelyn and hardly mentions books, being concerned mainly with the Royal Society, which here first received that title. Evelyn, like Pepys, seems to have thought more highly of the dedication than of the translation itself: Evelyn to Pepys, 12 August 1689 (Evelyn, *Diary and corr.*, ed. Wheatley, iii. 446). The book explains the principles on which

Naudé (d. 1653), the most distinguished French librarian of the time, arranged the library of Cardinal Mazarin. Evelyn meant it for the use of the gentlemen in the formation and arrangement of their collections: *Diary and corr.*, iv. 16. Pepys himself never used Naudé's system, which was meant for larger libraries than his. Naudé recommended separate subject- and author-catalogues (which Pepys by the 1690s, at any rate, adopted), but he also suggested arrangement by subject, whereas Pepys arranged his books according to size, and Naudé sneered at neat bindings, which Pepys delighted in. Cf. *The Library* (ser. 4), 12/383+; Sir G. Keynes, *Evelyn, . . . a bibliography* (1968 ed.), pp. 103+.

victuallers business, to put it into other hands, or more hands – which I do advise in, but I hope to do myself a jobb of work in it. So I walked through Westminster to my old house, the Swan, and there did pass some time with Sarah; and so down by water to Deptford and there to my Valentine's;[1] round about and next door on every side is the plague,[2] but I did not value it but there did what I would con ella; and so away to Mr. Evelings[3] to discourse of our confounded business of prisoners and sick and wounded seamen, wherein he and we are so much put out of order. And here he showed me his gardens, which are, for variety of Ever=greens and hedge of Holly, the finest things I ever saw in my life.[4] Thence in his coach to Greenwich, and there to my office, all the way having fine discourse of Trees and the nature of vegetables. And so to write letters I very late, to Sir W Coventry, of great concernment;[5] and so to my last night's lodging, but my wife is gone home to Woolwich.

The Bill, blessed be God, is less this week by 740 of what it was the last week.[6] Being come to my lodging,[7] I got something to eat, having eat little all the day, and so to bed – having this night renewed my promises of observing my vowes as I used to do, for I find that since I left them off, my minde is run a'wool-gathering and neglected my business.

6. Up; and having sent for Mr. Gawden, he came to me, and he and I largely discoursed the business of his victualling, in order to the adding of parteners to him, or other ways of altering it –

1. Mrs Bagwell.
2. See below, vii. 236 & n. 3.
3. Sayes Court, Deptford.
4. Evelyn in the 1664 edition of his *Sylva* (p. 66) gives the dimensions of this holly hedge as 160 ft long, 7 ft high and 5 ft thick; in the 1706 edition (p. 182) as 400 × 9 × 5 ft. Peter the Great, who lived at Sayes Court in 1698, is said to have had himself pushed through this hedge in a wheelbarrow, for fun.

5. A long letter, mainly about the navy victualling business and about Pepys's responsibility for stores; copy (in Pepys's s.h. and Hayter's l.h.) in NMM, LBK/8, pp. 242-4; printed in *Shorthand Letters*, pp. 55-9.
6. 4929 in 26 September-3 October, as opposed to 5533: GL, A.1.5, no. 96.
7. At Greenwich: see below, p. 261 & n. 3.

wherein I find him ready to do anything the King would have him do; so he and I took his coach, and to Lambeth and to the Duke of Albemarle about it; and so back again, where he left me – in our way discoursing of that business and contracting a great friendship with him; and I find he is a man most worthy to be made a friend, being very honest and grateful. And in the freedom of our discourse, he did tell me his opinion and knowledge of Sir W Pen, to be, what I know him to be, as false a man as ever was born, for so it seems he hath been to him. He did also tell me, discoursing how things are governed as to the King's Treasure, that having occasion for money in the country,[a] he did offer Alderman Maynell to pay him down money here, to be paid by the Receivers in some[b] county[1] in the country upon whom Maynell had assignements, in whose hands the money also lay ready. But Maynell refused it, saying that he could have his money when he would, and had rather it should lie where it doth then receive it here in town this sickly time, where he hath no occasion for it. But now the evil is, that he hath lent this money upon Tallys which are become payable, but he finds that nobody looks after it how long the money is unpaid and whether it lies dead in the Receivers hands or no; so the King, he pays Maynell 10 per cent, while the money lies in his Receivers hands to no purpose but the benefit of the Receiver.

I to dinner to the King's-head with Mr. Wooly, who is come to instruct me in the business of my goods, but gives me not so good comfort as I thought I should have had. But[c] however, it will be well worth my time, though not above 2 or 300*l*. He gone, I to my office, where very busy drawing up a letter by way of discourse to the Duke of Albemarle, about my conception how the business of the Victualling should be ordered,[2] wherein I have taken great pains, and I think have hitt the right, if they will but fallow it. At this very late, and so home to our lodgings to bed.

a repl. 'contrary'	*b* repl. 'place'	*c* repl. 'So'

---

1. Receivers of excise money.
2. Dated this day: PRO, SP 29/134 no. 46; summary in *CSPD 1665–6*, p. 7; copy (mostly in Hay-ter's hand, some in Pepys's) in NMM, LBK/8, pp. 245–7; printed in *Further Corr.*, pp. 54+. This letter was the result of an enquiry into naval vic-

7. Up, and to the office along with Mr. Childe, whom I sent for to discourse about the victualling business; who will not come into partenership (no more will Captain Beckford) but I do find him a mighty understanding man, and one I will keep a knowledge of.[1] Did business, though not much, at the office, because of the horrible Crowd and lamentable moan of the poor seamen that lie starving in the streets for lack of money – which doth trouble and perplex me to the heart. And more at noon, when we were to go through them; for then a whole hundred of them fallowed us – some cursing, some swearing, and some praying to us.

And that that made me more troubled, was a letter come this

---

tualling which had been going on since the end of August, occasioned by the failure of supplies in the course of the campaigns of this year: cf. Albemarle's letters, 4–9 October, in PRO, Adm. 106/11, ff. 122+. A decision had to be made quickly because the Board had to acquaint Gauden by Michaelmas of its victualling needs for the next year. Pepys now suggested a re-organisation, although (as he admits at 1 December) he knew little in detail about the business. He decided, despite Coventry's contrary opinion, that the addition of partners to Gauden (in sole charge since September 1660) would cause immediate delays without solving any root problems. He objected on similar grounds to a scheme of state management. He recommended in effect a combination of the traditional system of private contracting with the Commonwealth method of state management. The government was to appoint and pay a Surveyor-General who, by means of weekly reports from surveyors at each port, would keep a check on the supplies provided by the contractors. On

19 October Pepys wrote to Coventry proposing himself for the post, and was on 4 December appointed at a salary of £300 p.a. (PRO, Adm. 2/1725, f. 175*v*), to which Gauden latter added £500 p.a.: below, viii. 250. It is clear that as long as this system lasted – i.e. during the war, for the office was abolished in the summer of 1667 – a certain improvement resulted. For the sailor's point of view, see Edward Barlow's *Journal* (ed. Lubbock), passim; see also *CSPD 1664–5*, pp. 541, 552; ib., *1665–6*, p. 11; *Shorthand Letters*, pp. 64–6, 70–2; *Further Corr.*, pp. 51–3; *Cat.*, i. 152+; PL 2871, pp. 738–9; Tedder, pp. 112+, 146+. Cf. below, pp. 271, 279, 284.

1. Josiah Child was one of the most substantial merchants of his day, and wrote on the subject of trade. He had several times supplied victuals to the navy and was considered for appointment as official victualler in 1668: below, ix. 316; *DNB*; PRO, Adm. 20/3, p. 323. Thomas Beckford was appointed slopseller to the navy in February 1666: *CSPD Add. 1660–85*, p. 457.

noon from the Duke of Albemarle,[1] signifying the Duch to be in
sight, with 80 sail, yesterday morning off of Soldbay, coming
right into the bay; God knows what they will and may do to us,
we having no force abroad able to oppose them, but to be
sacrifized to them.　Here came Sir Wm. Rider to me, whom I
sent for about the victualling business also;[2] but he neither will
not come into partenership, but desires to be of the Commission,
if there be one.　Thence back the back-way to my office, where
very late, very busy[a] – but most of all when at night comes two
waggons from Rochester[b] with more goods from Captain Cocke;
and in housing them at Mr. Tookers lodgings, comes two of the
Custome-house to seize them, and did seize them, but I showed
them my Transire. However, after some heat and angry
words, we locked them up, and sealed up the key and did give it
to the constable to keep till Monday – and so parted.　But Lord,
to think how the poor constable came to me in the dark, going
home: "Sir," says he, "I have the Key, and if you would have me
do any service for you, send for me betimes tomorrow morning
and I will do what you would have me."　Whether the fellow
doth this out of kindness or knavery, I cannot tell, but it is pretty
to observe.

Talking with him in the highway, comes close by the bearers
with a dead corps of the plague; but Lord, to see what custom is,
that I am come almost to ⟨think⟩ nothing of it.

So to my lodging, and there with Mr. Hater and Will ending
a business of the state of the last six months' charge of the Navy,
which we bring to 1000000*l* and above[3] – and I think we do not
enlarge much in it, if anything.　So to bed.

a repl. 'business'　　　*b* repl. 'Cha'-

1. Albemarle to Navy Board, 7
October: PRO, Adm. 106/11, f. 122r.
2. Albemarle had suggested him:
Shorthand Letters, p. 57.
3. The account (covering 1 April–
30 September, amounting to
£1,006,075) was drawn up in preparation for the parliamentary session
due to begin on 10 October, at the
request of Sir P. Warwick (5
October); copy in PRO, Adm. 106/
3520, f. 26v. Cf. below, p. 257, n. 4.
The Commons granted £1¼m. (17
Car. II c.1), but asked for more
accounts: *CJ*, viii. 623.

8. *Lords day.* Up, and after being trimmed, to the office, whither I, upon a letter from the Duke of Albemarle to me to order as many ships forth out of the River as I can presently, to joyne to meet the Duch,[1] had ordered all the Captains of the ships in the River to come to me. I did some business with them, and so to Captain Cockes to dinner – he being in the country, but here his brother Salomon was,[2] and for guests, myself, Sir G Smith, and a very fine lady, one Mrs. Penington[3] – and two more Gentlemen. But, both [before] and after dinner, most excellent witty discourse with this lady, who is a very fine witty lady, one of the best I ever heard speak – and indifferent handsome. There after dinner an hour or two, and so to the office, where ended my business with the Captains; and I think of 22 ships, we shall make shift to get out seven (God help us – men being sick – or provisions lacking); and so to write letters to Sir Ph. Warwicke, Sir W. Coventry, and Sir G. Carteret to Court, about the last six months' accounts, and sent away by an express tonight.[4]

This day I hear the Pope is dead. And one said that the news is that the King of France is stobbed – but that the former is very true; which will do great things, sure, as to the troubling of that part of the world, the King of Spain being so lately dead.[5] And one thing more, Sir Martin Noell's lady is dead with grief, for the death of her husband and nothing else, as they say, in the world. But it seems nobody can make anything of his estate, whether he be dead worth anything or no, he having dealt in so many things, public and private, as nobody can understand whereabouts

---

1. Albemarle to Pepys, Cockpit, 7 October: PRO, Adm. 106/11, f. 124*r*.

2. This was his brother-in-law: Cocke had married Anna-Maria Solomons of Danzig.

3. Judith, daughter of Ald. Isaac Penington (Lord Mayor, 1642–3).

4. See above, p. 256 & n. 3. See Pepys to Warwick; copy in NMM, LBK/8, pp. 248–50 (in Hewer's hand; partially printed in *Further Corr.*, pp.

58–9). Concerning his estimate, Pepys pointed out that exact calculations are impossible in war conditions, and added notes on the difference in prices for naval goods caused by the war. He regretted he could not go to the court at Oxford, because of the approach of the Dutch fleet.

5. The news about the Pope and Louis XIV was untrue; Philip IV of Spain had died on 7/17 September.

his estate is – which is the fate of these great dealers at everything.[1]

So after my business being done, I home to my lodging and to bed.

9. Up, my head full of business, and called upon also by Sir Jo Shaw, to whom I did give a civil answer about our prize-goods, that all his dues as one of the Farmers of the Customes are paid; and showed him our Transire, with which he was satisfied and parted, ordering his servants to say the weight of them. I to the office, and there found an order for my coming presently to the Duke of Albemarle; and what should it be but to tell me that if my Lord Sandwich do not come to town, he doth resolve to go with the fleet to sea himself, the Dutch, as he thinks, being in the Downes; and so desired me to get a pleasure-boat for to take him in tomorrow morning, and do many other things, and with a great liking of me and my management especially, as that Cox-combe my Lord Craven doth tell me; and I perceive it, and I am sure take pains enough to deserve it.

Thence away, and to the office at London, where I did some business about my money and private accounts and there eat a bit of goose of Mr. Griffins; and so by water, it raining most miserably, to Greenwich, calling on several vessels in my passage. Being come there, I hear another seizure hath been made of our goods, by one Captain Fisher that hath been at Chatham by warrant of the Duke of Albemarle,[2] and is come in my absence to Tookers and viewed them, demanding the key of the constable, and so sealed up the door. I to the house; but there being no officers nor constable, could do nothing; but back to my office, full of trouble about this, and there late about business, vexed to see myself fall into this trouble and concernment in a thing that I want instruction from my Lord Sandwich whether I should

1. Noell (one of the greatest merchants and financiers of the century) had died of the plague on 29 September; his widow on 4 or 5 October. The wills of both were proved on 6 October and long wrangles followed. Noell left land in Staffordshire and Tipperary, plantations in the W. Indies, a mansion house in St Botolph's, Bishopsgate, interests in several government farms etc. He had been a member of the Royal African Company, the Levant Company and the E. India Company.

2. Albemarle was one of the Principal Commissioners for Prizes; Fisher a customs officer.

appear in or no. And so home to bed – ⟨having spent two hours, I and my boy, at Mr. Glanvills, removing of faggots to make room to remove our goods to; but when done, I thought it not fit to use it.⟩*a*

The news of the killing of the [King of] France is wholly untrue, and they say that of the Pope too.

10. Up, and receive a stop from the Duke of Albemarle of setting out any more ships or providing a pleasure-boat for himself, which I am glad of, and do see (what I thought yesterday) that this resolution of his was a sudden one and silly.[1] By and by comes Captain Cockes Jacob to tell me that he is come from Chatham this morning and that there are four waggons of goods at hand coming to town – which troubles me. I directed him to bring them to his maister's house. But before I could send him away to bring them thither, news is brought me that they are seized on in the town by this Captain Fisher, and they will carry them to another place. So I to them, and found our four waggons in the street, stopped by the church by this Fisher and company,*b* and 100 or 200 people in the streets gazing. I did give them good words, and made modest desires of carrying the goods to Captain Cockes; but they would have them to a house of their hiring, where in a barn the goods were laid. I had Transires to show for all, and the tale was right; and there I spent all the morning seeing this done – at which Fisher was vexed, that I would not let it be done by anybody else for the Merchant, and that I must needs be concerned therein – which I did not think fit to owne.

So that being done, I left the goods to be watched by men on their part and ours; and so to the office by noone, whither by and by comes Captain Cocke, whom I had with great care sent for by

a addition crowded in between paragraphs
b repl. same symbol badly formed

---

1. Cf. above, p. 257 & n. 1. From Albemarle's letter to Sandwich of this day, in which he announced his change of plan, it is clear that the squadron he had ordered consisted of only seven ships: Sandwich MSS, Letters from Ministers, i, f. 61r. Writing to Sandwich on this day, Pepys commented: 'I am confident it had been but to have discovered too much of our nakedness, for after all, a fleet could not have been got out, nor kept out' (*Shorthand Letters*, p. 60).

expresse the last night.   And so I with him to his house and there
eat a bit; and so by coach to Lambeth, and I took occasion first to
go to the Duke of Albemarle to acquaint him with something of
what had been done this morning in behalf of a friend absent,
which did give a good entrance and prevented their possessing the
Duke with anything of evil of me by their report; and by and by
in comes Captain Cocke and tells his whole story, so an order was
made for the putting him in possession, upon giving security to be
accountable for the goods – which for the present did satisfy us;
and so away, giving Locke,[1] that drew the order, a piece (Lord, to
see how unhappily a man may fall into a necessity of bribing
people to do him right in a thing wherein he hath done nothing
but fair, and bought dear); so to the office, there to write my
letters, and Cocke comes to tell me that Fisher is come to him, and
that he doubts not to cajolle Fisher and his companion and make
them friends with drink and a bribe.   This night comes Sir Chr.
Mings to towne and I went to see him; and by and by (he being
then out of the way) comes to see me.   He is newly come from
Court, and carries direction for the making a show of getting
out the fleet again to go fight the Dutch; but [says] that it will
end in a fleet of 20 good sailing frigates to go to the Norward or
Southward, and that will be all.[2]   I enquired, but he would not be
[thought] to know that he had heard anything at Oxford about
the business of the prize-goods, which I did suspect.[3]   But he
being gone, anon comes Cocke, and tells me that he hath been
with him a great while and that he finds him sullen[a] – and speaking
very high what disrespects he had received of my Lord, saying that
he hath walked three or four hours together at that Earles cabin
door for audience, and could not be received; which, if true, I am
sorry for.   He tells me that Sir G Askue says that he did from the

a l.h. repl. l.h. 'sullem'

---

1. Matthew Locke, Albemarle's
secretary.
2. As a result of this and of the
enthusiastic grant of money by the
Commons the rumour soon spread
to The Hague and Paris that the
English were refitting the warships
laid up for the winter, and preparing
a battle fleet of '117 ships of war and
eight fireships': *CSPVen. 1664–6*,
pp. 215, 216, 218.
3. Myngs and Ayscue, with two
other officers, had disapproved of
Sandwich's action in breaking bulk
and had refused their shares.   Myngs
had already been in trouble for the
same offence: Harris, ii. 9.

beginning declare against these goods, and would not receive his dividend, and that he and Sir W Pen are at odds about it – and that he fears Mings hath been doing ill offices to my Lord. I did tonight give my Lord an account of all this;[1] and so home and to bed.

11. Up, and so in my chamber stayed all the morning, doing something toward my Tanger accounts for the stating of them;[2] and also comes up my landlady, Mrs. Clerke, to make an agreement for the time to come; and I, for the having room enough, and to keep out strangers and to have a place to retreat to for my wife if the sickness should come to Woolwich, am contented to pay dear; so, for three rooms and a dining-room, and for linen and bread and beer and butter at nights and mornings, I am to give her 5*l*-10*s* per month – and I wrote, and we signed to an agreement.[3] By and by comes Cocke to tell me that Fisher and his fellow were last night mightily satisfied, and promised all friendship; but this morning he finds them to have new tricks and shall be troubled with them. So he being to go down to Erith with them this afternoon about giving security, I advised him to let them go by land; and so he and I (having eat something at his house) by water to Erith, but they got thither before us; and there we met Mr. Seamour, one of the Comissioners for Prizes, and a Parliament Man, and he was mighty high and had now seized our goods on their behalf – and he mighty imperiously would have all forfeited and I know not what.[4] I thought I was in the right in a thing I said, and spoke somewhat earnestly; so we took up one another very smartly – for which I was sorry afterward, showing thereby myself too much concerned. But nothing passed that I

1. Copy (in Hewer's hand), NMM, LBK/8, pp. 256–7; printed in *Short-hand Letters*, p. 59–61.
2. Cf. Pepys to Sir John Frederick, 11 October; BM, Add. 38849, f. 36*r*.
3. These lodgings were to serve Pepys until the following 7 January. (They were apparently those which Pepys had used on and off since 19 September and in which Hewer had a chamber.) The cost was high; the more informal arrangements made with the Sheldons at Woolwich for

Mrs Pepys's entertainment cost much less: below, p. 315. Mrs Clerke appears to have had one son (the boy Christopher), a daughter Sarah who lived with her, and a married daughter (the younger Mrs Daniel, wife of a naval lieutenant) who lived next door.
4. Edward Seymour was M.P. for Hindon, Wilts. His arrogance was notorious. He became Navy Treasurer and Speaker of the Commons in 1673.

valued at all. But I could not but think that a Parliament-man, in a serious discourse before such persons as we and my Lord Brouncker and Sir Jo Minnes, should quote *Hudibras*, as being the book I doubt he hath read most. They, I doubt, will stand hard for high security, and Cocke would have had me bound with him for his appearing, but I did stagger at it. Besides, Seymour doth stop the doing ⟨it⟩ at all, till he hath been with the Duke of Albemarle, so there will be another demurre. It growing late, and I having something to do at home, took my leave alone, leaving Cocke there for all night; and so, against tide and in the dark and very cold weather, to Woolwich, where we had appointed to keep the night*a* merrily; and so, by Captain Cockes coach, had brought a very pretty child (a daughter of one Mrs. Tookers, next door to my lodging), and so she and a daughter and kinsman of Mr. Petts made up a fine company at my lodgings at Woolwich, where my wife and Mercer and Mrs. Barbara[1] danced, and mighty merry we were, but especially at Mercer's dancing a Jigg, which she does the best I ever did see, having the most natural way of it and keeps time the most perfectly I ever did see. This night is kept, in lieu of yesterday, for my wedding-day of Ten Yeares[2] – for which God be praised – being now in an extreme good condition of health and estate and honour, and a way of getting more money – though at this hour under some discomposure, rather then dammage, about some prize-goods that I have bought of*b* the Fleete in partenership with Captain Cocke – and for the discourse about the world concerning my Lord Sandwich, that he hath done a thing so bad; and indeed it must needs have been a very rash act. And the rather, because of a parliament now newly met to give money and will have some account of what hath already been spent – besides the precedent for a General to take what prizes he pleases – and the giving a pretence to take away much more then he entended, and all will lie upon him. And not giving to all the Commanders, as well as the Flags, he displeases all them – and offends even some of them, thinking others to be better served then themselfs. And lastly, puts himself out of a power of begging anything again a great while of the King.

a MS. 'might'　　*b* repl. 'out'

---

1. Barbara Sheldon.　　　2. For the date of the wedding, see above, ii. 194, n. 3.

Having danced my people as long as I saw fit to sit up, I to bed, and left them to do what they would. I forgot that we had W Hewer there and Tom – and Golding, my barber at Greenwich, for our fiddler, to whom I did give x*s*.

12. Called up before day, and so I dressed myself and down, it being horrid cold, by water to my Lord Bruncker's ship,[1] who advised*ᵃ* me to do so, and it was civilly to show me what the King had commanded about the prize-goods, to examine most severely all that had been done in the taking out any, with or without order, without respect to my Lord Sandwich at all – and that he had been doing of it, and find him examining one man. And I do find that extreme ill use was made of my Lord's order, for they did toss and tumble and spoil and break things in hold, to a great loss and shame, to come at the fine goods, and did take a man that knew where the*ᵇ* fine goods were – and did this over and over again for many days – Sir W. Berkely being the chief hand that did it; but others did the like at other times. And they*ᶜ* did say in doing it, that my Lord Sandwichs back was broad enough to bear it. Having learned as much as I could, which was that the King and Duke are very severe in this point, whatever order they before had given my Lord in approbation of what he had done, and that all will come out, and the King see by the entries at the Custome-house what all doth amount to that had been taken. And so I took leave and by water, very cold, and to Woolwich – where it was now noon; and so I stayed dinner and talking part of the afternoon; and then by coach, Captain Cocke, to Greenwich, taking the young lady[2] home. And so to Cocke, and he tells me that he hath cajolled with Seymour, who will be our*ᵈ* friend; but that above all, Seymour tells him that my Lord Duke did show him today an order from*ᵉ* Court for having all respect paid to the Earle of Sandwich, and what goods had been delivered by his order – which doth overjoy us; and that tomorrow our goods

a repl. 'doth'   *b* repl. 'f'-   *c* repl. 'people'   *d* MS. 'to'
        e repl. 'made'

1. At Erith. (Hence the suggestion made in *Shorthand Letters*, p. 62, that these events belong to the 11th is mistaken.)

2. Frances Tooker, daughter of Pepys's neighbour: above, p. 262.

shall be weighed and he doubts not, possession tomorrow or next day. Being overjoyed at this, I to write my letters,[1] and at it very late. Good news this week that there are about 600 less dead of the plague then the last.[2] So home to bed.

13. Lay long; and this morning comes Sir Jer. Smith to see me in his way to Court, and a good man he is, and one that I must keep fair with – and will, it being I perceive my interest to have kindness with the Commanders. So to the office, and there very busy, till about noon comes Sir W Warren, and he goes and gets a bit of meat ready at the King's-head for us; and I by and by thither and we dined together. I am not pleased with him about a little business of Tanger that I put to him to do for me; but however, the hurt is not much, and his other matters of profit to me continue very likely to be good. Here we spent till 2 a-clock; and so I set him on shore, and I by water to the Duke of Albemarle, where I find him with Lord Craven and Lieutenant of the Tower about him; among other things, talking of ships to get of the King to fetch Coles for the poor of the city, which is a good work.[3] But Lord, to hear the silly talk between these three great people; yet I have no reason to find fault, the Duke and Lord Craven being my very great friends. Here did the business I came about, and so back home by water; and there Cocke comes to me and tells me that he is come to an understanding with Fisher, and that he must give him 100*l* and that he shall have his goods in possession tomorrow, they being all weighed today – which pleases me very well. This day the Duke tells me that there is no news heard of the Dutch, what they do or where they are; but believes that they are all gone home – for none of our Spyes can

---

1. E.g. to Sandwich about the distribution of the prize-goods: *Shorthand Letters*, pp. 62-4.

2. 4327 as against 4929: GL, A.1.5, no. 96.

3. Since 1554 a city tax had been levied to provide the poor with coal at less than market price: J. U. Nef, *Brit. coal ind.*, i. 196-7 etc. For this use of the King's ships to fetch the coal, see BM, Add. 18986, f. 397r (order of Navy Board, 24 April 1666, with reply from Sir John Robinson, Lieutenant of the Tower). The Lieutenant had control of storage, and arranged delivery from Tower Wharf to the churchwardens of each parish. For the government's measures ensuring a coal supply, see PRO, PC 2/58, ff. 53r, 64r, 226v; cf. also *Analytical index to . . . Remembrancia* (ed. W. H. and H. C. Overall), pp. 78-89. Clarendon (*Life*, iii. 192) mentions a similar case in 1667.

give us any tidings of them. Cocke is fain to keep these people, Fisher and his fellow, company night and day to keep them friends almost, and great troubles withal. My head is full of settling the victualling business also, that I may make some profit out of it, which I hope justly to do, to the King's advantage. Tonight came Sir Jo Bankes[1] to me upon my letter, to discourse it with him; and he did give me the advice I have taken, almost as fully as if I had been*a* directed by him what to write. The business also of my Tanger accounts to be sent to Court is upon my hands in great haste; besides, all my own proper accounts are in great disorder, having been neglected now above a Month; which grieves me, but it could not be settled sooner. These together, and the fear of the sickness, and providing for my family, do fill my head very full; besides the infinite business of the office, and nobody here to look after it but myself. So, late from my office, to my lodgings and to bed.

14. Up, and to the office, where mighty busy,*b* especially with Mr. Gawden, with whom I shall I think have much to do. And by*c* and by comes the Lieutenant of the Tower by my invitation yesterday, but I had got nothing for him; it is to discourse about the Coleshipps. So he went away to Sheriffe Hookers, and I stayed at the office till he sent for me at noon to dinner, I very hungry. When I came to the Sheriffes, he was not there, nor in many other places, nor could find him at all, so was forced to come to the office and get a bit of meat from the taverne,*d* and so to my business. By and by comes the Lieutenant and reproaches me with my not treating him as I ought, but all in jest; he, it seemed, dined with Mr. Adrian May. I very late, writing letters at the office, and much satisfied to hear from Captain Cocke that he had got possession of some of his goods to his own house and expected to have all tonight. The town, I hear, is full of talk that there are great differences in the fleet among the great Com-

---

a repl. 'b'-   *b* MS. 'business'   *c* repl. 'so'   *d* l.h. repl. s.h. 'cooks'

---

1. Sir John Bank(e)s, a wealthy E. India merchant and financier, for whom Pepys had a lifelong regard. In 1674 he defended Pepys in the Commons against the charge of Popery.

manders – and that Mings at Oxford did impeach my Lord of something, I think about these goods; but this is but talke.

But my heart and head tonight is full of the victualling business, being overjoyed and proud at my success in my proposal about it,[1] it being read before the King, Duke, and the Caball with complete applause and satisfactions.[2]   This, Sir G. Carteret and Sir W. Coventry both writ me, besides Sir W. Coventry's letters to the Duke of Albemarle, which I read yesterday – and I hope to find my profit in it also.   So late home to bed.

15.   *Lords day.*   Up, and while stayed for the barber, tried to compose a duo of Counterpoint; and I think it will do very well, it being by Mr. Berchensha's rule.[3]   By and by, by appointment comes Mr. Povy's coach, and, more then I expected, him himself to fetch me to Brainford; so he and I immediately set out, having drunk a draught of Mull'd Sacke, and so rode most nobly in his most pretty and best-contrived Charriott in the world, with many new conveniences, his never having, till now in a day or two, not yet finished – our discourse upon Tanger business – want of money – and then of public miscarriages[a] – nobody minding the public, but everybody himself and his lusts.   Anon we came to his house and there I eat a bit, and so with fresh horses, his noble fine[b] horses (the best confessedly in England, the King having none such), he sent me to Sir Rob. Viner's,[4] whom I met coming just from church; and so after having spent half an hour almost looking upon the horses with some gentlemen that were in company – he and I into his garden to discourse of money, but none is to be had – he confessing himself in great straits, and I believe it. Having this answer, and that I could not get better, we fell to public talk and to think how the fleet and seamen will be paid; which he protests he doth not think it possible to compass, as the world is now; no money got by trade, nor the persons that have it by them in the City to be come at.   The Parliament, it seems, have voted the King 1250000*l* at 50000*l* per month tax for the

1. See above, p. 255 & n. 1.
2. Cf. Albemarle to Pepys, 11 October: *CSPD 1665-6*, p. 11. 'Caball' here means inner council or cabinet: see below, p. 275.

3. See above, iii. 35, n. 1.   (E).
4. The goldsmith-banker; he lived at Swakeleys, Ickenham, Mdx.

war – and voted to assist the King against the Duch and all that
shall adhere to them – and thanks to be given him for his care of
the Duke of Yorke – which last is a very popular vote on the Dukes
behalf.[1]   He tells me how the taxes of the last assessment, which
should have been in good part gathered, are not yet laid, and
that even in part of the City of London[2] – and that the Chimny
money comes almost to nothing[3] – nor anything else looked
after.   Having done this, I parted, my mind not eased by any
money, but only that I had done my part to the King's service.
And so in a very pleasant evening, back to Mr. Povys and there
supped.   And after supper to talk and to sing, his man Dutton's
wife singing very prettily (a mighty fat woman), and I wrote[a] out
one song from her and pricked the Tune, being very pretty.   But
I did never hear one sing with so much pleasure to herself as this
lady doth, relishing it to her very heart – which was mighty
pleasant.

16.   Up about 7 a-clock; and after drinking, and I observing
Mr. Povy's being mightily mortifyed in his eating and drinking
and coaches ⟨and horses (he desiring to sell his best)⟩ and everything else, his furniture of his house – he walked with me to
Syon;[4] and there I took water, in our way he discoursing of the
wantonness of the Court and how it minds nothing else.   And I
saying that that would leave* the King shortly if he did not leave
it, he told me "No," for the King doth spend most of his time
in feeling and kissing them naked all over their bodies in bed –
and contents himself, without doing the other thing but as he
finds himself inclined; but this lechery will never leave him.
    Here I took boat (leaving him there) and down to the Tower,

---

a repl. 'took'

1. Parliament had met at Oxford
on the 9th, and these votes were
passed on the 10th and 11th: *CJ*,
viii. 614. By the 14th the bill
of supply (the Additional Aid: 17
Car. II c. 1) had already reached
committee stage. Pepys here gives
round figures.

2. The last assessment was the
Royal Aid, December 1664 (16–17
Car. II c. 1)—a grant of c. £2½m. to
cover costs of the war.   Its slowness

in producing cash led to the experiment of Exchequer credit: see below,
p. 292, n. 3.

3. In 1665 the returns of chimney
money (the Hearth Tax introduced in
1662) were particularly low because
of the plague, and because it was used
to repay the £100,000 lent by the
City of London: above, p. 211 &
n. 4.

4. Syon House, Isleworth, Mdx.

where I hear the Duke of Albemarle is. And I to Lumbard-streete, but can get no money.¹ So upon the Exchange, which is very empty, God knows, and but mean people there. The news for certain, that the Duch are come with their fleet before Margett, and some men were endeavouring*ᵃ* to come on shore when the post came away – perhaps to steal some sheep.² But Lord, how Colvill³ talks of the business of public Revenue like a madman, and yet I doubt all true; that nobody minds it, but that the King and Kingdom must speedily be undone – and rails at my Lord about the Prizes, but I think knows not my relation to him. Here I endeavoured to satisfy all I could people about bills of exchange from Tanger; but it is only with good words, for money I have not, nor can get. God knows what will become of all the King's matters in a little time, for he runs in debt every day, and nothing to pay them looked*ᵇ* after. Thence I walked to the Tower. But Lord, how empty the streets are, and melancholy, so many poor sick people in the streets, full of sores, and so many sad stories overheard as I walk, everybody talking of this dead, and that man sick, and so many in this place, and so many in that. And they tell me that in Westminster there is never a physitian, and but one apothecary left, all being dead⁴ – but that there are great hopes of a great decrease this week: God send it.

At the Tower found my Lord Duke⁵ and Duchesse at dinner, so I sat down. And much good cheer, the Lieutenant and his lady, and several officers with the Duke. But Lord, to hear the silly talk that was there would make one mad – the Duke having

a 'were endeavouring' repl. 'did land'   *b* repl. 'little'

1. For Pepys's efforts to cash the tallies he had drawn on 29 September, see his exchange of letters with John Colvill, Sir John Frederick and Nathaniel Herne printed in HMC, *Eliot Hodgkin*, pp. 164–6.

2. De Ruyter had sailed from the Texel on 11 October at the head of 90 ships, hoping to bring the English fleet to action. His force was soon dispersed by storms: below, p. 279. On the 15th his guns had played on Margate, damaging a few chimneys and killing two sheep. Cf. Marvell,

Third advice to a painter, ll. 351–2: 'Some sheep are stol'n, the Kingdom's all array'd,/And even Presbyt'ry's now call'd out for aid.' The news of a landing seems to have been a canard. See *CSPD 1665–6*, pp. 15, 25; *The Intelligencer*, 23 October, p. 1032; Tedder, p. 143.

3. John Colvill, goldsmith-banker.

4. Westminster, with its over-crowded alleys, was badly hit by the plague. Many physicians had left for the country.

5. Albemarle.

none almost but fools about him. Much of their talk about the
Duch coming on shore, which they believe they may some of
them have been – and stole sheep; and speak all in reproach of
them in whose hands the fleet is; but Lord help him, there is
something will hinder him and all the world in going to sea,
which is want of victualls, for we have not wherewith to answer
our *a* service. And how much better it would have been if the
Dukes advice had been taken, for the fleet to have gone presently*
out. But God help the King, while no better counsels are given,
and what is given no better taken. Thence after dinner, receiving
many commands from the Duke, I to our office on the Hill[1] and
there did a little business; and to Colvill's again, and so took
water at the Tower; and there met with Captain Cocke and he
down with me to Greenwich – I having received letters from my *b*
Lord Sandwich today,[2] speaking very high about the prize-goods,
that he would have us to fear nobody, but be very confident in
what we have and have done, and not to confess any fault or
doubt of what he hath done, for the King hath allowed it and doth
now confirm it; and sent orders, as he says, for nothing to be
disturbed that his Lordshipp hath ordered therein as to the division
of the goods to the fleet – which doth comfort us. But my Lord
writes to me that both he and I may hence learn by what we see
in this business. But that which pleases me best is that Cocke tells
me that he now understands that Fisher was set on in this business
by design of some of the Duke *c* of Albemarle's people, Warcupp[3]
and others, who lent him money to set him out in it, and he has
spent high – who now curse him for a rogue, to take 100*l* when
he might have had as well 1500*l*; and they are mightily fallen out
about it – which in due time shall be discovered. But that now
that troubles me afresh is, after I am got to the office at Greenwich,
that some new troubles are come, and Captain Cockes house is
beset before and behind with guards. And more, I do fear they

---

a repl. 'the'   *b* repl. 'the'   *c* repl. 'Mr.'

---

1. The Victualling Office on
Tower Hill.

2. Sandwich to Pepys, 14 October:
Rawl. A 174, f. 303*r*. 'The Kinge
hath Confirmed it and given mee
order to distribute these very Pro-
portions. . . . You are to owne the
Possession of them with Confidence. . . . Carry it high and
owne nothinge of basenesse or dis-
honor.'

3. Edmund Warcupp, a kinsman
of Albemarle, employed by the
Prize Commissioners.

may come to my office here to search for Cocke's goods and find some small things of my clerks – so I assisted them in helping to remove their small trade.   But by and by I am told that it is only the Custome-house men, who came to seize the things that did lie at Mr. Glanvilles, for which they did never yet see our Transire, nor did know of them till today – so that my fear is now over, for a Transire is ready for them.   Cocke did get a great many of his goods to London today – to the Stillyard; which place, however, is now shut up of the plague; but I was there, and we now make no bones of it.

Much talk there is of the Chancellors speech, and the King's, at the Parliaments meeting, which are very well liked.   And that we shall certainly, by their speeches, fall out with France at this time, together with the Dutch – which will find us work.[1]   Late at the office, entering my Journall for eight days past, the greatness of my business hindering me of late to put it down daily; but I have done it now very true and perticularly, and hereafter will, I hope, be able to fall into my old way*a* of doing it daily.

So to my lodging, and there had a good pullet to my supper; and so to bed, it being very cold again, God be thanked for it.[2]

17. Up, and all day long busy at the office, mighty busy – only, stepped to my lodging and had a fowl for my dinner.   And at night my wife and Mercer comes to me, which troubled me a little, because I am *b* to be mighty busy tomorrow all day, seriously about my accounts.   So late from my office to her, and supped and so to bed.

18. Up, and after some pleasant discourse with my wife (though my head full of business), I out and left her to go home, and myself to the office and thence by water to the Duke of Albemarles; and so back again, and find my wife gone.   So to my chamber at my lodgings and to*c* the making of my accounts up of Tanger, which I did with great difficulty, finding the

a repl. 'I'-   *b* repl. 'was'   *c* repl. 'so'

1. The King on 10 October had asked parliament for assistance 'against a more powerful Neighbour, if He shall prefer the Friendship of the Dutch before Mine'—a plea which the Chancellor elaborated: *LJ*, xi. 684–9.

2. The cold would reduce the virulence of the plague: cf. above, p. 93, n. 2.

difference between short and long reckonings where I have had occasion to mix my monies, as I have of late done my Tanger treasure upon other occasions, and other monies upon that. However, I was at it late, and did it pretty perfectly. And so after eating something, to bed – my mind eased of a great deal of figures and castings.

19. Up, and to my accounts again, and stated them very clear and fair*a*; and at noon dined at my lodgings, with Mr. Hater and W. Hewer at table with me – I being come to an agreement yesterday with my landlady for 6*l* per month for so many rooms for myself, them and my wife, and maid when she shall come – and to pay besides for my Dyet. After dinner I did give them my accounts and letters to write, against I went to the Duke of Albemarle this evening – which I did; and among other things, spoke to him for my wife's brother Balty to be of his guard, which he kindly answered that he should.[1] My business of the victualling[2] goes on as I would have it; and now my head is full how to make some profit of it to myself or people. To that end, when I came home, I wrote a letter to Mr. Coventry, offering myself to be the Surveyor Generall, and am apt to think he will assist me in it;[3] but I do not set my heart much on it, though it would be a good help. So back to my office, and there till past one before I could get all these letters and papers copied out, which vexed me. But so sent them away without hopes of saving the post, and so to my lodging to bed.

20. Up, and have my last night's letters brought back to me, which troubles me because of my accounts, lest they should be asked for before they come; which I abhorr, being more ready to give then they can be to demand them. So I sent away an express to Oxford with them, and another to Portsmouth with a copy of my letter to Mr. Coventry about my victuall[ing] business, for fear he should be gone from Oxford, as he entended, thither. So, busy all the morning; and at noon to Cocke and dined there – he and I alone – vexed that we are not rid of all our trouble about our

a MS. 'very clear and fair and clear'

1. After serving for about a year in the guards Balty was appointed a muster-master in the navy.
2. See above, p. 255 & n. 1.

3. Copy (in Pepys's hand) in NMM, LBK/8, pp. 263–4; printed in *Shorthand Letters*, pp. 70–2. For the sequel, see below, p. 280.

goods; but it is almost over. And in the afternoon to my lodging and there spent the whole afternoon and evening with Mr. Hater, discoursing of the business of the office – where he tells me that among other, Tho. Willson[1] doth now and then seem to hint that I do take too much business upon me, more then I can do, and that therefore some doth lie undone. This, I confess to my trouble, is true; but it arises from my being forced to take so much on me, more then is my proper task to undertake. But for this, at last I did advise to him to take another Clerke if he thinks fit; I will take care to have him paid. I discoursed also much with him about persons fit to be put into the Victualling business, and such as I could spare something out of their salaries for them; but without trouble I cannot, I see, well do it, because Tho. Willson must have the refusal of the best place, which is London, of 200*l* per annum[2] – which I did entend for Tooker,[3] and to get 50*l* per annum out of it as a help to Mr. Hater. How-[ever], I will try to do something of this kind for them.

Having done discourse with him late, I to enter my Tanger accounts fair, and so to supper and to bed.

21. Up, and to my office, where busy all the morning; and then with my two clerks home to dinner; and so back again to the office, and there very late, very busy; and so home to supper and to bed.

22. *Lords day.* Up, and after ready and going to Captain Cocke's, where I find we are a little further safe in some part of our goods, I to church, in my way meeting with some letters which make me resolve to go after church to my Lord Duke of Albemarle.[4] So after sermon I took Cockes chariot and to Lambeth; but in going, and getting over the water and through White-hall, I spent so much time, the Duke had almost dined. However, fresh meat was brought for me to his table and there I dined, and full of discourse and very kind. Here they are again

---

1. Clerk to Batten.
2. He had been a clerk to the Victualling Commission before 1660. For his appointment, see below, p. 280 & n. 3.
3. Since May, John Tooker had been a river-agent for the Board, with responsibility for putting stores and provisions on board warships.
4. Cf. Albemarle to Navy Board, 21 October; about supplies and the re-employment of seamen after sick-leave: *CSPD 1665–6*, p. 22.

talking of the prizes,*a* and my Lord did speak very broad that my Lord Sandwich and Pen should do what they would and answer for themselfs; for his part, he would lay all before the King. Here he tells me that the Duch Embassador at Oxford is clapped up; but since I hear it is not true.[1] Thence back again, it being evening before I could get home; and there, Cocke not being within, I and Mr. Salomon to Mr. Glanvill's; and there we found Cocke, and sat and supped and was mighty merry, with only Madam Penington, who is a fine witty lady. Here we spent the evening late, with great mirth; and so home and to bed.

23. Up, and after doing some business, I down by water, calling to see my wife, with whom very merry for ten minutes; and so to Erith, where my Lord Brouncker and I kept the office and despatched some business by appointment on the *Bizan.* Among other things, about the slopsellers who have trusted us so long; they are not able, nor can be expected to trust us further – and I fear this winter the fleet will be undone by that perticular.[2] Thence on board the East India ship, where his Lordshipp had provided a great dinner, and thither comes by and by Sir Jo. Minnes, and before him Sir W Warren – and anon a Perspective-glass maker, of whom we every one bought a pocket-glass.

But I am troubled with the much talk and conceitedness of Mrs. Williams and her impudence, in case she be not married to my Lord. They are getting themselfs ready to deliver the goods all out to the East India Company, who are to have the goods in their possession, and advance two-thirds of the moderate value thereof and sell them as well as they can, and the *b* King to give them 6 per cent for the use of the money they shall so advance.[3]

a repl. 'prs'-   *b* repl. 'give'

---

1. Van Gogh was recalled in December: *CSPVen. 1664–6,* p. 237. His secretary had been arrested at Colchester in July: *CSPD 1664–5,* p. 486.
2. In a memorandum of 26 October Pepys calculated that payment of £7000 in ready money to the two chief slopsellers, Burrows and Beckford, would see the navy through the winter: *Further Corr.,* p. 66.

3. The E. India Company sold the prize goods (i.e. those left after the seamen had taken their share) on 21–2 March 1666, for c. £155,000. The suggestion that the company should be employed was Coventry's. For the negotiation of the agreement, see BM, Harl. 1509, ff. 198+; *Cal. court mins E. India Co. 1664–7* (ed. Sainsbury), pp. 164, 172–7, 209, 420.

By this means, the Company will not suffer by the King's goods bringing down the price of their own.

Thence in the evening back again with Sir W Warren and Captain Taylor in my boat. And the latter went with me to the office, and there he and I reckoned, and I perceive I shall get a 100*l* profit by my services of late to him – which is a very good thing.[1] Thence to my lodging, where I find my Lord Rutherford, of which I was glad. We supped together and sat up late, he being a mighty wanton man with a daughter-in-law of my landlady's,[2] a pretty conceited woman, big with child; and he would be handling her breasts, which she coyly refused. But they gone, my Lord and I to business, and he would have me forbear paying Alderman[a] Backewell the money ordered him – which I, in hopes to advantage myself, shall forbear; but do not think that my Lord will do anything gratefully more to me then he hath done, nor that I shall get anything, as I pretended by helping him to interest for his last 7700*l*[3] – which I could do, and do him a courtesy too. Discourse being done, he to bed in my chamber, and I to another in the house.

24. Lay long, having a cold. Then to my Lord and sent him going to Oxford; and I to my office, whither comes Sir Wm. Batten, now newly from Oxford; I can gather nothing from him about my Lord Sandwich or the business of the prizes, he being close; but he showed me a bill which hath been read in the House, making all breaking of bulk for the time to come felony; but it is a foolish Act and will do no great matter – only, is calculated to my Lord Sandwich's case.[4] He showed me also a good letter

a   MS. 'Albem'-

---

1. Cf. above, p. 98 & n. 3.
2. This was presumably Mrs Daniel: cf. below, p. 336.
3. See above, p. 221 & n. 2.
4. The bill (which was supported by Coventry) had been committed on the 23rd, but nothing more was heard of it: *CJ*, viii. 615, 617, 619; Clarendon, *Life*, ii. 464, 469. Sandwich obtained a pardon to cover his own case: below, vii. 260 & n. 2.

printed, from the Bishopp of Munster to the States of Holland, showing the state of their case.[1]

Here we did some business and so broke up, and I to Cocke, where Mr. Eveling was, to dinner; and there merry, yet vexed again at public matters, and to see how little heed is had to the prisoners and sick and wounded.

Thence to my office; and no sooner there, but to my great surprise am told that my Lord Sandwich is come to town; so I presently to Boremans,[2] where he is, and there found him. He mighty kind to me, but no opportunity of discourse private yet, which he tells me he must have with me. Only, his business is sudden to go to the fleet to get out a few ships to drive away the Duch. I left him in discourse with Sir W. Batten and others, and myself to the office till about 10 at night; and so letters being done, I to him again to Captain Cockes, where he supped and lies – and never saw him more merry; and here is Ch. Herbert,[3] who the King hath lately knighted. My Lord, to my great content, did tell me before them, that never anything was read to the King and Council, all the chief ministers of state being there, as my letter about the victualling[4] was, and no more said upon it then a most thorough consent to every word was said, and direction that it be pursued and practised. After much mirth, and my Lord having travelled all night last night, he to bed and we all parted, I home.

25. Up, and to my Lord Sandwiches, where several commanders, of whom I took the state of all their ships, and of all could find not above four capable of going out – the truth is, the want of victuals being the whole overthrow of this year, both at sea and now at the Noure here and Portsmouth, where all the fleet lies. By and by comes down my Lord, and then he and I an hour

---

1. Christopher Bernard von Galen, Prince-Bishop of Münster (1650–78) was an ally of the English against the Dutch and had just invaded Overijssel and Groningen. The pamphlet referred to was *A letter sent by his Highness the Bishop and Prince of Münster to the Lords the States-General of the United Netherlands* (Oxford, 1665; 14 September), reciting his grievances against the common enemy.

2. See above, p. 208, n. 1.

3. Charles Harbord, jun., a close friend and *protégé* of Sandwich. This entry is important in dating his knighthood.

4. See above, p. 255 & n. 1.

together alone upon private discourse. He tells me that Mr. Coventry and he are not reconcilable, but declared enemies; the only occasion of it, he tells me, being his ill-usage from him about the*a* first Fight,[1] wherein he had no right done him (which me-thinks is a poor occasion, for in my conscience, that was no design of Coventry's); but however, when I asked my Lord whether it were not best, though with some condescensions, to be friends with him, he told me it was not possible, and so I stopped. He tells me, as very private, that there are great factions at the Court be-tween the King's party and the Duke of Yorkes, and that the King (which is a strange difficulty) doth favour my Lord in opposition to the Duke's*b* party. That my Lord Chancellor being, to be sure, the patron of the Duke's, it is a mystery whence it should be that Mr. Coventry is looked upon by him[2] as an enemy to him. That if he had a mind himself to be out of this imployment, as Mr. Coventry he believes wishes (and himself, and I do, doth encline to wish it also in many respects), yet he believes he shall not be able because of the King, who will keep him in on purpose in opposi-tion to the other party. That Prince Rupert and he are all pos-sible friends in the world. That Coventry hath aggravated this business of the prizes, though never so great plundering in the world as while the Duke and he were at sea.[3] And in Sir Jo. Lawsons time he could take and pillage and then sink a whole ship in the Streights, and Coventry say nothing to it.[4] That my Lord Arlington is his fast friend.[5] That the Chancellor is cold to him; and though I told him that I and the world do take my Lord Chancellor, in his speech the other day, to have said as much as

a repl. 'his'   *b* repl. 'King's'

---

1. See above, pp. 135 & n. 1.
2. The Lord Chancellor (Claren-don).
3. In the summer of 1665, when Coventry attended James as his secretary in the *Royal Charles*: Penn, ii. 320. There seems to be no evidence of plundering then.
4. Presumably during Lawson's voyage to the Mediterranean in

1661-2: the incident is untraced. For Sandwich's jealousy of Lawson, see above, iii. 121-2.
5. Clarendon's later account (*Life*, ii. 474) errs in stating that Arlington was now pressing, with Coventry, for Sandwich's removal. Sandwich wrote to Arlington on 27 October thanking him for his friendship: *CSPD 1665-6*, p. 32.

could be wished, yet he thinks he did not.[1] That my Lord
Chancellor doth from hence begin to be cold to him, because of
his seeing him and Arlington so great. That nothing at Court is
minded but faction[a] and pleasure, and nothing intended of general
good to the Kingdom by anybody heartily, so that he believes,
with me, in a little time confusion will certainly come over all the
nation. He told me how a design was carried on a while ago for
the Duke of Yorke to raise an army in the North, and to be General
of it, and all this without the knowledge or advice of the Duke of
Albemarle; which when he came to know, he was so vexed, they
were fain to let it fall to content him.[2] That his maching with the
family of Sir G. Carteret doth make the difference greater between
Coventry and him, they being enemies. That the Chancellor did,
as everybody else, speak well of me the other day, but yet was,
at the Committee for[b] Tanger, angry that I should offer to suffer
a bill of exchange to be protested. So my Lord did bid me take
heed, for that I might easily suppose I could not want enemies,
no more then others. In all, he speaks with the greatest trust and
love and confidence in what I say and do that a man can do.

After this discourse ended, we sat down to dinner, and mighty
merry – among other things, at the Bill brought into the House
to make it felony to break bulk[3] – which, as my Lord says well,
will make that no prizes shall be taken, or, if taken, shall be sunk
after plundered – and the Act for the method of gathering this
last 1250000*l* now voted, and how paid, wherein are several
strange imperfections.[4]

a preceded by blot   *b* blot below symbol

1. At the opening of parliament on
9 October, Clarendon had given a
favourable account of Sandwich's
handling of the fleet before the Texel,
of the attack on Bergen, and of the
capture of the E. Indiamen and finally
of his decision to make for port –
being 'by Tempest, and other
Reasons, which no Wisdom of his
could prevent, obliged to put into our
own Harbours': *LJ*, xi. 687. Clarendon's autobiography (*Life*, ii. 467+)
is also sympathetic to Sandwich.
2. These rumours were common in

1665–7, and were associated with
distrust of both James and of Clarendon. Albemarle's political neutrality
was regarded as a bulwark against any
dangerous intrusion of faction into
the armed forces: cf. Marvell, *Last
Instructions*, ll. 521–2. The Duke had
spent a large part of the summer
(5 August–23 September) at York:
Reresby, *Memoirs* (ed. A. Browning),
p. 55.
3. See above, p. 274, n. 4.
4. See below, p. 292 & n. 3.

After dinner my Lord by a Ketch down to Erith, where the *Bezan* was – it blowing these last two days, and now both night and day very hard Southwardly – so that it hath certainly drove the Duch off the coast.

My Lord being gone, I to the office and there find Captain Ferrer, who tells me his wife is come to town to see him, having not seen him since fifteen ⟨weeks⟩ ago, at his first going to sea last.¹ She is now at a Taverne and stays all night, so I was obliged to give him my house and chamber to lie in, which he, with great modesty and after much force, took; and so I got Mr. Evelings coach to carry her thither, and the coach coming back, I with Mr. Eveling to Deptford, where a little while with him doing a little business; and so in his coach back again to my lodgings, and there sat with Mrs. Ferrer two hours, and with my little girle, Mrs. Fran. Tooker, and very pleasant: anon the Captain comes, and then to supper, very merry; and so I led them to bed. And so to bed myself – having seen my pretty little girl home first, at the next door.

26. Up, and leaving my guests to make themselfs ready, I to the office; and thither comes Sir Jer. Smith and Sir Chr. Mings to see me, being just come from Portsmouth and going down to the fleet. Here I sat and talked with them a good while, and then parted, only Sir Chr. Mings and I together by water to the Tower. And I find him a very witty well-spoken fellow, and mighty free to tell his parentage, being a shoemaker's son,² to whom he is now going. And I to the Change – where I hear how the French have taken two and sunk one of our Merchant-men in the Streights and carried the ships to Toulon³ – so that there is no expectation but we must fall out with them. The Change pretty full, and the town begins to be lively again – though the streets very empty and most shops shut. So back again I, and took boat and called for Sir Chr. Mings at St. Katharines, who was fallowed

1. In attendance on Sandwich; some of Ferrer's accounts for this period are in Carte 223, f. 1r.

2. Doubt is thrown on the story of Myngs's humble birth by Sir J. Laughton in the *DNB*. But it is clear from a letter of Pepys (28 March 1665; NMM, LBK/8, p. 176) that

his father was a shoemaker and was then consulted by the Navy Board about the uses which leather shavings might be put to.

3. The Duc de Beaufort had fired on the merchantmen because they would not dip their flags to him: *CSPVen. 1664–6*, p. 217, 222.

with some ordinary friends, of which he says he is proud; and so down to Greenwich, the wind furious high, and we with our sail up till I made it be taken down. I took him, it being 3 a-clock, to my lodgings, and did give him a good dinner and so parted, he being pretty close to me as to any business of the fleet, knowing me to be a servant of my Lord Sandwiches. He gone, I to the office till night; and then they come and tell me my wife is come to town, so I to her, vexed at her coming; but it was upon innocent business, and so I was pleased and made her stay, Captain Ferrers and his lady being yet there. And so I left them to dance, and I to the office till past 9 at night; and so to them and there saw them dance very prettily, the Captain and his wife, my wife, and Mrs. Barbary[1] and Mercer, and my landlady's daughter; and then little Mrs. Fr. Tooker and her mother, a pretty woman, come to see my wife. Anon to supper, and then to dance again (Golding being our fidler, who plays very well and all tunes) till past 12 at night, and then we broke up and everyone to bed; we make shift for all our company – Mrs. Tooker being gone.

27. Up, and after some pleasant discourse with my wife, I out, leaving her and Mrs. Ferrers there; and I to Captain Cocke's, there to do some business; and then away with Cocke in his coach through Kent-street, a miserable, wretched, poor place, people sitting sick and muffled up with plasters at every four or five door. So to the Change, and thence I by water to the Duke of Albemarle; and there much company, but I stayed and dined, and he makes mighty much of me; and here he tells us the Dutch are gone, and have lost above 160 cables and anchors through the last foul weather.[2] Here he proposed to me from Mr. Coventry (as I had desired of Mr. Coventry) that I should be Surveyor Generall of the victualling business, which I accepted. But endeed, the terms in which Mr. Coventry proposes it for me are the most obliging that ever I could expect from any man, and more – it saying me to be the fittest man in England, and that he is sure, if I will undertake it, I will perform it – and that it will be also a very desirable thing that I might have this encouragement, my en-

---

1. Barbara Sheldon, niece of Mrs Pepys's host at Woolwich.

2. For these movements, see above, p. 268, n. 2; below, p. 291 & n. 1.

Anchors and cables lost in this way were sometimes recovered: cf. below, vii. 312.

couragement in the Navy alone being in no wise proportionable to my pains or deserts. This, added to the letter I had three days since from Mr. Southerne, signifying that the Duke of Yorke had in his master's absence opened my letter and commanded him to tell me that he did approve of my being the Surveyor general,[1] doth make me joyful*a* beyond myself, that I cannot express it; to see that as I do take pains, so God blesses me and hath sent me masters that do observe*b* that I take pains.

After having done here, I back by water and to London, and there met with Captain Cockes coach again, and I went in it to Greenwich and thence sent my wife in it to Woolwich. And I to the office, and thence home late with Captain Taylor; and he and I settled all accounts between us and I do find that I do get above*c* 120*l* of him for my services for him within these six months.[2] At it till almost one in the morning; and after supper he away and I to bed – mightily satisfied in all this and in a resolution I have taken tonight with Mr. Hater, to propose the port of London for the victualling business for Tho. Willson, by which it will be the better done, and I at more ease in case he should grumble.[3] So to bed.

28. Up, and sent for Tho. Willson and broke the victualling business to him; and he is mightily contented, and so am I that I have bestowed it on him. And so I to Mr. Boreman's, where Sir W. Batten is – to tell him what I had proposed to Tho. Willson, and the news also I have this morning from Sir W Clerke, which is, that notwithstanding all the care the Duke of Albemarle hath taken about the putting*d* the East India prize-goods into the East India Company's hands, and*e* my Lord Brouncker and Sir J. Mennes' having laden out a great part of the goods, an order is come from Court to stop all, and to have the

a repl. 'just'   *b* repl. 'see me'   *c* repl. 'about'
          d repl. 'see'   *e* repl. 'it'

---

1. James Southern was Coventry's secretary. For Pepys's appointment, see above, p. 254, n. 2.

2. Cf. above, p. 98 & n. 3.

3. Wilson (Batten's clerk) was appointed Surveyor of the Victual-ling in the port of London on 4 November, at a salary of £200 p.a.: Duke of York, *Mem. (naval)*, pp. 131–3. For his claims to the post, see above, p. 272 & n. 2.

goods delivered to the Sub-Commissioners of Prizes[1] – at which I am glad, because it doth vex this simple weak man and we shall have a little reparation for the disgrace my Lord Sandwich hath had in it. He tells me also that the Parliament hath given the Duke of Yorke 120000*l*,[2] to be paid him after the 1250000*l* is gathered upon the Tax which they have now given the King. He tells me that the Duch have lately lanched*a* sixteen new ships,[3] all which is great news.

Thence by Horsebacke with Mr. Deane to Erith, and so aboard my Lord Brouncker and dined; and very merry with him, and good discourse between them about ship-building. And after dinner and a little pleasant discourse, we away and by horseback again to Greenwich. And there I to the office very late, offering my persons for all the victualling ports, much to my satisfaction.[4] Also, much other business I did to my mind; and so, weary, home to my lodging; and there, after eating and drinking a little, I to bed. The King and Court, they say, have now finally resolved to spend nothing upon clothes but what is of the growth of England – which if observed, will be very pleasing to the people and very good for them.[5]

a strictly 'lanst'

---

1. Clarke's letter to Pepys (Cockpit, 27 October) is in PRO, SP 29/135, no. 90 (summary in *CSPD 1665-6*, p. 32). The sub-commissioners were those for London.

2. On 26 October: *CJ*, viii. 621.

3. These represented the completion of the first part of a programme of ship-building which, according to Downing, the English envoy, produced 48 new ships in 1663–5: HMC, *Heathcote*, p. 167; *CSPClar.*, v. 423, 484, 485, 486.

4. Copies (in Hayter's hand) of Pepys's letters of this date to Albemarle and to Coventry, nominating the surveyors and accepting the post of surveyor-general for himself, are in NMM, LBK/8, pp. 270–3; printed in *Further Corr.*, pp. 67–70.

5. On the 26th Arlington announced this decision to the Lord Mayor of London so that shopkeepers could plan their orders accordingly. The King had decided that once mourning for the King of Spain was over he would wear nothing 'inside or out' that was not of English manufacture, except linen and calicoes: *CSPD 1665-6*, p. 31. The gesture had little effect, and the renewed attempts made in parliament to achieve something of the sort resulted only in the act of 1667 requiring corpses to be shrouded in English wool. In April 1668 both houses resolved to ask the King and Court to wear only English products: *LJ*, xii. 228, 229. Cf. the King's attack on French fashions: below, vii. 324.

29. *Lords day.* Up, and being ready, set out with Captain Cocke in his coach toward Erith, Mr. Deane riding along with us – where we dined and were very merry. After dinner we fell to discourse about the Dutch, Cocke undertaking to prove that they were able to wage war with us three year together – which, though it may be true, yet, not being satisfied with his arguments, my Lord and I did oppose the strength of his arguments, which brought us to a great heat – he being a conceited man but of no Logique in his head at all, which made my Lord and I mirth. Anon we parted and back again, we hardly having a word all the way, he being so vexed at our not yielding to his persuasion. I was set down*a* at Woolwich town's-end and walked through the town in the dark, it being now night. But in the street did overtake and almost run upon two women, crying and carrying a man's Coffin between them: I suppose the husband of one of them, which methinks is a sad thing.

Being come to Sheldens, I find my people in the dark in the dining-room, merry and laughing, and I thought sporting one with another; which God help me, raised my jealousy presently. I came in in the dark, and one of them touching me (which afterward I found was Su),[1] made them shreeke; and so went out upstairs, leaving them to light a Candle – and to run out. I went out and was very vexed, till I found my wife was gone with Mr. Hill and Mercer this day to see me at Greenwich, and these*b* people were at supper; and the candle on a sudden falling out of the candlestick (which I saw as I came through the yard), and Mrs. Barbary[2] being there, I was*c* well at ease again – and so bethought myself what to do, whether to go to Greenwich or stay there. At last, go I would; and so with a lantern and three*d* or four people with me, among others, Mr. Browne[3] who was there, would go, I walked*e* with a Lanthorne – and discoursed with him about painting and the several sorts of it.

I came in good time to Greenwich, where I found Mr. Hill[4] with my wife – and very glad I was to see him. To supper and discourse of Musique, and so to bed, I lying with him, talking till

a preceding part of entry crowded into bottom of page   *b* repl. 'they'
      c repl. 'did'   *d* repl. 'for'   *e* repl. 'with'

1. A maidservant of the Pepyses.   3. Mrs Pepys's drawing master.
2. Barbara Sheldon.   4. Thomas Hill, merchant.

midnight about Berchenshaws music rules,[1] which I did to his great satisfaction inform him in; and so to sleep.

30. Up, and to my office about business. At noon to dinner, and after some discourse of music, he and I, I to the office awhile, and he to get Mr. Coleman[2] if he can, against night. By and by, I back again home, and there find him return[ed] with Mr. Coleman (his wife being ill) and Mr. Laneare[3] – with whom, with their Lute, we had excellent company and good singing till midnight, and a good supper I did give them. But Coleman's voice is quite spoiled; and when he begins to be drunk, he is excellent company, but afterward, troublesome and impertinent. Laneare sings, in a melancholy method, very well, and a sober man he seems to be. They being gone, we to bed; Captain Ferrer coming this day from my Lord, is forced to lodge here, and I put him to Mr. Hill.

31. Up, and to the office, Captain Ferrer's going back betimes to my Lord. I to the office, where Sir W Batten met me and did tell me that Captain Cockes black was dead of the plague – which I had heard of before but took no notice. By and by Captain Cocke came to the office, and Sir W. Batten and I did send to him that he would either forbear the office or forbear going to his own office. However, meeting yesterday the Searchers with their rods in their hands[4] coming from his house, I did overhear them*a* say that the fellow did not die of the plague. But he had I know been ill a good while, and I am told that his boy Jacke is also ill.

a repl. same symbol badly formed

1. See above, iii. 35, n. 1. (E).
2. Edward Coleman, musician, composer and singer; his wife was an actress and singer. (A).
3. Nicholas Lanier, Master of the King's Musick. (E).
4. The 'searchers of the dead', usually old women, were employed by parishes to examine corpses and ascertain the cause of death. On their unreliable diagnoses were based the figures of the Bills of Mortality.

In times of plague they were required to live at appointed places, to undertake no other work, to go abroad only on duty, and to carry tall white wands so that the public could avoid contact with them. The office was abolished in 1836. Bell, *Plague*, pp. 17–20, illust. opp. p. 104; *Orders by the Lord Maior . . . in A Collection of very valuable and scarce pieces relating to the Plague* (1721), p. 3.

At noon home to dinner, and then to the office again, leaving Mr. Hill, if he can, to get Mrs. Coleman at night. About 9 at night I came home, and there find Mrs. Pierce come, and little Franke Tooker and Mr. Hill and other people, a great many, dancing. Anon[a] comes Mrs. Coleman, with her husband and Laneare. The dancing ended, and to sing, which Mrs. Coleman doth very finely, though her voice is decayed as to strength; but mighty sweet, though saft – and a pleasant jolly woman, and in mighty good humour was tonight. Among other things, Laneare did at the request of Mr. Hill bring two or three the finest prints for my wife to see that ever I did see in all my life. But for singing, among other things, we got Mrs. Coleman to sing part of the Opera[1] (though she won't owne that ever she did get any of it without book, in order to the stage); but above all, her counterfeiting of Captain Cooke's part, in his reproaching his men with Cowardize, Base Slaves &c.,[2] she doth it most excellently: at it till past midnight, and then broke up and to bed. Hill and I together again – and being very sleepy, we had little discourse as we had the other night.

Thus we end the month merrily; and the more, for that after some fears that the plague would have encreased again this week, I hear for certain that there is above 400 [decrease] – the whole number being 1388; and of them, of the plague, 1031.[3]

Want of money in the Navy puts everything out of order. Men grow mutinous. And nobody here to mind the business of the Navy but myself. At least, Sir W. Batten for the few days he hath been here doth nothing. I in great hopes[b] of my place of Surveyor Generall of the Victualling, which will bring me 300*l* per annum.

---

a repl. 'with'　　　*b* repl. 'fears'

---

1. *The siege of Rhodes*, the opera by Davenant, in which Mrs Edward Coleman had sung the part of Ianthe in recitative when the first part of it was presented in 1656. She has therefore been occasionally described as the first Englishwoman to appear professionally on the stage, though she was a singer rather than an actress; see above, ii. 5 & n. 2. (A).

2. Possibly Solyman's passage beginning 'How cowardly my num'rous Slaves fall back' (1656 ed., p. 39; 1663 ed. pp. 40–1). The setting was by Henry Lawes. (E).

3. In the week 24–31 October, there was a decrease from the previous week of 390 in the deaths from plague: GL, A.1.5, no. 96.

1. Lay very long in bed, discoursing with Mr. Hill of most things of a man's life, and how little merit doth prevail in the world, but only favour – and that for myself, chance without merit brought me in, and that diligence only keeps me so, and will, living as I do among so many lazy people, that the diligent man becomes necessary, that they cannot do anything without him.   And so told him of my late business of the victualling and what cares I am in to keep myself, having to do with people of so different factions at Court, and yet must be fair with them all – which was very pleasant discourse for me to tell, as well, as he seemed to take it, for him to hear.

At last up, and it being a very foul day for rain and a hideous wind, yet having promised I would go, by water to Erith – and bearing sail, was in danger of oversetting – but made them take down their sail; and so, cold and wet, got thither as they had ended their dinner.   How[ever], I dined well.   And after dinner, all on shore, my Lord Brouncker with us, to Mrs. Williams's lodgings, and Sir W Batten, Sir Edmd Pooly and others; and there, it being my Lord's birthday, had everyone a greene riband tied in our hats, very foolishly, and methinks mighty disgracefully for my Lord to have his folly so open to all the world with this woman.   But by and by Sir W. Batten and I took coach, and home to Boremans;[1] and so going home by the backside, I saw Captain Cocke lighting out of his coach (he having been at Erith also with her, but not on board), and so he would come along with me home to my lodging; and there sat and supped and talked with us, but we were angry a little a while about our message to him the other day, about bidding him keep from[a] the office or his own office because of his black dying.   I owned it and the reason of it, and would have been glad he had been out of the house, but I could not bid him go; and so supped, and after much

a repl. 'to'

---

1. The house of George Boreman (Keeper of the Wardrobe, Greenwich Palace), where Batten lodged during the Plague.

other talk of the sad condition and state of the King's matters, we broke up, and my wife and I to bed.

This night, coming with Sir W. Batten into Greenwich, we called upon Collonell Clegatt, who tells us for certain that the King of Denmarke hath declared to stand for the King of England; but since, I hear it is wholly false.

2. Up, left my wife, and to the office; and there to my great content Sir W Warren came to me to settle the business of the Tanger boates,[1] wherein I shall get above 100*l*, besides a 100*l* which he gives me in the paying for them out of his own purse. He gone, I home to my lodgings to dinner; and there comes Captain Wager, newly returned from[a] the Streights, who puts me in great fears for our last[b] ships that went to Tanger with provisions, that they will be taken. A brave stout fellow this Captain is, and I think very honest.

To the office again after dinner, and there late, writing letters. And then about 8 at night set out from my office, and fitting myself at my lodging, entended to have gone this night in a ketch down to the fleet. But calling in my way at Sir Jo Minnes's, who is come up from Erith about something about the prizes – they persuaded me not to go till the morning, it being a horrible dark and a windy night.

So I back to my lodgings, and to bed.

3. Was called up about 4 a-clock, and in the dark by lanthorn took boat, and to the ketch and set sail – sleeping a little in the Cabbin till day; and then up, and fell to reading of Mr. Eveling's book about Paynting,[2] which is a very pretty book. Carrying good victuals, and Tom with me, I to breakfast about 9 a-clock, and then to read again, and came to the fleet about 12 – where

a repl. 'to'   *b* repl. 'new'

---

1. See above, p. 172 & n. 2.

2. Possibly a book lent by Evelyn, who had talked with Pepys on the subject of painting on 27 September. Evelyn's translation of Fréart's book (*An idea of the perfection of painting demonstrated*) was not published until 1668. It seems unlikely that Pepys was referring to Evelyn's *Sculptura* (1662; a small and slim octavo; PL 868), which was about engraving, and, to judge from the single shelf-mark in the PL copy in Pepys's hand, was a late acquisition in the library.

found my Lord (the *Prince* being gone in) on board the *Royall James*, Sir*ᵃ* Tho Allen commander; and with my Lord an hour alone, discoursing, which was my chief and only errand, about what was advisable for his Lordshipp to do in this state of things, himself being under the Duke of York and Mr. Coventrys envy and a great many more – and likely never to do anything honourably but he shall be envied, and the honour taken as much as can be from it. His absence lessens his interest at Court – and which is worst, we never able to set out a fleet fit for him to command; or if out, to keep them out, or fit them to do any great thing; or if that were so, yet nobody at home minds him or his condition when he is abroad; and lastly, the whole affairs of state looking as if they would all on a sudden break in pieces, and then what a sad thing it would be for him to be out of the way. My Lord did concur in everything, and thanked me infinitely for my visit*ᵇ* and counsel, telling me that in everything he concurs; but puts a query: What if the King will not think himself safe, if any man should go but him?¹ How he should go off then? To that, I had no answer ready but the making the King see that he may be of as good use to him here, while another goes forth. But for that, I am not able to say much. We*ᶜ* after this talked of some other little things, and so to dinner, where my Lord infinitely kind to me; and after dinner I rose and left him with some Commanders at the table, taking tobacco; and I took the *Bezan* back with me, and with a brave gale and tide reached up that night to the Hope, taking great pleasure in learning the seamen's manner*ᵈ* of singing when they sound the depths. And then to supper and to sleep,

《4.》 which I did most excellently all night, it being a horrible foul night for wind and rain. They sailed from midnight, and came to Greenwich about 5 a-clock in the morning – I, however, lay till about 7 or 8; and so to my office – my*ᵉ* head a little akeing, partly for want of natural rest – partly having so much business to do today, and partly from the news I hear, that one of

a repl. 'Captain'   *b* repl. 'fear'   *c* repl. 'Yet for all this'
d repl. symbol rendered illegible   *e* repl. 'serve'

---

1. The suggestion here appears to be that the King would fear assassination if the heir-presumptive, the Duke of York, were sent away in command of a fleet.

the little boys at my lodging is not well, and they suspect, by their sending for plaster and Fume,[1] that it may be the plague.   So I sent Mr. Hater and W Ewre to*ᵃ* speak with the mother – but they returned to me satisfied that there is no hurt nor danger, but the boy is well and offers to be searched.[2]   However, I was resolved myself to abstain coming thither for a while.

Sir W. Batten and myself at the office all the morning.   At noon with him to dinner at Boreman's, where Mr. Seymour[3] with us – who is a most conceited fellow, and not over-much in him.*ᵇ* Here Sir W. Batten told us (which I had not heard before) that the last sitting-day his cloak was taken from Mingo,[4] going home to dinner, and that he was beaten by the seamen, and swears he will come to Greenwich but no more to the office (till he can sit safe); after dinner, I to the office and there very late.   And much troubled to have 100 seamen all the afternoon there, swearing below and cursing us and breaking the glass windows; and swear they will pull the house down on Tuseday next.   I sent word of this to Court, but nothing will help it but money and a rope.[5] Late at night I to Mr. Glanvill's, there to lie for a night or two,[6] and to bed.

5.*ᶜ*   *Lords day.*   Up, and after being trimmed, by boate to the

a   repl. symbol rendered illegible   b   repl. ? 'tr'-   c   repl. '4'

---

1. Materials used to produce aromatic vapour.

2. I.e. for the buboes – the swellings which betokened bubonic infection: cf. above, p. 93, n. 2.

3. See above, p. 261, n. 4.

4. His negro servant.

5. Cf. Pepys to Coventry, 4 November: NMM, LBK/8, pp. 278–81 (copy in Hewer's hand, with note by Pepys); partially printed *Further Corr.*, pp. 74–5. Pepys describes the attack on Batten and his servant, and goes on: 'Nay at this instant while I am writeing the whole Company of the Breda . . . are now breakeing the Window of our Office and hath twice this day knocked

downe Marlow our Messenger, sweareing they will not budge without money. What meate they'l make of me anon you shall know by my next.' Later, in the same letter: 'Since the Fore=part of my letter, I have given my Breda=blades an answer that they are parted with. . . '. Riots of unpaid seamen were not uncommon in this and later periods. The screen in front of the 18th-century Admiralty building is said to have been designed to protect the officials from attack: Ehrman, p. 132.

6. He left there on the 9th. For Glanville, see above, p. 243, n. 6.

Cockepitt, where I heard the Duke of Albemarle's chaplain[1] make a simple sermon. Among other things, reproaching the imperfection of humane learning, he cried – "All our physicians can't tell what an ague is, and all our Arithmetique is not able to number the days of a man" – which, God knows, is not the fault of arithmetique, but that our understandings reach not that thing.

To dinner, where a great deal of silly discourse. But the worst is, I hear that the plague encreases much at Lambeth, St. Martins, and Westminster, and fear it will all over the City.[2] Thence I to the Swan, there thinking to have seen Sarah, but she was at church; and so by water to[a] Deptford, and there made a visit to Mr. Evelings, who, among other things, showed me most excellent painting in little – in distemper, Indian Incke – water colours – graveing; and above all, the whole secret of Mezzo Tinto and the manner of it, which is very pretty, and good things done with it.[3] He read to me very much also of his discourse he hath been many years and now is about, about Guardenage; which will be a most noble and pleasant piece.[4] He[b] read me part of a play or two of his making,[5] very good, but not as he conceits them, I think, to be. He showed me his *Hortus hyemalis*; leaves laid up in a book of several plants, kept dry, which preserve Colour however, and look very finely, better than any herball.[6] In fine, a most excel-

a repl. 'home to Lambeth and to Mr. Glanvi'-   b repl. 'And'

1. There were several: the best-known was Thomas Gumble, biographer of his patron.

2. See below, p. 295 & n. 5.

3. The earliest mezzotints had been done in the 1640s. Prince Rupert had made important experiments in the process, and imparted his technical knowledge to Evelyn in 1661: see Evelyn, *Sculptura* (1662; ed. Bell, 1906), and O. Pissaro in *Walpole Soc.*, 36/1–9. (OM).

4. *Elysium Britannicum*, begun c. 1659 and never finished. A printed broadsheet giving a prospectus of the work had been distributed to his friends some time before January 1660: Rawl. A 185, f. 40r; Thomas Browne, *Works* (ed. Keynes), vi. 299+. For his other works on gardening,

see Evelyn, i. 124+; Sir G. Keynes, *Evelyn . . . a bibliography* (1968 ed.), pp. 45+, 147+.

5. One was probably 'Thersander', a tragi-comedy in verse completed in 1663 but never published. Christ Church, Oxford, Evelyn MSS 41.

6. A large folio volume of plants collected by Evelyn at Padua, 1645, is now in the library of Christ Church, Oxford; (*Hortus Hyemalis, sive Collectio Plantarum* D. 16). Cf. Evelyn, ii. 466 & n. 5; C. E. Raven, *Engl. naturalists from Neckam to Ray*, p. 77, n. 8; Gunther, iii. 201+. These collections were fairly common; John Locke made one which is still preserved in the Bodleian: MSS Locke, c. 41, b. 7.

lent person he is, and must be allowed a little for a little conceited-ness; but he may well be so, being a man so much above others. He read me, though with too much gusto, some little poems of his own, that were not transcendent, yet one or two very pretty Epigrams: among others, of a lady looking in at a grate and being pecked at by an Eagle that was there.[1]

Here comes in in the middle of our discourse, Captain Cocke, as drunk as a dog, but could stand and talk and laugh. He did so joy himself in a brave woman that he had been with all the after-noon, and who should it be but my Lady Robinson. But very troublesome he is with his noise and talk and laughing, though very pleasant.

With him in his coach to Mr. Glanvills, where he sat with Mrs. Penington and myself a good while, talking of this fine woman again, and then went away. Then the lady and I to very serious discourse; and among other things, of what a bonny lass my Lady Robinson is, who is reported to be kind to the prisoners, and hath[a] said to Sir G. Smith, who is her great Chrony: "Look, there is a pretty man; I could be contented to break a command-ment with him" – and such loose expressions she will have often.

After an hour's talk, we to bed – the lady mightily troubled about a little pretty bitch she hath, which is very sick and will eat nothing. And the jest was, I could hear her in her chamber bemoaning the bitch; and by and by taking her to bed with her, the bitch pissed ⟨and shit⟩ abed, and she was fain to rise[b] and had coals out of my chamber to dry the bed again. This night, I had a letter that Sir G Carteret would be in town tomorrow, which did much surprize me.

a repl. 'is'   *b* MS. 'raise

---

1. Evelyn preserved a number of his English and Latin poems in a small MS. volume now at Christ Church (Evelyn MSS 124). Among them (lightly struck through in pencil) is *Celia afraid of an Eagle*: 'Faire   Celia   do   you   wonder why / This royal Bird presumes so nigh? / He struggles onely thro' his Grate / To shew himselfe legiti-mate, / Finding in this imprison'd place / No other Sunn to prove his race. / Fly not so fast tho' you have read / How he once trust up *Gany-mede*. / Think you he hold Commis-sion now / Or like designe to seize on you? / If the Gold Messenger presumes / On Such a Rape to try his plumes / Though he beare Lightning free from harme / Your brighter Eyes will prove to warme.'

6.[a] Up, and to my office, where busy all the morning; and then to dinner to Captain Cockes with Mr. Eveling, where very merry; only, vexed after dinner to stay too long for our coach. At last, however, to Lambeth, and thence the Cockepitt, where we find Sir G. Carteret come, and in with the Duke and the East India Company about settling the business of the Prizes, and they have gone through with it.

Then they broke up, and Sir G. Carteret came out and thence through[b] the garden to the water-side, and by water, I with him in his boat, down with Captain Cocke to his house at Greenwich. And while supper was getting ready, Sir G. Carteret and I did walk an hour in the garden before the house, talking of my Lord Sandwich's business – what enemies he hath and how they have endeavoured to bespatter him; and perticularly about his leaving of 30 ships of the enemy, when Pen would have gone and my Lord called him back again – which is most false.[1] However, he says it was purposed by some hot-heads in the House of Commons to have, at the same time when they voted a present to the Duke of Yorke, to have voted 10000*l* to the Prince and half a Crowne to my Lord of Sandwich – but nothing came of it.[2] But for all this, the King is most firme to my Lord, and so is my Lord Chancellor and my Lord Arlington. The Prince in appearance kind. The Duke of Yorke, silent, says no hurt, but admits others to say it in his hearing. Sir W Pen, the falsest rascal that ever was in the world; and that this afternoon the Duke of Albemarle did tell him that Pen was a very cowardly rogue, and one that hath brought all these roguish fanatic captains into the fleet, and swears he shall never go out with the fleet again. That Sir W. Coventry is most kind to[c] Pen still, and says nothing nor doth anything openly to the prejudice of my Lord. He agrees with me that it is impossible for the King [to] set out a fleet again the next year, and

a repl. '5'   *b* repl. 'by water'   *c* repl. 'for all'

---

1. On 24 October Sandwich had hurried from Oxford to London on receiving news from Penn that a fleet of 30 Dutchmen was off the Gunfleet. He gathered together a badly equipped squadron and was off the Nore by 29 October. A storm scattered the Dutch and Sandwich found little to do except to play his guitar. Harris, ii. 20; cf. *CSPD 1665–6*, p. 28; Carte 75, ff. 375r, 380r.

2. Cf. above, p. 281 & n. 2. There appears to be no other trace of this proposal concerning Sandwich.

that he fears all will come to ruine, there being no money in prospect but these prizes, which will bring, it may be, 20000*l*;[1] but that will signify nothing in the world for it. That this late act of Parliament for bring[ing] the money into the Exchequer and making of it payable out there [is] intended as a prejudice to him,[2] will be his convenience* hereafter and ruine the King's business – and so I fear it will, and do wonder Sir W. Coventry would be led by Sir G Downing to persuade the King and Duke to have it so, before they had thoroughly weighed all circumstances.[3]   That for my Lord, the King hath said to him lately that I was an excellent officer, and that my Lord Chancellor doth, he thinks, love and esteem*a* of me as well as he doth of any man in England that he hath no more acquaintance with.

So having done, and received from me the sad news that we are like to have no money here a great while, not even of the very prizes, I set up my rest in giving up the King's service to be ruined; and so in to supper, where pretty merry; and after supper

a repl. 'es'—

---

1. In fact the navy received £100,000 from the two Dutch E. India prizes: Harris, ii. 12. Albemarle had expected £200,000: BM, Harl. 1509, f. 206*r*.

2. Carteret.

3. The Act for an Additional Aid of £1¼ m. (17 Car. II c. 1, passed on 31 October), promoted by Downing and Coventry, with the King's help but without co-operation from the Council, was a new venture in English public finance, and for all Pepys's and Carteret's fears, proved a great success. Put into effect after 25 December, it provided for the appropriation of supplies to war purposes, allowing loans and goods to be advanced on its credit. The principal of the loans was to be repaid to creditors in strict rotation. Carteret stood to lose his Treasurer's poundage on all the goods which would now be paid for directly by the Exchequer,

as well as his profits from discount transactions with the bankers. The latter too were distrustful of the act: below, p. 311 & n. 2. Pepys, after his initial distrust, came to approve of it, though not so far as to venture any of his own money. He persuaded Warren to send in over £3000-worth of timber on its credit (below, p. 330), and he cashed one of Warren's repayment orders, making a handsome profit: below, vii. 90 & n. 1. The act led to the introduction of assignable Treasury orders, and to the use of appropriation in the Poll Tax of 1666 and the Eleven Months Assessment of 1666. For its working, see below, pp. 327, 330, 341; *Further Corr.*, pp. 83, 86, 91, 92; *A state of the case* (1666); *Hist. Essays* (ed. T. F. Tout and J. Tait), pp. 419+; C. D. Chandaman, *Engl. public revenue 1660–88*, esp. p. 178+.

late to Mr. Glanvills, and Sir G. Carteret to bed. I also to bed, it being very late.

7.[a] Up, and to Sir G. Carteret, and with him, he being very passionate to be gone, with[out] staying a minute for breakfast, to the Duke of Albemarle; and I with him by water and with Fen. But among other things, Lord, to see how he wondered to see the river so empty of boats – nobody working at the Custome-house Keys. And how fearful he is, and vexed that his man, holding a wine-glass in his hand for[b] him to drink out of[c], did Cover his hands, it being a cold, windy, rainy morning, under the watermans Coate, though he brought the waterman from six or seven miles up the River too.[1] Nay, he carried this glass with him for his man to let him drink out of at the Duke of Albemarle, where he intended to dine, though this he did to prevent sluttery; for, for the same reason, he carried a napkin with him to Captain Cocke, making him believe that he should eat with foul linen. Here he with the Duke walked a good while in the parke, and I with Fen – but cannot gather that he entends to stay with us, nor thinks anything at all of ever paying one farding of money more to us here, let what will come of it.

Thence in, and Sir W Batten comes in by and by; and so staying till noon, and there being a great deal of company there, Sir W. Batten and I took leave of the Duke and Sir G. Carteret, there being no good to be done more for money; and so over the River and by Coach to Greenwich, where at Boremans we dined, it being late. Thence, my head being full of business, and mind out of order for thinking of the effects which will arise from the want of money, I made an end of my letters by 8 a-clock; and so to my lodging and there spent the evening till midnight talking with Mrs. Penington, who is a very discreet, understanding lady; and very pretty discourse we had, and great variety. And she tells me, with great sorrow, her bitch is dead this morning – died in her bed. So broke up, and to bed.

8.[d] Up, and to the office, where busy, among other things, to look my warrants for the settling of the victualling business, the

a repl. '6'   b repl. 'to dr'–   c repl. 'out'   d repl. '7'

---

1. Carteret was fearful of infection.

warrants being come to me for the Surveyors of the ports, and that for me also to be Surveyor Generall. I did discourse largely with Tom Willson about it, and doubt not to make it a good service to the King as well, as the King gives us very good salaries.[1] It being a fast-day,[2] all people were at Church and the office quiet, so I did much business. And at noon adventured to my old Lodgeing and there eat; but am not yet well satisfied, not seeing of Christopher,[3] though they say he is abroad. Thence after dinner to the office again, and thence am sent for to the King's-head by my Lord Rutherford, who, since I can hope for no more con-venience*from him, his business is troublesome to me;[4] and there-fore I did leave him as soon as I could, and by water to Deptford and there did order my matters so, walking up and down in the fields till it was dark night, that je alloy[a] à la maison of my valen-tine,[5] and there je faisais whatever je voudrais avec her. And about 8 at night did take water, being glad I was out of the town, for the plague, it seems, rages there more then ever. And so to my lodgings, where my Lord had got a supper, and the mistress of the house and her daughters. And here stayed Mrs. Pierce to speak with me about her husband's business, and I made her sup with us; and then at night my Lord and I walked with her home, and so back again. My Lord and I ended all we had to say as to his business overnight, and so I took leave and went again to Mr. Glanvile's;[b] and so to bed, it being very late – to bed.

9. Up, and did give the servants something at Mr. Glanvills and so took leave, meaning to lie tonight at my own lodging. To my office, where busy with Mr. Gawden running over the vic-tualling business; and he is mightily pleased that this course is

a l.h. repl. s.h. 'alloy'   *b* repl. 'B'-

---

1. Copies of the warrants appoint-ing Pepys and Wilson (4 November) are in PRO, Adm. 1725, ff. 175*v*-176*r*; Duke of York, *Mem. (naval)*, pp. 131–3. Pepys received £300 p.a., Wilson £200 p.a.

2. The monthly fast for the Plague, ordered by a proclamation of 6 July 1665 to be held on the first Wednes-day of each month. In this month

the date had been altered to the second Wednesday, since 1 November hap-pened to be All Saints' Day: pro-clamation, 26 September (Steele no. 3437).

3. The small son of Pepys's land-lady, Mrs Clerke; Pepys feared he had the plague.

4. See above, pp. 221 & n. 2.

5. Mrs Bagwell: above, p. 35.

taking, and seems sensible of my favour and promises kindness to me. At noon by water to the King's-head at Deptford,[1] where Captain Taylor invites Sir W. Batten, Sir Jo. Robinson (who came in with a great deal of company from Hunting and brought in a hare alive, and a great many silly stories they tell of their sport, which pleases them mightily, and me not at all, such is the different sense of pleasure in mankind)[2] and others, upon the score of a survey of his new ship.[3] And strange it is, to see how a good dinner and feasting reconciles everybody, Sir W. Batten and Sir Jo Robinson being now as kind to him, and report well of his ship and proceedings and promise money, and Sir W. Batten is a solicitor for him, that it is a strange thing to observe – they being the greatest enemies he had, and yet I believe hath, in the world in their hearts.[4]

Thence after dinner stole away, and to my office, where did a great deal of business till midnight; and then to Mrs. Clerkes to lodge again. And going home, W. Hewer did tell me my wife will be here tomorrow, and hath put away Mary; which vexes me to the heart, I cannot help it, though it be a folly in me; and when I think seriously on it, I think my wife means no ill design in it, or if she do, I am a fool to be troubled at it, since I cannot help it.[5]

The Bill of Mortality, to all our griefs, is encreased 399 this week,[6] and the encrease general through the whole city and suburbs, which makes us all sad.

10. Up, and enter all my Journall since the 28th of October, having every day's passage well in my head, though it troubles me to remember it; and what I was forced to, being kept from my lodging, where my books and papers are, for several days. So to

1. In Church St: Boyne, p. 359.
2. Cf. Pepys's dislike of cock-fighting and bear-baiting: above, iv. 425–6; below, vii. 245–6. For hunting in and around London, see N. Brett-James, *Growth of Stuart London*, pp. 55, 450.
3. Built by Capt. John Taylor to replace the *London*; later named the *Loyal London*. For Robinson's letter (9 November) reporting the survey,

see *CSPD 1665–6*, pp. 46–7.
4. Batten had opposed Taylor's appointment as Navy Commissioner at Harwich: above, v. 326.
5. This last phrase appears to be an echo of the aphorism of Epictetus: cf. above, iii. 194 & n. 1.
6. From 1031 (24–31 October) to 1414 (31 October–7 November): GL, A.1.5, no. 96.

my office – where, till 2 or 3 a-clock, busy before I could go to
my lodging to dinner.   Then did it, and to my office again.   In
the evening news is brought me my wife is come; so I to her, and
with her spent the evening, but with no great pleasure, I being
vexed about her putting away of Mary in my absence; but yet I
took no notice of it at all – but fell into other discourse; and she
told me, having herself been this day at my house at London
(which was boldly done) to see Mary have her things, that Mr.[a]
Harrington our neighbour, and East Country merchant, is dead at
Epsum of the plague.[1]   And that another neighbour of ours, Mr.
Hallworthy,[2] a very able* man, is also dead, by a fall in the
country from his horse, his foot hanging in the stirrup and his
brains beat out.   Here we sat talking; and after supper, to bed.

11.   I up, and to the office (leaving my wife in bed) and there
till noon; then to dinner and back again to the office – my wife
going to Woolwich again and I staying very late at my office;
and so home to bed.

12.   *Lords day.*   Up, and invited by Captain Cocke to dinner.
So after being ready, I went to him, and there he and I and Mr.
Yard (one of the Guiny Company) dined together, and very
merry.   After dinner I by water to the Duke of Albemarle and
there had a little discourse and business with him, chiefly to receive his commands about Pilotts to be got for our Hambrough
ships, going now at this time of the year Convoy to the merchant-
ships that have lain, with great pain and charge, some three and
some four months, at Harwich for a convoy.[b3]   They hope here the
plague will be less this week.   Thence back by water to Captain
Cockes, and there he and I spent a great deal of the evening, as we
had done of the day, reading and discoursing over part of Mr.

a repl. 'she'   b repl. same symbol badly formed

---

1. This was untrue: Harrington
did not die until 1669. He was
William, younger brother of the
author of *Oceana*, and lived in Mark
Lane.
2. Richard Hollworthy, merchant.
3. Sandwich was ordered on the

15th to convoy them, but soon afterwards left the fleet to go to Oxford.
They did not set off until 8 December:
CSPD 1665-6, p. 59. Warren, the
merchant most concerned, later made
heavy charges for demurrage: PL
2874, pp. 487+.

Stillingfleete's *Origines Sacræ*,[1] wherein many things are very good – and some frivolous. Thence by and by, he and I to Mrs. Peningtons, thinking to have spent the evening with her, but she was gone to bed; so we back and walked a while, and then to his house and to supper; and then broke up, and I home to my lodging to bed.

13. Up, and to my office, where busy all the morning; and at noon to Captain Cockes to dinner as we had appointed, in order to settle our business of accounts. But here came in an Alderman, a merchant, a very merry man, and we dined; and he being gone – after dinner Cocke and I walked into the garden and there, after a little discourse, he did undertake under his hand to secure me in 500*l* profit for my share of the profit of what we bought of the prize-goods; we agreed upon the terms, which were easier on my side then I expected; and so, with extraordinary inward joy, we part till the evening. So I to the office, and among other business, prepared a deed for him to sign and seal to me about our agreement, which at night I got him to come and sign and seal. And so he and I to Glanvills, and there he and I sat talking and playing with Mrs. Penington, whom we found undressed in her smock and petticoats by the fireside; and there we drank and laughed, and she willingly suffered me to put my hand in her bosom very wantonly, and keep it there long – which methought was very strange, and I looked upon myself as a man mightily deceived in a lady, for I could not have thought she could have suffered it, by her former discourse with me – so modest she seemed, and I know not what. We stayed here late; and so home, after he and I had walked till past midnight, a bright moonshine, clear, cool night, before his door by the water; and so I home after one of the clock.

14. Called up by break of day by Captain Cocke by agreement, and he and I in his coach through Kent Streete (a sad place through the plague, people sitting sick and with plasters about them in the street, begging) to Viners and Colvills about money business; and so to my house there and took 300*l*, in order to the

1. Edward Stillingfleet, *Origines Sacrae, or A rational account of the grounds of Christian faith, as to the* *truth and divine authority of the scriptures* . . . (1663; 619 pp.); PL 1274.

carrying it down to my Lord Sandwich, in part of the money I am to pay for Captain Cocke by our agreement. So I took it down, and down went to Greenwich to my office, and there sat busy till noon; and so home to dinner, and thence to the office again, and by and by to the Duke of Albemarles by water, late – where I find he had remembered that I had appointed to come to him this day about money, which I excused not doing sooner. But I see, a dull fellow as he is, doth sometimes remember what another thinks he minded not. My business was about getting money of the East India Company.[1] But Lord, to see how the Duke himself magnifies himself in what he had done with that Company, and my Lord Craven, what the King could have done without my Lord Duke; and a deal of stir, but most mightily, what a brave fellow I am. Back by water, it raining hard, and so to the office and stopped my going, as I entended, to the Buoy of the Noure; and great reason I had to rejoice at it, for it proved the night of as great a Storme as was almost ever remembered.[2] Late at the office, and so home to bed.

This day, calling at Mr. Rawlinson's to know how all did there, I hear that my pretty grocer's wife, Mrs. Beversham, over the way there, her husband is lately dead of the plague at Bow, which I am sorry for, for fear of losing her neighbourhood.

15. Up, and all the morning at the office busy; and at noon to the Kings-head Taverne, where all the Trinity-house dined today to choose a new Maister in the room of Hurlestone that is dead. And Captain Crispe is chosen. But Lord, to see how Sir W. Batten governs all and tramples upon Hurlstone; but I am confident that company will grow the worse for that man's death, for now Batten, and in him a lazy, corrupt, doting rogue, will have all the sway there.[3]

1. The money was for the prize-goods; see above, p. 273 & n. 3.
2. Dr D. J. Schove writes: 'Pepys exaggerates; but the gales of this month were at their worst from the 14th to the 17th: cf. *Oxford Gazette*, 20 November. Sir William Petty's ship was lost off Yarmouth, 14–15

November: J. Gadbury, *Nauticum Astrologicum* (1710), p. 63.'
3. The election was at Deptford. Capt. Nicholas Crisp had been an Elder Brother only since the previous April. Batten had been Master, 1663–4.

After dinner, who comes in but my Lady Batten and a troop of a dozen women almost; and expected, as I found afterward, to be made mighty much of, but nobody minded them. But the best Jest was, that when they saw themselfs not regarded, they would go away; and it was horrible foul weather, and my Lady Batten walking through the dirty lane with new spick-and-span white shoes, she dropped one of her Galloshes in the dirt, where it stuck, and she forced to go home without one – at which she was horrible vexed, and I led her. And after vexing her a little more in mirth, I parted, and to Glanvills, where I knew Sir Jo Robinson, Sir G Smith and Captain Cocke were gone. And there, with the company of Mrs. Penington (whose father I hear was one of the Court of Justice, and died prisoner, of the stone, in the Towre),[1] I made them against their resolutions to stay from hour to hour till it was almost midnight, and a furious dark and rainy and windy stormy night; and which was best, I, with drinking small beer, made them all drunk drinking wine, at which Sir Jo Robinson made great sport. But they being gone, the lady and I very civilly sat an hour by the fireside observing the Folly of this Robinson, that makes it his work to praise himself and all he says and doth – like a heavy-headed coxcomb.

The plague, blessed be God, is decreased near 400; making the whole this week but 1300 and odd – for which the Lord be praised.[2]

16. Up, and fitted myself for my Journy down to the Fleete; and sending my money and boy down by water to Eriffe, I borrowed a horse of Mr. Boreman's son, and after having sat an hour laughing with my Lady Batten and Mrs. Turner and*a* eat and drank with them, I took horse and rode to Eriffe; where after making a little visit to Madam Williams, who did give me information of W Hows having bought eight bags of precious

a repl. 'laughing'

---

1. Sir Isaac Penington, puritan Lord Mayor of London 1642–3, and member of the regicide tribunal (though he did not sign the warrant for execution), had died in the Tower in December 1661 after just over one year's imprisonment.

2. Total burials during 7–14 November were 1359, of which 1050 were of plague victims, who had numbered 1414 in the previous week: GL, A.1.5, no. 96.

stones, taken from about the Dutch Viceadmirall's neck, of which there*ᵃ* were eight Dyamonds, which cost him 4000*l* sterling in India and hoped to have made 12000*l* here for them[1] – and that this is told by one that sold him one of the bags, which hath nothing but rubys in it, which he hath for 35*s* – and that it will be proved he hath made 125*l* of one stone that he bought.   This she desired, and I resolved, I would give my Lord Sandwich notice of. So I on board my Lord Bruncker, and there he and Sir Edmd Pooly carried me down into the Hold of the India Shipp, and there did show me the greatest wealth lie in confusion that a man can see in the world – pepper scatter[ed] through every chink, you trod*ᵇ* upon it; and in cloves and nutmegs, I walked above the knees – whole rooms full – and silk in bales, and boxes of Copper-plate, one of which I saw opened.

Having seen this, which was as noble a sight as ever I saw in my life, I away on board the other ship in despair, to get the pleasure-boat of the gentlemen there to carry me to the fleet.   They came, Mr. Ashburnham and Collonell Wyndham[2] – but pleading the King's business, they did presently* agree I should have it.   So I presently on board and got under sail, and had a good bedd by the shift of Wyndhams;   and so sailed all night and got down to

《17.》 Quinbrough water, where all the great ships are now come;   and there on board my Lord, and was soon received with great content.   And after some little discourse, he and I on board Sir W Pen and there held a council of Warr about many wants of the fleet, but chiefly how to get Slopps and*ᶜ* victuals for the fleet now going out to convoy our Hambrough Ships, that have been so long detained, for four or five months, for want of Convoy;   which we did accomodate one way or other,[3]

a repl. 'eight'   *b* repl. same symbol badly formed   *c* repl. 'and money'

---

1. Howe's plunder seems to have been worth far less: below, vii. 22. But he had used Sandwich's seal to author-ise the sale: Pepys to Sandwich, 20 November 1665, Sandwich MSS, Letters from Ministers, i, f. 75r–v.   He had also taken spices, allegedly for Sand-wich's table: ib., ii, f. 56r.

2. William Ashburnham, Cofferer of the King's Household, and Col. Edmund Wyndham.

3. Cf. Pepys to Coventry, 18 November, reporting this council, 'I must confess it is a deadening employment to keepe a dying Fire alive with ones Chopps, for want of Bellows and fresh Coles': Longleat, Coventry MSS 97, f. 5r. The meeting was held on board Penn's ship because of his indisposition: *Further Corr.*, p. 79.

and so after much chatt, Sir W. Penn did give us a very good
and neat dinner, neater I think then ever I did see at his own
house at home in my life, and so was the other I eat with him.
After dinner, much talk; and among*a* other things, he and I about
his money for his prize-goods, wherein I did give him a cool
answer but so as we did not disagree in words much; and so let
that fall, and so fallowed my Lord Sandwich, who was gone a little
before me on board the *Royall James*. And there spent an hour,
my Lord playing upon the Gittarr, which he now commends
above all Musique in the world, because it is bass enough for a
single voice, and is so portable, and manageable without much
trouble. That being done, I got my Lord to be alone, and so I fell
to acquaint him with W How's business, which he had before
heard a little of from Captain Cocke but made no great matter of
it; but now he doth, and resolves nothing less then to lay him by
the heels and seize on all he hath – saying that for these year or two
he hath observed him so proud and conceited, he could not en-
dure him. But though I was not at all displeased with this,*b* yet
I prayed him to forbear doing anything therein till he heard from
me again about it and I had made more enquiry into the truth
of it; which he agreed to. Then we fell to public discourse –
wherein was principally this – he cleared it to me, beyond all
doubt, that Coventry is his enemy and hath been long so. So
that I am over that; and my Lord told it me upon my proposal of
a friendship between them, which he says is impossible. And
methinks that my Lord's displeasure about the report in print of
the first Fight was not of his making[1] – but I perceive my Lord
cannot forget it, nor the other think he can. I showed him how
advisable it were, upon almost any terms, for him to get quite off
the sea imployment. He answers me again, that he agrees to it
but thinks the King will not let him go off.*c* He tells me he lacks
now my Lord Orery to solicit it for him, who is very great with
the King.[2] As an infinite secret, my Lord tells me the factions are
high between the King and the Duke, and all the Court are in an

a MS. 'about'   b MS.? 'us'   c MS. 'on'

1. See above, p. 135 & n. 1.
2. Orrery (since c. 1658 a political
associate of Sandwich, and since May
1665 a Privy Councillor) was now in
Ireland as President of Munster.

According to both Clarendon and
Burnet, he was over-zealous in build-
ing up a court interest for himself:
Life, ii. 86–7; Burnet, i. 480.

uproare with their loose amours – the Duke of York being in love desperately with Mrs. Stewart. Nay, that the Duchesse herself is fallen in love with her new Maister of the Horse, one Harry Sidny, and another Harry Savill[1] – so that God knows what will be the end of it. And that the Duke is not so obsequious as he used to be, but very high of late – and would be glad to be in the head of an army as generall; and that it is said that he doth propose to go and command under the King of Spayne in Flanders. That his amours to Mrs. Stewart are told the King – so that all is like to be nought among them.

That he knows that the Duke of Yorke doth give leave to have him spoken slightly of in his own hearing, and doth not oppose it, and told me from what time he hath observed this to begin. So that upon the whole, my Lord doth concur to wish with all his heart that he could with any honour get from off the imployment. After he had given thanks to me for my kind visit and good counsel, on which he seems to set much by, I left him; and so away to my *Bezan* againe – and there to read in a pretty French book, *La Nouvelle Allegorique*, upon the strife between Rhetorique and its enemies[2] – very pleasant. So after supper to sleep; and sailed all night, and came to Erith before break of day.

18. About 9 of the clock I went on shore there (calling by the way only to look upon my Lord Brouncker) to give Mrs. Williams an account of her matters; and so hired an ill-favourd hoss and away to Greenwich to my lodgings, where I hear how

---

1. They were friends, and both were in the Duke's service. Henry Sidney ('handsome Sidney', son of Robert, 2nd Earl of Leicester) was 'the best-looking fellow in the whole of England': Gramont, p. 284. For his alleged affair with the Duchess, see below, vii. 8; Gramont, pp. 278+. Henry Savile was brother of George Savile, later Marquis of Halifax. Of his alleged affair there is no mention in Gramont; Clarendon (admittedly no friend) has a vague reference to his 'incredible confi-

dence and presumption': *Life*, ii. 489.

2. Antoine Furetière, *Nouvelle Allégorique, ou Histoire des derniers troubles arrivez au royaume d'éloquence*; a small and popular work first published in Paris in 1658; not in the PL. Under cover of a fable telling how the land of a Princess (Rhetoric) was invaded by the forces of a villain (Pedantry), Furetière ingeniously defended many of his literary values. See the modern edition (Geneva, 1967) by E. van Ginneken.

rude the Souldiers have been in my absence, swearing what they would do with me – which troubled me; but however, after eating a bit, I to the office and there very late writing letters, and so home and to bed.

19. *Lords day.* Up, and after being trimmed, I alone by water to Erith, all the way with my song-book singing of Mr. Laws's long recitative Song in the beginning of his book.*ᵃ*1   Being come there on board my Lord Brouncker, I find Captain Cocke and other company (the lady not well), and mighty merry we were, Sir Edmd Pooly being very merry, and a right-English gentleman and one of the discontented Cavaliers that thinks their Loyalty is not considered.² After dinner, all on shore to my Lady Williams and there drank and talked; but Lord, the most impertinent bold woman with my Lord that ever I did see. I did give her an account again of my business with my Lord touching W How, and she did give me some more information about it and examination taken about it; and so we parted, and took boat and to Woolwich, where we found my wife not well of them* – and I, out of humour, begun to dislike her painting, the last things not pleasing me so well as the former – but I blame myself for my being so little complaisant.   So without eating or drinking, there being no wine (which vexed me too), we walked with a lanthorn to Greenwich and eat something at his³ house; and so home to bed.

20.   Up before day, and wrote some letters to go to my Lord; among others, that about W How, which I believe will turn him out.⁴   And so took horse for Nonesuch, with two men with me, and the ways very bad, and the weather worse for wind and rain.

a repl. 'second'

1. Quite possibly Henry Lawes's three collections of *Ayres and dialogues* (1653, 1655, 1658) bound together: see above, p. 27, n. 3. The first song in the 1653 book is Lawes's famous 'Ariadne'. (E).

2. Pooley (M.P. for Bury St Edmunds, Suff.) had been forced to compound for his Suffolk estate in 1646. By 1667 at latest he held a clerkship of the Privy Council and several minor fiscal posts. For the Cavaliers' discontents, see above iv. 373–4; below, p. 330 & n. 1.

3. Cocke's.

4. Sandwich MSS, Letters from Ministers, i, f. 75r. Howe was not dismissed from Sandwich's service, but was not employed again in the navy during the diary period. For his examination, see below, p. 333.

But we got in good time thither, and I did get my Tallys got ready,[1] and thence, with as many as would go, to Yowell; and there dined very well, and I saw my Besse, a very well-favoured country lass there. And after being very merry and having spent a piece, I took horse, and by another way met with a very good road; but it rained hard and blew, but got home very well. Here I find Mr. Deering come to trouble me about business – which I soon despatched; and parted, he telling me that Luellin[2] hath been dead this fortnight of the plague in St. Martin's lane – which much surprized me.

21. Up, and to the office, where all the morning doing business. And at noon home to dinner, and quickly back again to the office, where very busy all the evening; and late, sent a long discourse to Mr. Coventry by his desire, about the regulateing of the*a* method of our payment of bills in the Navy – which will be very good; though it may be he did ayme principally at striking at Sir G Carteret.[3] So, weary, but pleased with this business being over, I home to supper and to bed.

a repl. 'our p'-

1. At the Exchequer. The tallies were for Tangier payments: see HMC, *Eliot Hodgkin*, pp. 166–7.

2. Peter Luellin, Dering's clerk; an old colleague of Pepys in the Exchequer.

3. A copy of this letter, in several hands (together with a memorandum by Pepys: 'Sir Wm. Coventry's proposicions touching paying of bills in Course, and my reflections thereon'), is in NMM, LBK/8, pp. 294–303. The Navy Board's orders in this matter (22 June and 30 December 1665) are in PRO, Adm. 106/3520, ff. 26r, 27r. In June, on Carteret's initiative, the Board had begun to prepare to pay its bills in course by numbering them in the order in which they were received. The scheme was now more than ever necessary if merchants were to be persuaded to provide supplies on the credit of parliament under the recent act of supply (see above, p. 292 & n. 3). But Carteret would lose his poundage (Pepys in a letter of 14 December offered him the consolation that this would be more than offset by the Duke's increased regard for him). The scheme was adopted in December and came into force on 1 January 1666. Pepys thought that payment in course, though desirable, was impracticable in the face of the difficulty of finding cash. See below, p. 323 & n. 3; p. 336 & n. 2; *Further Corr.*, pp. 76, 88–9, 114; Duke of York, *Mem. (naval)*, pp. 136–41 (where the Duke's instructions of 8 December are misdated 8 October); BM, Add. 36782, ff. 28v–29v; Tanner 45, ff. 41–2.

22. Up, and by water to the Duke of Albemarle and there did some little business – but most to show myself, and mightily I am yet in his and Lord Cravens books; and thence to the Swan and there drank, and so down to the bridge, and so to the Change, where spoke with many people and about a great deal of business, which kept me late. I heard this day that Mr. Harrington is not*ᵃ* dead of the plague as we believed; at which I was very glad – but most of all to hear that the*ᵇ* plague is come very low; that is, the whole under 1000 and the plague 600 and odd[1] – and great hopes of a further decrease, because of this day's being a very exceeding hard frost – and continues freezing.[2] This day the first of the *Oxford Gazettes* came out, which is very pretty, full of news, and no folly in it – wrote by Williamson.[3] Fear that our Hambrough ships at last cannot go, because of the great frost which we believe it is there. Nor are our ships cleared at the Pillow,[4] which will keep them there too, all this winter I fear.

From the Change, which is pretty full again, I to my house and there took some things, and so by water to my lodging at Greenwich and dined; and then to the office a while and at night home to my lodgings, and took T Willson and T Hater with me and

a repl. 'doing'   *b* repl. 'it'

---

1. The figures were 905 and 652 respectively for 14–21 November: GL, A.1.5, no. 96.
2. For the effects of cold weather on the disease, see above, p. 93, n. 2.
3. Pepys is comparing the new journal with the work of L'Estrange: q.v. above, iv. 297 n. 2. The first number, undated, appeared on 16 November in Oxford; the reference here may be to the second (16–20 November) which was reprinted in London. For its authorship, see P. Fraser, *Intelligence of Secretaries of State*, pp. 48–9. Williamson (Arlington's secretary) allowed it to be understood that he wrote it, but his share was rather that of supplier of news, and the earlier numbers before February 1666 were written by Henry

Muddiman. No. 24 of the *Gazette* was first published in London and entitled *The London Gazette*; the first of a series which has continued ever since. For most of the period until 1688 it was the only printed newspaper available to the public. In the PL is a series running from 7 November 1665 to 3 January 1704 (PL 2078–90) in uniform binding. Pepys also kept four volumes of the newsbooks which were the *Gazette*'s predecessors, covering 1 January 1660 to 1 January 1666: PL 1744–7. For a general account, see P. M. Handover, *Hist. of London Gazette, 1665–1965*.
4. Pillau, nr Königsberg, E. Prussia; the ships required passports giving customs clearance.

there spent the evening till midnight, discoursing and settling of our Victualling business, that thereby I might draw up instructions for the Surveyours, and that we might be doing something to earne our money. This done,[a] I late to bed. Among other things, it pleased me to have it demonstrated that a purser without professed cheating is a professed loser, twice as much as he gets.[1]

23. Up betimes, and so being trimmed, I to get papers ready against Sir H. Cholmly come to me by appointment, he being newly come over from Tanger. He did by and by come, and we settled all matters about his money; and he is a most satisfied man in me, and doth declare his resolution to give me 200*l* per annum.[2] It continuing to be a great frost (which gives us hope for a perfect cure of the plague), he and I to walk in the park, and there discoursed with grief of the calamity of the times; how the King's service is performed, and how Tanger is governed by a man,[3] who, though honourable, yet doth mind his ways of getting, and little else compared, which will never make the place flourish. I brought him home and had a good dinner for him; and there come by chance Captain Cuttance – who tells me how W. How is laid by the heels, and confined to the *Royall Katharin* and his things all seized. And how also, for a Quarrell (which endeed my

a repl. 'day'

---

1. Cf. Pepys to Batten, 21 April 1666: 'Is it not manifest . . . that a purser (with the utmost of his present allowed profits) must be a knave or be undon . . .?' (*Further Corr.*, p. 129). And cf. the pursers' petition of 1639: 'We are poor men, bred fit for service of consequence, but so poorly paid that we cannot exist without the continuance of what has ever been tolerated' (qu. Michael Lewis, *England's Sea-officers*, p. 245). Pursers' pay was small and they had to enter into bond for the performance of their duties, the amount varying (like their pay) with the rate of their ship. The worst of the tricks of the trade included the cashing of pay-tickets for non-existent sea-

men. But pursers were allowed to make a profit from the sale of victuals and slops, sharing the proceeds, more often than not, with their captains and the contractors. For examples of their 'cheating', see J. Hollond, *Discourses* (ed. Tanner), p. 163 & n.; for Pepys's reform of the system, see below, vii. 1 & n. 1.

2. Cholmley was building the mole at Tangier. He had now returned because of the death of a nephew: [Cholmley,] *A short account of the progress of the mole*, [?1680], p. 3. His gratuities to Pepys turned out to be rather less than he promised: below, vii. 18–19.

3. Lord Belasyse.

Lord the other night told me), Captain Ferrers, having cut all over the back of another of my Lord's servants, is parted from my Lord. I sent for little Mrs. Fr. Tooker; and after they were gone, I sat dallying with her an hour, doing what I would with my hand about her – and a very pretty creature it is. So in the evening parted, and I to the office, where late writing letters; and at my lodging later, writing for the last twelve days my Journall, and so to bed. Great expectation what mischief more the French will do us*a* – for we must fall out. We in extraordinary lack of money and everything else to go to sea the next year. My Lord Sandwich is gone from the Fleete yesterday toward Oxford.

24. Up, and after doing some business at the office, I to London; and there in my way, at my old Oyster-shop in Gracious-streete, bought two barrels of my fine woman of the shop, who is alive after all the plague – which now is the first observation or enquiry we make at London concerning everybody we knew before it. So to the Change, where very busy with several people, and mightily glad to see the Change so full, and hopes of an abatement still the next week. Off the Change, I went home with Sir G Smith[1] to dinner, sending for one of my barrel[s] of oysters, which were good, though come from Colchester, where the plague hath been so much.[2] Here a very brave dinner, though no invitation; and Lord, to see how I am treated, that come from so mean a beginning, is matter of wonder to me. But it is God's great mercy to me – and His blessing upon my taking pains and being punctual in my dealings. After dinner, Captain Cocke and I about some business; and then with my other barrel of oysters home to Greenwich, sent them by water to Mrs. Penington, while he and I landed and visited Mr. Eveling – where most excellent discourse with him; among other things, he showed me a Lieger of a Treasurer of the Navy, his great-grand-

a repl. 'our'

1. A merchant of the Royal African Company. On the day after this dinner, he wrote asking Pepys for a favour for the company: *CSPD 1665–6*, p. 74.
2. The plague had struck Colchester in August. It abated in the winter, but broke out again in the following summer. See R. Josselin, *Diary* (ed. Hockcliffe), pp. 148+; below, vii. 193 & n. 4.

father,[1] just 100 years old; which I seemed mighty fond of, and he did present me with it; which I take as a great rarity, and he hopes to find me more, older then it. He also showed us several letters of the old Lord of Liecesters in Queen Elizabeth's time[2] – under the very handwriting of Queen Elizabeth and Queen Mary Queen of Scotts and others, very venerable names. But Lord, how poorly methinks they wrote in those days, and on what plain uncut paper. Thence, Cocke having sent for his coach, we to Mrs. Penington, and there sat and talked and eat our oysters with great pleasure; and so home to my lodging late, and to bed.

25. Up, and busy at the office all day long, saving dinner time; and in the afternoon also very late at my office – and so home to bed. All our business is now about our Hambrough Fleete, whether it can go or no this year, the weather being set in frosty[3] – and the whole stay being for want of Pilotts now; which I have wrote to the Trinity-house about, but have so poor an account from them, that I did acquaint Sir W Coventry at Court with it this post.[4]

1. *Recte* his wife's great-great-grandfather, Benjamin Gonson, Treasurer of the Navy 1549–77, whose daughter Thomazine had married Sir Richard Browne, grandfather of Evelyn's father-in-law, who was also Sir Richard Browne: Evelyn, iv. 303, n. 3; 304, n. 1. Pepys's collection of Elizabethan naval papers became considerable before his death. The ledger alluded to here may be Rawl. A 200 (1562–3), or ib., 202 (1573–4). In c. 1689 Pepys possessed eight other volumes of Gonson's accounts: list in Rawl. D 794, f. 1r. Pepys in 1669–70 used an Elizabethan ledger to confound his critics on the Brooke House Committee, when the argument turned on precedents: PL 2874, p. 436.

2. Evelyn had inherited these from his wife's great-grandfather, Sir Richard Browne (d. 1604), who appears to have entered public service through the patronage of Robert

Dudley, 1st Earl of Leicester (d. 1588). See Evelyn, iv. 303 & n. 3. In 1681 Evelyn lent to Pepys these and other Elizabethan state papers in his possession, and never asked for them back: *Diary and corr. of J. Evelyn* (ed. Wheatley), iii. 406–10; *Private Corr.*, i. 14–21. They are still in the PL in three large MS. volumes ('Original Papers of State', PL 2502–4), each volume inscribed on the title-page: 'The Gift of my hond. & learned Friend John Evelyn Esqre of Says-Court.' They are calendared in HMC, *Pepys*: see esp. pp. 96–7, 177, 182.

3. Cf. James Askew to Pepys, London, 24 November: *CSPD 1665–6*, p. 71.

4. Copy (in Hewer's hand) NMM, LBK/8, pp. 307–8; printed (incompletely) in *Further Corr.*, pp. 80–1. The ships were still without pilots on 5 December, three days before they sailed: ib., p. 84.

26. *Lords day.* Up, though very late abed, yet before day, to dress myself to go toward Erith – which I would do by land, it being a horrible cold frost to go by water. So borrowed two horses of Mr. Howell and his friend, and with much ado set out, after my horses being frosted[1] (which I know not what it means to this day), and my boy having lost one of my spurs and stockings,[2] carrying them to the smith's. But I borrowed a stocking, and so got up, and Mr. Tooker with me, and rode to Erith; and there on board my Lord Bruncker met Sir W Warren upon his business, among others, and did a great deal; Sir J. Mennes, as God would have it, not being there to hinder us with his impertinences.*[3] Business done, we to dinner very merry, there being there Sir Edm. Pooly, a very worthy Gentleman. They are now come to the copper-boxes in the prizes,[a] and hope to have ended all this week. After dinner took leave, and on shore to Madam Williams to give her an account of my Lord's letter to me about How, who he hath clapped by the heels on suspicion of having the Jewells. She did give me my Lord Bruncker's examination of the fellow, that declares his having them. And so away, Sir W Warren riding with me, and the way being very bad, that is, hard and slippery[b] by reason of the Frost, so we could not come to past Woolwich till night. However, having a great mind to have gone to the Duke of Albemarle, I endeavoured to have gone further; but the night came on, and no going, so I light and sent my horse by Tooker, and returned on foot to my wife at Woolwich – whom I found as I had directed, a good dinner to be made against tomorrow and invited guests in the yard; meaning to [be] merry in order to her taking leave, for she intends to come in a day or two to me for altogether. But here they tell me one of the houses behind them is infected; and I was fain to stand there a great while to have their back-door opened (but they could not, having locked them fast against any passing through); so was forced to pass by them again, close to their sick-beds which they

a repl. 'prize'   *b* repl. same symbol badly formed

---

1. Protected against slipping by frost-nails, roughing, etc. Howell was probably Richard Howell, timber merchant, with whom Pepys did much business.

2. Leather riding-stockings covering the knees.

3. Brouncker and Mennes were in charge of the two Dutch prizes at Erith: cf. above, p. 234.

were removing out of the house – which troubled me. So I
made them uninvite their guests – and to resolve of coming all
away to me tomorrow.   And I walked with a Lanthorn, weary
as I was, to Greenwich; but it was a fine walk, it being a hard
frost.   And so to Captain Cocke's, but he I found had sent for
me to come to him to Mrs. Penington's; and there I went, and
we were very merry and supped.   And Cock being sleepy, he
went away betimes; I stayed alone, talking and playing with her
till past midnight – she suffering me a hazer whatever ego voulus
avec ses mamelles – and I had almost led her by *a* discourse to make
her tocar mi cosa naked, which ella did presque and did not
refuse.   Much pleased with her company, we parted, and I home
to bed at past one, all people being in bed, thinking I would have
stayed out of town all night.

27.   Up, and being to go to wait on the Duke of Albemarle,
who is to go out of town to Oxford tomorrow, I being unwilling to go by water, it being bitter cold, walked it with my
landlady's little boy Christopher *b* – to Lambeth, it being a very
fine walk – and calling at Half-the-way[1] and drank.   So to the
Duke of Albemarle, who is visited by everybody against his
going – and mighty kind to me; and upon my desiring his Grace
to give me his kind word to the Duke of Yorke, if *c* any occasion
there were of speaking of me – he told me he had reason to do,
for there had been nothing done in the Navy without me.   His
going, I hear, is upon putting the sea-business into order, and as
some say, and people of his own family, that he is agog to go to
sea himself the next year.   Here I met with a letter from Sir G.
Carteret, who is come to Cranborne, that he will be here this
afternoon and desires me to be with him – so the Duke would
have me dine with him.   So it being not dinner time, I to the
Swan, and there found Sarah *d* all alone in the house and I had the
opportunity a hazer what I tena a mind á hazer con ella, only con
my hands – but she was vexed at my offer a tocar la under *e* sus
jupes; but I did once, nonobstant all that.   So away to the Duke
of Albemarle again, and there to dinner; he most exceeding *f*

_a_ MS. 'to'　　　_b_ MS. 'Chyistopher'　　　_c_ repl. 'of'　　　_d_ s.h.
　　　　　_e_ repl. 'to'　　　_f_ repl. 'serve'

_____

1. The Halfway House, Rotherhithe.

kind to me, to the observation of all that are there. At dinner
comes Sir G. Carteret, and dines with us. After dinner, a great
deal alone with Sir G. Carteret, who tells me that my Lord hath
received still worse and worse usage from some base people about
the Court. But the King is very kind, and the Duke doth not
appear the contrary, and my Lord Chancellor swore to him "By
[God], I will not forsake my Lord of Sandwich." Our next discourse is upon this Act for money, about which Sir G. Carteret
comes to see what money can be got upon it – but none can be
got; which pleases him the thoughts of, for if the Exchequer
should succede in this, his office would fail.[1] But I am apt to think,
at this time of hurry and plague and want of trade, no money will
be got upon a new way which few understand. We walked,
Cocke and I, through the parke with him; and so we being to
meet the*a* Vice-chamberlain tomorrow at Nonsuch to treat with
Sir Rob Long about the same business – I into*b* London, it being
dark night, by a Hackny Coach, the first I have durst to go in
many a day, and with great pain now for fear. But it being unsafe to go by water in the dark, and frosty, cold, and unable, being
weary with my morning walk, to go on foot, this was my only
way. Few people yet in the streets, nor shops open, here and
there twenty in a place almost, though not above 5 or 6 a-clock at
night. So to Viner's, and there heard of Cocke and found him at
the Popes-head, drinking with Temple. I to them – where the
Goldsmiths do decry the new Act for money to be all brought into
the Exchequer and paid out thence – saying they will not advance
one farding upon it. And endeed, it is their interest to say and do
so.[2] Thence Cocke and I to Sir G Smiths, it being now night,
and there up to his chamber and sat talking, and I barbing against
tomorrow. And anon, at 9 at night, comes to us Sir G Smith
and the Lieutenant of the Tower, and there they sat talking and
drinking till past midnight, and mighty merry we were – the
Lieutenant of the Tower being in a mighty vein of singing; and

a repl. 'him'   *b* repl. 'by water'

---

1. See above, p. 292 & n. 3.
2. They were offered 6% under
the act, instead of their usual 10%, and
would possibly suffer competition
from public subscription. None of
their existing loans to the government
were transferred to the funds raised by
the act.

he hath a very good eare and strong voice, but no manner of skill. Sir G Smith showed me his lady's closet, which was very fine. And after being very merry – here I lay in a noble chamber, and mighty highly treated – the first night I have lain in London a long time.

28.   Up before day, and Cocke and I took a hackney-coach, appointed with four horses to take us up, and so carried us over London-bridge.   But there thinking of some business, I did light at the foot of the bridge, and by help of a candle at a Stall where some pavers were at work, I wrote a letter to Mr. Hater;   and never knew so great an instance of the usefulness of carrying pen and ink and wax about one.[1]   So we, but way being very bad, to Nonsuch, and thence to Sir Rob. Long's house[2] – a fine place, and dinner-time ere we got thither (but we had breakfasted a little at Mr. Gawdens, he being out of town though;   and there borrowed Dr. Taylors Sermons,[3] and is a most excellent book and worth my buying), where had a very good dinner and curiously dressed. And here a couple of ladies, kinswomen of his, not handsome though, but rich, that knew me by report of The Turner, and mighty merry we were.

After dinner, to talk of our business, the act of Parliament; where in short, I see Sir R Long mighty fierce in the great good qualities of it;   but in that and many other things he was stiff in, I think without much judgment or the judgment I expected from him – and already they have evaded the necessity of bringing people into the Exchequer with their bills to be paid there.

Sir G Carteret is tickeled* at this, yet resolves with me to make the best use we can of this act for the King;   but all our care, we

1. Pepys was no longer using his silver fountain-pen: cf. above, iv. 264 & n. 1.

2. Worcester House. In 1663 the King had leased to Long (Auditor of the Receipt in the Exchequer) the reversion of the mansion, of the park (Worcester Park, near Ewell, Surrey, originally the Great Park of Nonsuch) and of the Great Park Meadow. Long took full possession in 1670 after the death of the Queen Mother:

CTB, i. 167; VCH, *Surrey*, iii. 268–9; O. Manning and W. Bray, *Hist. Surrey* (1804–14), ii. 606.

3. Jeremy Taylor's ΣΥ΄ΜΒΟΛΟΝ ΘΕΟΛΟΓΙΚΟ΄Ν: *or A collection of polemical discourses, wherein the Church of England in its worst as well as more flourishing condition, is defended . . . against . . . Papists . . . and the Fanaticks . . .* (1657); PL 2640 (3rd ed. 1674).

think, will not render it as it should be. He did again, here alone, discourse with me about my Lord, and is himself strongly for my Lord's not going to sea, which I am glad to hear and did confirm him in it. He tells me too, that he talked[a] last night with the Duke of Albemarle about my Lord Sandwich, by the bye making him sensible that it is his interest to preserve his old friends – which he confessed he had reason to do, for he knew ill offices were doing of him, and that he honoured my Lord Sandwich with all his heart. After this discourse we parted, and all of us broke up – and we parted.

Captain Cocke and I through Wandsworth; drank at Sir Allen Broderick's,[1] a great friend and comrade of Cocke's, whom he values[b] above the world for a witty companion, and I believe he is so. So to Fox hall, and there took boat[c] and down to the Old Swan, and thence to Lumbard-street, it being dark night. And thence to the Tower, took boat, and down to Greenwich, Cocke and I. He home, and I to the office, where did a little business, and then to my lodgings, where my wife is come, and I am well pleased with it; only, much trouble in these lodgings we have, the mistress of the house being so deadly dear in everything we have – so that we do resolve to remove home as soon as we know how the plague goes this week, which we hope will be a good decrease. So to bed.

29. Up, my wife and I talking how to dispose of our goods, and resolved upon sending our two maids, Alce (who hath been a day or two at Woolwich with my wife, thinking to have had a feast there)[d] and Susan home. So my wife, after dinner, did take them to London with some goods. And I in the afternoon, after doing other business, did go also by agreement to meet Captain Cocke; and from him to Sir Rogr Cuttance about the [money] due from Cocke to him for the late prize-goods – wherein Sir Rog. is troubled that he hath not payment as agreed,[2] and the other that he must pay without being secured in the quiet possession of them. But some accomodacion to both, I think, will be

a repl. 'hath'   b repl. 'doth'   c repl. 'coach'
d   bracket misplaced after 'Susan'

1. Courtier; he had inherited a   2. See above, pp. 230, 240.
house at Wandsworth, Surrey.

found. But Cocke doth*ᵃ* tell me that several have begged so much of the King, to be discovered out of stolen prize-goods, and so I am afeared we shall hereafter have trouble, therefore I will get myself free of them as soon as I can, and my money paid.[1] Thence home to my house, calling my wife, where the poor wretch is putting things in a way to be ready for our coming home; and so by water together to Greenwich, and so spent the night together.

30. Up, and at the office all the morning. At noon comes Sir Tho. Allen and I made him dine with me, and very friendly he is; and a good man I think, but one that professes he loves to get and to save.[2] He dined with my wife and me and Mrs. Barbary, whom my wife brings along with her from Woolwich for as long as she stays here. In the afternoon to the office, and there very late writing letters; and then home, my wife and people sitting up for me, and after supper, to bed. Great joy we have this week in the weekly Bill, it being come to 544 in all, and but 333 of the plague[3] – so that we are encouraged to get to London as soon as we can. And my father writes as great news of joy to them, that he saw Yorkes waggon go again this week to London, and was full of passengers – and tells me that my aunt Bell hath been dead of the plague these seven weeks.

a repl. 'did'

---

1. Pepys sold his interest in the goods to Cocke, and, as a result, his name does not appear among those listed in the prize officers' report (February 1666) on the affair: PRO, SP 29/149, no. 89.

2. This was the admiral, Sir Thomas Allin. Before entering naval service he had been a merchant and shipowner in Lowestoft. For his greed, see R. Ollard, *Pepys*, p. 240.

3. For the week 21–8 November. In the previous week the figures had been 905 and 652: GL, A.1.5, no. 96.

DECEMBER

1. This morning to the office, full of resolution to spend the whole day at business. And there, among other things, I did agree with Poynter[1] to be my clerk for my Victualling business. And so I all alone all the day long, shut up in my little closet at my office, drawing up instructions which I should long since have done for my Surveyors of the Ports[2] – Sir W. Coventry desiring much to have them, and he might well have expected them long since. After dinner to it again; and at night had long discourse with Gibbson, who is for Yarmouth, who makes me understand so much of the victualling business and the pursers trade, that I am shamed I should go about the concerning myself in a business which I understand so very very little of, and made me distrust all I had been doing today.[3] So I did lay it by till tomorrow morning, to think of it fresh. And so home, by promise to my wife to have mirth there; so we have our neighbours, little Mis Tooker and Mrs. Daniels, to dance; and after supper I to bed and left them merry below, which they did not part from till 2 or 3 in the morning.

2. Up, and discoursing with my wife, who is resolved to go to London for good and all this day, we did agree upon giving Mr. Sheldon 10*l*, and Mrs. Barb. two pieces.[4] And so I left her to go down thither to fetch away the rest of the things and pay him the money; and so I to the office, where very busy, setting Mr. Poynter to write out my last night's work; which pleases me this

---

1. Thomas Pointer, of the Navy Office; on 22 December Pepys transferred him to the service of the Comptroller.

2. Issued on 7 December over the name of the Duke of York: copy (certified by Pepys) in BM, Add. 19399, f. 99r. Coventry approved them on the day of issue: *CSPD 1665–6*, p. 92.

3. Richard Gibson, Surveyor of Victualling at Great Yarmouth, Norf.,

1665–7, had been a purser since 1652. He was to have a successful career becoming chief clerk to three successive Clerks of the Acts (1672–7) and clerk to Pepys as Secretary for Admiralty Affairs, 1684–9.

4. Mrs Pepys and her maid had stayed at the house of William Sheldon (Clerk of the Cheque, Woolwich) since 9 July. Barbara Sheldon was his niece.

day, but yet it is pretty to reflect how much I am out of countenance with what I had done up[on] Gibsons discourse with me,
for fear I should have done it sillily.   But Poynter likes them, and
Mr. Hater also; but yet I am afeared lest they should do it out of
flattery, so conscious I am of my ignorance.

Dined with my wife at noon, and took leave of her, she being
to go to London, as I said, for altogether; and I to the office, busy
《3.》 till past one in the morning, it being Lords day; and up and
dressed – and to church, thinking to have sat with Sir James
Bunce to hear his daughter and her husband[1] sing, that are so much
commended; but was prevented by being invited into Collonell
Cleggatts pew.   However, there I sat near Mr. Laneare, with whom
I spoke, and in sight by chance, and very near, my fat brown beauty
of our parish, the rich merchant's lady, a very noble woman[2] –
and of Madam Pierce.   A good sermon of Mr. Plumes'; and so to
Captain Cocke's and there dined with him and Collonell Wyndham, a worthy gentleman, whose wife was nurse to the present
King, and one that while she lived, governed him and everything
else, as Cocke says, as a minister of state, the old King putting
mighty weight and trust upon her.[3]   They talked[a] much of
matters of state and persons, and perticularly how my Lord Berkely hath all along been a fortun[ate], though a passionate and but
weak man as to policy; but as a kinsman[b] brought in and promoted by my Lord of St. Albans, and one that is the greatest
vapourer in the world;[4] this, Collonell Wyndham says – and one
to whom only, with Jacke Ashburnham and Collonell Legg, the
King's removal to the Isle of Wight from Hampton Court was
communicated, and though betrayed by their knavery, or at[c] best

----

a repl. 'tell me'   *b* MS. 'kinswoman'   *c* MS. 'all'

----

1. Their name was Chamberlain.
The church was the parish church of
St Alfege, Greenwich.

2. Anne, wife of John Lethieulier,
merchant, of St Olave's.   Cf. below,
p. 328.

3. She was Christabella, wife of
Col. Edmund Wyndham.   Clarendon complained of her influence:
'a woman of great rudeness and a
country pride': *Hist.*, iv. 22, 23.

4. There is a confusion here

between the 1st Baron Berkeley of
Stratton and the 9th Baron Berkeley
(of Berkeley).   It was the latter who
was a relative of St Albans (their
mothers were first cousins), but the
reference is clearly enough to the
former.   It was he who was a great
braggart (cf. above, p. 38 & n. 1),
and it was he who (as the entry goes
on to say) took a leading part in
Charles I's escape to the Isle of Wight.

by their ignorance. Insomuch that they have all solemnly charged one another with their failures therein, and have been at daggers-drawing publicly about it; yet now none greater friends in the world.[1]

We dined, and in comes Mrs. Owen, a kinswoman of my Lord Bruncker's, about getting a man discharged, which I did for her. And by and by Mrs. Pierce, to speak with me (and Mary my wife's late maid, now gone to her) about her husband's business of money.[2] And she tells us how she prevented Captain Fisher the other day in[a] his purchase of all her husband's fine goods, as pearls and silks, that he had seized in a apothecary's house, a friend of theirs. But she got in, and broke them open and removed all, before Captain Fisher came the next day to fetch them away – at which he is stark mad.

She went home, and I to my lodgings. At night by agreement I fetched her again with Cockes coach. And he came, and we sat and talked together, thinking to have had Mrs. Coleman and my songsters, her husband and Laneare, but they failed me. So we to supper, and as merry as was sufficient, and my little pretty Mis[3] with me. And so after supper walked Pierce home, and so back and to bed. But Lord, I stand admiring of the wittiness[b] of her little boy, which is one of the wittiest boys, but most confident that ever I did see of a child of nine year old or

---

a repl. ? 'with'   *b* repl. 'witness'

---

1. In November 1647 Charles I escaped from Hampton Court and travelled to Titchfield House, Hants., where he hoped to get into touch with Col. Robert Hammond, parliamentary governor of the Isle of Wight, and arrange a passage to France. The three royal servants here mentioned had accompanied him. William Legge stayed with the King at Titchfield, while Ashburnham and Berkeley went across to make arrangements with Hammond. It was Berkeley, it seems, who was mainly responsible for letting Hammond know of the King's whereabouts before getting assurances from

him of the King's safety. Hammond did not play their game, but came to Titchfield and took Charles off into custody at Carisbrooke. Ashburnham's defence of his conduct was published in 1648, and Berkeley's in 1699; both are reprinted in Ashburnham, *Narrative* (2 vols, 1830): see esp. ii. 108+, and App. vi. See also Clarendon (*Hist.*, iv. 263+), who unjustly casts the blame on Ashburnham.

2. This was money due for the purchase of Pepys's prize-goods: above, p. 230.

3. Frances Tooker.

under in all my life, or endeed one twice his age almost; but all
for roguish wit.

So to bed.

4.   Several people to me about business; among*a* others, Captain Taylor, intended Storekeeper for Harwich,[1] whom I did give
some assistance in his despatch – by lending him money.   So out,
and by water to London, and to the Change and up and down
about several businesses.   And after the observing (God forgive
me) one or two of my neighbour hermosa mohers come to town,
which did please me very well, home to my house*b* at the office,
where my wife had got a dinner for me.   And it was a joyful
thing for us to meet here – for which God be praised.   Here was
her brother, come to see her and speak with me about business –
it seems my recommending of him hath not only obtained pre-
sently* being admitted into the Duke of Albemarle's guard and
present pay[2] – but also, by the Dukes and Sir Ph. Howards directions, to be put as a right-hand man, and other marks of special
respect; at which I am very glad, partly for him, and partly to see
that I am reckoned something in my recommendations – but wish
he may carry himself that I may receive no disgrace by him.   So
to the Change, and up and down again in the evening about
business – and to meet Captain Cocke, who waited for Mrs.
Pierce (with whom he is mightily stricken) to receive and hide
for her her rich goods she saved the other day from seizure.
Upon the Change today, Colvill tells me from Oxford that the
King in person hath justified my Lord Sandwich to the highest
degree – and is right in his favour to the uttermost.   So late by
water home, taking a barrel of oysters with me; and at Greenwich
went and sat with Madam Penington, con laquelle je faisais
almost whatever je voudrais – con mi mano, sino tocar la chose
même; and I was very near it, and made her undress her head and
set dishevelled all night, sporting till two in the morning; and so
away to my lodging, almost cloyed with this dalliance, and so to

a repl. same symbol badly formed   *b* repl. 'home'

1. Capt. Silas Taylor now replaced
John Brown, suspended (and later
dismissed) for embezzlement. He
is to be distinguished from Capt.

John Taylor, Navy Commissioner
at Harwich.

2. For Balty's appointment, see
above, p. 271 & n. 1.

bed.   ⟨Over-fasting all the morning hath filled me mightily with
wind, and nothing else hath done it, that I fear a fit of the Cholique.⟩

5.   Up, and to the office, where very busy about several
businesses all the morning.   At noon, empty, yet without stomach, to dinner, having spoiled myself with fasting yesterday,
and so filled with wind.   In the afternoon by water, calling Mr.
Stevens (who is with great trouble paying of seamen of their
tickets at Depford),[1] and to London to look for Captain Kingdon,[2] whom we found at home about 5 a-clock.   I wooed him,
and he promised to fallow us presently to the East India-house to
sign papers tonight, in order to the settling the business of my
receiving money for Tanger.   We went and stopped the officers
there to shut up.   He made us stay above an hour.   I sent for
him; he comes, but was not found at home, but abroad on other
business – and brings a paper saying that he had been this hour
looking for the Lord Ashlys order.[3]   When he looks for it, that
is not the paper – he would go again to look; kept us waiting till
almost 8 at night.   Then was I to go home by water, this weather
and dark, and to write letters by the post – besides keeping the
East India officers there so late.   I sent for him again; at last he
comes and says he cannot find the paper (which is a pretty thing,
to lay orders for 100000*l* no better);[4]   I was angry; he told me I
ought to give people ease at night, and all business was to be done
by day.   I answered him sharply, that I did [not] make, nor any
honest man, any difference between night and day in the King's
business, and this was such – and my Lord Ashly should know;
he answered me short; I told him I knew the time (meaning the
Rump's time) when he did other men's business with more dili-

---

1. On 2 December Anthony
Stevens had written to Pepys asking
for a guard and also, if possible, for
Pepys's own presence at the pay table
'if only for a little time, to lay an
awe upon the spirits of the soldiers':
CSPD 1665–6, p. 83.
2. Richard Kingdon, a sub-com-
missioner of prizes; his office until
1667 was in E. India House.   Pepys
was to be paid from prize money.

3. Ashley was Treasurer of the prize
commission.
4. The Treasury had borrowed
£100,000 from the E. India Company
on the security of the Dutch prize
ships: *Cal. court mins E. India
Company 1664–7* (ed. Sainsbury),
pp. 174–6.

gence.[1]   He cried, "Nay, say not so," and stopped his mouth, not one word after.   We then did our business without the order in less then eight minutes, which he made me, to no purpose, stay above two hours for the doing.   This made me*a* mad; and so we exchanged notes, and I had notes for 14000*l* of the Treasurer of the Company;   and so away, and by water to Greenwich and wrote my letters, and so home late to bed.

6.   Up betimes, it being Fast day,[2] and by water to the Duke of Albemarle, who came to town from Oxford last night.   He is mighty brisk, and very kind to me and asks my advice principally in everything.   He surprizes me with the news that my Lord Sandwich goes Embassador to Spayne speedily – though I know not whence this arises, yet I am heartily glad of it.[3]   He did give me several directions what to do;   and so I home by water again, and to church a little, thinking to have met Mrs. Pierce in order to our meeting at night.   But she not there, I home – and dined; and comes presently by appointment my wife.   I spent the afternoon upon a song of Solyman's words*b* to Roxolana that I have set;[4]   and so with my wife walked, and Mercer, to Mrs. Pierces, where Captain Rolt and Mrs. Knipp,[5] Mr. Coleman and his wife, and Laneare, Mrs. Worship, and her singing daughter met;   and by and by unexpectedly comes Mr. Pierce from Oxford.   Here

a MS. 'him'   *b* repl. same symbol badly formed

1. Kingdon had been an official of The Admiralty Committee under the Protectorate and in 1659-60, and Comptroller of the prize commission during the First Dutch War.

2. For the Plague; held on the first Wednesday of each month: above, p. 155, n. 4.

3. By 31 December it was clear to Pepys that this appointment was a method of getting Sandwich out of the way while the prize-goods scandal blew over.   He seems to have received the appointment in November; he sailed from Portsmouth on 2 March 1666, and returned in September 1668.

4. The passage was that beginning 'Beauty retire' from Davenant's

Siege of Rhodes, Pt II, Act IV, sc. 2. Pepys now made of it a declamatory song of which he was extremely proud, and which has become his best-known musical composition. For the MS., see PL 2803, pp. 210-12 (with a bass line which is possibly by Pepys: below, p. 324). The Hayls portrait (1666; above, vol. i, front.) shows him holding a copy. For a modern edition, see Sir Frederick Bridge, *S. Pepys lover of musique,* opp. p. 123. (E).

5. Elizabeth (?) Knepp, an actress in the King's company.   Pepys was very fond of her, and in August 1666, he agreed to have her son named Samuel: below, vii. 196 & n. 2.

the best company for Musique I ever was in in my life, and wish I could live and die in it, both for music and the face of Mrs. Pierce and my wife and Knipp, who is pretty enough, but the most excellent mad-hum[ou]rd thing; and sings the noblest that ever I heard in my life, and Rolt with her, some things together most excellently – I spent the night in an ectasy almost; and having invited them to my house a day or two hence, we broke up – Pierce having told me that he is told how the King hath done my Lord Sandwich all the right imaginable, by showing him his countenance before all the world on every occasion, to remove thoughts of discontent – and that he*a* is to go Embassador; and that the Duke of Yorke is made Generall of all forces by land and sea, and the Duke of Albemarle Lieutenant-Generall; whether the two latter alterations be so true or no, he knows not, but he is told so[1] – but my Lord is in full favour with the King. So*b* all home and to bed.

7. Up, and to the office, where very busy all day. Sir G. Carteret's letter tells me my Lord Sandwich is, as I was told, declared Embassador-Extraordinary to Spayne, and to go with all speed away – and that his enemies have done him as much good as he could wish. At noon late to dinner; and after dinner spent till night with Mr. Gibson and Hater, discoursing and making myself more fully [understand] the trade of pursers and what fittest to be done in their business;[2] and so to the office till midnight, writing letters; and so home, and after supper with my wife, about one a-clock to bed.

a repl. 'is'   *b* repl. 'then'

1. Cf. the similar rumour in September 1668: W. Westergaard (ed.), *First Triple Alliance*, pp. 14–15. On neither occasion was the rumour true. Albemarle remained Captain-General for life (the patent had been granted on 3 August 1660). On Albemarle's death in 1670 James advised his brother not to appoint a successor, the trust being too great for a mere subject: *Life* (ed. J. S. Clarke, 1816), i. 446–7, 494–5. But Monmouth was appointed.

2. On 5 December the Duke of

York had asked the Board to study methods of simplifying pursers' accounts, asking that they be required to make them up every time their ships came into port so that the length of period covered should be reduced: Tanner 45, f. 35r. Writing to Coventry on the 12th, Pepys said he had 'collected a little volume of observation' about 'the purser's trade': *Further Corr.*, p. 88. This was the basis of his proposals of 1 January 1666: see below, vii. 1 & n. 1.

8. Up, well pleased in my mind about my Lord Sandwich, about whom I shall know more anon from Sir G. Carteret, who will be in town – and also that the Hambrough [ships], after all difficulties, are got out;[1] God send them good speed. So after being trimmed – I by water to London to the Navy Office, there to give order to my maid to buy things to send down to Greenwich for supper tonight; and I also to buy other things, as oysters and lemons (6*d* per piece) and oranges, 3*d*. That done, I to the Change; and among many other things, especially for getting of my Tanger money paid, I by appointment met Mr. Gawden; and he and I to the Pope's-head tavern, and there he did give me alone a very pretty dinner. Our business, to talk of his matters and his supply of money, what was necessary for us to talk on before the Duke of Albemarle this afternoon and Sir G. Carteret. After that, I offered it to pay him the 4000*l*[a] remaining of his 8000*l* for Tanger; which he took with great kindness, and prayed me most frankly to give him a note for 3500*l*, and accept the other 500*l* for myself – which, in good earnest, was against my judgment to do, for expected about 100*l* and no more; but however, he would have me do it, and owns very great obligations to me; and the man endeed I love, and he deserves it. This put me into great joy, though with a little stay to it till we have time to settle it; for, for so great a sum, I was fearful any accident might by death or otherwise defeat me, having not now time to change papers. So we rose, and by water to White-hall, where we find Sir G. Carteret with the Duke, and also Sir G Downing, whom I had not seen in many years before. He greeted me very kindly, and I him; though methinks I am touched that it should be said that he was my Maister heretofore, as doubtless he will.[2] So to talk of our Navy business, and perticularly money business, of which there is little hopes of any present supply upon[b] this new Act, the goldsmiths being here (and Alderman Backewell, newly

a repl. '2000'   *b* repl. 'for all'

---

1. Cf. above, p. 300.
2. Pepys had been clerk to Downing in the Exchequer, c. 1656–60. He reports this conversation in greater detail in a letter to Coventry, 9 December: *Further Corr.*, pp. 86–7.

Downing (envoy-extraordinary to the United Provinces) had been in England since August: *CSPVen. 1664–6*, p. 195. It was his initiative which had inspired the recent financial reforms: see above, p. 292, n. 3.

come from Flanders),[1] and none offering any. So we rose without doing more then my stating the case of the Victualler: that whereas there is due to him on the last year's declaration, 80000*l*, and the charge of this year's amounts to 420000*l* and odd – he must be supplied between this and ⟨the end of⟩ January with 150000*l*, and the remainder in 40 weeks by weekly payments, or else he cannot go through his business.[2]

Thence, after some discourse with Sir G. Carteret, who, though he tells me that he is glad of my Lord's being made Embassador, and that it is the greatest courtesy his enemies could do him, yet I find he is not heartily merry upon it, and that it was no design of my Lord's friends but the prevalence of his enemies – and that the Duke of Albemarle and Prince Robert are like to go to sea together the next year. I pray God, when my Lord is gone, they do not fall hard upon the Vice chamberlain, being alone and in so envious a place, though by this late Act and the instructions now a-brewing for our office as*a* to method of payments, will destroy the profit of his place of itself, without more trouble.[3]

Thence by water down to Greenwich, and there find all my company come; that is, Mrs. Knipp (and a n ill, melancholy, jealous-looked fellow, her husband,[4] that spoke not a word to us all the night), Pierce and his wife, and Rolt, Mrs. Worship and her daughter, Coleman and his wife, and Laneare; and to make us perfectly happy, there*b* comes by chance to town, Mr. Hill to see us. Most excellent Musique we had in abundance, and a good supper – dancing – and a pleasant Scene of Mrs. Knip's rising sick from table – but*c* whispered me it was for some hard word or other her husband give her just now, when she laughed and was more merry then ordinary – but we got her in humour again, and mighty merry, spending the night till 2 in the morning with

a repl. 'may'   *b* repl. 'drops in'   *c* repl. 'up'

1. See above, p. 150, n. 1.

2. On 7 January a warrant was issued for the payment to Gauden of £100,000 to cover the cost of sea-victuals for 35,000 men for one year. Imprests for a further £300,000 followed on 23 February. *CSPD 1665-6*, p. 193; PRO, Adm. 20/7/2, p. 587.

3. For the instructions, see above, p. 304 & n. 3. A fourteen-point draft (5 December) had just arrived in the office: Tanner 45, ff. 41-2. It was later revised: see below, p. 336 & n.2. For Carteret's losses, see above, p. 292 & n. 3.

4. A horse-dealer.

most complete content as ever in ⟨my⟩ life, it being encreased by
my day's work with Mr. Gawden.   Then broke up – and we to
bed, Mr. Hill and I – whom I love more and more, and he us.

9.   Called up betimes by my Lord Brouncker, who is come to
town from his long Water worke at Erith last night[1] – to go with
him to the Duke of Albemarle, which by his coach I did – our
discourse upon the ill posture of the times through lack of money.
At the Dukes did some business, and I believe he was not pleased
to see all the Duke's discourse and applications to me and every-
bodys else.   Discoursed also with Sir G. Carteret about office
business, but no money in view.   Here my Lord and I stayed and
dined, the Vice-Chamberlain taking his leave.   At[a] table, the
Duchesse, a damned ill-looked woman, complaining of her Lord's
going to sea the next year, said these cursed words – "If my Lord
had been a coward he had gone to sea no more it may be; then he
might have been excused and made an Embassador" (meaning my
Lord Sandwich); this made me mad, and I believe she perceived
my countenance change, and blushed herself very much.   I was
in hopes others had not minded it; but my Lord Bruncker, after
we were come away, took notice of the words to me with displeasure.
    Thence after dinner away by water, calling and taking leave of
Sir G. Carteret, whom we found going through at White-hall;
and so over to Lambeth and took coach and home; and so to the
office, where late writing letters; and then home to Mr. Hill and
sang, among other things, my song of *Beauty returne*,[2] which he
likes; only, excepts against two notes[b] in the bass, but likes the
whole very well.   So, late to bed.

10.   *Lords day*.   Lay long talking, Hill and I, with great pleasure, and then up; and being ready, walked to Cocke's for some
news, but heard none; only, they would have us stay their dinner,
and sent for my wife, who came, and very merry we were –
there being Sir Edm. Pooly and Mr. Eveling.   Before we had
dined comes Mr. Andrews, whom we had sent for to Bow, and

---

a repl. 'setting out'   *b* repl. 'or three'

1. He was custodian of one of the   2. *Recte* 'Beauty   Retire':   q.v.
E. India ships: above, p. 234.   above, p. 320, n. 4.   (E).

so after dinner, home; and there we sang some things, but not with much pleasure, Mr. Andrews being in so great haste to go home, his wife looking every hour to be brought to bed. He gone, Mr. Hill and I continued our Musique, one thing after another, late till supper; and so to bed with great pleasure.

11. Lay long, with great pleasure talking. So I left him, and to London to the Change. And after discoursed with several people about business, met Mr. Gawden at the Pope's-head, where he brought Mr. Lewes and T. Willson to discourse about the victualling business and the alteration of the pursers' trade; for something must be done to secure the King a little better, and yet that they may have wherewith to live. After dinner I took him aside and perfected to my great joy my business with him, wherein he deals most nobly, in giving me his hand for the 4000*l* and would take my note but for 3500*l*. This is a great blessing, and God make me thankful truly for it. With him till it was dark, putting in writing our discourse about victualling; and so parted, and I to Viners and there evened all accounts and took up my notes*a* from him, setting all straight between us to this day. The like to Colvill, and paying several bills due from me on the Tanger account. Then late met Cocke and Temple[1] at the Pope's-head, and there had good discourse with Temple – who tells me that of the 80000*l* advanced already by the East India Company,[2] they have had 45000*l* out of their hands. He discoursed largely of the quantity of money coyned, and what may*b* be thought the real sum of money in the Kingdom. He told me too, as an instance of the thrift used in the King's business, that the tolls, and the interest of the money rising to the King for the money he borrowed while the new invention of the Mill money was perfected,[3] cost him 35000*l*. And in mirth tells me that the new-fashion money is good for nothing but to help the Prince;* if he can secretly get copper-plates shut up in silver,[4] it shall never be discovered, at least not in his age.

Thence Cocke and I by water, he home and I home, and

a repl. 'house'   *b* repl. 'did'

---

1. Chief clerk to Sir Robert Vyner, goldsmith-banker.

2. See above, p. 319 & n.4.

3. In 1663: see above, iii. 265 & n. 2.

4. I.e. plated with silver.

there sat with Mr. Hill and my wife supping, talking, and singing till midnight, and then to bed.

⟨That I may remember it the more perticularly, I thought fit to insert this additional Memorandum*ᵃ* of Temple's discourse this night with me, which I took in writing from his mouth.

Before the Harp=and=Crosse Mony was cried down,[1] he and his fellow-goldsmiths did make some perticular trials what proportion that money bore to the old King's money, and they found that generally it came to, one with another, about 25*l*. in every 100*l*.

Of this money there was, upon the calling it in, 650000*l* at least brought into the Tower. And from thence computes that the whole money of England must be full 1625000*l*. But for all this, believes that there is above 3000000*l*, he supposing that about the King's coming in (when he begun to observe the quantity of the new money) people begun to be fearful of this money's being cried down, and so picked it out and set it a-going as fast as they could, to be rid of it. And he thinks 3000000*l* the rather, because if there were but 1625000*l*, the King, having 2000000*l* every year, would have the whole money of the Kingdom in his hands in eight years.

He tells me about 350000*l* sterling was coined out of the French money, the proceed of Dunkirke;[2] so that with what was coined of the cross-money, there is new-coined about 1000000*l* – besides the gold, which is guessed at 500000*l*. He tells*ᵇ* me that though the King did deposit the French money in pawn all the while for the 350000*l*, he was forced to borrow thereupon, till the tools could be*ᶜ* made for the new Minting in the present form. Yet the interest he paid for that time came to 35000*l* – Viner having, to his knowledge, 10000*l* for the use of 100000*l* of it.⟩

a made on small memorandum-sheet stuck alongside entry
b repl. 'tol'-   *c* 'be' repeated

---

1. The Commonwealth coinage ('Harp and Cross money': q.v. above, iv. 148, n. 2) was demonetized in 1661-2. The figures given in this entry are not very different from those given above at iv. 148, v. 23; in *CSPD 1675-6*, p. 456, ib., *1689-90*, p. 373; and in M. Folkes, *Table of Engl. silver and gold coins* (1745), pp. 96 n., 111 n., 112 n. For a summary of the amounts coined in 1649-57 and in 1663-9, see Longleat, Coventry MSS 12, ff. 7*r*, 54*r*.
2. For the coining of the Dunkirk money in 1662-3, see Sir A. E. Feavearyear, *Pound Sterling*, pp. 96-7, 109, n.1. Cf. *CTB*, i. 459.

12. Up and to the office, where my Lord Bruncker met me, and among other things, did finish a contract with Cocke for hemp, by which I hope to get my money due from him paid presently.[1] At noon home to dinner, only eating a bite, and with much kindness taking leave of Mr. Hill, who goes away today; and so I by water, saving * my tide through bridge, and to Sir G Downing by appointment at Charing-Crosse – who did at first mightily please me with informing me thoroughly the virtue and force of this act; and endeed, it is ten times better then ever I thought could have been said of it.[2] But when *a* he came to impose upon me that without more ado I must get by my credit people to serve in goods, and lend money upon it, and none could do it better then I, and the King should give me thanks perticularly in it – and I could not get him to excuse me, but I must come to him, though to no*b* purpose, on Saturday, and he is sure I will bring him some bargains or other made upon this act, it vexed me more then all the pleasure I took before, for I find he will be troublesome to me in it, if I will let him have as much of my time as he would*c* have. So late I took leave, and in the cold (the weather setting in cold) home to the office; and after my letters being wrote,*d* home to supper and to bed – my wife being also gone to London.

13. Up betimes, and finished my journall for five days back; and then after being ready, to my Lord Bruncker by appointment, there to order the disposing of some money that we have come into the office; and here to my great content I did get a bill of imprest to Captain Cocke, to pay myself in part of what is coming to me from him for my Lord Sandwiches satisfaction and my*e* own, and also another payment or two wherein I am concerned. And having done that, did go to Mr. Pierce's, where he and his

a repl. 'y'- *b* repl. 'new' *c* repl. 'could' *d* repl. 'writ'
      e repl. 'his'

---

1. A contract with Cocke and Gauden for hemp and tallow was concluded in January 1666: *CSPD 1665-6*, p. 135.

2. Downing's views are referred to by Pepys in his letters to Coventry (9, 12 December): *Further Corr.*, pp. 86, 87.

wife made me drink some Tea;[1] and so he and I by water together to London.   Here, at a Taverne in Cornehill, he and I did
agree upon my delivering up to him a bill of Captain Cockes, put
into my hand for Pierces use – up[on] evening of reckonings about
the prize-goods; and so away to the Change, and there hear the
ill news, to my great and all our great trouble, that the plague is
increased again this week,[2] notwithstanding there hath been a day
or two great frosts; but we hope it is only the effects of the late
close warm weather, and if the frosts continue the next week, may
fall again; but the town doth thicken so much with people, that
it is much if the plague do not grow again upon us.   Off the
Change, invited by Sheriffe Hooker, who keeps the poorest mean
dirty table, in a dirty house,[3] that ever I did see any sheriff of
London – and a plain ordinary silly man I think he is, but rich.
Only, his son, Mr. Lethulier, I like, for a pretty civil understanding merchant, and the more, by much, because he happens to be
husband to our noble fat brave lady in our parish that I and my
wife admire so.   Thence away to the Pope's-head tavern, and
there met first with Captain[a] Cocke, and despatched my business
with him to my content, he being ready to sign his bill of imprest
of 2000*l* and give it me in part of his payment to me, which glads
my heart.   He being gone, comes Sir Wm Warren, who advised
with me about several things about getting money, and 100*l* I
shall presently have of him.[4]   We advised about a business of insurance, wherein something may be saved to him and got to me;[5]
and to that end, he and I did take a coach at night and to the
Cockepitt, there to get the Duke of Albemarle's advice for our
insuring some of our Sownd Goods coming home under Harmans
convoy, but he proved shy of doing it without knowledge of the

a repl. 'Sir'

---

1. An expensive rarity. Perhaps
Pierce (as purser of Sandwich's ship,
the *Royal Charles*) had acquired it as
prize from the Dutch E. Indiamen
(see above, p. 230). It was possibly
used on this occasion as a medicine
against the plague.
   2. 243 died from plague during
5–12 December; 210 during the

previous week: GL, A.1.5, no. 96.
   3. A small house (of eight hearths)
in Eastcheap North, near Three
Kings Court in the parish of St
Clement. John Lethieulier (his son-
in-law) had a house with 16 hearths.
(R).
   4. See above, p. 286.
   5. See below, p. 329 & n. 2.

Duke of Yorke; so we back again, and calling at my house to see my wife, who is well (though my great trouble is that our poor little parish is the greatest number this week in all the city within the walls, having six (from one the last week);[1] and so by water to Greenwich, leaving Sir W. Warren at home, and I straight to my Lord Brouncker, it being late, and concluded upon insuring something, and to send to that purpose to Sir W. Warren to come to us tomorrow morning. So I home and, my mind in great rest, to bed.

14. Up, and to the office a while with my Lord Brouncker, where we directed Sir W Warren in the business of the insurance as I desired,[2] and ended some other businesses of his; and so at noon, I to London, but the Change was done before I got thither. So I to the Pope's-head tavern, and there find Mr. Gawden and Captain Beckeford and Nich Osborne going to dinner and I dined with them, and very exceeding merry we were, as I had been a great while. And dinner being done, I to the East India-house and there had an Assignment on Temple for my 2000*l* of Captain Cockes, which joyed my heart; and so having seen my wife in the way, I home by water, and to write my letters and then home to bed.

15. Up, and spent all the morning with my Surveyors of the Ports for the victualling, and there read to them what instructions I had provided for them,[3] and discoursed largely much of our business and the business of the pursers.[4] I left them to dine with my people, and I to my Lord Brunckers, where I met with a great good dinner, and Sir Tho. Teddiman, with whom my Lord and I were to discourse about the bringing of W How to a trial for his Jewells.[5] There till almost night, and so away toward the office and in my way met with Sir James Bunch, and after asking what news, he cried (I know [not] whether in earnest or jest): "Aye," says he, "this is the time for you," says he, "that were for Oliver heretofore; you are full of imployment, and we poor Cavaliers sit

1. There were 57 plague deaths altogether in the parishes within the walls.

2. On the 15th Pepys and Brouncker laid out £500 in insurance

of the Gothenburg fleet: BM, Add. 28084, f. 8*r*.

3. See above, p. 315 & n. 2.

4. See below, vii. 1 & n. 1.

5. See above, p. 300 & n. 1.

still and can get nothing"[1] – which was a pretty reproach, I thought, but answered nothing to it, for fear of making it worse. So away, and I to see Mrs. Penington; but company being to come to her, I stayed not, but to the office a little; and so home, and after supper to bed.

16. Up, and met at the office, Sir W. Batten with us – who came from Portsmouth on Monday last, and hath not been with us to see or discourse with us about any business till this day. At noon to dinner ⟨(Sir W. Warren with me)⟩,[a] one bite; and thence I by water, it being a fearful cold snowing day, to Westminster to White-hall[b] stairs; and thence to Sir G. Downing, to whom I brought the happy news of my having contracted, as we did this day with Sir W Warren, for a ship's loading of Norway goods here, and another at Harwich, to the value of above 3000*l*; which is the first that hath been got upon the New=act and he is over-joyed with it,[2] and tells me he will do me all the right at[c] Court about it in the world, and I am glad I have it to write to Sir W Coventry tonight.[3] He would fain have me come, in 200*l*, to lend upon the act; but I desire to be excused in doing that,[4] it being to little purpose for us that relate to the King to do it, for the sum gets the King no courtesy nor Credit. So I parted from him and walked to Westminster-hall, where Sir W. Warren, who came along with me, stayed for me; and there I did see Betty

a insertion repl. 'so back to the office'   *b* repl. 'the New Exchange'   *c* MS. 'to'

---

1. Bunce and four others had been discharged from the aldermen's bench as royalists by parliament in 1649. The complaint here voiced was commonly made, but much exaggerated by Cavaliers: cf. above, p. 303 & n. 2. In 1660–1 similar grumbles (particularly about court posts) had been widespread, but an investigation ordered by Ormond (Lord Steward) had revealed in 1661 that out of 298 newly-appointed Household officers only two had been Cromwellians – a porter and a scullery-man: P. H. Hardacre, *Royalists during Puritan Revolution*, p. 147.

2. For the contract, see *CSPD 1665–6*, p. 134, no. 238; details in *Shorthand Letters*, p. 74 (Pepys to Carteret, 16 December). Warren lent more on the act than any other merchant. He appears to have been repaid in 1669: PRO, E 403/2119.

3. Copy (in Hayter's hand) in NMM, LBK/8, pp. 326–7; printed in *Further Corr.*, pp. 89–91.

4. But writing to Carteret on this subject on this same day Pepys congratulated him on his prudence in lending £1000: *Shorthand Letters*, p. 74.

Howlet, come after the sickness to the Hall. I had not opportunity to salute her as I desired, but was glad to see her, and a very pretty wench she is. Thence back, landing at the Old Swan and taking boat again at Billingsgate and setting ashore at home; and I*ᵃ*, lying down close in my boat, and there, without use of my hand, had great pleasure, and the first time I did make trial*ᵇ* of my strength of fancy of that kind without my hand, and had it complete avec la fille que I did see au-jour-dhuy in Westminster hall. So to my office and there wrote my letters; and so home to supper and to bed, it being a great frost. News is come today of our Sound Fleete being come¹ – but I do not know what Sir W. Warren hath insured.

17. *Lords day.* After being trimmed, word brought me that Cutler's² coach is by appointment come to the Isle of Doggs for me; and so I over the water, and in his coach to Hackny, a very fine, cold, clear, frosty day. At his house, I find him with a plain little dinner – good wine and welcome. He is still a prating man, and the more I know him, the less I find in him. A pretty house he hath here indeed – of his own building – his old mother was an object at dinner that made me not like it; and after dinner, to visit his sick wife I did not also take much joy in. But very friendly he is to me, not for any kindness I think he hath to any man, but thinking me, I perceive, a man whose friendship is to be looked after. After dinner back again, and to Deptford to Mr. Evelins, who was not within; but I had appointed my Cosen Tho. Pepys of Hacham to meet me there, to discourse about getting his 1000*l* of my Lord Sandwich³ – having now an opportunity of my having above that sum in my hand of his. I find this a dull fellow still in all his discourse, but in this he is ready enough to imbrace what I counsel him to, which is to write importunately to my Lord and me about it, and I will look after it. I do again and again declare myself a man unfit to be security for such a sum. He walked with me as far as Deptford upper-town, being mighty

---

a MS. 'I to the office'   *b* repl. same symbol badly formed

1. It anchored in the Thames mouth on the 15th: *CSPD 1665-6*, p. 103.
2. William Cutler, merchant. He dealt (among other things) in hemp.
3. See below, vii. 31 & n. 3.

respectful to me; and there parted – he telling me that this town is still very bad of the plague. I walked to Greenwich; first, to make a short visit to my Lord Brouncker; and next, to Mrs. Penington and spent all the evening with her, with the same freedom I used to have, and very pleasant company. With her till one of the clock in the morning and past; and so to my

《18.》 lodgings to bed, and betimes up, it being a fine frost, and walked it to Redriffe,*a* calling and drinking at Halfway-house, thinking indeed to have overtaken some of the people of our house, the women who were to walk the same walk – but I could not. So to London, and there visited my wife and was a little displeased to find she is so forward, all of a spurt, to make much of her brother and sister since my last kindness to him in getting him a place. But all ended well presently, and I to the Change, and up and*b* down to Kingdon and the goldsmiths to meet Mr. Stephens, and did get all my money matters most excellently cleared, to my complete satisfaction. Passing over Cornhill, I spied young Mrs. Daniel and Sarah, my landlady's daughters,[1] who are come as I expected to town; and did see they spied me, and I dogged them to St. Martins, where I passed by them, buying shoes, and walked down as low as Ducke-lane and enquired ⟨for⟩ some Spanish books; and so back again, and they were gone; so to the Change, hoping to see them in the street; and missing them, went back again thither and back to the Change, but no sight of them; so I went after my business again, and though late, was*c* sent to by Sir W. Warren (who heard where*d* I was) to entreat me to come dine with him, hearing I lacked a dinner, at the Pope's-head – and there with Mr. Hinton the goldsmith and others, very merry. But Lord, to see how Dr. Hinton[2] came in with a gallant or two from Court, and doth so call Cosen Mr. Hinton the goldsmith; but I, that know him to be a beggar and a knave, did make great sport in my mind at it.

After dinner Sir W. Warren and I alone in another room a little while, talking*e* about business; and so parted, and I thence, my mind full of content in my day's work, home by water to

---

a repl. 'Depford'	*b* repl. 'an'	*c* repl. 'did'	*d* repl. 'of'
e repl. same symbol badly formed

---

1. See above, p. 261, n. 3.	2. John Hinton, physician-in-ordinary to the King.

Greenwich, the River beginning to be very full of Ice, so as I was a little frighted.[1] But got home well, it being Darke. So having no mind to do any business, went home to my lodgings and there got little Mrs. Tooker, and Mrs. Daniel the daughter, and Sarah to my chamber to Cards and sup with me – when in comes Mr. Pierce to me, who tells me how W How hath been examined on shipboard by my Lord Bruncker today, and others. And that he hath charged him, out of envy, with sending goods under my Lord's seal and*a* in my Lord Bruncker's name, thereby to get them safe passage – which he tells me is false, but that he did use my name to that purpose, and hath acknowledged it to my Lord Brouncker. But doth also confess to me, that for one parcel he thinks he did use my Lord Brouncker's name; which vexes me mightily, that my name should be brought in question about such things, though I did not say much to him of my discontent till I have spoke with my Lord Brouncker about it. So he being gone, being to go to Oxford tomorrow, we to cards again late; and so broke up, I having great pleasure with my little girl, Mrs. Tooker.

19. Up, and to the office, where all the morning. At noon by agreement comes Hacham Pepys to dine with me. I thought to have had him to Sir Jo Mines to a good venison pasty with the rest of my fellows, being invited; but seeing much company, I went away with him and had a good dinner at home. He did give me letters he hath wrote to my Lord and Moore about my Lord's money, to get it paid to my cousin; which I will make good use of. I made mighty much of him, but a sorry dull fellow he is, fit for nothing that is ingenious; nor is there a turd of kindness or service to be had from him. So I shall neglect him, if I could get but him satisfied about this money, that I may be out of bonds for my Lord to him. To see that this fellow could desire me to help him to some imployment, if it were but of 100*l* per annum, when he is not worth less then, I believe, 20000*l*. He gone, I to Sir Jo Minnes, and thence with my Lord Brouncker on board the *Bezan* to examine W How again, who I find upon this trial, one of much more wit and ingenuity in his answers then

a repl. 'to'

---

1. The river-ice thawed on the 27th.

ever I expected, he being very cunning and discreet and well-spoken in them. I said little to him or concerning him. But Lord, to see how he writes to me [now]adays, and styles me "My Honour" – so much is a man subjected and dejected under afflictions as to flatter me in that manner on this occasion. Back with my Lord to Sir Jo Mines, where I left him and the rest of a great deal of company; and so I to my office, where late writing letters, and then home to bed.

20. Up, and was trimmed, but not time enough to save my Lord Brouncker's coach or Sir Jo Mines, and so was fain to walk to Lambeth on foot; but it was a very fine frosty walk, and great pleasure in it – but troublesome getting over the River for Ice. I to the Duke of Albemarle, whither my Brethren were*a* all come but I was not too late. There we sat in discourse upon our Navy businesses an hour; and thence in my Lord Brouncker's coach alone, he walking before (while I stayed a while talking with Sir G Downing about the Act, in which he is horrid troublesome), to the Old Exchange – whence I took Sir Ellis Layton to Captain Cockes, where my Lord Brouncker and Lady Williams dine, and we all mighty merry – but Sir Ell. Layton one of the best companions at a meal in the world.[1] After dinner I to the Exchange to see whether my pretty seamstress[2] be come again or no, and I find she is; so I to her, saluted her over her counter in the open Exchange above, and mightily joyed to see her, poor pretty woman – I must confess I think her a great beauty. After laying out a little money*b* there for two pair of thread stockings, cost 8*s*, I to Lomb[a]rdstreete to see some businesses to right there at the goldsmiths; among others, paying in 1258*l* to Viner for my Lord Sandwich's use upon Cocke's account.[3] I was called by my Lord Brouncker in his coach, with his mistress and Mr. Cottle the lawyer, our acquaintance at Greenwich; and so home to Greenwich, and thence I to Mrs. Penington, and have a supper from the King's-head for her and there mighty merry and free, as I used to be with her. And at last, late, did pray her to undress herself

a MS. 'where'   *b* repl. 'more'

1. Leighton was a courtier holding several offices; since 1664 he had been one of the secretaries to the prize office. For his wit, cf. v. 300.

2. Mary Batelier.

3. For the prize goods: see above, pp. 238–9.

into her nightgown, that I might see how to have her picture drawn carelessly (for she is mighty proud of that conceit),[1] and I would walk without in the street till she had done.   So I did walk forth, and whether I made too many turns or no in the dark cold frosty night between the two walls up to the park gate, I know not, but she was gone to bed when I came again to the house upon pretence of leaving some papers there, which I did on purpose by her consent.   So I away home, and was there sat up for, to be spoken with by young Mrs. Daniel to pray me to speak for her husband to be a Lieutenant.   I had the opportunity here of kissing her again and again, and did answer that I would be very willing to do him any kindness; and so parted, and I to bed – exceedingly pleased in all my matters of money this month or two, it having pleased God to bless me with several opportunities of good sums, and that I have them in effect all very well paid, or in my power to have.   But two things trouble me: one, the sickness is encreased above 80 this week (though in my own parish, not one hath died, though six the last week);[2] the other most of all, which is that I have had so complexed an account for these last two months, for variety of layings out up[on] Tanger occasions and variety of gettings, that I have not made*a* even with myself now these three or four months; which doth trouble me mightily, fearing that I shall hardly ever come to understand them thoroughly again, as I used to do my accounts when I was at home.

21.   At the office all the morning.   At noon all of us dined at Captain Cockes at a good chine of beef and other good meat, but being all frost-bitten, was most of it unroast; but very merry, and

a repl. 'made'

---

1. The fashion for female portraits to be painted in *déshabillé* can be traced back to occasional examples in the work of Van Dyck, but became a very marked feature of Restoration portraiture and is particularly associated with Lely; in some of his portraits the vogue was carried to extremes and caused the most common of all criticism levelled against him, voiced by such varied writers as Pope, Horace Walpole and Byron.

Walpole (*Anecdotes of painting*, ed. Wornum, ii. 77–8) quotes a Puritan tract of 1678 (Cooke's *Just and reasonable reprehension of naked breasts and shoulders*) against the flagrant display of female charms in contemporary portraiture. (OM).

2. The increase in the total number of deaths from all causes, 12–19 December, was 83; the increase in plague burials 38: GL, A.1.5, no. 96.

a good dish of fowl we dressed ourselfs.   Mr. Eveling there, in
very good humour.   All the afternoon till night, pleasant, and
then I took my leave of them and to the office, where I wrote my
letters, and away home, my head full of business and some
trouble for my letting my accounts go so far; but I have made an
oath this night for the drinking no wine, &c., on such penalties,
till I have passed my account and cleared all.[1]   Coming home
and going to bed, the boy tells me his sister Daniel hath provided
me a supper of little birds, killed by her husband; and I made
her sup with me, and after supper were alone a great while and I
had the pleasure of her lips – she being a pretty woman, and one
whom a great belly becomes as well as ever I saw any.   She gone,
I to bed.   This day I was come to by Mrs. Burrows of Westminster, Lieutenant Burrows (lately dead) his widow, a most
pretty woman, and my old acquaintance.   I had a kiss or two of
her, and a most modest woman she is.

22.   Up betimes, and to my Lord Brouncker to consider the
late instructions sent us, of the method of our signing bills hereafter and paying them.[2]   By and by by agreement, comes Sir Jo
Mines and Sir W. Batten; and then to read them publicly, and
consider of putting them in execution.   About this all the morning.   And it appearing necessary for the Controller to have
another clark, I recommend Poynter to him,[a] which he accepts,
and I by that means rid of one that I fear would not have been fit
for my turn – though he writes very well.[3]   At noon comes Mr.
Hill to town, and finds me out here and brings Mr. Houbland,[4]
who met him here.   So I was compelled to leave my Lord and
his dinner and company, and with them to the Beare[5] and dined
with them and their brothers, of which Hill had his, and the other

a repl. 'them'

1. Cf. below, vii. 15, 23, 25, 65–6.
He did not clear his private accounts
until 5 March 1666.
2. The Board sent its comments to
the Duke of York on 23 December,
and in consequence a revised version
of the instructions was issued on the
26th: Tanner 45, ff. 51–2. Cf.
above, p. 304 & n. 3; p. 323 & n. 3.
3. Examples of his handwriting

are in Tanner 44, ff. 40*r*, 44*r*.
4. James Houblon, jun., merchant,
who was to become an intimate
friend of Pepys.   He and his two
younger brothers, Peter and John,
were important figures in the Spanish
trade.
5. In Bear St, Greenwich: E.
Hasted, *Hist. Kent* (ed. Drake), p. 104.

two of his – and mighty merry and very fine company they are, and I glad to see them. After dinner I forced to take leave of them, by being called upon by Mr. Andrews, I having sent for him; and by a fine glosse did bring him to desire tallies for what orders I have to pay him and his company for Tanger victualls;[1] and I by that means cleared to myself 210*l*, coming to me upon their two orders, which is also a noble addition to my late profits, which have been very considerable of late; but how great, I know not till I come to cast up my accounts; which burdens my mind that it should be so backward, but I am resolved to settle to nothing till I have done it.

He gone, I to my Lord Brouncker and there spent the evening, by my desire, in*a* seeing his Lordship open to pieces and make up again his Wach, thereby being taught what I never knew before; and it is a thing very well worth my having seen, and am mightily pleased and satisfied with it. So I sat talking with him till late at night – somewhat vexed at a snappish answer Madam Williams did give me to herself, upon my speaking a free word to her in mirth, calling her a mad Jade. She answered, we were not so well acquainted yet. But I was more [vexed] at a letter from my Lord Duke of Albemarle today, pressing us to continue our meetings for all Christmas,[2] which, though everybody entended not to have done, yet I am concluded* in it, who intended nothing else. But I see it is necessary that I do make often visits to my Lord Duke, which nothing shall hinder after I have evened my accounts; and now the River is frozen, I know not how to get to him.

Thence to my lodging, making up my Journall for eight or nine days; and so my mind being eased of it, I to supper and to bed.

The weather hath been frosty these eight or nine days, and so we hope*b* for an abatement of the plague the next week; or else God have mercy upon us, for the plague will certainly continue the next year if it doth not.*c*

---

a repl. 'his'   *b* symbol blotted   *c* repl. 'it'

---

1. The sum was close on £5000 for victuals and demurrage: PRO, AO 1/310/1220.

2. Albemarle pointed out that the dockyards were having only three days' holiday and that much had to be done before the end of March: *CSPD 1665–6*, p. 112.

23. At my office all the morning, and home to dinner, my head full of business, and there my wife finds me unexpectedly. But I not being at leisure to stay or talk with her – she went down by coach to Woolwich, thinking to fetch Mrs. Barbary to carry her to London to keep her Christmas with her – and I to the office; this day one came to me with four great turkeys, as a present from Mr. Deane at Harwich – three of which my wife carried in the evening home with her to London in her coach (Mrs. Barbary not being to be got so suddenly, but will come to her the next week); and I at my office late, and then to my lodging to bed.

24. *Sunday*. Up betimes; to my Lord Duke [of] Albemarle by water – and after some talk with him about business of the office*a* with great content; and so back again and to dinner, my landlady and her daughters with me,[1] and had mincepies; and very merry at a mischance her young son had, in tearing of his new coat quite down the outside of his sleeve in the whole cloth – one of the strangest mishaps that ever I saw in my life. Then to church, and placed myself in the parson's pew under the pulpit to hear Mrs. Chamberlin in the next pew sing (who is daughter to Sir James Bunch), of whom I have heard much; and endeed, she sings very finely. And from church met with Sir W Warren, and he and I walked together, talking about his and my businesses, getting of money as fairly as we can. And having set him part of his way home, I walked to my Lord Bruncker, whom I heard was at Alderman Hookers, hoping to see and*b* salute Mrs. Lethulier[2] – whom I did see in passing, but no opportunity of beginning acquaintance, but a very noble lady she is, however the silly alderman got her. Here we sat talking a great while, Sir The. Biddulph and Mr. Vaughan, a son-in-law of Alderman Hooker's. Thence with my Lord Brouncker home, and sat a little with him and so home*c* to bed.

25. *Christmas Day*. To church in the morning, and there saw a wedding in the church, which I have not seen many a day, and the young people so merry one with another; and strange, to see

a repl. symbol made illegible   *b* blot below symbol   *c* repl. 'him'

1. See above, p. 261, n. 3.   2. See above, p. 316 & n. 2.

what delight we married people have to see these poor fools de-
coyed into our condition, every man and wife gazing and smiling
at them. Here I saw again my beauty Lethulier. Thence to my
Lord Brouncker by invitation, and dined there – and so home to
my lodgings to settle myself to look over and settle my papers,
both of my accounts private and those of Tanger, which I have let
go so long that it were impossible for any soul, had I died, to
understand them or ever*a* come to any good end in them. I hope
God will never suffer me to come to that disorder again.

26. Up, and to the office, where Sir Jo. Minnes and my Lord
Brouncker and I met, to give our directions to the Comanders of
all the ships in the River to bring in lists of their ships' companies,
with entries, discharges, &c, all the last voyage[1] – where young
Seamour, among twenty that stood bare, stood with his hat on, a
proud saucy young man. Thence with them to Mr. Cuttles,[2]
being invited, and dined nobly and neatly – with a very pretty
house, and a fine Turret at top, with windeing stairs, and the finest
prospect I know about all Greenwich, save the top of the hill –
and yet in some respects better then that. Here I also saw some
fine writing-work and Flourishing of Mr. Hore;[3] he, one that I
knew long ago, an acquaintance of Mr. Tomson's*b* at Westminster, that is*c* this man's clerk. It is the stories of the several
Archbishops of Canterbury, engrossed in vellum to hang up in
Canterbury Cathedrall in tables, in lieu of the old ones, which are
almost worn out.[4] Thence to the office a while, and so to Captain Cockes and there talked, and home to look over my papers,
and so to bed.

a repl. 'every' *b* repl. 'Tomsoms' *c* MS. 'his'

1. Almost 60 captains (from Woolwich, Deptford and above Lime-
house) were summoned to attend:
a list of their names and those of their
ships, with a few notes, is in PRO,
SP 29/140, no. 18 (in Pepys's hand,
dated this day).

2. Mark Cottle, lawyer, of Greenwich; Registrar of the Prerogative
Court of the Archbishop of Canterbury.

3. Richard Hoare, a clerk in the
Prerogative Court of Canterbury.
Cf. above, i. 132–3 & n.

4. They are not mentioned in the
inventories (1662 and 1689) printed
in J. Wickham Legg and W. H. St
John Hope, *Inventories of Canterbury*.
The cathedral was being extensively
refurnished at this time: see C. E.
Woodruff and W. Danks, *Memorials
of Canterbury*, pp. 338–41.

27. Up, and with Cocke by coach to London. There home to my wife, and angry about her desiring a maid yet, before the plague is quite over; it seems Mercer is troubled that she hath not one under her, but I will not venture my family by encreasing it before it be safe. Thence about many businesses, perticularly with Sir W Warren on the Change; and he and I dined together and settled our Tanger matters, wherein I get above 200*l* presently.* We dined together at the Pope's-head to do this. And thence to the goldsmiths, I to examine the state of my matters there too; and so with him to my house, but my wife was gone abroad to Mrs. Mercer's, so we took boat. And it being dark, and the thaw having broke the ice but not carried it quite away, the boat did pass through so much of it all along, and that with the Crackeling and noise, that it made me fearful endeed; so I forced the watermen to land us on Redriffe side, and so walked together till Sir W. Warren and I parted near his house; and thence I walked quite over the fields home, by light of link, ⟨one of⟩ my watermen carrying it and I reading by the light of it, it being a very fine clear dry night. So to Captain Cocke's and there sat and talked, especially with his counsellor, about his prize-goods, that hath done him good turns, being of the company with Captain Fisher: his name, Godderson. Here I supped, and so home to bed – with great content that the plague is decreased to 152 – the whole being but 330.[1]

28. Up, and to the office – and thence, with a great deal of business in my head, dined alone with Cocke. So home alone, strictly about my accounts, wherein I made a good beginning; and so after letters wrote by the post, to bed.

29. Up betimes, and all day long within-doors upon my accounts public and private; and find the ill effects of letting them go so long without evening, that no soul could have ever understood them but myself, and I with much ado. But however, my regularity in all I did and spent doth help me, and I hope to find them well. Late at them, and to bed.

1. During 19–26 December: GL, A.1.5, no. 96.

30. Up, and to the office. At noon home to dinner, and all the afternoon to my accounts again; and there find myself, to my great joy, a great deal worth above 4000*l*, for which the Lord be praised – and is principally occasioned by my getting 500*l* of Cocke for my profit in his bargains of prize goods, and from Mr. Gawden's making me a present of 500*l* more when I paid him 8000*l* for Tanger. So to my office to write letters, then to my accounts again, and so to bed, being in great ease of mind.

31. *Lords day*. All the morning in my chamber, writing fair the state of my Tanger accounts,[1] and so dined at home. In the afternoon to the Duke of Albemarle, and thence back again by water, and so to my chamber to finish the entry of my accounts and to think of the business I am next to do, which is the stating my thoughts and putting in order my collections about the business of Pursers, to see where the fault of our present constitution relating to them lies, and what to propose to mend*a* it. And upon this late, and, with my head full of this business, to bed.

Thus ends this year, to my great joy, in this manner: –

I have raised my estate from 1300*l* in this year to 4400*l*. I have got myself greater interest, I think, by my diligence; and my imployments encreased by that of Treasurer for Tanger and Surveyor of the Victuals.

It is true we have gone through great melancholy because of the great plague, and I put to great charges by it, by keeping my family long at Woolwich, and myself and another part of my family, my clerks, at my charge at Greenwich, and a maid at London. But I hope the King will give us some satisfaction for that. But now the plague is abated almost to nothing, and I entending to get to London as fast as*b* I can, my family, that is, my wife and maids, having been there*c* these two or three weeks. The Duch war goes on very ill, by reason of lack of money; having none to hope for, all being put into disorder by a new Act that is made as an experiment to bring Credit to the Exchequer,

a repl. 'mind'   *b* repl.? 'with'   *c* repl. 'these'

---

1. They cover 19 October–31 December 1665 and (with a letter of 16 January 1666 from Pepys to the Tangier committee) are in PRO, C 279/6, ff. 7–10.

for goods and money to be advanced upon the credit of that Act.[1]
I have never lived so merrily (besides that I never got so much) as
I have done this plague-time, by my Lord Brouncker's and Captain Cocke's good company, and the acquaintance of Mrs. Knipp,
Coleman and her husband, and Mr. Laneare; and great store of
dancings we have had at my cost (which I was willing to indulge
myself and wife) at my lodgings. The great evil of this year, and
the only one endeed, is the fall of my Lord of Sandwich, whose
mistake about the Prizes hath undone him, I believe, as to interest
at Court; though sent (for a little palliateing it) Imbassador into
Spayne, which he is now fitting himself for. But the Duke of
Albemarle goes with the Prince to sea this next year, and my Lord
very meanly spoken of; and endeed, his miscarriage about the
prize-goods is not to be excused, to suffer a company of rogues to
go away with tcn times as much as himself, and the blame of all to
be deservedly laid upon him.

My whole family hath been well all this while, and all my
friends I know of, saving my aunt Bell, who is dead, and some
children of my Cosen Sarah's,[a] of the plague. But many of such
as I know very well, dead. Yet to our great joy, the town fills
apace, and shops begin to be open again. Pray God continue the
plague's decrease – for that keeps the Court away from the place
of business, and so all goes to wrack as to public matters, they at
this distance not thinking of it.[b]

a repl. 'Joyces'   *b* followed by one blank page

---

1. The Additional Aid: q.v. above, p. 292 & n. 3. In the first week of its operation (30 December–5 January) £14,070 was lent; ultimately loans in money and goods totalled c. £300,000. The city was unwilling to make any advances under the act until July 1666. See H. G. Rose-veare, 'The advancement of the King's credit' (unpub. thesis, Univ. Cambridge, 1962), App. I.

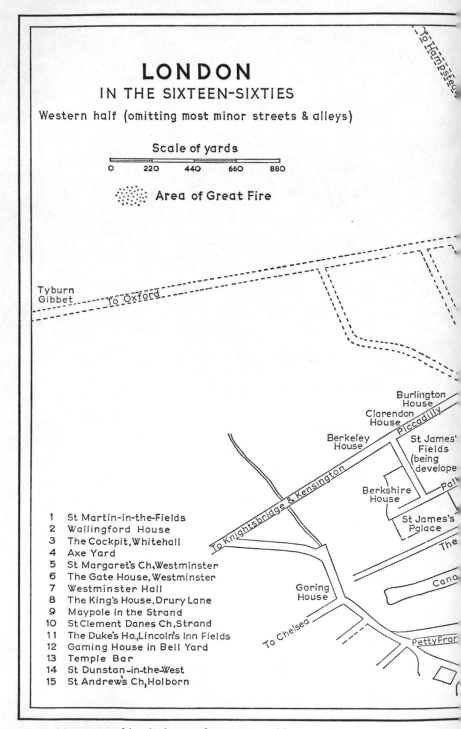

LONDON
IN THE SIXTEEN-SIXTIES

Western half (omitting most minor streets & alleys)

Scale of yards

0   220   440   660   880

Area of Great Fire

To Hampstead

Tyburn Gibbet   To Oxford

Burlington House
Clarendon House
Berkeley House
St James' Fields (being develope
Berkshire House
St James's Palace
Piccadilly

To Knightsbridge & Kensington

Goring House

To Chelsea

Pal

The

Cana

PettyFrar

1   St Martin-in-the-Fields
2   Wallingford House
3   The Cockpit, Whitehall
4   Axe Yard
5   St Margaret's Ch, Westminster
6   The Gate House, Westminster
7   Westminster Hall
8   The King's House, Drury Lane
9   Maypole in the Strand
10   St Clement Danes Ch, Strand
11   The Duke's Ho., Lincoln's Inn Fields
12   Gaming House in Bell Yard
13   Temple Bar
14   St Dunstan-in-the-West
15   St Andrew's Ch, Holborn

Map prepared by the late Professor T. F. Reddaway

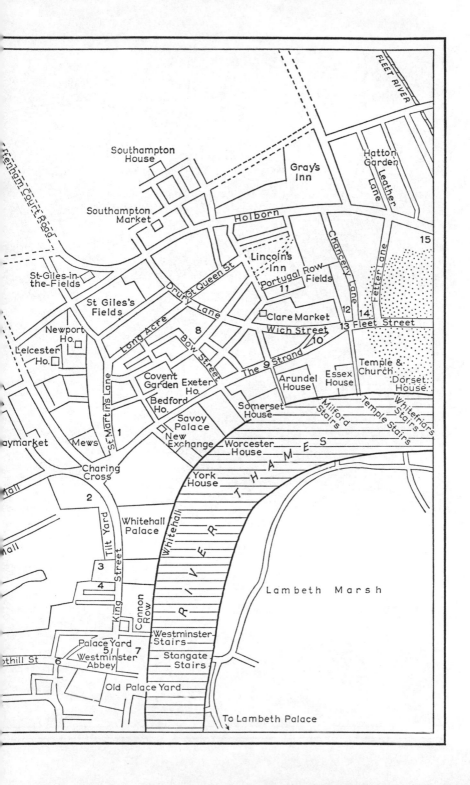

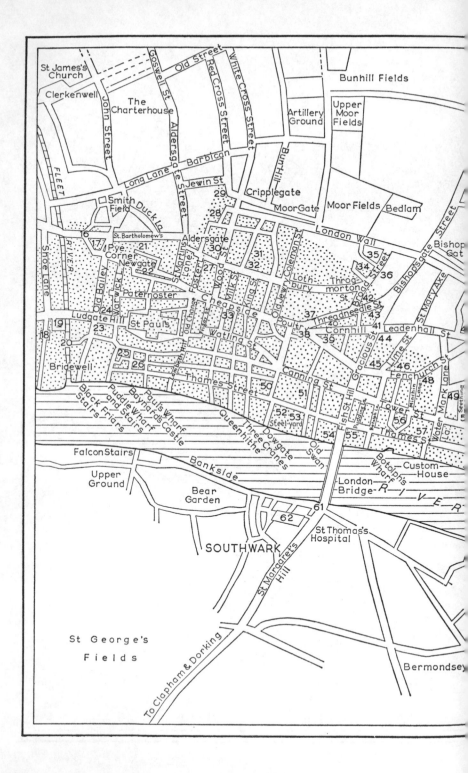

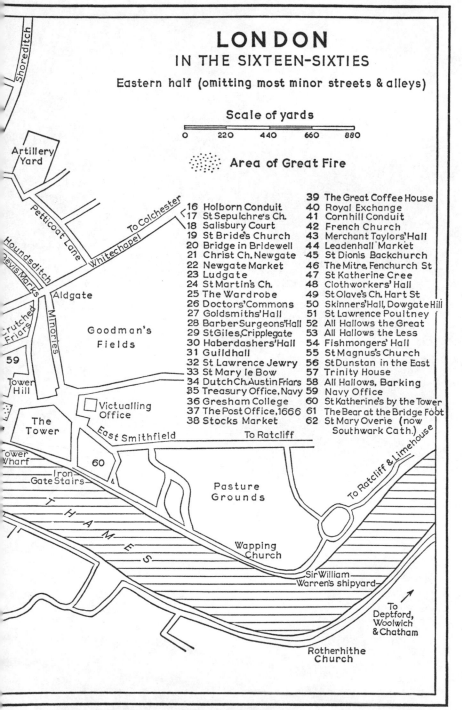

LONDON
IN THE SIXTEEN-SIXTIES

Eastern half (omitting most minor streets & alleys)

Scale of yards

0   220   440   660   880

Area of Great Fire

16 Holborn Conduit
17 St Sepulchre's Ch.
18 Salisbury Court
19 St Bride's Church
20 Bridge in Bridewell
21 Christ Ch. Newgate
22 Newgate Market
23 Ludgate
24 St Martin's Ch.
25 The Wardrobe
26 Doctors' Commons
27 Goldsmiths' Hall
28 Barber Surgeons' Hall
29 St Giles, Cripplegate
30 Haberdashers' Hall
31 Guildhall
32 St Lawrence Jewry
33 St Mary le Bow
34 Dutch Ch. Austin Friars
35 Treasury Office, Navy
36 Gresham College
37 The Post Office, 1666
38 Stocks Market

39 The Great Coffee House
40 Royal Exchange
41 Cornhill Conduit
42 French Church
43 Merchant Taylors' Hall
44 Leadenhall Market
45 St Dionis Backchurch
46 The Mitre, Fenchurch St
47 St Katherine Cree
48 Clothworkers' Hall
49 St Olave's Ch. Hart St
50 Skinners' Hall, Dowgate Hill
51 St Lawrence Poultney
52 All Hallows the Great
53 All Hallows the Less
54 Fishmongers' Hall
55 St Magnus's Church
56 St Dunstan in the East
57 Trinity House
58 All Hallows, Barking
59 Navy Office
60 St Katherine's by the Tower
61 The Bear at the Bridge Foot
62 St Mary Overie (now
    Southwark Cath.)

Shoreditch

Artillery Yard

Petticoat Lane

To Colchester

Whitechapel

Houndsditch

Trevis Marks

Aldgate

Crutched Friars

Minories

59

Tower Hill

The Tower

Goodman's Fields

Victualling Office

East Smithfield

To Ratcliff

Tower Wharf

Iron-Gate Stairs

60

T H A M E S

Pasture Grounds

Wapping Church

To Ratcliff & Limehouse

Sir William Warren's shipyard

To Deptford, Woolwich & Chatham

Rotherhithe Church

Map prepared by the late Professor T. F. Reddaway

SELECT LIST OF PERSONS

ADMIRAL, the: James, Duke of York, Lord High Admiral of England

ALBEMARLE, 1st Duke of (Lord Monke): Captain-General of the Kingdom

ARLINGTON, 1st Earl of (Sir Henry Bennet): Secretary of State

ASHLEY, 1st Baron (Sir Anthony Ashley Cooper, later 1st Earl of Shaftesbury): Chancellor of the Exchequer

ATTORNEY-GENERAL: Sir Geoffrey Palmer

BACKWELL, Edward: goldsmith-banker

BAGWELL, Mrs: Pepys's mistress; wife of ship's carpenter

BALTY: Balthasar St Michel; brother-in-law; minor naval official

BATTEN, Sir William: Surveyor of the Navy

BETTERTON (Baterton), Thomas: actor in the Duke's Company

BIRCH, Jane: maidservant

BOOKSELLER, my: Joseph Kirton (until the Fire)

BOWYER, my father: Robert Bowyer, senior Exchequer colleague

BRISTOL, 2nd Earl of: politician

BROUNCKER (Bruncker, Brunkard, Brunkerd), 2nd Viscount: Commissioner of the Navy

BUCKINGHAM, 2nd Duke of: politician

CARKESSE (Carcasse), James: clerk in the Ticket Office

CARTERET, Sir George: Treasurer of the Navy and Vice-Chamberlain of the King's Household

CASTLEMAINE, Barbara, Countess of: the King's mistress

CHANCELLOR, the: *see* 'Lord Chancellor'

CHILD, the: usually Edward, eldest son and heir of Sandwich

CHOLMLEY, Sir Hugh: courtier, engineer

COCKE, George: hemp merchant

COFFERER, the: William Ashburnham

COMPTROLLER (Controller), the: the Comptroller of the Navy (Sir Robert Slingsby, 1660–1; Sir John Mennes, 1661–71)

COVENTRY, Sir William: Secretary to the Lord High Admiral, 1660–7; Commissioner of the Navy; occasionally called 'Mr.' after knighted, 1665

CREED, John: household and naval servant of Sandwich

CREW, 1st Baron: Sandwich's father-in-law; Presbyterian politician

CUTTANCE, Sir Roger: naval captain

DEANE, Anthony: shipwright

DEB: *see* 'Willet, Deborah'

DOWNING, Sir George: Exchequer official, Envoy-Extraordinary to the United Provinces, and secretary to the Treasury Commission

DUKE, the: usually James, Duke of York, the King's brother; occasionally George (Monck), Duke of Albemarle

DUKE OF YORK: *see* 'James, Duke of York'

EDWARD, Mr: Edward, eldest son and heir of Sandwich

EDWARDS, Tom: servant

EVELYN, John: friend, *savant*; Commissioner of Sick and Wounded

FENNER, Thomas (m. Katherine Kite, sister of Pepys's mother): uncle; ironmonger

FERRER(s), Capt. Robert: army captain; Sandwich's Master of Horse

FORD, Sir Richard: Spanish merchant

FOX, Sir Stephen: Paymaster of the Army

GAUDEN, Sir Denis: Navy victualler

GENERAL(s), the: Albemarle, Captain-General of the Kingdom, 1660–70; Prince Rupert and Albemarle, Generals-at-Sea in command of the Fleet, 1666

GIBSON, Richard: clerk to Pepys in the Navy Office

GWYN, Nell: actress (in the King's Company) and King's mistress

HARRIS, Henry: actor in the Duke's Company

HAYTER, Tom: clerk to Pepys in the Navy Office

HEWER, Will: clerk to Pepys in the Navy Office

HILL, Thomas: friend, musician, Portuguese merchant

HINCHINGBROOKE, Viscount (also 'Mr Edward', 'the child'): eldest son of Sandwich

HOLLIER (Holliard), Thomas: surgeon

HOLMES, Sir Robert: naval commander

HOWE, Will: household and naval servant of Sandwich

JAMES, DUKE OF YORK: the King's brother and heir presumptive (later James II); Lord High Admiral

JANE: usually Jane Birch, maidservant

JOYCE, Anthony (m. Kate Fenner, 1st cousin): innkeeper

JOYCE, William (m. Mary Fenner, 1st cousin): tallow-chandler

JUDGE-ADVOCATE, the: John Fowler, Judge-Advocate of the Fleet

KNIPP (Knepp), Mrs: actress in the King's Company

LADIES, the young/the two/the: often Sandwich's daughters

LAWSON, Sir John: naval commander

LIEUTENANT OF THE TOWER: Sir John Robinson

L'IMPERTINENT, Mons.: [?Daniel] Butler, friend, ? clergyman

LORD CHAMBERLAIN: Edward Mountagu, 2nd Earl of Manchester; Sandwich's cousin

LORD CHANCELLOR: Edward Hyde, 1st Earl of Clarendon (often called Chancellor after his dismissal, 1667)

LORD KEEPER: Sir Orlando Bridgeman

LORD PRIVY SEAL: John Robartes, 2nd Baron Robartes (later 1st Earl of Radnor)

LORD TREASURER: Thomas Wriothesley, 4th Earl of Southampton

MARTIN, Betty (*née* Lane): Pepys's mistress; shopgirl

MENNES (Minnes), Sir John: Comptroller of the Navy

MERCER, Mary: maid to Mrs Pepys

MILL(E)S, Rev. Dr John: Rector of St Olave's, Hart St; Pepys's parish priest

MONCK (Monke), George (Lord): soldier. *See* 'Albemarle, 1st Duke of'

MONMOUTH, Duke of: illegitimate son of Charles II

MOORE, Henry: lawyer; officer of Sandwich's household

MY LADY: usually Jemima, wife of Sandwich

MY LORD: usually Sandwich

NELL, NELLY: usually Nell Gwyn

PALL: Paulina Pepys; sister (sometimes spelt 'pall')

PEARSE (Pierce), James: courtier, surgeon to Duke of York, and naval surgeon

PENN, Sir William: Commissioner of the Navy and naval commander (father of the Quaker leader)

PEPYS, Elizabeth (*née* St Michel): wife

PEPYS, John and Margaret: parents

PEPYS, John (unm.): brother; unbeneficed clergyman

PEPYS, Tom (unm.): brother; tailor

PEPYS, Paulina (m. John Jackson): sister

PEPYS, Capt. Robert: uncle, of Brampton, Hunts.

PEPYS, Roger: 1st cousin once removed; barrister and M.P.

PEPYS, Thomas: uncle, of St Alphege's, London

PETT, Peter: Commissioner of the Navy and shipwright

PICKERING, Mr (Ned): courtier, 1662–3; Sandwich's brother-in-law and servant

POVEY, Thomas: Treasurer of the Tangier Committee

PRINCE, the: usually Prince Rupert

QUEEN, the: (until May 1662) the Queen Mother, Henrietta-Maria, widow of Charles I; Catherine of Braganza, wife of Charles II (m. 21 May 1662)

RIDER, Sir William: merchant

ROBERT, Prince: Prince Rupert

RUPERT, Prince: 1st cousin of Charles II; naval commander

St MICHEL, Alexandre and Mary: parents-in-law

St MICHEL, Balthasar ('Balty'; m. Esther Watts): brother-in-law; minor naval official

SANDWICH, 1st Earl of: 1st cousin once removed, and patron; politician, naval commander and diplomat

SHIPLEY, Edward: steward of Sandwich's household

SIDNY, Mr: Sidney Mountagu, second son of Sandwich

SOLICITOR, the: the Solicitor-General, Sir Heneage Finch

SOUTHAMPTON, 4th Earl of: Lord Treasurer

SURVEYOR, the: the Surveyor of the Navy (Sir William Batten, 1660–7; Col. Thomas Middleton, 1667–72)

TEDDIMAN, Sir Thomas: naval commander

THE: Theophila Turner

TREASURER, the: usually the Treasurer of the Navy (Sir George Carteret, 1660–7; 1st Earl of Anglesey, 1667–8); sometimes the Lord Treasurer of the Kingdom, the Earl of Southampton, 1660–7

TRICE, Tom: relative by marriage; civil lawyer

TURNER, John (m. Jane Pepys, distant cousin): barrister

TURNER, Betty and The[ophila]: daughters of John and Jane Turner

TURNER, Thomas: senior clerk in the Navy Office

VICE-CHAMBERLAIN, the: Sir George Carteret, Vice-Chamberlain of the King's Household and Treasurer of the Navy

VYNER, Sir Robert: goldsmith–banker

WARREN, Sir William: timber merchant

WARWICK, Sir Philip: Secretary to the Lord Treasurer

WIGHT, William: uncle (half-brother of Pepys's father); fishmonger

WILL: usually Will Hewer

WILLET, Deborah: maid to Mrs Pepys

WILLIAMS ('Sir Wms. both'): Sir William Batten and Sir William Penn, colleagues on the Navy Board

WREN, Matthew: Secretary to the Lord High Admiral, 1667–72

SELECT GLOSSARY

A Large Glossary (of words, phrases and proverbs in all languages) will be found in the *Companion*. This Select Glossary is restricted to usages, many of them recurrent, which might puzzle the reader. It includes words and constructions which are now obsolete, archaic, slang or dialect; words which are used with meanings now obsolete or otherwise unfamiliar; and place names frequently recurrent or used in colloquial styles or in non-standard forms. Words explained in footnotes are not normally included. The definitions given here are minimal: meanings now familiar and contemporary meanings not implied in the text are not noted, and many items are explained more fully in *Companion* articles ('Language', 'Food', 'Drink', 'Music', 'Theatre' etc.), and in the Large Glossary. A few foreign words are included. The spellings are taken from those used in the text: they do not, for brevity's sake, include all variants.

ABLE: wealthy
ABROAD: away, out of doors
ACCENT (of speech): the accentuation and the rising and falling of speech in pronunciation
ACCOUNTANT: official accountable for expenditure etc.
ACTION: acting, performance
ACTOR: male or female theatrical performer
ADDES: adze
ADMIRAL SHIP: flagship carrying admiral
ADMIRATION; ADMIRE: wonder, alarm; to wonder at
ADVENTURER: investor, speculator
ADVICE: consideration
AFFECT: to be fond of, to be concerned
AFFECTION: attention
AIR: generic term for all gases
ALPHABET: index, alphabetical list
AMBAGE: deceit, deviousness
AMUSED, AMUZED: bemused, astonished
ANCIENT: elderly, senior

ANGLE: gold coin worth *c.* 10*s.*
ANGELIQUE: small archlute
ANNOY: molest, hurt
ANOTHER GATE'S BUSINESS: different altogether
ANSWERABLE: similar, conformably
ANTIC, ANTIQUE: fantastic
APERN: apron
APPRENSION: apprehension
APPROVE OF: criticise
AQUA FORTIS (FARTIS): nitric acid
ARTICLE: to indict
ARTIST: workman, craftsman, technician, practitioner
ASPECT (astrol.): position of stars as seen from earth
ASTED: Ashtead, Surrey
AYERY: airy, sprightly, stylish

BAGNARD: bagnio, prison, lock-up
BAILEY, BAYLY: bailiff
BAIT, BAYTE: refreshment on journey (for horses or travellers). *Also* v.
BALDWICK: Baldock, Herts.
BALLET: ballad

BAND: neckband
BANDORE: musical instrument resembling guitar
BANQUET: course of fruits, sweets and wine; slight repast
BANQUET-, BANQUETTING-HOUSE: summer-house
BARBE (s.): Arab (Barbary) horse
BARBE (v.): to shave
BARN ELMS: riverside area near Barnes, Surrey
BARRICADOES (naval): fenders
BASE, BASS: bass viol; thorough-bass
BASTE HIS COAT: to beat, chastise
BAVINS: kindling wood, brush-wood
BAYLY: see 'Bailey'
BEARD: facial hair, moustache
BEFOREHAND, to get: to have money in hand
BEHALF: to behave
BEHINDHAND: insolvent
BELL: to throb
BELOW: downstream from London Bridge
BELOW STAIRS: part of the Royal Household governed by Lord Steward
BEST HAND, at the: the best bargain
BEVER: beaver, fur hat
BEWPERS: bunting, fabric used for flags
BEZAN, BIZAN (Du. *bezaan*): small yacht
BIGGLESWORTH: Biggleswade, Beds.
BILL: (legal) warrant, writ; bill of exchange; Bill of Mortality (weekly list of burials; *see* iii. 225, n. 2)
BILLANDER (Du. *bijlander*): bilander, small two-masted merchantman
BIRD'S EYE: spotted fabric
BLACK (adj.): brunette, dark in hair or complexion
BLACK(E)WALL: dock on n. shore of Thames below Greenwich used by E. Indiamen
BLANCH (of coins): to silver
BLIND: out of the way, private, obscure

BLOAT HERRING: bloater
BLUR: innuendo; charge
BOATE: boot or luggage compartment on side of coach
BODYS: foundations, basic rules; structure; (of ship) sectional drawings
BOLTHEAD: globular glass vessel with long straight neck
BOMBAIM: Bombay
BORDER: *toupée*
BOTARGO: dried fish-roe
BOTTOMARYNE, BOTTUMARY, BUMMARY: mortgage on ship
BOWPOTT: flower pot
BRAINFORD: Brentford, Mdx
BRAMPTON: village near Huntingdon in which Pepys inherited property
BRANSLE: branle, brawl, group dance in triple measure
BRAVE (adj.): fine, enjoyable
BRAVE (v.): to threaten, challenge
BREAK BULK: to remove part of cargo
BREDHEMSON, BRIGHTHEMSON: Brighton, Sussex
BREW AS SHE HATH BAKED, let her: let her accept the consequences of her own wilful actions
BRIDEWELL-BIRD: jailbird
BRIDGE: usually London Bridge; also jetty, landing stairs
BRIG, BRIGANTINE: small vessel equipped both for sailing and rowing
BROTHER: brother-in-law; colleague
BRUMLY: Bromley, Kent
BRUSH (s.): graze
BUBO: tumour
BULLEN: Boulogne
BULLET: cannon-ball
BURNTWOOD: Brentwood, Essex
BURY (of money): pour in, salt away, invest
BUSSE: two- or three-masted fishing boat

CABALL: inner group of ministers; knot
CABARETT (Fr. *cabaret*): tavern

CAKE WILL BE DOE, all my: all my plans will miscarry

CALES: Cadiz

CALICE, CALLIS: Calais

CALL: to call on/for; to drive

CAMELOTT, CAMLET, CAMLOTT: robust light cloth made from wool or goat hair

CANAILLE, CHANNEL, KENNEL: drainage gutter (in street); canal (in St James's Park)

CANCRE: canker, ulcer, sore

CANNING ST: Cannon St

CANONS: boot-hose tops

CANTON (heraldic): small division of shield

CAPER (ship): privateer

CARBONADO: to grill, broil

CARESSE: to make much of

CARRY (a person): to conduct, escort

CAST OF OFFICE: taste of quality

CATAPLASM: poultice

CATCH: round song; (ship) ketch

CATT-CALL: whistle

CAUDLE: thin gruel

CELLAR: box for bottles

CERE CLOTH: cloth impregnated with wax and medicaments

CESTORNE: cistern

CHAFE: heat, anger

CHALDRON: $1\frac{1}{3}$ tons (London measure)

CHAMBER: small piece of ordnance for firing salutes

CHANGE, the: the Royal (Old) Exchange

CHANGELING: idiot

CHANNELL: see 'Canaille'

CHANNELL ROW: Cannon Row, Westminster

CHAPEL, the: usually the Chapel Royal, Whitehall Palace

CHAPTER: usually of Bible

CHARACTER: code, cipher; verbal portrait

CHEAP (s.): bargain

CHEAPEN: to ask the price of, bargain

CHEQUER, the: usually the Exchequer

CHEST, the: the Chatham Chest, the pension fund for seamen

CHILD, with: eager, anxious

CHIMNEY/CHIMNEY-PIECE: structure over and around fireplace

CHIMNEY-PIECE: picture over fireplace

CHINA-ALE: ale flavoured with china root

CHINE: rib (beef), saddle (mutton)

CHOQUE: a choke, an obstruction

CHOUSE: to swindle, trick

CHURCH: after July 1660, usually St Olave's, Hart St

CLAP: gonorrhoea

CLERK OF THE CHEQUE: principal clerical officer of a dockyard

CLOATH (of meat): skin

CLOSE: shutter; (of music) cadence

CLOUTERLY: clumsily

CLOWNE: countryman, clodhopper

CLUB (s.): share of expenses, meeting at which expenses are shared. Also v.

CLYSTER, GLISTER, GLYSTER: enema

COACH: captain's state-room in large ship

COCK ALE: ale mixed with minced chicken

COCKPIT(T), the: usually the theatre in the Cockpit buildings, Whitehall Palace; the buildings themselves

COD: small bag; testicle

CODLIN TART: apple (codling) tart

COFFEE: coffee-house

COG: to cheat, banter, wheedle

COLEWORTS: cabbage

COLLAR DAY: day on which knights of chivalric orders wore insignia at court

COLLECT: to deduce

COLLIER: coal merchant; coal ship

COLLOPS: fried bacon or other meat

COLLY-FEAST: feast of collies (cullies, good companions) at which each pays his share

COMEDIAN: actor

COMEDY: play

COMFITURE (Fr. *confiture*): jam, marmalade

COMMEN/COMMON GUARDEN: Covent Garden

COMMONLY: together

COMPLEXION: aspect

COMPOSE: to put music to words. *Also* Composition

CONCEIT (s.): idea, notion

CONCLUDE: to include

CONDITION (s.): disposition; social position, state of wealth

CONDITION (v.): to make conditions

CONDITIONED: having a (specified) disposition or social position

CONGEE: bow at parting

CONJURE: to plead with

CONJUROR: fortune-teller operating by conjuration of spirits

CONSIDERABLE: worthy of consideration

CONSTER: to construe, translate

CONSUMPTION: (any) wasting disease. *Also* Consumptive

CONTENT, by/in: by agreement, without examination, at a rough guess

CONVENIENCE: advantage

CONVENIENT: morally proper

CONVERSATION: demeanour, behaviour; acquaintance, society

COOLE: cowl

CORANT(O): dance involving a running or gliding step

COSEN, COUSIN: almost any collateral relative

COUNT: to reckon, estimate, value

COUNTENANCE: recognition, acknowledgement

COUNTRY: county, district

COURSE: career, way of life

COURSE, in: in sequence

COURSE, of: as usual

COURT-DISH: dish with a cut from every meat

COY: disdainful; quiet

COYING: stroking, caressing

CRADLE: fire-basket

CRAMBO: rhyming game

CRAZY: infirm

CREATURE (of persons): puppet, instrument

CRUMB, get up one's: to improve one's station

CRUSADO: Portuguese coin worth 3s.

CUDDY: room in a large ship in which the officers took their meals

CULLY: dupe; friend

CUNNING: knowledgeable; knowledge

CURIOUS: careful, painstaking, discriminating; fine, delicate

CURRANT: out and about

CUSTOMER: customs officer

CUT (v.): to carve meat

CUTT (s.): an engraving

DAUGHTER-IN-LAW: stepdaughter

DEAD COLOUR: preparatory layer of colour in a painting

DEAD PAYS: sailors or soldiers kept on pay roll after death

DEALS: sawn timber used for decks, etc.

DEDIMUS: writ empowering J.P.

DEFALK: to subtract

DEFEND: to prevent

DEFY (Fr.): to mistrust. *Also* Defyance

DELICATE: pleasant

DELINQUENT: active royalist in Civil War and Interregnum

DEMORAGE: demurrage, compensation from the freighter due to a shipowner for delaying vessel beyond time specified in charter-party

DEPEND: to wait, hang

DEVISE: to decide; discern

DIALECT: jargon

DIALL, double horizontal: instrument telling hour of day

DIRECTION: supervision of making; arrangement

DISCOVER: to disclose, reveal

DISCREET: discerning, judicious

DISGUST: to dislike

DISPENSE: outgoings

DISTASTE (s.): difference, quarrel, offence. *Also* v.

DISTINCT: discerning, discriminating

DISTRINGAS: writ of distraint

DOATE: to nod off to sleep

DOCTOR: clergyman, don

DOE: dough. *See* 'All my cake . . .'

DOGGED: determined

DOLLER: *see* 'Rix Doller'

DORTOIRE: dorter, monastic dormitory

DOTY: darling

DOWNS, the: roadstead off Deal, Kent

DOXY: whore, mistress

DRAWER: tapster, barman

DRESS: to cook, prepare food

DROLL: comic song

DROLLING, DROLLY: comical, comically

DRUDGER: dredger, container for sweetmeats

DRUGGERMAN: dragoman, interpreter

DRY BEATEN: beaten without drawing blood

DRY MONEY: hard cash

DUANA: divan, council

DUCCATON: ducatoon, large silver coin of the Netherlands worth 5s. 9d.

DUCKET(T): ducat, foreign gold coin (here probably Dutch) worth 9s.

DUKE'S [PLAY] HOUSE, the: playhouse in Lincoln's Inn Fields used by the Duke of York's Company from June 1660 until 9 November 1671; often called 'the Opera'. Also known as the Lincoln's Inn Fields Theatre (LIF)

DULL: limp, spiritless

EARTH: earthenware

EASILY AND EASILY: more and more slowly

EAST INDIES: the territory covered by the E. India Company, including the modern sub-continent of India

EAST COUNTRY, EASTLAND: the territory (in Europe) covered by the Eastland Company

EFFEMINACY: love of women

ELABORATORY: laboratory

ELECTUARY: medicinal salve with a honey base

EMERODS: haemorrhoids

ENTENDIMIENTO (Sp.): understanding

ENTER (of horse): to break in

ENTERTAIN: to retain, employ

EPICURE: glutton

ERIFFE: Erith, Kent

ESPINETTE(S): *see* 'Spinet'

ESSAY: to assay

EVEN (adv.): surely

EVEN (of accounts): to balance

EVEN (of the diary): to bring up to date

EXCEPT: to accept

EXPECT: to see, await

FACTION: the government's parliamentary critics

FACTIOUS: able to command a following

FACTOR: mercantile agent

FACTORY: trading station

FAIRING: small present (as from a fair)

FAIRLY: gently, quietly

FALCHON: falchion, curved sword

FAMILY: household (including servants)

FANCY (music): fantasia

FANFARROON: fanfaron, braggart

FASHION (of metal, furniture): design, fashioning

FAT: vat

FATHER: father-in-law (similarly with mother etc.)

FELLET (of trees): a cutting, felling

FELLOW COMMONER: undergraduate paying high fees and enjoying privileges

FENCE: defence

FERRANDIN, FARRINDIN, FARANDINE: cloth of silk mixed with wool or hair

FIDDLE: violin; occ. treble viol

FINE (s.): payment for lease
FINE FOR OFFICE (v.): to avoid office by payment of fine
FIRESHIP: ship filled with combustibles used to ram and set fire to enemy
FITS OF THE MOTHER: hysterics
FLAG, FLAGGMAN: flag officer
FLAGEOLET: end-blown, six-holed instrument
FLESHED: relentless, proud
FLOOD: rising tide
FLOWER: beautiful girl
FLUXED (of the pox): salivated
FLYING ARMY/FLEET: small mobile force
FOND, FONDNESS: foolish; folly
FOND: fund
FORCE OUT: to escape
FORSOOTH: to speak ceremoniously
FORTY: many, scores of
FOXED: intoxicated
FOX HALL: Vauxhall (pleasure gardens)
FOY: departure feast or gift
FREQUENT: to busy oneself
FRIENDS: parents, relatives
FROST-BITE: to invigorate by exposure to cold
FULL: anxious
FULL MOUTH, with: eagerly; openly, loudly

GALL: harass
GALLIOTT: small swift galley
GALLOPER, the: shoal off Essex coast
GAMBO: Gambia, W. Africa
GAMMER: old woman
GENERAL-AT-SEA: naval commander (a post, not a rank)
GENIUS: inborn character, natural ability; mood
GENT: graceful, polite
GENTILELY: obligingly
GEORGE: jewel forming part of insignia of Order of Garter
GERMANY: territory of the Holy Roman Empire
GET WITHOUT BOOK: to memorise
GIBB-CAT: tom-cat

GILDER, GUILDER: Dutch money of account worth 2s.
GIMP: twisted thread of material with wire or cord running through it
GITTERNE: musical instrument of the guitar family
GIVE: to answer
GLASS: telescope
GLEEKE: three-handed card game
GLISTER, GLYSTER: see 'Clyster'
GLOSSE, by a fine: by a plausible pretext
GO(O)D BWYE: God be with ye, goodbye
GODLYMAN: Godalming, Surrey
GOODFELLOW: convivial person, good timer
GOODMAN/GOODWIFE (Goody): used of men and women of humble station
GOOD-SPEAKER: one who speaks well of others
GORGET: neckerchief for women
GOSSIP (v.): to act as godparent, to attend a new mother; to chatter. Also s.
GOVERNMENT: office or function of governor
GRACIOUS-STREET(E): Gracechurch St
GRAIN (? of gold): sum of money
GRAVE: to engrave
GREEN (of meat): uncured
GRESHAM COLLEGE: meeting-place of Royal Society; the Society itself
GRIEF: bodily pain
GRUDGEING, GRUTCHING: trifling complaint, grumble
GUEST: nominee; friend; stranger
GUIDE: postboy
GUN: flagon of ale; cannon, salute
GUNDALO, GUNDILOW: gondola
GUNFLEET, the: shoal off Essex coast

HACKNEY: workhorse; vehicle
HAIR, against the: against the grain
HALF-A-PIECE: gold coin worth c. 10s.
HALF-SHIRT: short shirt
HALFE-WAY-HOUSE: Rotherhithe tav-

ern halfway between London Bridge and Deptford

HALL, the: usually Westminster Hall

HAND: cuff

HANDSEL: to try out, use for first time

HAND-TO-FIST: hastily

HANDYCAPP: handicap, a card game

HANG IN THE HEDGE: to be delayed

HANGER: loop holding a sword; small sword

HANGING JACK: turnspit for roasting meat

HANK: hold, grip

HAPPILY: haply, perchance

HARE: to harry, rebuke

HARPSICHON, HARPSICHORD: keyboard instrument of one or two manuals, with strings plucked by quills or leather jacks, and with stops which vary the tone

HARSLET: haslet, pigmeat (esp. offal)

HAT-PIECE: protective metal skull-cap

HAVE A HAND: to have leisure, freedom

HAWSE, thwart their: across their bows

HEAD-PIECE: helmet

HEART: courage

HEAVE AT: to oppose

HECTOR: street-bully, swashbuckler

HERBALL: botanical encyclopaedia; *hortus siccus* (book of dried and pressed plants)

HERE (Du. *heer*): Lord

HIGH: arrogant, proud, high-handed

HINCHINGBROOKE: Sandwich's house near Huntingdon

HOMAGE: jury of presentment at a manorial court

HONEST (of a woman): virtuous

HOOKS, off the: out of humour

HOPE, the: reach of Thames downstream from Tilbury

HOPEFUL: promising

HOUSE: playhouse; parliament; (royal) household or palace building

HOUSE OF OFFICE: latrine

HOY: small passenger and cargo ship, sloop-rigged

HOYSE: to hoist

HUMOUR (s.): mood; character, characteristic; good or ill temper

HUMOUR (v.): to set words suitably to music

HUSBAND: one who gets good/bad value for money; supervisor, steward

HYPOCRAS: hippocras, spiced wine

ILL-TEMPERED: out of sorts, ill-adjusted (to weather etc.; cf. 'Temper')

IMPERTINENCE: irrelevance, garrulity, folly. *Also* Impertinent

IMPOSTUME: abscess

IMPREST: money paid in advance by government to public servant

INDIAN GOWN: loose gown of Indian style, material, or pattern

INGENIOUS, INGENUOUS: clever, intelligent

INGENUITY: wit, intelligence; freedom

INSIPID: stupid, dull

INSTITUCIONS: instructions

INSTRUMENT: agent, clerk

INSULT: to exult over

INTELLIGENCE: information

IRISIPULUS: erysipelas

IRONMONGER: often a large-scale merchant, not necessarily a retailer

JACK(E): flag used as signal or mark of distinction; rogue, knave. *See also* 'Hanging Jack'

JACKANAPES COAT: monkey jacket, sailor's short close-fitting jacket

JACOB(US): gold sovereign coined under James I

JAPAN: lacquer, lacquered

JARR, JARRING: quarrel

JEALOUS: fearful, suspicious, mistrustful. *Also* Jealousy

JERK(E): captious remark

JES(S)IMY: jasmine

JEW'S TRUMP: Jew's harp

JOCKY: horse-dealer

JOLE (of fish): jowl, a cut consisting of the head and shoulders. *See also* 'Pole'

JOYNT-STOOL: stout stool with stretchers, held together by joints

JULIPP: julep, a sweet drink made from syrup

JUMBLE: to take for an airing

JUMP WITH: to agree, harmonise

JUNK (naval): old rope

JURATE (of Cinque Ports): jurat, alderman

JUSTE-AU-CORPS: close-fitting long coat

KATCH: (ship) ketch

KENNEL: *see* 'Canaille'

KERCHER: kerchief, head-covering

KETCH (s.): catch, song in canon

KETCH (v.): to catch

KING'S [PLAY] HOUSE, the: playhouse in Vere St, Clare Market, Lincoln's Inn Fields, used by the King's Company from 8 November 1660 until 7 May 1663; the playhouse in Bridges St, Drury Lane, used by the same company from 7 May 1663 until the fire of 25 January 1672. Also known as the Theatre Royal (TR)

KITLIN: kitling, kitten, cub

KNOT (s.): flower bed; difficulty; clique, band

KNOT (v.): to join, band together

KNOWN: famous

LACE: usually braid made with gold- or silver-thread

LAMB'S-WOOL: hot ale with apples and spice

LAMP-GLASS: magnifying lens used to concentrate lamp-light

LANDS: framing members of ship

LAST: load, measure of tar

LASTOFFE: Lowestoft, Suff.

LATITUDINARIAN: liberal Anglican

LAVER: basin of fountain

LEADS: flat space on roof top, sometimes boarded over

LEAN: to lie down

LEARN: to teach

LEAVE: to end

LECTURE: weekday religious service consisting mostly of a sermon

LESSON: piece of music

LETTERS OF MART: letters of marque

LEVETT: reveille, reveille music

LIBEL(L): leaflet, broadside; (in legal proceedings) written charge

LIE UPON: to press, insist

LIFE: life interest

LIGHT: window

LIGNUM VITAE: hard W. Indian wood with medicinal qualities, often used for drinking vessels

LIMB: to limn, paint

LIME (of dogs): to mate

LINK(E): torch

LINNING: linen

LIPPOCK: Liphook, Hants.

LIST: pleasure, desire

LOCK: waterway between arches of bridge

LOMBRE: *see* 'Ombre'

LONDON: the city of London (to be distinguished from Westminster)

LOOK: to look at/for

LUMBERSTREETE: Lombard St

LUTE: pear-shaped plucked instrument with six courses of gut strings and a turned-back peg-box; made in various sizes, the larger instruments having additional bass strings

LUTESTRING: lustring, a glossy silk

LYRA-VIALL: small bass viol tuned for playing chords

MAD: whimsical, wild, extravagant

MAD (v.): to anger

MADAM(E): prefix used mainly of widows, elderly/foreign ladies

MAIN (adj.): strong, bulky

MAIN (s.): chief purpose or object

MAISTER: expert; professional; sailing master

MAKE (s.): (of fighting cocks) match, pair of opponents

MAKE (v.): to do; to copulate

MAKE LEGS: to bow, curtsey

MAKE SURE TO: to plight troth

MALLOWS: St Malo

MAN OF BUSINESS: executive agent, administrator

MANAGED-HORSE (cf. Fr. *manège*): horse trained in riding school

MANDAMUS: royal mandate under seal

MARGARET, MARGETTS: Margate, Kent

MARGENTING: putting margin-lines on paper

MARK: 13*s*. 4*d*.

MARMOTTE (Fr., term of affection): young girl

MARROWBONE: Marylebone, Mdx

MASTY: burly

MATCH: tinderbox and wick

MATHEMATICIAN: mathematical instrument-maker

MEAT: food

MEDIUM: mean, average

METHEGLIN: strong mead flavoured with herbs

MINCHIN-LANE: Mincing Lane

MINE: mien

MINIKIN: thin string or gut used for treble string of lute or viol

MISTRESS (prefix): used of unmarried girls and women as well as of young married women

MISTRESS: sweetheart

MITHRYDATE: drug used as an opiate

MODEST (of women): virtuous

MOHER (Sp. *mujer*): woman, wife

MOIS, MOYS: menstrual periods

MOLD, MOLDE, MOLLE (archit.): mole

MOLEST: to annoy

MOND: orb (royal jewel in form of globe)

MONTEERE, MOUNTEERE: huntsman's cap; close-fitting hood

MONTH'S MIND, to have a: to have a great desire

MOPED: bemused

MORECLACK(E): Mortlake, Surrey

MORENA (Sp.): brunette

MORNING DRAUGHT: drink (sometimes with snack) usually taken mid-morning

MOTHER-IN-LAW: stepmother (similarly with 'father-in-law' etc.)

MOTT: sighting line in an optical tube

MOYRE: moire, watered silk

MUM: strong spiced ale

MURLACE: Morlaix, Brittany

MUSCADINE, MUSCATT: muscatel wine

MUSIC: band, choir, performers

MUSTY: peevish

NAKED BED: without nightclothes/curtains

NARROWLY: anxiously, carefully

NAUGHT, NOUGHT: worthless, bad in condition or quality, sexually wicked

NAVY: Navy Office

NAVY OFFICERS: Principal Officers of the Navy – i.e. the Comptroller, Treasurer, Surveyor, Clerk of the Acts, together with a variable number of Commissioners; members of the Navy Board. Cf. 'Sea-Officers'

NEARLY: deeply

NEAT (adj.): handsome

NEAT (s.): ox, cattle

NEITHER MEDDLE NOR MAKE: to have nothing to do with

NEWSBOOK: newspaper (weekly, octavo)

NICOTIQUES: narcotics, medicines

NIGHTGOWN(E): dressing gown

NOISE: group of musical instruments playing together

NORE, the: anchorage in mouth of Thames

NORTHDOWNE ALE: Margate ale

NOSE: to insult, affront

NOTE: thing deserving of note; note of credit

NOTORIOUS: famous, well-known

OBNOXIOUS: liable to
OBSERVABLE (adj.): noteworthy, notorious
OBSERVABLE (s.): thing or matter worthy of observation
OFFICE DAY: day on which a meeting of the Navy Board was held
OLEO (Sp. *olla*): stew
OMBRE (Sp. *hombre*): card game
ONLY: main, principal, best
OPEN: unsettled
OPERA: spectacular entertainment (involving use of painted scenery and stage machinery), often with music
OPERA, the: the theatre in Lincoln's Inn Fields. *See* 'Duke's House, the'
OPINIASTRE, OPINIASTREMENT (Fr.): stubborn, stubbornly
OPPONE: to oppose, hinder
ORDER: to put in order; to punish
ORDINARY (adj.): established
ORDINARY (s.): eating place serving fixed-price meals; peace-time establishment (of navy, dockyard, etc.)
OUTPORTS: ports other than London
OVERSEEN: omitted, neglected; guilty of oversight
OWE: to own

PADRON (?Sp., ?It. *patrone*): master
PAGEANT: decorated symbolic float in procession
PAINFUL: painstaking
PAIR OF OARS: large river-boat rowed by two watermen, each using a pair of oars. Cf. 'Scull'
PAIR OF ORGANS/VIRGINALS: a single instrument
PALACE: New Palace Yard
PALER: parlour
PARAGON: heavy rich cloth, partly of mohair
PARCEL: share, part; isolated group
PARK, the: normally St James's Park (Hyde Park is usually named)
PARTY: charter-party
PASSION: feeling, mood

PASSIONATE: touching, affecting
PATTEN: overshoe
PAY: to berate, beat
PAY [HIS] COAT: to beat, chastise
PAY SICE: to pay dearly (sixfold)
PENDANCES, PENDENTS: lockets; earrings
PERPLEX: to vex
PERSPECTIVE, PERSPECTIVE GLASSES: binoculars
PESLEMESLE: pall-mall, early form of croquet
PETTY BAG: petty cash
PHILOSOPHY: natural science
PHYSIC: laxative, purge
PHYSICALLY: without sheets, uncovered
PICK: pique
PICK A HOLE IN [HIS] COAT: to pick a quarrel, complain
PICKAROON (Sp. *picarón*): pirate, privateer
PIECE: gold coin worth *c.* 20*s.*
PIECE (PEECE) OF EIGHT: Spanish silver coin worth 4*s.* 6*d.*
PIGEON: coward
PINK(E): small broad-beamed ship; poniard, pointed weapon
PINNER: coif with two long flaps; fill-in above low *décolletage*
PIPE: measure of wine (*c.* 120 galls.)
PIPE (musical): flageolet or recorder
PISTOLE: French gold coin worth 16*s.*
PLACKET: petticoat
PLAIN: unaffected
PLAT(T): plate, plan, chart, map; arrangement; level; [flower] plot
PLATERER: one who works silver plate
PLAY (v.): to play for stakes
POINT, POYNT: piece of lace
POINT DE GESNE: Genoa lace
POLE: head; head-and-shoulder (of fish); poll tax
POLICY: government; cunning; self-interest
POLLARD: cut-back, stunted tree
POMPOUS: ceremonious, dignified
POOR JACK: dried salt cod

POOR WRETCH: poor dear

POSSET: drink made of hot milk, spices, and wine (or beer)

POST (v.): to expose, pillory

POST WARRANT: authority to employ posthorses

POSY: verse or phrase engraved on inside of ring

POWDERED (of meat): salted

PRACTICE: trick

PRAGMATIC, PRAGMATICAL: interfering, conceited, dogmatic

PRATIQUE: ship's licence for port facilities given on presentation of clean bill of health

PRESBYTER JOHN: puritan parson

PRESENT (s.): shot, volley

PRESENT, PRESENTLY: immediate, immediately

PRESS BED: bed folding into or built inside a cupboard

PREST MONEY (milit., naval): earnest money paid in advance

PRETTY (of men): fine, elegant, foppish

PREVENT: to anticipate

PRICK: to write out music; to list

PRICK OUT: to strike out, delete

PRINCE: ruler

PRINCIPLES (of music): natural ability, rudimentary knowledge

PRISE, PRIZE: worth, value, price

PRIVATE: small, secret, quiet

PRIZE FIGHT: fencing match fought for money

PROPRIETY: property, ownership

PROTEST (a bill of exchange): to record non-payment

PROUD (of animals): on heat

PROVOKE: to urge

PULL A CROW: to quarrel

PURCHASE: advantage; profit; booty

PURELY: excellently

PURL(E): hot spiced beer

PUSS: ill-favoured woman

PUT OFF: to sell, dispose of

PYONEER: pioneer (ditch digger, labourer)

QU: cue

QUARREFOUR: crossroads

QUARTER, to keep a: to make a disturbance

QUARTERAGE: any salary or sum paid quarterly

QUEST HOUSE: house used for inquests, parish meetings

QUINBROUGH: Queenborough, Kent

QUINSBOROUGH: Königsberg, E. Prussia

RACE: to rase, destroy

RAKE-SHAMED: disreputable, disgraceful

RARE: fine, splendid

RATE: to berate, scold

RATTLE: to scold

RATTOON: rattan cane

READY: quick, accomplished

REAKE: trick

RECEPI: writ of receipt issued by Chancery

RECITATIVO (stilo r.): the earliest type of recitative singing

RECONCILE: to settle a dispute, to determine the truth

RECORDER: family of end-blown, eight-holed instruments (descant, treble, tenor, bass); P played the treble

RECOVER: to reconcile

RECOVERY (legal): process for re-establishment of ownership

REDRIFFE: Rotherhithe, Surrey

REFERRING: indebted, beholden to

REFORM: to disband

REFORMADO: naval/military officer serving without commission

REFRESH (of a sword): to sharpen

RELIGIOUS: monk, nun

REPLICACION (legal): replication, plaintiff's answer to defendant's plea

RESEMBLE: to represent, figure

RESENT: to receive

RESPECT: to mean, refer to

RESPECTFUL: respectable

REST: wrest, tuning key

RETAIN (a writ): to maintain a court action from term to term

REVOLUTION: sudden change (not necessarily violent)

RHODOMONTADO: boast, brag

RIGHT-HAND MAN: soldier on whom drill manoeuvres turn

RIGHTS, to: immediately, directly

RINGO: eryngo (sea-holly)

RIS (v.): rose, risen

RISE: origin

RIX DOLLER: Dutch or N. German silver coin (*Rijksdaalder, Reichsthaler*) worth *c.* 4*s.* 9*d.*

ROCKE: distaff

ROMANTIQUE: having the characteristics of a tale (romance)

ROUNDHOUSE: uppermost cabin in stern of ship

ROYALL THEATRE, the: see 'Theatre, the'

RUB(B): check, stop, obstacle

RUFFIAN: pimp, rogue

RUMP: remnant of the Long Parliament

RUMPER: member or supporter of the Rump

RUNLETT: cask

RUNNING: temporary

SACK: white wine from Spain or Canaries

SALT: salt-cellar

SALT-EELE: rope's end or leather belt used for punishment

SALVE UP: to smooth over

SALVO: excuse, explanation

SARCENET: thin taffeta, fine silk cloth

SASSE (Du. *sas*): sluice, lock

SAVE: to be in time for

SAY: fine woollen cloth

SCALE (of music): key; gamut

SCALLOP: scalloped lace collar

SCALLOP-WHISK: see 'Whiske'

SCAPE (s.): adventure

SCAPE (v.): to escape

SCARE-FIRE: sudden conflagration

SCHOOL: to scold, rebuke

SCHUIT (Du.): Dutch canal boat, barge

SCONCE: bracket, candlestick

SCOTOSCOPE: portable *camera obscura*

SCOWRE: to beat, punish

SCREW: key, screw-bolt

SCRUPLE: to dispute

SCULL, SCULLER: small river-boat rowed by a single waterman using one pair of oars. Cf. 'Pair of oars'

SEA-CARD: chart

SEA-COAL: coal carried by sea

SEA-OFFICERS: commissioned officers of the navy. Cf. 'Navy Officers'

SECOND MOURNING: half-mourning

SEEL (of a ship): to lurch

SEEM: to pretend

SENNIT: sevennight, a week

SENSIBLY: perceptibly, painfully

SERPENT: variety of firework

SERVANT: suitor, lover

SET: sit

SET UP/OFF ONE'S REST: to be certain, to be content, to make an end, to make one's whole aim

SEWER: stream, ditch

SHAG(G): worsted or silk cloth with a velvet nap on one side

SHEATH (of a ship): to encase the hull as a protection against worm

SHIFT (s.): trial; dressing room

SHIFT (v.): to change clothes; to dodge a round in paying for drinks (or to get rid of the effects of drink)

SHOEMAKER'S STOCKS: new shoes

SHOVE AT: to apply one's energies to

SHROUD: shrewd, astute

SHUFFLEBOARD: shovelboard, shove-ha'penny

SHUTS: shutters

SILLABUB, SULLYBUB, SYLLABUB: milk mixed with wine

SIMPLE: foolish

SIT: to hold a meeting

SIT CLOSE: to hold a meeting from which clerks are excluded

SITHE: sigh

SKELLUM: rascal, thief

SLENDERLY: slightingly
SLICE: flat plate
SLIGHT, SLIGHTLY: contemptuous; slightingly, without ceremony
SLIP A CALF/FILLY: to abort
SLOP(P)S: seamen's ready-made clothes
SLUG(G): slow heavy boat; rough metal projectile
SLUT (not always opprobrious): drudge, wench
SMALL (of drink): light
SNAP(P) (s.): bite, snack, small meal; attack
SNAP (v.): to ambush, cut down/out/off
SNUFF: to speak scornfully
SNUFFE, take/go in: to take offence
SOKER: old hand; pal; toper
SOLD(E)BAY: Solebay, off Southwold, Suff.
SOL(L)ICITOR: agent; one who solicits business
SON: son-in-law (similarly with daughter etc.)
SON-IN-LAW: stepson
SOUND: fish-bladder
SOUND, the: strictly the navigable passage between Denmark and Sweden where tolls were levied, but more generally (and usually in Pepys) the Baltic
SPARROWGRASS: asparagus
SPEAK BROAD: to speak fully, frankly
SPECIALITY: bond under seal
SPECIES (optical): image
SPEED: to succeed
SPIKET: spigot, tap, faucet
SPILT, SPOILT: ruined
SPINET: single-manual wing-shaped keyboard instrument with harpsichord action
SPOIL: to deflower; injure
SPOTS: patches (cosmetic)
SPRANKLE: sparkling remark, *bon mot*
SPUDD: trenching tool
STAIRS: landing stage
STAND IN: to cost
STANDING WATER: between tides

STANDISH: stand for ink, pens, etc.
STATE-DISH: richly decorated dish; dish with a round lid or canopy
STATESMAN: Commonwealth's-man
STATIONER: bookseller (often also publisher)
STEEPLE: tower
STEMPEECE: timber of ship's bow
STICK: blockhead
STILLYARD, the: the Steelyard
STOMACH: courage, pride; appetite
STONE-HORSE: stallion
STOUND: astonishment
STOUT: brave, courageous
STOWAGE: storage, payment for storage
STRAIGHTS, STREIGHTS, the: strictly the Straits of Gibraltar; more usually the Mediterranean
STRANG: strong
STRANGERS: foreigners
STRIKE (nautical): to lower the topsail in salute; (of Exchequer tallies) to make, cut
STRONG WATER: distilled spirits
SUBSIDY MAN: man of substance (liable to pay subsidy-tax)
SUCCESS(E): outcome (good or bad)
SUDDENLY: in a short while
SUPERNUMERARY: seaman extra to ship's complement
SURLY: imperious, lordly
SWINE-POX: chicken-pox
SWOUND: to swoon, faint
SYMPHONY: instrumental introduction, interlude etc., in a vocal composition

TAB(B)Y: watered silk
TABLE: legend attached to a picture
TABLE BOOK: memorandum book
TABLES: backgammon and similar games
TAILLE, TALLE (Fr. *taille*): figure, shape (of person)
TAKE EGGS FOR MONEY: to cut one's losses, to accept something worthless

TAKE OUT: to learn; perform

TAKE UP: to patch up, reform

TAKING (s.): condition

TALE: reckoning, number

TALL: fine, elegant

TALLE: see 'Taille'

TALLY: wooden stick used by the Exchequer in accounting

TAMKIN: tampion, wooden gun plug

TANSY, TANZY: egg pudding flavoured with tansy

TARGET: shield

TARPAULIN: 'tar', a sea-bred captain as opposed to a gentleman-captain

TAXOR: financial official of university

TEAR: to rant

TELL: to count

TEMPER (s.): moderation; temperament, mood; physical condition

TEMPER (v.): to moderate, control

TENDER: chary of

TENT: roll of absorbent material used for wounds; (Sp. *tinto*) red wine

TERCE, TIERCE: measure of wine (42 galls.; one-third of a pipe)

TERELLA: terrella, spherical magnet, terrestrial globe containing magnet

TERM(E)S: menstrual periods

THEATRE, the: before May 1663 usually Theatre Royal, Vere St; afterwards usually Theatre Royal, Drury Lane (TR)

THEM: see 'Those'

THEORBO: large double-necked tenor lute

THOSE: menstrual periods

THRUSH: inflammation of throat and mouth

TICKELED: annoyed, irritated

TICKET(T): seaman's pay-ticket

TILT: awning over river-boat

TIMBER: wood for the skeleton of a ship (as distinct from plank or deals used for the decks, cabins, gun-platforms etc.)

TIRE: tier

TOKEN, by the same: so, then, and

TONGUE: reputation, fame

TOPS: turnovers of stockings

TOUCHED: annoyed

TOUR, the: coach parade of *beau monde* in Hyde Park

TOWN(E): manor

TOWSE: to tousle/tumble a woman

TOY: small gift

TOYLE: foil, net into which game is driven

TRADE: manufacture, industry

TRANSIRE: warrant allowing goods through customs

TRAPAN, TREPAN: (surg.) to perforate skull; cheat, trick, trap, inveigle

TREASURY, the: the Navy Treasury or the national Treasury

TREAT: to handle (literally)

TREAT, TREATY: negotiate, negotiation

TREBLE: treble viol

TRIANGLE, TRYANGLE: triangular virginals

TRILL(O): vocal ornament consisting of the accelerated repetition of the same note

TRIM: to shave

TRUCKLE/TRUNDLE-BED: low bed on castors which could be put under main bed

TRY A PULL: to have a go

TUITION: guardianship

TUNE: pitch

TURK, the: used of all denizens of the Turkish Empire, but usually here of the Berbers of the N. African coast, especially Algiers

TURKEY WORK: red tapestry in Turkish style

TURKY-STONE: turquoise

TUTTLE FIELDS: Tothill Fields

TWIST: strong thread

UGLY: awkward

UMBLES (of deer): edible entrails, giblets

UNBESPEAK: countermand

UNCOUTH: out of sorts or order, uneasy, at a loss

UNDERSTAND: to conduct oneself properly; (s.) understanding

UNDERTAKER: contractor; parliamentary manager

UNHAPPY, UNHAPPILY: unlucky; unluckily

UNREADY: undressed

UNTRUSS: to undo one's breeches, defecate

UPPER BENCH: name given in Interregnum to King's Bench

USE: usury, interest

USE UPON USE: compound interest

VAPOURING: pretentious, foolish

VAUNT: to vend, sell

VENETIAN CAP: peaked cap as worn by Venetian Doge

VESTS: robes, vestments

VIALL, VIOL: family of fretted, bowed instruments with six gut strings; the bowing hand is held beneath the bow and the instrument held on or between the knees; now mostly superseded by violin family

VIRGINALS: rectangular English keyboard instrument resembling spinet; also generic term for all plectral keyboard instruments

VIRTUOSO: man of wide learning

WAISTCOAT, WASTECOATE: warm undergarment

WAIT, WAYT (at court etc.): to serve a turn of duty (usually a month) as an official

WARDROBE, the: the office of the King's Great Wardrobe, of which Lord Sandwich was Keeper; the building at Puddle Wharf containing the office; a cloak room, dressing room

WARM: comfortable, well-off

WASSAIL, WASSELL: entertainment (e.g. a play)

WASTECLOATH: cloth hung on ship as decoration between quarter-deck and forecastle

WATCH: clock

WATER: strong water, spirits

WAY, in/out of the: accessible/inaccessible; in a suitable/unsuitable condition

WAYTES: waits; municipal musicians

WEATHER-GLASS(E): thermometer (or, less likely, barometer)

WEIGH (of ships): to raise

WELLING: Welwyn, Herts.

WESTERN BARGEMAN (BARGEE): bargee serving western reaches of Thames

WESTMINSTER: the area around Whitehall and the Abbey; not the modern city of Westminster

WHISKE: woman's neckerchief

WHITE-HALL: royal palace, largely burnt down in 1698

WHITSTER: bleacher, launderer

WIGG: wig, cake, bun

WILDE: wile

WIND (s.): wine

WIND LIKE A CHICKEN: to wind round one's little finger

WINDFUCKER: talkative braggart

WIPE: sarcasm, insult

WISTELY: with close attention

WIT, WITTY: cleverness, clever

WONDER: to marvel at

WOODMONGER: fuel merchant

WORD: utterance, phrase

WOREMOODE: wormwood

WORK: needlework. *Also* v.

YARD: penis

YARE: ready, skilful

YILDHALL: Guildhall

YOWELL: Ewell, Surrey